Other Kaplan Books on Improving Your English

Essential Review for the TOEIC
Success with American Idioms
Success with Business Words
Success with Legal Words
Success with Medical Words
Success with Words for the TOEFL
TOEFL

Other Kaplan Books on University Admissions

Access America's Guide to Studying in the USA
College Catalog
Guide to College Selection
Get into College Toolkit
ACT 1999
SAT 1999
SAT Math Workbook
SAT Verbal Workbook
Graduate School Admissions Adviser
Business School Admissions Adviser
GMAT 1998–1999
GRE 1998–1999

TOEFL*
FOR THE
COMPUTER

Marilyn J. Rymniak

Gerald Kurlandski

K. Aaron Smith

Alyssa S. Goldberg

and the Staff of
Kaplan Educational Centers

Simon & Schuster

*TOEFL is a registered trademark of Educational Testing Service (ETS), which is not affiliated with this product.

Kaplan Books
Published by
Kaplan Educational Centers and Simon & Schuster
1230 Avenue of the Americas
New York, NY 10020

For bulk sales to schools, colleges and universities, please contact the Vice President for Special Markets, Simon & Schuster, 1633 Broadway, 8th Floor, New York, NY 10019.

Manufactured in the United States of America
Published Simultaneously in Canada

Project Editor: Julie Schmidt
Production Editor: Maude Spekes
Page Layout and Design: Amparo Graf
Illustrations: Bola Famuyiwa
Managing Editor: David Chipps
Desktop Publishing Manager: Michael Shevlin
Executive Editor: Del Franz

CD-ROM Development Team:
Producer: Robert Garrelick
Project Manager: Karen Fallowes
Lead Programmer/Designer: Hristina Le Blanc
Editor/Formatter/Graphic Artist: Joseph Wilson
Consulting Programmer/Designer: Bill Shander

Special thanks to: Jude Bond, Richard Christiano, Carol Hirsch, Kate Holum, Lin Lougheed, Alison May, Tatyana Miller, Krista Pfeiffer, Jeff Samson, and Linda Volpano

January 1999

10 9 8 7 6 5 4 3 2 1

ISBN: 0-684-85534-8

CONTENTS

PART FOUR: PRACTICE TEST TWO

PART FIVE: ANSWER KEYS AND SCORE CONVERSION CHART

ABOUT THE AUTHORS

Marilyn J. Rymniak

Rymniak is the executive director of International Products and Programs at Kaplan Educational Centers. For 25 years she has been a foreign language/ESL specialist and a leader in the international education field, holding national and regional positions with NAFSA: Association of International Educators and TESOL. A sociolinguist and international and comparative educator by training, she has taught in, administered, and developed curricula for campus-based intensive English Programs in California and New York, including those at the University of California at San Diego, the University of California at Los Angeles, University of California at Irvine, the California State System, and Manhattanville College. She has held overseas teaching and curriculum development positions in Spain, France, England, Iran, and Saudi Arabia. Rymniak, who was a Fulbright scholar in Germany, can communicate in six languages. She also sits on the Board of Directors of Metro International in New York City and is an intercultural communication trainer for BDx InterFace, Inc. of Connecticut.

Gerald Kurlandski

Kurlandski, who was a Fulbright scholar and Peace Corps volunteer, has been educated as a teacher of English to speakers of other languages. He has taught ESL courses and developed curricula for several colleges and universities in the United States, as well as in Portugal and Morocco. He has also written a reading textbook for use in Moroccan universities and speaks Moroccan Arabic and French. He is a former ESL specialist at Kaplan Educational Centers.

K. Aaron Smith

A theoretical linguist and classical language enthusiast, Smith has taught TOEFL Prep and ESL for many years and has developed second-language curricula for university-bound international students. He is fluent in Spanish, German, and Portuguese and is a Latin scholar. He is the former associate director for International Products and Programs at Kaplan Educational Centers.

Alyssa S. Goldberg

Goldberg received a master of arts degree in communications from the University of Wisconsin and has taught ESL at the university level and in IEPs for nine years. She is the current associate director for International Products and Programs at Kaplan Educational Centers, and has created an extensive computer-based TOEFL curriculum for the company.

A SPECIAL NOTE
ON STUDYING IN THE U.S.A.

If you are not from the United States, but want to attend a United States college or university, here are the steps you need to take:

➤ If English is not your first language, start there. You will probably need to take the TOEFL or show some other evidence that you are very proficient in English. Usually an applicant's TOEFL scores are submitted as part of the university application. You should, of course, prepare for the TOEFL itself, but TOEFL preparation alone is probably not going to give you the scores you need to get into an American university. A good base in all aspects of English is necessary.

➤ Depending on the university, some undergraduate applicants may also be required to take the SAT (formerly known as the Scholastic Assessment Test). Applicants for graduate programs may have to take the GRE (Graduate Record Exam); applicants for Masters in Business Administration programs may have to take the GMAT (Graduate Management Admissions Test); and law school applicants will probably have to take the LSAT (Law School Admissions Test).

➤ Selecting the correct school can be difficult. Get help from a counselor or use the information in and advice of the experts in a Kaplan book such as *Guide to College Selection, Graduate School Admissions Adviser,* or *Business School Admissions Adviser.* Since admission to many undergraduate and graduate programs is quite competitive, you should select three or four programs and complete an application for each one. You need to begin the application process at least a year in advance, especially if you are overseas. Find out application deadlines for the schools you are interested in, and plan accordingly.

➤ Higher education in the United States is generally very expensive in comparison to university education in other countries. International students generally have to show at the time that they apply that they have sufficient funds to pay for the costs of a year's studies in the United States. On the undergraduate level, there are few scholarships given to international students. Advanced-degree students, however, may find that there are opportunities for research grants, teaching assistantships, and practical training or work experience in U.S. graduate departments. To be eligible for these, a student will first have to be accepted into the college or university in question. For more information on funding for higher education in the United States, see Kaplan's *Scholarships* or *Yale Daily News Guide to Fellowships and Grants.*

➤ Finally, after you are accepted into a university, you will need to obtain an I-20 Certificate of Eligibility in order to receive an F-1 Student Visa to study in the United States. This can be obtained from the school which you are going to attend.

Access America English Language Programs

If you need more help with English language learning, TOEFL preparation, or the complex process of university admissions, you may be interested in Kaplan's Access America® program.

Kaplan created Access America to assist international students and professionals who want to enter the United States university system. The program was designed for students who have received the bulk of their primary and secondary education outside the United States in a language other than English. Access America also has programs for obtaining professional certification in the United States. A brief description of some of the help available through Access America follows.

The Access America Certificate Program in English for University Admission

The Access America Certificate Program in English for University Admission is a comprehensive English language training program that prepares serious students for admission to an accredited American university. Using a content-based approach to studying English, this course trains students in three main areas:

- Academic English for university admissions
- TOEFL test-taking skills and strategies
- University admissions counseling and placement

This course is designed for international students at the high-intermediate, advanced, and super-advanced levels of English proficiency who have as their end goal admission into a university degree program. Some American universities will accept Kaplan's Certificate of High Achievement in English for University Admissions in lieu of a TOEFL score. This means that they trust the Kaplan Certificate as a reliable evaluation of a student's readiness for university work. A list of schools providing TOEFL waivers for Kaplan's certificate will be provided upon request.

In this course, students use actual material written for native speakers of English and work on improving the following critical skills:

(1) Listening and lecture notetaking skills
(2) Extended and rapid textbook reading skills

(3) Vocabulary enhancement for developing nativelike intuition about words
(4) Understanding and applying English grammar in a real context
(5) Effective use of a monolingual dictionary
(6) Time management skills for academic study
(7) Computer literacy and computer keyboarding skills
(8) Successfully taking the TOEFL (on paper and on computer) and other standardized test skills
(9) Functional conversation performance skills
(10) Learning strategies

Graduate School/GRE (Graduate Record Exam) Preparation

If your goal is to enter a master's or Ph.D. program in the United States, Kaplan will help you achieve a high GRE score, while helping you understand how to choose a graduate degree program in your field.

USMLE (United States Medical Licensing Exam) and Other Medical Licensing

If you are an international medical graduate who would like to be certified by the Educational Commission for Foreign Medical Graduates (ECFMG) and obtain a residency in a United States hospital, Kaplan will help you achieve a passing score on all three steps of the USMLE.

If you are an international nurse who wishes to practice in the United States, Kaplan will help you achieve a passing score on the NCLEX (Nursing Certification and Licensing Exam) or CGFNS (Commission on Graduates of Foreign Nursing Schools) exam. Kaplan will also provide you with the English and cross-cultural knowledge you will need to be an effective nurse.

Business Accounting/CPA (Certified Public Accounting)

If you are an accountant who would like to be certified to do business in the United States, Kaplan will help you achieve a passing score on the CPA Exam, and will assist you in understanding accounting procedures in the United States.

Applying to Access America

To get more information, or to apply for admission to any of Kaplan's programs for international students or professionals, you can write to us at:

Kaplan Educational Centers
International Admissions Department
888 Seventh Avenue
New York, NY 10106

You can call us at 1-800-527-8378 from within the United States, or at 1-212-262-4980 outside the United States. Our fax number is 1-212-957-1654. Our e-mail address is world@kaplan.com. You can also get more information or even apply through the Internet at http://www.kaplan.com/intl.

USER'S GUIDE FOR THE COMPUTER-BASED TOEFL CD-ROM

If you are worried because the new computer-based TOEFL includes unfamiliar question types, you are in luck! Kaplan's *Mastering the Computer-Based TOEFL® Test* CD-ROM, combined with the information you will cover in the course of working through this book, will give you the edge you need to conquer both your fears and the computer-based TOEFL (as well as many other types of computer-based or computer adaptive tests). This CD-ROM, which you will find attached to the back cover of this book, is the result of months of research, development, and testing by Kaplan Educational Centers' Technology and ESL divisions—both staffed by recognized experts in their fields.

Before you install the CD-ROM, read through the User's Guide provided here. You should also check out the introductory sections on the computer-based TOEFL test that precede each set of Power Lessons. These materials offer details about the new question types you will answer, and will help you to master the mechanics of taking the test on computer as well as its content.

NOTE: This CD-ROM also includes audio recordings for the Listening Power Lessons and Practice Tests. DO NOT attempt to play this disc on a regular music CD player.

NOTE: Technical Support for the CD-ROM is available Monday through Friday from 6 A.M. to 6 P.M. EST at 1-970-339-7142.

System Requirements

WINDOWS™

Windows 3.1 or higher, 486 SX or higher, 50MHz, 25 MB hard disk space, 8 MB available RAM, 640x480/256 colors, 2x CD-ROM, 16-bit audio, speakers or headphones

MACINTOSH®

Macintosh OS 7.0 or higher, 68040 or higher, 25 MB hard disk space, 8 MB available RAM, 640x480/256 colors, 2x CD-ROM, 16-bit audio, speakers or headphones

Installing and Launching the Software

This application requires QuickTime™ software, which has been included on the CD-ROM. If you do not have QuickTime installed, or are not sure if you do or not, choose to install QuickTime.

WINDOWS 3.1, 3.11

(1) Exit out of all open applications (make sure you have no applications running).
(2) Insert *Kaplan's Mastering the Computer-Based TOEFL Test* CD-ROM into your CD-ROM drive.
(3) Choose Run from the File menu of the Program Manager and type d:\Kapsetup.exe (where d: is your CD-ROM drive).
(4) Press OK and follow the prompts.
(5) You are now ready to use the software. You must have the CD-ROM in your computer when using the software, even though you have installed information onto your hard drive. To run the program after installation, choose the Kaplan program group from the Program Manager and select the Mastering the Computer-Based TOEFL Test icon.
(6) At the title screen, click the mouse once anywhere on the screen to go on. Use the right-facing arrow at the top right of the next few screens to go through the introduction and get to the Main Menu.

WINDOWS 95 or Higher

(1) Exit out of all open applications (make sure you have no applications running).
(2) Insert *Kaplan's Mastering the Computer-Based TOEFL Test* CD-ROM into your CD-ROM drive.
(3) From the Start Menu, choose Run and type (or browse for) d:\Kapsetup.exe (where d: is your CD-ROM drive).
(4) Press OK and follow the prompts.
(5) You are now ready to use the software. You must have the CD-ROM in your computer when using the software, even though you have installed information on your hard drive. To run the program, go to the Start Menu, choose Programs, then Kaplan, then Mastering the Computer-Based TOEFL Test.
(6) At the title screen, click the mouse once anywhere on the screen to go on. Use the right-facing arrow at the top right of the next few screens to go through the introduction and get to the Main Menu.

MACINTOSH

(1) Quit out of all open applications (make sure you have no applications running).

(2) Insert *Kaplan's Mastering the Computer-Based TOEFL Test* CD-ROM into your CD-ROM drive.

(3) Double-click the Kaplan Mastering TOEFL Install icon.

(4) Follow the prompts.

(5) When Kaplan files are done installing, the installer will determine if you need to install QuickTime. If so, you will be prompted to do so.

(6) When QuickTime installation is complete, you will be forced to restart your computer.

(7) You are now ready to use the software. You must have the CD-ROM in your computer when using the software, even though you have installed information on your hard drive. To launch the program, double-click the Kaplan Mastering the TOEFL Test icon.

(8) At the title screen, click the mouse once anywhere on the screen to go on. Use the right-facing arrow at the top right of the next few screens to go through the introduction and get to the Main Menu.

USING THE APPLICATION—MAJOR SECTIONS OF THE SOFTWARE

At the Main Menu, you will have three options:

- Familiarize yourself with the different types of questions and strategies for answering these questions
- Learn more about Access America programs provided by Kaplan Educational Centers and about computer-based testing
- Take a full-length practice computer-based TOEFL test

Strategies and Practice

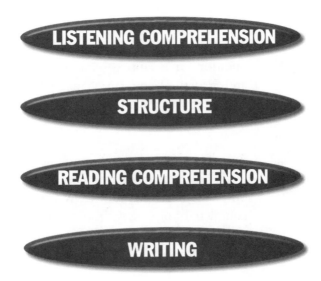

LISTENING COMPREHENSION

STRUCTURE

READING COMPREHENSION

WRITING

Kaplan Strategies for Listening, Structure, Reading, and Writing will walk you through strategies for approaching each section and answering its questions, and will provide a short set of practice questions. You will get feedback on your performance and the correct answers to the practice questions. For more information on the format of the test, you can contact ETS to receive a free copy of their CD-ROM Sampler, which includes in-depth tutorials (the same ones you'll see on test day) on the new computer-based TOEFL test. Write to TOEFL Order Services, P.O. Box 6161, Princeton, NJ 08541-6161. You can also order the CD-ROM or download the tutorial from the Web at www.toefl.org.

These button descriptions will help you navigate through the strategies and practice questions.

Tutorial Screens:

Navigates forward and backward through the screens.

Exits *Mastering the Computer-Based TOEFL Test*.

Returns to the Main Menu screen.

Question Screens:

Available in all test areas. Click this to go on the next question. In adaptive sections (Listening Comprehension and Structure) you can change your response after clicking next, but you must confirm your response to go on to the next question.

Available in Listening Comprehension and Structure test areas. You must click this after clicking Next in order to go on to the next question. In Writing, click this when you've completed your essay. You cannot change your answer or return to the item after clicking on Confirm. Confirm saves your response, and sends you to the next item.

Available only in the Reading test area. Goes back to the previous question.

Review Screens:
You must complete the practice questions before you can access these screens.

Available from the Feedback and Answers areas. Goes to the beginning of the strategies for that section.

Shows analysis of your performance for the section of the practice questions you are reviewing.

Shows the questions, your responses to them, and the correct answers in the section you are reviewing.

Typing Test
This typing test goes with the Writing section of Kaplan's Mastering the Computer-Based TOEFL Test CD-ROM. *Type the essay below as quickly and accurately as you can. After 5 minutes have passed, your essay will be checked for its accuracy, and your typing speed will be calculated by the CD-ROM. This information will help you decide whether you should hand write the essay portion of the TOEFL or type it directly onto the computer.*

It is important for all TOEFL test-takers to be able to use the computer. Not only are computers used for the actual TOEFL test, they are an important part of everyday life for a student. From typing papers to finding out in which building your class is being held, computers are indispensable for today's university student.

Whether you are studying art history or zoology, business or medicine, the laws of man or the laws of nature, your professor will expect you to turn in assignments that have been typed on a computer. Gone are the days of handwritten essays on notebook paper. Be sure to practice using an American keyboard whenever you can. The keys may be laid out differently from keyboards in your own country, so pay close attention. Also, word-processing programs vary from one to another. The TOEFL word-processing program is probably very different from any you have seen before. Make sure you use the "help" button on your screen if you do not know how to perform a particular function.

Typing test continued on next page

Many institutions disseminate a great deal of important information via the internet. You will be given an e-mail account when you begin your studies and will use it often to communicate with fellow students, professors and university administrators. Most universities also maintain a web page, that is, a particular site on the internet where you can find information ranging from a class syllabus to recreational activities on campus. For more information on many universities, you can check out Kaplan's web site at http://www.kaplan.com.

(end of test)

Access America

ACCESS AMERICA

If you are considering studying or attending school in the United States, this section will give you valuable information about the U.S. educational system. It also contains information about Kaplan programs, and more details and strategies for taking computer-based exams.

These button descriptions will help you navigate through information in this section.

Shows a list of all topics available to review.

In subsections with video and text, plays the video.

In subsections with video and text, displays the text.

Full-Length Practice Test

Once you've worked with the strategies and practice questions and feel comfortable with the interface and mechanics of taking the test on the computer, you can take a full-length test that follows the format of the actual computer-based TOEFL exam. While the test will not be officially scored, it will consist of all four sections and be timed as the real exam would be.

At the end of the test, you will receive an analysis of your test performance in several key areas. Use this feedback to adjust your test-taking strategies and zero in on your weaker areas. The feedback is broken down as follows:

(1) Overall

Shows a breakdown of right, wrong, and omitted items for each section.

(2) Content

Shows the percentage correct you received in key content areas. Use this as a guide for further study; you'll want to concentrate more on areas in which you did not score well.

(3) Timing

The pace of this test is the same as what you could expect on test day. If you're having trouble finishing the test, see whether your time investment is paying off. We'll tell you the 5 questions on which you spent the most and the least time. How did you do on these questions? If you tend to get them wrong despite spending a large amount of time on them, consider a change in test-taking strategy.

To take the full-length test:

(1) Click the Full-Length Test button on the Main Menu.

(2) A Login window will appear. Click the button "Add New User." Type in any 8-digit number (the number cannot begin with a zero) and click OK. You only need to add yourself once. To review, resume, or reset your test, select your ID from the list, click Select User, and enter your name.

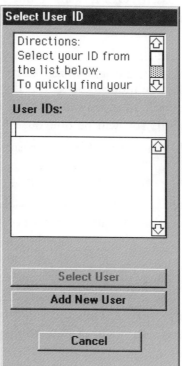

(3) At the next window, enter your name (remember exactly what you type; you will need it to access your test results at a later time). Click OK.

KAPLAN

(4) You can now click Continue to begin the full-length test, or you can click Main Menu to take it at some other time. Follow all on-screen instructions.

(5) Since stamina is a big part of taking the TOEFL test, you are encouraged to complete the test at one sitting with one short break in the middle, as you would if taking the actual test. However, we allow you to exit the test and early and resume at a later time. There are two ways to exit early:

- *From the middle of a section* (Windows users press the Esc key or Control-Q, Macintosh users press Command-period). **Your answers to that section will not be saved.** All completed sections will be saved. You will be quit out of the *Mastering the Computer-Based TOEFL Test* software completely (not recommended).
- *Between sections* (click the Exit button at the end of a section instead of continue). All of your work will be saved and you can resume taking the test at a later time. You will returned to the Main Menu of the software.

(6) To resume taking the test, go to the login screen and click the 8-digit number you already entered, click Select User, and enter your name.

These button descriptions will help you navigate through the full-length practice test.

Question Screens:

After reading the directions, click this to begin the section.

Available in Reading only. Click this after scrolling through the passage to get to the first question.

Available in all test areas. Click this to go on the next question. In adaptive sections (Listening Comprehension and Structure) you can change your response after clicking next, but you must confirm your response to go on to the next question.

Available in Listening Comprehension and Structure test areas. You must click this after clicking Next in order to go on to the next question. In Writing, click this when you've completed your essay. You cannot change your answer or return to the item after clicking on Confirm. Confirm saves your response, and sends you to the next item.

Available only in the Reading test area. Goes back to the previous question.

Review Screens

You must complete the entire test before you can use these buttons.

Available after completing the full-length test. Brings you to the Overall Feedback screen.

Shows the questions, your responses to them, and the correct answers in each section of the full-length test.

Shows an analysis of your content mastery and test-taking skills for each section of full-length test.

Shows general feedback (number of right, wrong, and omitted questions) for all sections of the full-length test.

Available in Listening Analysis only. Replays the audio so you can read the transcript for each question while listening to it.

AUDIO FOR BOOK PRACTICE

All of the audio files that are referenced throughout this book are located on the CD-ROM. **The CD-ROM must be played on a computer and cannot be used with a regular music CD player.**

(1) Insert *Kaplan's Mastering the Computer-Based TOEFL Test CD-ROM* into your CD-ROM drive.
(2) Navigate to the folder called "Audio" on the CD-ROM.
(3) Double-click the file referenced in the text of the book. The QuickTime MoviePlayer will launch (if you are prompted about purchasing QuickTime 3.0 Pro, click "Later"), and a control bar will appear:

The only button you will need on the control bar is: play/pause. Click the right arrow to begin playing the sound. If it is too loud or too soft, you'll need to adjust your computer's volume. On Windows, do this through Sounds in the Control Panel or, if available, on the Task Bar. On Macintosh, do this through Sound in the Control Panels. (If you use the volume button on the QuickTime controller, you will need to adjust the volume of each file individually.) There is no need to start/stop playback after each question. The audio file includes time to respond that approximates the pace of the actual test.

When you are done listening to a file, you can open the next one by choosing Open from the File menu in the QuickTime MoviePlayer. (If you double-click the next file, the QuickTime MoviePlayer will relaunch.) Then, navigate to the Kaplan CD-ROM, and select the desired audio file. If you are done with audio files for now, you can Quit out of the QuickTime movie player.

The audio files do not necessarily appear in the same order in the text as they do on the CD-ROM. The text will direct you to the appropriate audio track numbers on the CD-ROM.

The audio files for the paper-based practice tests are named:

Test_1A.mov	Test_2A.mov
Test_1B.mov	Test_2B.mov
Test_1C.mov	Test_2C.mov

The audio files for the Power Lessons are named:

Listening Power Lesson One:

Track_1.mov
Track_2.mov
Track_3.mov
Track_4.mov
Track_5.mov
Track_6.mov
Track_7.mov

Listening Power Lesson One Vocabulary: Track_8.mov

Listening Power Lesson Two:

Track_9.mov
Track_10.mov
Track_11.mov
Track_12.mov
Track_13.mov

Listening Power Lesson Two Vocabulary: Track_14.mov

Listening Power Lesson Three:

Track_15.mov
Track_16.mov
Track_17.mov
Track_18.mov
Track_19.mov

Listening Power Lesson Three Vocabulary: Track_20.mov

Reading Power Lesson One Vocabulary: Track_21.mov

Reading Power Lesson Two Vocabulary: Track_22.mov

PART ONE:

UNDERSTANDING THE TOEFL

GETTING STARTED

WHOM THIS BOOK IS FOR

This book was written with a particular group in mind: students who are preparing for the Test of English as a Foreign Language (TOEFL) on their own. Self-study students will appreciate the clear, carefully written lessons as well as the fact that answer keys are provided for all of the exercises and practice tests.

TOEFL for the Computer is filled with information on the new computer-based TOEFL exam. Those who plan to take the paper-based test will also find it useful. However, if the computer-based TOEFL exam is not offered in your country, we recommend that you buy Kaplan's *TOEFL* book instead of, or in addition to, this one. *TOEFL* concentrates exclusively on the paper-based exam and offers more paper-based test strategies and practice exams than we are able to provide in this book.

This book assumes that the student using it has a good grasp of the English language. Students who have a previous TOEFL score of below 440 should probably improve their basic knowledge of the language before attempting to devote themselves to TOEFL preparation.

How This Book Will Help You

This book will improve your TOEFL score in two ways. First, it takes a very practical view of the TOEFL. One TOEFL exam is not very different from any other, and the authors of this book have spent years teaching TOEFL preparation and administering these exams. They have also read numerous studies of the TOEFL and of the kind of language that it tests. The very organization of this book has been shaped by this experience.

Basically, *TOEFL for the Computer* is organized around the kinds of questions the TOEFL asks. For example, there is a section of this book designed to help students master the "What is his or her job?" type of question that is often asked in the Listening Comprehension section of the TOEFL. Other sections teach students to recognize and be prepared for distractors—answers that look correct but are actually what the makers of the TOEFL use to mislead test takers.

But the authors' experience has also taught them the limitations of this approach. The TOEFL tests English language proficiency, and although practice tests and strategy lessons can improve a student's score somewhat, the best way for students to really bring their test scores up is to improve their English-language ability as a whole. This is especially true with regard to vocabulary, which is far more important for high TOEFL scores than many people realize. For this reason, this book takes a unique approach: It emphasizes vocabulary building in every lesson, and even provides students with a special section at the back of the book designed to help students learn the kinds of words they need for the TOEFL.

What Is the TOEFL?

This section of the book is meant to give you a clear understanding of exactly what the Test of English as a Foreign Language is—and exactly what it is not. There is an expression in English that states, "Know thy enemy." This means that the best way to defeat an opponent is to know as much as possible about that opponent.

To get the best possible TOEFL score possible, you should know the TOEFL as well as the people at Kaplan do—and we know the TOEFL inside and out!

Some Basic Information on the TOEFL

The Test of English as a Foreign Language (TOEFL) is designed to test your ability to understand standard North American English. It is written and administered by the Educational Testing Service (ETS), a private, not-for-profit company based in Princeton, New Jersey. The TOEFL was developed to help American and Canadian colleges and universities evaluate the level of English language proficiency of the international students they want to admit. You may need a certain TOEFL score to get into a particular college or university. However, even a great TOEFL score does not guarantee that you will get into the college of your choice. Nor does a great TOEFL score guarantee academic success. To succeed in school, you also need to know how to communicate in English.

The TOEFL is one of several standardized tests that measure a student's proficiency level in English. A standardized test:

➤ Consists of different types of multiple-choice questions
➤ Is given to a large number of people at the same time
➤ Is graded by computer
➤ Is timed

Because Kaplan has studied and analyzed many TOEFL exams, we can explain to you the form of the test and the kinds of questions that will appear on it, as well as help you develop skills and strategies for taking it. This will allow you to work more efficiently when the time comes to take the actual TOEFL exam.

Beginning in 1998, the TOEFL will be offered as a computerized test in many areas of the world. However, in certain countries, the paper-based TOEFL will continue to be used. In the pages that follow we will discuss in detail the differences between the paper-based and the computer-based TOEFL and what you can expect from each.

Basic Sections of the TOEFL

In both the paper-based and the computer-based TOEFL exams, each section tests particular skills in English communication:

Listening Comprehension

The questions in the Listening Comprehension section test your understanding of English grammar, idioms, and vocabulary. They also test your ability to distinguish between words with similar sounds. And since you have only about 12 seconds to answer each question, your ability to concentrate and your ability to distinguish between words with similar sounds will also be very important.

Structure and Written Expression (Simply Called Structure on the Computer-Based TOEFL)

The questions in the Structure section focus on grammar and word choice. This section stresses grammar, but your vocabulary plays a large role in doing well here, especially when you are asked to make a correct word choice.

Reading Comprehension

In the Reading Comprehension section, you must read a number of passages and answer 7 to 10 questions for each passage about what you have read. You will be asked about the content of what you read, and about the meanings of words as they are used in a passage.

TWE (called Writing on the Computer-Based TOEFL)

The TWE or Writing section of the TOEFL is a 30-minute section that tests your ability to write in English. This includes the ability to come up with and organize ideas, support your ideas with examples and/or evidence, and to write in standard English in response to an assigned topic.

PAPER-BASED TOEFL

The paper-based TOEFL will continue to be administered until at least the year 2000 in the following countries:

Bangladesh	Japan	People's Republic of China
Bhutan	Korea	Taiwan
Cambodia	Laos	Thailand
Hong Kong	Macao	Vietnam
India	Pakistan	

In addition to these countries, all Institutional TOEFLs will continue to be paper-based, regardless of the country in which they are administered. The Institutional TOEFL, as its name implies, is given by an institution or school to its own students. This exam has the same form, content, and level of difficulty as the official TOEFL and is also produced and distributed by ETS, but is considered unofficial by ETS for college or university admissions from overseas. Some universities will, however, accept the score of an Institutional TOEFL conditionally while waiting for your official score.

Again, for more in-depth information on the paper-based TOEFL than we can provide in this book, you can turn to Kaplan's book called *TOEFL*, available in countries in which the computer-based TOEFL is not yet offered.

Form and Content

The paper-based TOEFL is approximately two hours long and consists of 140 multiple-choice questions. If you include the time it takes to fill in forms and listen to directions, you will spend about three hours at the test site.

Paper-based TOEFL questions are divided into three sections: Section I, Listening Comprehension; Section II, Structure and Written Expression; and Section III, Reading Comprehension. Each section is timed separately. You have approximately 30 to 40 minutes to work on Section I, 25 minutes to work on Section II, and 55 minutes to work on Section III. Once you are done with a section, you cannot return to it.

Listening Comprehension

In Section I, Listening Comprehension, which consists of 50 questions, you listen to spoken English and answer questions that test how well you understood what you heard. This section consists of three parts: A, B, and C. In part A, you hear 30 short conversations and answer a question about each one. In part B, you hear three or four longer conversations and answer a few questions about each one. In part C, you listen to three or four talks of about a minute each and answer several questions about each one.

Structure and Written Expression

In Section II, Structure and Written Expression, which consists of 40 questions, you are asked to either complete a sentence, or identify an error in a sentence. The first 15 questions are sentence completion, in which you will see a sentence with a blank space. You will be presented with four answer choices from which you will choose one. The remaining 25 questions are error identification, in which each question consists of a sentence that contains four underlined words or phrases, labeled A, B, C, and D. One of these four words or phrases is incorrect, and you must identify it.

Reading Comprehension

In the Reading Comprehension section you must read 5 or 6 reading passages and answer 50 questions about what you have read. You will be asked about the content of what you read and the meanings of the words as they are used in a passage. Questions include four answer choices from which you select the best answer.

TWE

The TWE (Test of Written Expression) is an optional section of the paper-based TOEFL that tests your ability to respond to a question in essay form using standard English. You are given a choice of two topics, from which you pick one. You must write your essay by hand.

Computer-Based TOEFL

The computer-based TOEFL employs two types of computerized testing: computer adaptive testing (CAT) and computer-linear testing. Before we take a closer look at the different sections of the computer-based TOEFL, let's take a moment to clarify the differences between these two types of testing.

Computer Adaptive Testing

Computer adaptive testing is a complex system for determining your proficiency level in the English language. The following is a very simplified explanation of how computer adaptive and computer-based testing determine your TOEFL score.

Computer adaptive tests, or CATs, are quite different from the paper-and-pencil standardized tests you have probably seen in the past. For example, you might have taken the TOEFL before July 1998 early on a Saturday morning with a huge room full of other test takers, all of whom were given identical tests with questions that ranged in difficulty from easy to hard. The CAT is a computer-based test that you take at a special test center, by yourself, at a time you schedule.

The major difference between the tests is that the CAT "adapts" to your performance. Each test taker is given a different mix of questions depending on how well he or she is doing on the test. This means the questions get harder or easier depending on whether you answer them correctly or not. Your score is not directly determined by how many questions you get right, but by the difficulty level of the questions you answer correctly.

Computer Adaptive Test Scoring

When you start a section, the computer:

- Assumes you have a medium level score as defined by ETS's TOEFL division
- Gives you a medium difficulty question; about half the people who take the test would get this question right, and half would get it wrong

What happens next depends on whether you answered the question correctly. If you answer the question correctly:

- Your score goes up
- You are given a slightly harder question

If you answer a question incorrectly:

- Your score goes down
- You are given a slightly easier question

This continues for the rest of the test. Every time you get the question right, the computer raises your score, then gives you a slightly harder question. Every time you get a question wrong, the computer lowers your score, then gives you a slightly easier question. In this way the computer tries to "home in" on your score.

Theoretically, as you get to the end of a section, you will reach a point at which every time the computer raises the difficulty level of a question, you get it wrong, but every time it lowers the difficulty level of a question, you get it right. Your score at this point will supposedly be an accurate measure of your ability.

Sample Computer Adaptive Test
To do your best on a CAT, you must have a grasp of the mechanics by which it finds your score. Take a look at the adaptive test on the following pages. It follows the same sort of rules the CAT does in assigning a score and a new question.

As you answer the questions, notice what happens to your score as you get questions right or wrong, and what happens to the difficulty level of the questions if you get them right or wrong.

Pick an answer for question 1,
then check the answer on the page
following the test.

Each time you get a question
right, follow the 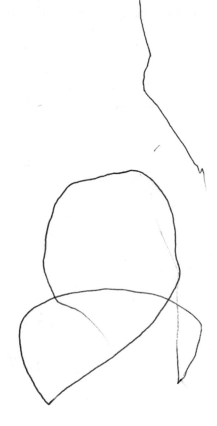 arrow.

Each time you get a question
wrong, follow the ⊗ arrow.

Your current score is the value in
the oval.

WORLD CAPITALS ADAPTIVE TEST

2. What is the capital of Norway?

    Copenhagen
    Lillehammar
    Oslo
    Narvik
    Stockholm

227

✓

⊗

✓

START HERE

1. What is the capital of the People's
   Republic of China?

    Shanghai
    Hong Kong
    Beijing
    Nanking
    Taipei

177

⊗

2. What is the capital of Mexico?

    Guadalajara
    Mexicali
    Mexico City
    Tenotchtitlan
    Tijuana

123

✓

⊗

4. What is the capital of Eritrea?

Asmara
Berbera
Bosasu
Masawa
Mogadishu

287 → ✓ → **300**
287 → ✗ → **277**

3. What is the capital of Australia?

Canberra
Melbourne
Perth
Porpoise Spit
Sydney

263 ✓

263 ✗

4. What is the capital of Brazil?

Amazonia
Brasilia
Buenos Aires
Rio de Janeiro
São Paulo

237 → ✓ → **247**
237 → ✗ → **223**

4. What is the capital of Kenya?

Harare
Kampala
Lusaka
Mombasa
Nairobi

213 → ✓ → **223**
213 → ✗ → **200**

3. What is the capital of Portugal?

Florence
Madrid
Le Paz
Lisbon
São Paulo

187 ✓

187 ✗

4. What is the capital of Vietnam?

Bangkok
Hanoi
Ho Chi Minh City
Hue
Phnom Penh

160 → ✓ → **173**
160 → ✗ → **150**

4. What is the capital of Iceland?

Ålborg
Birkenstock
Reykjavik
Trondheim
Björk

187 → ✓ → **200**
187 → ✗ → **173**

3. What is the capital of Spain?

Barcelona
Bilbao
Granada
Madrid
Seville

163 ✓

163 ✗

4. What is the capital of Austria?

Berlin
Bonn
Prague
Linz
Vienna

140 → ✓ → **150**
140 → ✗ → **127**

3. What is the capital of France?

Madrid
Marseilles
Louisville
Paris
The Hague

83 ✓

83 ✗

4. What is the capital of Japan?

Helsinki
Kyoto
Nakasone
Osaka
Tokyo

113 → ✓ → **127**
113 → ✗ → **100**

4. What is the capital of the U.S.A.?

Washington, D.C.
Chicago
New York
Ottowa
Austin

53 → ✓ → **67**
53 → ✗ → **40**

Answer Key for Sample Test

Question 1:   The capital of the People's Republic of China is Beijing.

Question 2:   The capital of Norway is Oslo.
The capital of Mexico is Mexico City.

Question 3:   The capital of Australia is Canberra.
The capital of Portugal is Lisbon.
The capital of Spain is Madrid.
The capital of France is Paris.

Question 4:   The capital of Eritrea is Asmara.
The capital of Brazil is Brasilia.
The capital of Kenya is Nairobi.
The capital of Vietnam is Hanoi.
The capital of Iceland is Reykjavik.
The capital of Austria is Vienna.
The capital of Japan is Tokyo.
The capital of the U.S.A. is Washington, D.C.

How Does This Test Relate to the Real CAT Sections of the TOEFL?
So, how did you do? Of course you will never see questions like this on the TOEFL; we used this simple example to illustrate a few important points about the computer adaptive test. Here's what you might have noticed:

1. The questions get progressively easier or harder depending on your performance.
The first question was of average difficulty. If you got it right, your next question was one that most people found a little harder. If you got it wrong, the next question was a little easier. This was true for every subsequent question as well. The effect is cumulative. If you keep getting questions right, the questions keep getting harder. If you keep getting questions wrong, the questions keep getting easier. The same thing will happen on the actual CAT sections of the TOEFL.

2. Questions at the start of the test are worth more than questions at the end of the test.
Say, for example, on the World Capitals test, you got question 1 and 2 right and questions 3 and 4 wrong. Even though you got two questions right and two questions wrong, you would have gotten a score of 223—an above average score. Because the first two questions were worth more than the last two questions, you gained a lead that could not be eroded by two mistakes. This is also why people can get the same number of questions right on a CAT and still get different scores. (If you got two right then two wrong, you got a 223; if you got two wrong and two right you got a 127.) It is as important where you got the questions right or wrong as how many you got right or wrong.

On the real CAT sections of the TOEFL, the computer makes large jumps to find your approximate scoring level quickly, then makes much smaller jumps to fine-tune your score. Take a look at the following graph. It illustrates how your score might rise and fall on a real CAT. Notice how large the jumps are at the beginning compared to those at the end. On the TOEFL you have to start strong—the early questions have the greatest effect on your score.

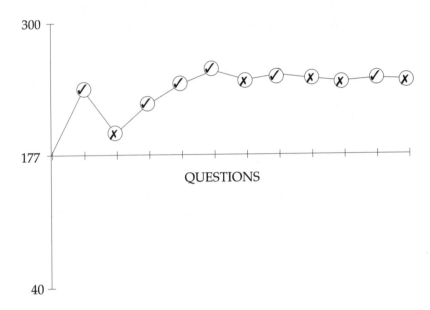

CAT Law of Diminishing Returns

In general, each succeeding question you are given is worth less to your score than the previous question in the section. If you get a question wrong at the start of the test, you will have to get several questions right later on simply to undo the damage.

3. You must answer each question in the order it is given to you.
The structure of the test means you must take the questions one at a time, as they are given to you. You can't skip around on the CAT sections of the TOEFL; if you are stuck, you have to guess an answer if you want to move on.

Computer-Linear Testing

Computer-linear testing is similar to computer adaptive testing in that you record your answer on the computer; however, in computer-linear testing, the test does not adjust for your level. You will be given a set number of questions to answer. In a computer-linear testing situation, you can skip a question and come back to it later, but we don't recommend doing this as it is very easy to lose your place in the exam.

Form and Content of the Computer-Based TOEFL

The length of the computer-based TOEFL is more flexible than the paper-based TOEFL. You will have up to three-and-a-half hours to complete the exam, which includes time for a break. Your appointment for the exam will cover a four-and-a-half hour time slot; this is to allow ample time to do the necessary paperwork. When you begin a section, the total number of questions will appear at the top of the screen. On each question screen you will be provided with information telling you which question you are currently on and how many questions there are in total.

Computer-based TOEFL questions are divided into four sections: Section I, Listening Comprehension; Section II, Structure; Section III, Reading Comprehension; and Section IV, Writing. Each section is timed separately. You have 40 or 60 minutes to work on Section I, 15 or 20 minutes to work on Section II, 70 or 90 minutes to work on Section III, and 30 minutes to work on Section IV. Once you are done with a section, you cannot return to it.

The following is a general overview of each section of the computer-based TOEFL. For more detailed information on what you can expect from the computer-based versions of these different sections, check out the Listening, Structure, Reading, and Writing Power Lessons later in this book.

Listening Comprehension

The Listening Comprehension section of the computer-based TOEFL is computer adaptive. You will have 40 or 60 minutes to complete Section I, Listening Comprehension. This section consists of 30 or 50 questions in which you listen to spoken English and answer questions that test how well you understood what you heard. This section consists of two parts: A and B. In part A you will hear a number of short conversations anywhere from 6 to 20 seconds long and be asked to answer a question about each one. In part B you will hear 2 or 3 longer conversations from 30 seconds to 1 minute and a few long talks that are 1.5 to 2.5 minutes long. You will be asked to answer 4 or 5 questions about each one. The subject matter for these questions is academic or university related. Computer-based listening comprehension questions may appear in the following formats:

- Four choice
- Multiple answer (pick two of four choices)
- Ordering or matching questions (click on one element, then click on another to create a match)
- Graphic region selection (click on a picture or element in a picture)

Structure

The Structure section of the computer-based TOEFL, Section II, is computer adaptive. You will have 15 or 20 minutes to complete this section. It consists of 20 or 25 questions in which you either complete a sentence or identify an error.

There are two question formats mixed together here:

- Four choice
- Click on underlined word

Reading Comprehension

The Reading Comprehension section of the computer-based TOEFL, Section III, is computer linear. You will have 70 or 90 minutes to complete it. You must read 5 to 8 academic reading passages and will be asked a number of questions about the content of what you read and the meanings of the words as they are used in the passage. The total number of questions will be either 44 or 60. The computer-based Reading Comprehension section includes slightly longer passages than the paper-based test. You must read off of the screen and will need to scroll in order to read the entire passage. There are four question formats:

- Four choice
- Click on word, paragraph, or sentence
- Insert text
- Graphic region choice

Assessment of Written English

The Writing section of the computer-based TOEFL is required of all TOEFL test-takers. You will have 30 minutes to write an essay in response to a single question that will appear on the screen. You can either type your answer on the computer or hand write your essay on a separate sheet of paper. The results from this section will be combined with those from the Structure section to give a final scaled score. The computer does not figure out your grade on this section; it must be graded the old-fashioned way—by human beings who are specifically trained to score your essay.

ADMINISTRATION OF THE TOEFL

Recent changes in the administration of the TOEFL include:

- When and where students take the TOEFL
- The number of questions a student must answer
- The duration of the exam
- The overall scaled score
- Format

ETS has a contract with Sylvan Technology Centers to administer the computer-based TOEFL exam. Each of the centers is set up according to strict regulations. Even the furniture, color of the walls, and number of computers available are the same in each center!

Probably the number one change is the fact that you can now take the TOEFL any day of the year (except Sundays and holidays) and you have a choice of morning or afternoon to take your test. You should register early to take the test—Sylvan Technology Centers can only accommodate up to 15 test takers at one time, and you may be taking your exam next to other students who are taking other ETS standardized tests. You can still take the test once per calendar month, but if you register for a test twice in one month, you will not receive a score for the second exam and your money will not be refunded.

You cannot eat, drink, or smoke while taking the test. Your personal belongings can be stored in a locker provided to you by the testing center. You should not bring anything but yourself into the testing center—no pencils, pens, paper, calculators, books of any kind, dictionaries, electronic equipment, watches with calculators, pagers, or translators. Finally, you will not get any scratch paper and you are not permitted to take notes during the exam. If you choose to hand write your essay, you will be given paper at that time.

How to Register for the TOEFL

To register to take the TOEFL, you need to fill out the form in the *Bulletin of Information*, which also contains a list of all the test dates for the TOEFL, the TWE, and the TSE. Copies of the *Bulletin* are usually obtainable at United States educational commissions, United States Information Service (USIS) offices and libraries, binational centers, and private English language schools.

If you cannot get a copy of the *Bulletin of Information* locally, you can write to:

TOEFL/TSE Publications
P.O. Box 6154
Princeton, NJ 08541-6154 USA
Phone: (609) 771-7100
Fax: (609) 771-7500
E-mail: toefl@ets.org

Test Day Tips

(1) Arrive at the test center at least a half hour before your scheduled test time in order to check in. If you arrive late for your appointment, you may not be able to take the test at that time and your registration fee will not be refunded.

(2) Make sure you bring proper photo identification with you to the testing center. There are strict requirements for the Photo Identification section. In the United States you can use your passport as official photo identification (exceptions apply to U.S. citizens, naturalized citizens, immigrants, refugees, or members of the U.S. Armed Forces). If you are taking the exam outside of the United States, you can use your passport as photo ID. Be sure to read the latest ETS bulletin to see what the acceptable alternative identifications are for the region in which you are taking the exam, if you do not currently hold a passport.

(3) You will also need your appointment confirmation number, which is given to you when you register for the exam.

(4) Compose a list of institutions to which you would like to automatically send your test scores. You can have scores automatically sent to four institutions at no additional charge.

SCORING

When you take an official TOEFL, ETS will send reports of your score directly to the institutions you choose, and to you, about one month after you take the test. You will receive four scores, one for each of the three TOEFL sections, and most importantly, a three-digit total score.

Your total score is based on the number of correct answers you identified, adjusted (the technical word for this is *scaled*) for the difficulty level of the particular TOEFL you took. Statistically speaking, a TOEFL score is not precise. ETS says that TOEFL scores have a plus or minus 14-point margin of error, which means that if you get a 500, your real proficiency in English ranges from 486–514. Some schools may take this fact into account when evaluating your English for admission.

The total score is reported on a 200–677 scale, and the scores for each section are reported on a scale of 20–68. Most students get a total score of between 440 and 580. The score you need to get depends on the admissions requirements of the college or university you are trying to get into.

The chart on the following page will give you an idea of how TOEFL scores measure English proficiency. Remember that the lowest score possible is 200, and the highest score possible is 677.

TOEFL SCORE	PROFICIENCY LEVEL	PROFICIENCY DESCRIPTION
380	Elementary Proficiency	Able to satisfy basic survival requirements and maintain very simple face-to-face conversations on familiar topics; thinks in native language and translates into English.
450	Intermediate Proficiency	Can initiate and maintain predictable face-to-face conversations; range and control of language limited; demonstrates emerging, but not consistent, basic grammar; can read very simple English texts.
550	Working Proficiency	Able to satisfy routine social demands; facility with concrete subject matter and language; usually thinks in English, occasionally resorts to translation; needs more practice in academic-level reading.
630	Advanced Working Proficiency	Approaching native proficiency in English; able to satisfy most academic requirements with language usage that is often, but not always, acceptable and effective; effective use of language may deteriorate under tension or pressure.

Passing TOEFL Score

There is no "passing" or "failing" score on the TOEFL. The test measures English language proficiency only and it is up to the individual college or university to set its own minimum TOEFL score for admission. Minimum scores can vary from a low of 450 to a high of 630 or more. A score of 677 is considered perfect.

Keep in mind that schools with low TOEFL admissions score requirements may also have lower academic standards. In many colleges, to major in communications, journalism, public relations, marketing, advertising, and English/American literature, you need a TOEFL score of 600. The most prestigious American universities require a paper-based TOEFL score of 600 or more for all students admitted. Most top-tier master of business administration (MBA) programs require a TOEFL score of 600 in addition to good GMAT scores.

Paper-Based Scores versus Computer-Based Scores

The concordance table on the following pages will tell you how paper-based TOEFL scores compare with computer-based TOEFL scores. For more details on how each section is scored, read through the introductory pages of each Power Lesson section carefully.

TOEFL CONCORDANCE TABLE TOTAL SCORE COMPARISON

Paper-Based TOEFL	Computer-Based TOEFL	Paper-Based TOEFL	Computer-Based TOEFL	Paper-Based TOEFL	Computer-Based TOEFL
677	300	553	217	430	117
673	297	550	213	427	113
670	293	547	210	423	113
667	290	543	207	420	110
663	287	540	207	417	107
660	287	537	203	413	103
657	283	533	200	410	103
653	280	530	197	407	100
650	280	527	197	403	97
647	277	523	193	400	97
643	273	520	190	397	93
640	273	517	187	393	90
637	270	513	188	390	90
633	267	510	180	387	87
630	267	507	180	383	83
627	263	503	177	380	83
623	263	500	173	377	80
620	260	497	170	373	77
617	260	493	167	370	77
613	257	490	163	367	73
610	253	487	163	363	73
607	253	483	160	360	70
603	250	480	157	357	70
600	250	477	153	353	67
597	247	473	150	350	63
593	243	470	150	347	63
590	243	467	147	343	60
587	240	463	143	340	60
583	237	460	140	337	57
580	237	457	137	333	57
577	233	453	133	330	53
573	230	450	133	327	50
570	230	447	130	323	50
567	227	443	127	320	47
563	223	440	123	317	47
560	220	437	123	313	43
557	220	433	120	310	40

TOEFL CONCORDANCE TABLE TOTAL SCORE RANGE COMPARISON

Paper-Based TOEFL	Computer-Based TOEFL	Paper-Based TOEFL	Computer-Based TOEFL
660–677	287–300	460–477	140–153
640–657	273–283	440–457	123–137
620–637	260–270	420–437	110–123
600–617	250–260	400–417	97–107
580–597	237–247	380–397	83–93
560–577	220–233	360–377	70–80
540–557	207–220	340–357	60–70
520–537	190–203	320–337	47–57
500–517	173–187	310–317	40–47
480–497	157–170		

TOEFL Concordance Table Section Scaled Scores

LISTENING COMPREHENSION		STRUCTURE/WRITING		READING	
Paper-Based TOEFL	Computer-Based TOEFL	Paper-Based TOEFL	Computer-Based TOEFL	Paper-Based TOEFL	Computer-Based TOEFL
68	30	68	30	67	30
67	30	67	29	66	29
66	29	66	28	65	28
65	28	65	28	64	28
64	27	64	27	63	27
63	27	63	27	62	26
62	26	62	26	61	26
61	25	61	26	60	25
60	25	60	25	59	25
59	24	59	25	58	24
58	23	58	24	57	23
57	22	57	23	56	22
56	22	56	23	55	21
55	21	55	22	54	21
54	20	54	21	53	20
53	19	53	20	52	19
52	18	52	20	51	18
51	17	51	19	50	17
50	16	50	18	49	16
49	15	49	17	48	16
48	14	48	17	47	15
47	13	47	16	46	14
46	12	46	15	45	13
45	11	45	14	44	13
44	10	44	14	43	12
43	9	43	13	42	11
42	9	42	12	41	11
41	8	41	11	40	10
40	7	40	11	39	9
39	6	39	10	38	9
38	6	38	9	37	8
37	5	37	9	36	8
36	5	36	8	35	7
35	4	35	8	34	7
34	4	34	7	33	6
33	3	33	7	32	6
32	3	32	6	31	5
31	2	31	6		

FREQUENTLY ASKED QUESTIONS

Q: How will studying from a book help me prepare for the computer-based TOEFL?
Well, there are really two answers to this question. The first is that even though the format of the test is different on the computer-based TOEFL—for example, you may be asked to click on a graphic element or choose two out of four answer choices—the skills being tested remain the same. In the Listening Comprehension section the main difference is that all of the audio clips (short and long conversations and lectures) are set within a university context. The location and vocation type questions on the paper-based TOEFL will not appear on the computer-based TOEFL. However, it is not a waste of time to practice these skills as they will be useful to you in your everyday English communication. The Structure section of the computer-based TOEFL is virtually identical to the paper-based exam, except that sentence completion and error identification questions are not segregated. Reading is actually a little easier on the computer-based exam, as the computer will highlight or otherwise indicate the section of the passage in which the answer can be found for certain question types. As for the writing section, it is your choice whether you will keyboard or hand write your response, and this book provides a great deal of focused writing practice.

The second answer to the question is that many students will still be required to take the paper-based exam. Anyone taking the TOEFL in the countries listed earlier in this book will still need to take the paper-based exam, as will any test-takers whose university requires an institutional TOEFL.

Q: How often can I take the computer-based TOEFL?
You can take the computer-based TOEFL only once per calendar month. If you register for the computer-based TOEFL twice in one month, your second score will not be recorded and you will have wasted your time and money. Be sure to check with ETS when scheduling your exam to make sure a sufficient amount of time has passed since your last exam.

Q: Is the TOEFL written or administered by the U.S. government's Department of Education?
No. The U.S. government has nothing to do with the TOEFL. The TOEFL is administered by the Educational Testing Service. ETS is a private, nongovernmental, not-for-profit organization that writes, manages, and administers standard exams for American college and university entrance.

Q: Is it possible to use a TOEFL score from a test taken a long time ago?
Not usually, no. Admissions officers want to know what your current English level is, so most admissions officers require a recent TOEFL score taken within the previous six months when they consider a candidate for admission.

Schools frequently have this rule because TOEFL scores can drop 30 to 60 points on average if a person takes a break of longer than two months from intensive English study. This is especially true if a student's level of English proficiency has not yet reached the 550 level.

Q: Can students prepare for the TOEFL in the same way that they study for a typical college exam?

No. Most exams test a student's knowledge of a set of information. There may or may not be a lot of information that the student needs to know, but it is always a finite amount. A student can make a list of information that he or she must learn and study it item by item.

The TOEFL, on the other hand, tests English proficiency. A language cannot be summed up in a list. The best way to improve your TOEFL scores is by improving your overall proficiency in the language.

Another way to improve your TOEFL score is to become very familiar with the exam. You should take several practice exams and you should know what kinds of questions and general topics to expect. You can also learn certain test-taking strategies—ways of finding the correct answer more quickly.

This book will help you do both. The unique emphasis on vocabulary will get you started on learning the kinds of words you need for success on the TOEFL . . . and in a real American college or university. At the same time, this book will give you the test-taking practice and the strategies you need to get the very best TOEFL score possible for you!

YOU'RE IN CHARGE!

This section is entitled "You're in Charge!" because we want to emphasize that you must take control of your own English learning. In addition to introducing you to the TOEFL, giving you practice tests, and suggesting test-taking strategies, this book will show you how to take charge of your own English learning.

The Limitations of Test Preparation without Intensive English Study

For a good TOEFL score, it is essential that you become familiar with the test and the kinds of questions it asks. This is true whether you are taking the paper-based or the computer-based TOEFL. A student who takes the test without this kind of preparation will not do as well as he or she would have with test preparation. So test preparation helps. The creators of this course have seen students' scores jump as much as 50 points (40) (computer-based TOEFL equivalents appear in parentheses) in a short, ten-week, 40-hour course.

The problem is that an increase of 30 (20), 40 (30), or even 50 (40) points may not be enough. If a student starts with a proficiency level of 440 (123), a jump of 50 points will not be sufficient for him or her to get into a university that requires a score of 550 (213) for admission. Even worse, a second or third TOEFL preparation course almost never improves a student's score as much as the first. So our imaginary student, who jumped from a 450 (133) to a 490 (163) after just ten weeks of TOEFL preparation, may have only a score of 500 (173) after two or three more courses—still not enough to get into the university he or she wants to attend.

What this student needs is more knowledge of English, not more TOEFL preparation. Too many learners of English don't understand this, and they continue to spend more money on too many TOEFL-preparation courses, or worse, they become frustrated and abandon their dreams of studying in the United States.

ETS, the makers of the TOEFL exam, once conducted a study that showed that, on average, an increase of 40 points on the TOEFL requires about 300 hours of intensive English study. The details of the study are shown in the graph below.

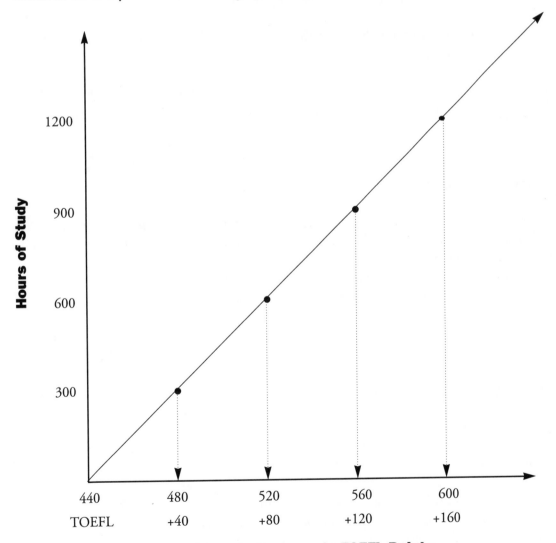

Average Increase in TOEFL Points

The Importance of Vocabulary

Look at the sentences below. They could all easily appear on the TOEFL exam. Do any of the underlined words seem incorrect to you?

She wants to marry as <u>tall a man</u> as possible.

You'll just have to <u>make do with what</u> you have.

Don't <u>talk with your mouth full</u>.

The French <u>founded</u> the city in 1678.

The fact is, there is nothing wrong with any of these sentences, no matter how strange they may look to a nonnative English speaker.

The point of the little test you just took is to show that even though no section of the TOEFL is called "Vocabulary," there is no doubt that vocabulary plays an important—perhaps the most important—role in every section.

Perhaps you're thinking, "Sure, I can see why vocabulary is important in the Reading Comprehension section, but why is it so important in the Listening Comprehension or Structure sections?"

Of course, the Listening Comprehension section tests your listening skills. But how can you expect to answer questions about what you have heard if you do not know the meaning of what is said? Moreover, in the Structure section (the grammar section) of the TOEFL, getting the correct answer often depends more on your knowledge of English idioms than your knowledge of English grammar. Even more often, it depends on your knowing whether something "sounds right" or not.

Look at the sentences above again. Do the underlined words "sound right" to you? If one or more of them sounds wrong, then you need to add that expression to your English vocabulary.

Keep in mind that vocabulary does not involve only individual words. It also includes idioms (like *to keep your head,* meaning "not to panic"), phrasal verbs (like *do something over,* meaning "to do something a second time"), and collocations (words that often appear together, like *sparsely populated,* meaning "having a low population"). Vocabulary, for the purposes of TOEFL, means using words the way real people use them.

The vocabulary sections in this book show you how words are used, and are followed by exercises that give you practice using the new words and expressions in real sentences. This approach will not only help you remember the words and expressions, but also develop a sense of what "sounds right" in English. It will also give you a good beginning to go out and take charge of your own vocabulary building by collecting English words and expressions that you encounter in films, television shows, books, magazines, and newspapers.

The Importance of Reading

Like vocabulary, reading is at the heart of the TOEFL exam, basically because it is at the heart of good academic skill preparation. Success on the TOEFL, and in any American college or university, depends heavily on a student's ability to read well.

Many students find the Reading Comprehension section of the TOEFL extremely difficult. To make matters worse, the Reading Comprehension section comes at the end of the exam, when concentration requires real effort. The best way to prepare for this section, and for your academic studies in general, is to do a lot of reading in English on your own.

Varying the content of your reading as much as possible is strongly recommended. This means that your reading should not be limited to one topic or style. For example, if you read a lot of literature, you should try to read science articles from a general-interest magazine like *Newsweek*. On the other hand, if you love science, read some short stories or a Hemingway novel. As you may already know from your native language, these are two very different types of reading.

The reason for this advice is that the Reading Comprehension section of the TOEFL requires the test taker to read an extremely varied amount of topics, from literature to geology to American history. If you can't read many different types of writing well—if you aren't familiar with different styles of writing and the different kinds of vocabulary belonging to different topics—you will probably not do well on the TOEFL.

Here is a list of the topics most often found in the reading section of the TOEFL, with a percentage indicating how frequently they appear.

➤ Natural and physical sciences (40%)
➤ American and natural history (30%)
➤ Biography (15%)
➤ Social science (10%)
➤ General interest (5%)

To get started, look for the chapter entitled "Recurring Topics and Related Vocabulary" later in this book. But remember that this is only a start: It's your job to *take charge* by going out and reading as much and as widely as you can in English.

THE TOEFL STUDY PLAN

In this section we offer a plan to the self-study student who is preparing for the TOEFL by himself or herself. To be as prepared as possible for the TOEFL, a student should go through every section of this book. The TOEFL Study Plan below offers advice on how to do that. How long it takes the student to go through all the lessons depends on how much time he or she spends on them per day.

(1) Study the chapter "TOEFL Test Strategies," and the "computer-based TOEFL" sections at the beginning of the Listening, Structure, and Reading Power Lessons.

Test strategies are suggestions on how to take the TOEFL. They can improve student scores significantly. The computer-based TOEFL sections will tell you how to tackle different types of questions on this exam.

(2) Take the Diagnostic Test (Practice Test One).

Use the answer key and the conversion chart at the end of the book to give yourself a grade for each section as well as an overall grade for the test. Decide on your areas of weakness.

(3) Begin a program of extensive reading in English.

Read widely—about many different topics, including the topics given in the "Recurring Topics and Related Vocabulary" section towards the back of the book. Begin collecting vocabulary words and expressions from the reading. You should do this even if the Reading Comprehension section was not the part of the exam you did most poorly in.

(4) Go through half of the Power Lessons.

The Power Lessons could be done in any order: listening first, then grammar, then reading; or, alternatively, a student could do one listening lesson and three grammar lessons, followed by one reading lesson. And don't forget the writing exercises in the Writing Power chapter, particularly if you are taking the computer-based TOEFL test, for which an essay is compulsory.

As you go through the Power Lessons of this book, you should take charge of your English acquisition by doing additional work in these areas. If the Listening Comprehension section was very difficult for you, schedule time to watch movies or TV programs in English, or to listen to English-language cassettes. If the Structure section was especially difficult, get a good reference grammar book and learn more about the grammar structures you got wrong on the practice test. If the Reading Comprehension section was your problem, go through the practice test and identify the topics that gave you the most trouble. Then go to an English language library or bookstore to get books and/or magazines on the troublesome topics.

(5) Take Practice Test Two or the computer-based TOEFL practice test.

If you are taking the paper-based exam, do Practice Test Two at this point in order to gain more familiarity with the paper-based exam format, especially if you have limited time in which to prepare for the test. If you are taking the computer-based TOEFL exam, try the full-length computer-based practice test on the CD-ROM included with this book. Use the answer key and the conversion chart at the back of the book, and/or the concordance charts on pages 19–20 to give yourself a grade for each section as well as an overall grade for the test.

Are your areas of weakness the same as after the first practice test? If so, you need more practice. Identify a new set of areas of weakness, and devote additional time to these.

(6) Finish the Power Lessons.

Don't forget to continue doing additional reading and vocabulary building as you work through the Power Lessons.

(7) Take Practice Test Two or the computer-based TOEFL practice test.

If at step (5) you did Practice Test Two, try the computer-based TOEFL test now to give yourself additional practice in TOEFL test taking. Keep in mind, however, that the test format and strategies you will find here are somewhat different than those you will encounter on the paper-based exam. Likewise, if at step (5) you did the computer-based TOEFL practice test, try your luck at Practice Test Two now.

(8) Do the "Recurring TOEFL Topics and Related Vocabulary" section towards the back of the book.

Make sure your outside reading covers these topics.

TOEFL FACT SHEET

The following is an overview of the differences between the paper-based TOEFL and the computer-based TOEFL.

Paper-Based TOEFL

Total number of questions: 140
Duration: 2—2.5 hours (3—3.5 hours at test site)
Overall scaled score: 300 to 677
Format: Three scored sections, each with a subscore of 30 to 68

Section I: Listening Comprehension

Number of questions: 50
Duration: 30 or 40 minutes
Part A—Short conversations (30 questions)
Part B—Longer conversations (8 questions)
Part C—Talks (12 questions)

Section II: Structure and Written Expression

Number of questions: 40
Duration: 25 minutes
Part A—Sentence completion (15 questions)
Part B—Error identification (25 questions)

Section III: Reading Comprehension

Number of questions: 50
Duration: 55 minutes
5 or 6 reading passages (8 to 12 questions per passage)

Computer-Based TOEFL

Total number of questions: varies
Duration: varies—2.25 hours to 3 hours (up to 4.5 hours at test site)
Overall scaled score: 0 to 300
Format: Four sections. Sections I, II, and III have subscores of 0 to 30. Section IV has subscores of 0 to 6.

Section I: Listening Comprehension

Number of questions: 30 or 50
Duration: 40 or 60 minutes
Part A—Short conversations
Part B—Longer conversations and talks
Computer adaptive

Section II: Structure

Number of questions: 20 or 25
Duration: 15 or 20 minutes
Sentence completion and error identification questions are mixed together.

Section III: Reading Comprehension

Number of questions: 44 or 60. Test taker will see the total number of questions displayed on screen prior to beginning this section.
Duration: 70 or 90 minutes
5 to 8 reading passages (8 to 12 questions per passage)

Section IV: Writing

Number of questions: 1
Duration: 30 minutes

KAPLAN'S TOEFL TEST STRATEGIES

An examination is meant to test a person's knowledge or skills in a particular area. But sometimes two people with the same knowledge may not receive the same score on an exam. This is because only one of them knows *how* to do well on the exam.

That's what test-taking strategies are: methods of taking exams that lead to greater success. This book is designed to give you every advantage on the TOEFL. Of course, we want to improve your English proficiency—that's the job of the Power Lessons. But we also want to give you the test-taking strategies you need in order to get the very best TOEFL score possible for you.

In this section, we offer you a number of different types of test strategies. These strategies will help you to improve your score dramatically on both the paper-based and the computer-based versions of the TOEFL exam. For more specific information on how to do your best on each section of the computer-based TOEFL, turn to the introductory pages of the Power Lessons. For example, to find out more about listening comprehension computer-based test strategies, turn to the "Listening Comprehension for the Computer-Based TOEFL" section of the Listening Power Lessons.

To benefit as much as you can from all of these strategies, you should review them before you take every practice exam. Review them again before you take the official TOEFL.

OVERALL TEST STRATEGIES

The paper-based TOEFL and the computer-based TOEFL are very different. If you are planning to take the paper-based exam, you will need to memorize the paper-based test strategies below, while the computer-based strategies will help you do better on the computer-based TOEFL exam.

Paper-Based Test Strategies:

- Know the directions ahead of time.
- Leave no blanks. Guess if you don't know the answer.
- Budget your time.
- Read all the answer choices before selecting the best one.
- Mark your answer sheet correctly.
- Develop your stamina.

Computer-Based Test Strategies:

- Know the directions ahead of time.
- Know how to use the computer ahead of time. Practice scrolling and using the mouse and the keyboard.
- Leave no blanks. Guess if you don't know the answer. For Sections I & II, you cannot skip a question. For Section III you should not skip even though you can return to questions. Failure to complete Section IV will result in a score of zero.
- Budget your time.
- Read all the answer choices before selecting the best one.
- Develop your stamina (this version of the test is much longer than the paper-based test).

Know the Directions Ahead of Time

Make absolutely sure you know the directions for each section of the TOEFL. Read and reread the directions given on the practice tests in this book, or on the computer-based TOEFL tutorial CD-ROM distributed by ETS. Contact ETS at 1 (609) 771-7100 for a free copy of this CD-ROM; you can also visit their Web site at http://www.toefl.org. Once you learn how to do the questions, you won't have to read the directions during the real TOEFL exam. This means that on the Structure sections as well as the Reading Comprehension section, you can begin the test immediately instead of reading the directions. This will save you a lot of time.

Know How to Use the Computer Ahead of Time

Try to use computers whenever possible. Most Kaplan centers are equipped with computer equipment and will have some TOEFL practice programs for you to work on. You can also practice the skills you will need for taking the computer-based TOEFL on any computer that uses a mouse. Public libraries in most cities will have computers that you can use for free. Surfing the Internet is a great way to practice the computer skills you will need for this test because many sites ask you to click on buttons or pictures, have long blocks of text that require you to scroll, and have audio clips and places in which you can write your own text. Plus, since most of the Internet is in English, this is a great opportunity to practice your language skills as well!

Leave No Blanks; Guess If You Don't Know the Answer

If you leave a blank answer on the paper-based TOEFL, you can easily lose your place and misgrid the remainder of the section on which you are working. Leaving blanks is a bad idea, even though you risk giving wrong answers by filling them in. Remember that you are not penalized for getting a wrong answer—in fact, you have a 25 percent chance of getting the question right, compared to 0 percent if you leave it blank.

A wise test taker will make educated guesses on the TOEFL. This means using what you already know to eliminate answers that you know are wrong. Each section of this book will help you with strategies for making educated guesses on the various sections of the test. Another point to consider when making an educated guess is that you will rarely see more than four consecutive identical answers. If you are certain about your answers to questions 21–24, and they are all (C), but in question 25 you are not sure if the answer is (C) or (D), you should select (D).

Suppose that on the entire exam you get six or seven questions correct by guessing. That can raise your score by 25 to 30 points. In fact, guessing is so important that we suggest that in the last two minutes of every section of the test, you stop working on the questions and make guesses for every unanswered question on the answer sheet. When you do this, always guess (B) or (C), because on past TOEFLs these have been the most common answers.

Finally, on the paper-based TOEFL, each question is worth approximately 4.5 points. You should answer questions with the goal of getting points, not getting the questions correct. Of course you want to select the right answers to as many questions as possible, but what you really want is to get the highest score possible. Sometimes you may have to guess on a hard question in order to have enough time to answer the other questions in that section.

On the computer-based TOEFL, you will not have the opportunity to leave "blanks" in the Listening Comprehension and Structure sections of the exam. Because your score is determined through adaptive means (see the section in the previous chapter explaining computer-adaptive testing), the level of each question is determined by whether or not the previous question was answered correctly. In fact, if you fail to click on at least one answer, you will not be permitted to go on to the next question, and the computer will give you a message saying that you must make a selection.

In computer adaptive testing, your goal is to answer as many questions as possible at the highest level of difficulty. Because the bigger jumps in your score are determined by the earlier questions in these tests, it is better to spend a little more time on the first third of the set of questions. If you still have some questions left at the end and you have very little time left, try clicking on either of the two middle choices. If you must click on two, try the second and fourth answer choice. If it is a matching question, drag the first item to the middle slot, the second item to the third, and the third item to the first. These are only guessing strategies, so don't rely on them throughout the test—only use them if you absolutely do not know the answer and cannot make an educated guess!

Read All the Answer Choices Before Selecting the Best One
Don't pick the first answer choice that "looks good." Read all the answer choices and then pick the best answer. Many of the wrong answers on the TOEFL have been purposely written to confuse you. We call these types of wrong answers "distractors." In order to distinguish the distractors from the right answer, you must always read all the answer choices.

Mark Your Answer Sheet Correctly

If you are taking the paper-based TOEFL, your test will be scanned by a machine and that machine cannot think like a human being. If you make a mistake, erase the mark completely. Do not make any stray marks on the answer sheet. Do not mark more than one answer; if you do, it will be scored as a wrong answer. Don't misgrid. Misgridding is marking an answer in the wrong row or column. For instance, if you accidentally mark the answer to question 5 in the row for question 6, you have misgridded. Misgridding is very easy to do when you are in a hurry, and it can cost you many points. The machine that grades your test will not be able to "understand" the mistake you made.

Fortunately, if you are taking the computer-based TOEFL, the problems of incomplete erasures, double answers, and misgridding have been eliminated. Double-check to see that you clicked on the right answer before moving on to the next question, though.

Develop Your Stamina

There are no rests or breaks between sections for the paper-based TOEFL. The computer-based TOEFL does allow a ten-minute break between the Listening Comprehension section and the remainder of the test. Section III is long on the paper-based exam and even longer on the computer-based test. You need to keep working even if you are tired. Take as many practice tests as you can as if they were real tests. Do not let yourself be distracted. Try to stick to the amount of time that it takes for each section. Do not get up for a break, a snack or even to use the bathroom! You need to increase your ability to sit in one place for an extended period.

Other Tips

Eat a good breakfast on the day of your test, but nothing greasy or unusual. The test is long and hunger can be very distracting. If you are a person who gets hungry easily, it might be a good idea to eat an apple or some bread just before the test begins. Don't drink too much coffee or tea beforehand; a lot of caffeine (or any other drug, for that matter) is a bad idea. Finally, remember that if you are taking the computer-based TOEFL, there is no food or drink allowed in the testing center.

PART TWO:

TOEFL
DIAGNOSTIC
TEST (PRACTICE
TEST ONE)

Answer Grid for Practice Test One

1 | LAST NAME | FIRST NAME | MI

A B C D E F G H I J K L M N O P Q R S T U V W X Y Z

2 TODAY'S DATE

MONTH	DAY	YEAR
JAN		
FEB		
MAR	0 0	0 0
APR	1 1	1 1
MAY	2 2	2 2
JUNE	3 3	3 3
JULY	4 4	4
AUG	5 5	5
SEPT	6 6	6
OCT	7 7	7
NOV	8 8	8
DEC	9 9	9

SECTION 1
1–50: A B C D

SECTION 2
1–50: A B C D

SECTION 3
1–50: A B C D

IMPORTANT INFORMATION

USE ONLY A NO. 2 OR HB PENCIL TO COMPLETE THIS ANSWER SHEET. DO NOT USE INK.

MARK ONE AND ONLY ONE ANSWER TO EACH QUESTION.

BE SURE TO FILL IN COMPLETELY THE SPACE FOR YOUR INTENDED ANSWER CHOICE.

IF YOU ERASE, DO SO COMPLETELY.

MAKE NO STRAY MARKS.

RIGHT MARK: ●

WRONG MARK: ⊘ ⊗ ⊙

DIRECTIONS FOR THE TOEFL DIAGNOSTIC TEST (PRACTICE TEST ONE)

This diagnostic test, Practice Test One, is intended as a tool to help guide you in your TOEFL preparation. Ideally, you should take this test before you go through any of the Power Lessons, Practice Test Two, or the computer-based practice test on the CD-ROM.

Although this diagnostic test is paper-based, it covers the same basic content that is covered in the computer-based TOEFL exam. Therefore, even if you plan to take the computer-based version of the exam, Practice Test One will give you a good indication of the kinds of questions you can expect. It will also help you to identify potential areas of weakness. Based on how you do on the different sections of Practice Test One, you can decide which areas you need to spend most time on in your TOEFL studies. For example, if your score is not as high as you would like it to be for the Reading Comprehension section of the diagnostic test, you should pay particularly close attention to the Reading Power Lessons in this book.

Make this practice test as much like a real TOEFL test as possible. This means that you must find a space of about two-and-a-half hours during which you can take the practice test completely uninterrupted. Do not take breaks between the three sections of the practice test; you are not allowed breaks during the real TOEFL, so you need to build up your mental stamina.

Particularly if you are taking the paper-based TOEFL, it is strongly recommended that you use the answer grid provided, as you would have to use a similar grid if you took the real paper-based exam. You should give yourself about 20 minutes to fill out the form. It is important that you do this because you do not want to be confused by any of the questions or by the format of the form. Being confused by the information form of the real TOEFL might make you a little nervous—a bad way to begin a two- to three-hour exam. Although it may at first seem an unnecessary bother, recording your answers here will give you important practice in avoiding misgridding. Misgridding occurs when a test taker writes the answer to one question in the row for a different question. Misgridding can cause you to lose a lot of time on the paper-based TOEFL, or, worse, it can cause you to score far lower than you should.

Before you take the practice test, you should carefully read the section of this book entitled "TOEFL Test Strategies." Then, as you take the test, try to give yourself practice using these strategies as well. They can really improve your score.

As you take Practice Test One, give yourself only the allotted time for each section of the test. Stop when your time is up. Then use the answer key and conversion chart at the back of the book to give yourself a TOEFL score. (Don't forget to check the Listening Comprehension script immediately following the test if you don't understand why you got a particular Listening Comprehension answer wrong.) Finally, use this practice test to guide your TOEFL preparation by following the suggestions in the "TOEFL Study Plan" in the chapter called "Getting Started."

Directions and examples will be provided at the beginning of each section of all the practice tests in this book. However, we have also provided a set of more general directions on the following pages. These TOEFL test directions are similar to those you would read prior to taking an actual paper-based TOEFL exam. These directions are provided only once in this book; Practice Test Two, which is also paper-based, will not ask you to read these directions.

Test of English as a Foreign Language

General Instructions

This is a test of your English language ability. There are three sections. Each section has its own directions and sample questions. Make sure you understand the directions before you begin any section of the test.

You should work carefully, but be sure not to spend too much time on any single question. If you finish a section early, you may return to your answers for that section only. You are not allowed to go to any other section of the test.

Try to answer every question. Your score is based on the number of questions you answer correctly. If you are not certain you know the right answer to a question, you should make the best guess that you can. You will not lose points because of wrong answers, so you should answer every question, even if you have to guess.

You must answer all the questions on the separate answer grid. Do not answer the questions in this test booklet. When you mark your answers on the separate answer grid, you must:

➤ Use a medium-soft black lead pencil (No. 2 or HB).

➤ On the answer grid, find the number of the question you are answering, and mark the appropriate oval: (A), (B), (C), or (D). You are not allowed to make any changes after the time for a section of the test has ended.

➤ Give only one answer to each question.

➤ Take care to completely fill the oval with a dark mark, so that the letter inside the oval cannot be seen. The scoring machine may not be able to read light or incomplete marks correctly.

➤ Erase all marks outside of the oval completely. If you want to change your answer, completely erase the old answer.

The ovals on the answer grid may be arranged horizontally or vertically. Look at the example below for correct and incorrect ways of marking both of these formats. It is very important that you fill in the ovals on the answer grid in the correct way.

Vertical Answers

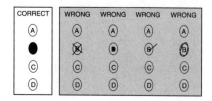

Horizontal Answers

Some of the material in this test may have been adapted from previously published materials. The ideas contained here do not necessarily represent the opinions of the Educational Testing Service.

LISTENING COMPREHENSION

Directions: Listening Comprehension Section

In this section of the test, you will demonstrate your ability to understand conversations and talks in English. You will find the audio tracks for this section on the CD-ROM included with this book. There are three parts to this section, with different directions for each part. Answer all the questions according to what the speakers say or imply. When you take the actual TOEFL test, you will not be allowed to take notes or write in your test book. Try to work on this sample test in the same way.

PART A

Test_1A.mov

Directions: In Part A, you will hear two people having short conversations. After each conversation, you will hear a question. The conversations and questions will not be repeated. After you hear a question, read the four possible answers and choose the best answer. Then, on one of the answer sheets at the back of this book, find the number of the question and fill in the space that corresponds to the letter of the answer you have chosen.

Here is an example.

On the recording, you hear:

In your book, you read:

(A) He is too tired to walk in the park.
(B) He agrees to go walking in the park with her.
(C) He is not Jim. His name is Pete.
(D) He doesn't know what to do.

Sample Answer

● Ⓑ Ⓒ Ⓓ

You learn from the conversation that the man is "beat," an idiomatic expression meaning "very tired." Therefore, the best answer to the question, "What does the man say?" is (A).

1. (A) It was nicer when she moved in.
   (B) It was hard to find.
   (C) It was not a nice place at first.
   (D) The man has seen it before.

2. (A) He won't hire anyone.
   (B) The woman won't get the job.
   (C) The job application was incomplete.
   (D) He can't tell her anything.

3. (A) The man should talk to his mother.
   (B) The man should call his mother later.
   (C) The man's mother will not be in.
   (D) Anyone could call his mother.

4. (A) He doesn't like rain.
   (B) He likes soccer very much.
   (C) The game isn't important.
   (D) He doesn't like to watch soccer.

5. (A) She looks old enough.
   (B) She looks younger than 21.
   (C) The man looks older than she does.
   (D) She looks older than 21.

6. (A) He enjoys sports.
   (B) He doesn't like his team.
   (C) He doesn't want to lose.
   (D) He is not athletic.

7. (A) Wait for better weather.
   (B) Don't skate so early.
   (C) Skate with a friend.
   (D) Buy a new pair of skates.

8. (A) at a restaurant
   (B) in a kitchen
   (C) at a theater
   (D) at a grocery store

9. (A) She has never seen the man.
   (B) She doesn't know any European History.
   (C) She and the man were classmates.
   (D) She doesn't remember the man.

10. (A) Jeremy's brother
    (B) Jeremy
    (C) the woman
    (D) the man

11. (A) She's glad he called.
    (B) She thought he would call.
    (C) She's angry because he didn't call.
    (D) She doesn't mind that he didn't call.

12. (A) in an airplane
    (B) in a truck
    (C) at a sporting event
    (D) in a department store

13. (A) He is very unhappy with the test.
    (B) He doesn't have another chance to take the test.
    (C) He plans on taking the test again.
    (D) He is satisfied with the score.

14. (A) in the woods
    (B) at a library
    (C) at a soccer game
    (D) in a restaurant

15. (A) She found a great parking place.
    (B) The park was wonderful.
    (C) She didn't enjoy the trip.
    (D) She could not find the place.

16. (A) He actually earned money in Europe.
    (B) It's impossible to save money there.
    (C) He doesn't know much about the cost.
    (D) Europe is not that expensive.

17. (A) She thinks the man is joking.
    (B) She thinks the car is dangerous.
    (C) It's the kind of car she wants.
    (D) The car is very unappealing to her.

18. (A) why Joe's mistakes bother her
    (B) why Joe eats that way
    (C) how Joe would correct his mistake
    (D) why Joe's habit upsets her

19. (A) The book is no longer in most stores.
    (B) The book was written many years ago.
    (C) She's been looking for the book for years.
    (D) The print in the book is rare.

20. (A) He's willing to make a deal.
    (B) He will give it to her.
    (C) He wants to know why she needs it.
    (D) He doesn't have it now.

21. (A) Sally took them from her.
    (B) She felt silly taking them.
    (C) The notes were a group effort.
    (D) Sally actually wrote the notes.

22. (A) It wasn't the dining hall.
    (B) He's not through eating.
    (C) He didn't like the meat.
    (D) The beef was excellent.

23. (A) It's the first thing she ever made.
    (B) Her maid knitted it for her.
    (C) It didn't take very long.
    (D) She didn't make it herself.

24. (A) It was a bad day for a date.
    (B) Kelly forgot about the date.
    (C) It was his worst date ever.
    (D) The date wasn't too bad.

25. (A) who has the clamp
    (B) where they should camp
    (C) where the lamps go
    (D) whether it's damp

26. (A) It was a very easy class.
    (B) He finds calculus to be useful.
    (C) The class was not worth it.
    (D) He tries hard in school.

27. (A) He bought some farmland.
    (B) There's a lot of food.
    (C) She wants one more thing.
    (D) Everything is very fresh.

28. (A) a parking garage
    (B) a car showroom
    (C) a car wash
    (D) a police station

29. (A) He is brilliant.
    (B) He looks like Shakespeare.
    (C) His question is difficult.
    (D) She is not amused by his answer.

30. (A) He misses his hometown.
    (B) He has been sick at home.
    (C) Nothing is the matter with him.
    (D) He is tired of his current apartment.

PART B

Test_1B.mov

<u>Directions</u>: On this part of the test, you will hear slightly longer conversations. After each conversation, you will hear several questions. Neither the conversations nor the questions will be repeated.

After you hear a question, read the four possible answers in this book and choose the best one. Then, on your answer sheet, find the number of the question and fill in the space that corresponds to the letter of the answer you have chosen.

Remember *that you cannot take notes or write on the test pages in any way.*

31. (A) the man's wife
    (B) the woman's sons
    (C) the man's daughter
    (D) the woman's driver

32. (A) They still don't know for certain.
    (B) just some scratches and bruises
    (C) a broken leg
    (D) serious injuries

33. (A) A car ran a red light.
    (B) A bicyclist ran into a car.
    (C) A car ran into a bicyclist.
    (D) A parked car coasted down a hill.

34. (A) the condition of the driver
    (B) possible damage to the car
    (C) the cost of the x rays
    (D) the woman's poor attitude

35. (A) a rock star
    (B) a teacher
    (C) a horse trainer
    (D) an opera singer

36. (A) He strained himself.
    (B) He is sick.
    (C) He can't sing.
    (D) He hurt it when he ate.

37. (A) She liked it.
    (B) She didn't like it.
    (C) She didn't notice it.
    (D) It was more trouble than it was worth.

38. (A) all of it
    (B) all of it, except for the man's solo
    (C) none of it
    (D) some of it, including the man's solo

PART C

Test_1C.mov

<u>Directions</u>: On this part of the test, you will hear several talks. After each talk, you will hear some questions. Neither the talks nor the questions will be repeated.

After you hear a question, read the four possible answers in this book and choose the best one. Then, on your answer sheet, find the number of the question and fill in the space that corresponds to the letter of the answer you have selected.

Here is an example.

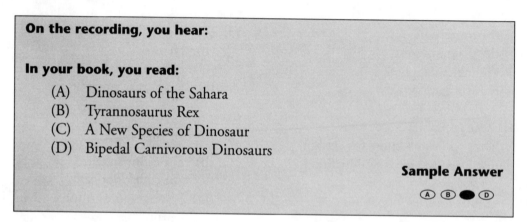

On the recording, you hear:

In your book, you read:

(A) Dinosaurs of the Sahara
(B) Tyrannosaurus Rex
(C) A New Species of Dinosaur
(D) Bipedal Carnivorous Dinosaurs

Sample Answer

Ⓐ Ⓑ ● Ⓓ

The best answer to the question, "What would be a good title for this talk?" is (C), "A new species of dinosaur."

Remember *you should not take notes or write on your test pages.*

39. (A) her large body of work
     (B) the novel *Uncle Tom's Cabin*
     (C) the work she did in the antislavery movement
     (D) her novels, which describe nineteenth century New England life

40. (A) prejudiced
     (B) charming
     (C) dedicated
     (D) wealthy

41. (A) immediately after publishing *Uncle Tom's Cabin*
    (B) after the liberation of the slaves
    (C) before the Civil War
    (D) when she joined the antislavery movement

42. (A) It was not abolitionist propaganda.
    (B) The characters were real.
    (C) It would be her last work.
    (D) It was a very risky venture.

43. (A) a pound of lobster for $12.95
    (B) a pound of spaghetti for $5.95
    (C) a pound of lobster for $5.95
    (D) a pound of spaghetti for $12.95

44. (A) seafood
    (B) vegetarian dishes
    (C) italian food
    (D) chinese dishes

45. (A) elegant
    (B) informal
    (C) low class
    (D) foreign

46. (A) imported wines
    (B) vegetarian dishes
    (C) large servings of beer
    (D) meals for kids

47. (A) the different places where American folk can be found
    (B) community parades and what they tell us about
    (C) the convergence of cultures in New York City
    (D) the many forms of modern-day American folklore

48. (A) a history class
    (B) a sociology class
    (C) a Spanish class
    (D) a psychology class

49. (A) West Indies
    (B) New York
    (C) Puerto Rico
    (D) on a farm

50. (A) reggae
    (B) New York
    (C) a spirit of independence
    (D) cardboard

STRUCTURE AND WRITTEN EXPRESSION

⏱ Time allowed for this section: 25 minutes

Directions: Structure and Written Expression Section

This section is designed to measure your ability to recognize language that is appropriate for standard written English. There are two types of questions in this section, with special directions for each type.

PART A

<u>Directions</u>: Questions 1–15 are incomplete sentences. Beneath each sentence you will see four words or phrases, marked (A), (B), (C), and (D). Choose the one word or phrase that best completes the sentence. Then, on your answer grid, find the number of the question and fill in the space that corresponds to the letter of the answer you have chosen. Fill in the space so that the letter inside the oval cannot be seen.

Example I

> Geysers have often been compared to volcanoes ----- they both emit hot liquids from below the earth's surface.
>
> (A) due to
> (B) because
> (C) in spite of
> (D) regardless of
>
> **Sample Answer**
>

The sentence should read, "Geysers have often been compared to volcanoes because they both emit hot liquids from below the earth's surface." Therefore, you should choose answer (B).

Example II

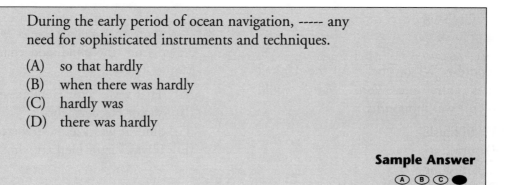

During the early period of ocean navigation, ----- any need for sophisticated instruments and techniques.

(A)   so that hardly
(B)   when there was hardly
(C)   hardly was
(D)   there was hardly

Sample Answer

Ⓐ Ⓑ Ⓒ ●

The sentence should read, "During the early period of ocean navigation, there was hardly any need for sophisticated instruments and techniques." Therefore, you should choose answer (D).

Now begin work on the questions.

1. ----- the Boston Red Sox have often been outstanding, they haven't won the World Series since 1918.

   (A) However
   (B) Yet
   (C) That
   (D) Although

2. ----- many computer software programs that possess excellent word-processing capabilities.

   (A) There are
   (B) The
   (C) There is a lot of
   (D) Some

3. Many Middle Eastern diplomats still feel that the United States is intent ----- the ultimate policeman in the region.

    (A) to being
    (B) being
    (C) be
    (D) on being

4. Woodrow Wilson believed the United States' entry into World War I would ----- the war in months.

    (A) to finish
    (B) finish
    (C) finishing
    (D) will had finished

5. ----- of New York's Erie Canal greatly enhanced trade in the upstate region.

    (A) The complete
    (B) Completing
    (C) A completing
    (D) The completion

6. After ----- the skin, a leech is best removed by the application of either salt or heat.

    (A) it attaches to
    (B) attaching it
    (C) its attaching to
    (D) where it attaches to

7. ----- east of the Mississippi River.

    (A) Indigo was grown usually
    (B) Usually grown was Indigo
    (C) Indigo usually grown
    (D) Indigo was usually grown

8. ----- wrote the operetta *Babes in Toyland,* drawn from the childhood characters of Mother Goose.

    (A) That was Victor Herbert who
    (B) Victor Herbert who
    (C) Since it was Victor Herbert
    (D) It was Victor Herbert who

9. Some of the oldest and most widespread creation myths are ----- involving the all-giving "Earth Mother."

    (A) those
    (B) them
    (C) they
    (D) their

10. In -----, compact disk technology has almost made record albums obsolete.

    (A) the decade from
    (B) the decade since
    (C) the past decade
    (D) decade ago the

11. In the first few months of life, an infant learns how to lift its head, how to smile, and -----.

    (A) how its parents to recognize
    (B) how to recognize its parents
    (C) to be recognizing its parents
    (D) the recognizing of its parents

12. Juana Inéz de la Cruz ----- Mexico's greatest female poet.

    (A) considered
    (B) considered to be
    (C) is considered to be
    (D) is consideration

13. Because the metal mercury ----- in direct proportion to temperature, it was once used as the indicator in common thermometers.

    (A) is expanding
    (B) expands
    (C) is expanded
    (D) expanded

14. ----- what is now San Salvador, Christopher Columbus believed that he had found Japan.

    (A) He reached
    (B) When did he reach
    (C) Having reached
    (D) Whether he reached

15. The principal purpose of aviation medicine is ----- by people aboard an aircraft in flight.

    (A) to study the stress experienced
    (B) study the experienced stress
    (C) to study stress experiencing
    (D) studying the stress experience

PART B

<u>Directions:</u> In questions 16–40 each sentence has four underlined words or phrases. The four underlined parts of the sentence are marked (A), (B), (C), and (D). Identify the one underlined word or phrase that must be changed in order for the sentence to be grammatically correct. Then, on your answer grid, find the number of the question and fill in the space that corresponds to the letter of the answer you have chosen.

Example I

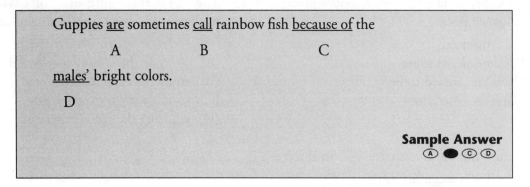

The sentence should read, "Guppies are sometimes called rainbow fish because of the males' bright colors." Therefore, you should choose (B).

Example II

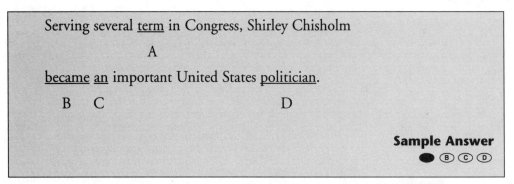

The sentence should read, "Serving several terms in Congress, Shirley Chisholm became an important United States politician." Therefore, you should choose answer (A).

Now begin work on the questions.

16. The dwarf lemon tree, <u>grown</u> in many
                          A
    areas of the world, <u>bears fruit</u> when it is
                         B
    less <u>than</u> six inches in <u>high</u>.
         C   D

17. <u>The</u> brain is composed of a mass of <u>softly</u>
    A   B
    <u>gray matter</u> in the skull <u>that</u> controls
     C   D
    our intelligence.

18. <u>Polluter</u> is a topic of such <u>importance</u>
    A   B
    today that even elementary school
    children are <u>well informed</u> about <u>its</u>
                  C   D
    dangers.

19. <u>Best</u> represented in a famous <u>oil painting</u>
    A   B
    by da Vinci, *The Last Supper* <u>it</u> is an
                                    C
    important part <u>of the history</u> of
                    D
    Christianity.

20. Together <u>with</u> his friend Little John,
                 A
    Robin Hood <u>are</u> <u>fondly</u> <u>remembered</u>
                B   C   D
    <u>today</u> by millions of people.
     D

21. In Vermont, the sap <u>the</u> maple <u>tree is</u> the
                         A   B
    <u>primary</u> ingredient <u>in</u> producing maple
     C   D
    syrup.

22. After <u>to have</u> <u>won</u> the 1945 Pulitzer Prize
          A   B
    for *A Bell for Adano*, John Hersey <u>wrote a</u>
                                         C
    nonfiction book <u>about</u> the bombing of
                     D
    Japan.

23. The <u>smallest</u> of the hummingbirds beat
        A
    their wings 70 <u>times</u> <u>a second</u> and are
                    B   C
    about two <u>inched</u> long.
               D

24. Quality, price, and <u>located</u> <u>are</u> often con-
                         A   B
    sidered <u>to be</u> the primary concerns
             C
    <u>in buying</u> a house.
     D

25. The <u>name</u> "America" <u>comes of</u> the <u>name</u>
        A   B   C
    of Amerigo Vespucci, <u>who</u> was a 16th-
                          D
    century Italian explorer.

26. Marie Curie <u>won</u> two Nobel Prizes for
           A
<u>their</u> discoveries of <u>radioactivity</u> and
 B   C
<u>radioactive</u> elements.
    D

27. The <u>developing</u> of the submarine was
         A
hindered by <u>the</u> lack of <u>a power source</u>
          B   C
that could <u>propel</u> an underwater vessel.
         D

28. Although humans have <u>highly developed</u>
                        A
brains, <u>most</u> animals have <u>more acute</u>
       B   C
senses <u>than them</u>.
    D

29. The movement of <u>the stars</u> was first
               A
noticed by <u>early</u> travelers, <u>who</u> used the
       B   C
stars to guide <u>its</u> way across the sea.
         D

30. <u>Those who</u> have seen <u>what</u> is <u>believed to be</u>
    A   B   C
Noah's Ark say it is <u>the largest</u> than a modern
                D
battleship.

31. <u>It is implicit</u> in the Constitution of the
    A
United States <u>that</u> one has <u>a right</u> to <u>their</u>
           B   C   D
privacy.

32. Although scientists <u>have been</u> successful
                  A
<u>about finding</u> treatments for cancer, they
    B
<u>haven't</u> yet discovered <u>a</u> cure.
  C   D

33. In the 18th century, standard college
curriculums <u>included</u> a heavy <u>emphasis on</u>
         A   B
<u>classical</u>, mathematics, and <u>religion</u>.
  C   D

34. <u>As</u> the <u>numbered</u> of nonnative speakers
  A   B
rises, the demand <u>for</u> teachers of English
               C
as a second language <u>will</u> increase.
               D

35. There is <u>much</u> bird migration above the
        A
equator, <u>where</u> the Pole Star can be seen,
       B
than <u>below</u> the equator, where <u>it</u> cannot be
    C   D
seen.

36. Although <u>most</u> people believe that
          A
    diamonds are the <u>costliest</u> gems, <u>emeralds</u>
               B   C
    are actually the <u>valuablest</u>.
              D

37. <u>In the summer</u>, Ann Arbor, along with
       A
    Ypsilanti, Saline, and Pontiac, <u>are</u> flooded
                      B
    with runaways <u>fleeing</u> the boredom of
              C
    their lives in Cincinnati and <u>its</u> suburbs.
                     D

38. A recent article in *The New York Times*
    reported that the typical business graduate
    of 1990 is <u>less likely</u> <u>to be</u> willing to work
            A   B
    <u>long hours</u> for the sake of advancement
     C
    than <u>their</u> 1970 counterpart.
        D

39. The dietary habits of <u>a</u> given child often
                 A
    <u>has little</u> to do with <u>that child's</u> eating
     B   C
    habits <u>as an adult</u>.
        D

40. One of the <u>claims</u> made against science is
           A
    <u>that data</u> are often manipulated to prove a
     B
    scientist's thesis, rather than <u>studying it</u>
                        C
    for possible <u>contradictions</u>.
            D

READING COMPREHENSION

🕐 **Time allowed for this section: 55 minutes**

<u>Directions</u>: In this section you will read several passages. Each one is followed by several questions about it. For this section, you are to choose the one best answer, (A), (B), (C), or (D), to each question. Then, on your answer grid, find the number of the question and fill in the space that corresponds to the letter of the answer you have chosen.

Answer all the questions following a passage on the basis of what is stated or implied in that passage.

Read the following passage.

One of the most successful communal experiments in the New World was that of the Shakers, a sect that fled from England to
Line New York State in 1774 in order to escape
(5) religious bigotry. In America, they adopted the name Shaker, once used derisively by the English to describe the dance they performed when in a state of religious ecstasy. At the movement's peak, in the decade prior
(10) to the Civil War, there were 6,000 Shakers in 18 communities throughout the eastern states. Since then, however, the Shakers have almost dwindled away. Today, only two active Shaker communities remain, with a
(15) total membership of eighteen, all female. The Shakers are resigned to the death of their sect, as they have never believed that everyone could be persuaded to share their beliefs.

Example 1

Where did the Shaker movement begin?

(A)   The eastern states
(B)   The New World
(C)   New York
(D)   England

Sample Answer

The passage states that the Shaker sect fled from England to New York State in 1774. Therefore, you should have chosen answer (D).

Example II

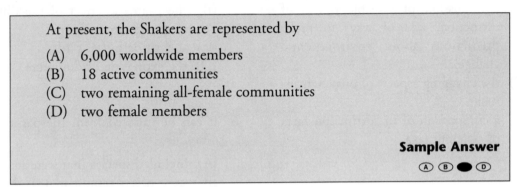

At present, the Shakers are represented by

(A)   6,000 worldwide members
(B)   18 active communities
(C)   two remaining all-female communities
(D)   two female members

Sample Answer
Ⓐ Ⓑ ● Ⓓ

According to the passage, only two active Shaker communities remain, with a total membership of 18, all female. Therefore, you should have chosen answer (C).

Now begin work on the questions.

Questions 1–12 refer to the following passage.

The reasons for the extinction of a species, and for the rapid rates of change in our environment, are currently a focus of much
Line scientific research. An individual species'
(5) susceptibility to extinction depends on at least two things: the taxon (the biological group—kingdom, phylum, class, order, family, or genus) to which a species belongs, and the overall rate of environmental
(10) change. Fossil evidence shows that more mammals and birds become extinct than do mollusks or insects. Studies of the extinction of the dinosaurs and other reptiles during the Cretaceous Period show that a
(15) changing environment affects different taxa in different ways. Some may be dramatically affected; others less so.

The best way to answer the question of what causes an extinction is to combine
(20) fields of inquiry and viewpoints. Using the fossil record and historical documentation, the different rates of extinction of various taxa and different responses to environmental change can be detected. Then, the
(25) evolutionary development of the different species can be compared and traits that may be disadvantageous can be singled out. Finally, researchers can use mathematical formulas to determine whether a popula-
(30) tion is likely to adapt itself to the changing environment or disappear. Hopefully, as more of this information is collected, specialists in different fields—physiological and behavioral ecology, population ecology,
(35) community ecology, evolutionary biology and systematics, biogeography, and paleobiology—will work together to make predictions about the broader changes that might occur in the ecosystem.

1. Which of the following is the main topic of the passage?

    (A) assessment of the work of specialists concerned with ecology
    (B) a discussion of possible causes of extinction, and of ways to make predictions about environmental change
    (C) the changing aspects of our environment
    (D) a comparison of the extinction rates of different taxa

2. The word *susceptibility* in line 5 is closest in meaning to

    (A) insensitivity
    (B) receptiveness
    (C) immunity
    (D) vulnerability

3. An example of a taxon would be

    (A) a phylum
    (B) the rate of environmental change
    (C) a fossil
    (D) studies of extinction

4. The author compares mammals and birds to

    (A) mollusks and insects
    (B) phylum and class
    (C) dinosaurs and reptiles
    (D) ecologists and biologists

5. It can be inferred from the passage that a significant event of the Cretaceous Period was

    (A) the appearance of many taxa
    (B) the dramatic effect of the dinosaur on the environment
    (C) the extinction of birds
    (D) the extinction of dinosaurs

6. It can be inferred from the passage that dinosaurs

    (A) included species that were mammals
    (B) were better represented in the fossil record than other species
    (C) possessed disadvantageous traits
    (D) were not susceptible to extinction

7. The word *dramatically* in lines 16–17 means

    (A) strongly
    (B) inspiringly
    (C) flimsily
    (D) visually

8. The word *fields* in line 20 is closest in meaning to

    (A) areas
    (B) meadows
    (C) studies
    (D) careers

9. From the passage it can be inferred that disadvantageous traits are

   (A) occurring at different rates
   (B) a contributing cause of extinction
   (C) adaptable
   (D) learned by mathematical formulas

10. The expression *singled out* in line 27 is closest in meaning to

   (A) isolated
   (B) blamed
   (C) seen
   (D) divided

11. According to the passage, the likelihood of a population becoming extinct can be

   (A) lessened by the efforts of a few concerned specialists
   (B) unaffected by environmental change
   (C) determined by mathematical formulas
   (D) almost impossible to ascertain

12. The word *broader* in line 38 is closest in meaning to

   (A) fatter
   (B) extra
   (C) wider
   (D) many

Questions 13–23 refer to the following passage.

The Quakers, also called the Society of Friends, are a Christian group that arose in the mid-seventeenth century in England and the
Line American colonies. Quakerism came into
(5) being in England on or around 1652, when George Fox began to organize converts to preach his doctrine of "God in every man." The Friends were silent at their meetings, waiting for the "inward light." They believed peo-
(10) ple should sense God inside of themselves, without church buildings, appointed preachers, written liturgy, or many of the outward trappings associated with Christianity.

The Society of Friends is part of the left wing
(15) of the seventeenth-century English Puritan movement; in America, Quakers were persecuted by Puritans. Quakers experienced much official persecution, including imprisonment and execution, for their belief that worship of
(20) God should be very personal. The term "Quaker" may refer to their penchant for "quaking" during religious services, or it may be a derogatory reference to supposed Quaker cowardliness and belief in pacifism.
(25) Quakerism in the American colonies existed mainly in the northeast. The American Quaker population surged after 1682 when Quaker William Penn founded the state of Pennsylvania as a haven for Quakers and a
(30) "holy experiment" in religious toleration. Quakers were prominent and powerful in the Pennsylvania state government in the period before the American Revolution. During and after the Revolution, Friends concerned them-
(35) selves with the plight of Native Americans. They also worked with escaped slaves and for the abolition of slavery. They continue to be known for their efforts at social reform.

13. In which of the following publications would this passage be most likely to appear?

    (A) an anthology of English literature
    (B) an introductory American history book
    (C) a book about Eastern religions
    (D) a basic math textbook

14. The word *their* in line 8 refers to

    (A) trappings
    (B) preachers
    (C) religious services
    (D) the Friends

15. The word *persecuted* in lines 16–17 is closest in meaning to

    (A) scrutinized
    (B) lauded
    (C) harassed
    (D) believed

16. Where in the passage does the author give an example of Quaker involvement in social issues?

    (A) lines 6–7
    (B) lines 16–17
    (C) lines 27–29
    (D) lines 33–34

17. Which of the following would be an example of "the outward trappings associated with Christianity" referred to in lines 12–13?

    (A) clergy
    (B) silent, leaderless worship
    (C) concern for social reform
    (D) the doctrine of "God in every man"

18. It can be inferred from the passage that early Quakers experienced official persecution because

    (A) they were known for "quaking" during religious services
    (B) they helped found the state of Pennsylvania
    (C) they came to America from England
    (D) their religious beliefs were considered subversive

19. Why does the author mention execution in lines 18–19?

    (A) It is an example of the persecution Quakers faced.
    (B) It is an outward trapping of Christianity.
    (C) This serves as an example of William Penn's policies.
    (D) Many religions were concerned with this issue.

24. The degree of viscosity in newly issued lava is a critical determinant of

    (A) the chemical nature of the magma
    (B) whether the lava will be red or white-hot
    (C) the ultimate nature of the hardened lava field
    (D) the viscosity of the liquid rock

25. The chemical composition of a hardened field

    (A) has nothing to do with the viscosity of the liquid rock
    (B) will cause the crusting phenomena common in hardened lava
    (C) is important in shaping the ultimate appearance of the field
    (D) depends upon the degree of viscosity of the original liquid rock

26. In line 20, the word *issues* most nearly means

    (A) is dormant
    (B) heats up
    (C) traverses
    (D) comes out

27. Knots of surface rocks are characteristic of

    (A) all types of ultimate lava fields
    (B) the initial stage of some lava field formation
    (C) the end result of some highly viscous flows
    (D) only highly liquid, wavelike lava forms

28. If the hardened lava presents a smoother, wavelike surface it is likely that

    (A) it was not initially a highly liquid lava
    (B) it results from a highly liquid lava
    (C) its final form will be rough and difficult to traverse
    (D) at issue, it was red-hot

29. The primary function of this passage is to

    (A) explain the primary chemical components of lava, including silica and oxides
    (B) predict when volcanic lava will appear
    (C) warn of the limitations of viscosity and chemical analysis
    (D) discuss two crucial determinants of a hardened lava field's character

30. The word *exhibit* in line 32 is closest in meaning to

    (A) give off
    (B) put on
    (C) show
    (D) cause

31. This passage would most likely appear in which type of publication?

    (A) an introductory college textbook on geography
    (B) the national events section of a local newspaper
    (C) an introductory college textbook on geology
    (D) a tourist brochure for a volcanic region

KAPLAN

Questions 32–42 refer to the following passage.

The period of the Revolution was a time of contrasts in American fashion. In urban centers, women enjoyed a wide range of
Line expression in the fashions available to them,
(5) even though shortages might force a young lady to wear an outfit made from the bright red uniform of her British beau. The patriots, however, tended to scorn fashion as frivolous in time of war. In remote areas,
(10) patriotic groups led boycotts of British goods and loomed their own woolen cloth.

In selecting clothes, stylish American ladies depended on "fashion babies"—foot-high dolls illustrating the latest Paris styles.
(15) This infatuation with the fashion trends of the "continent" remained intact well into the twentieth century. Indeed even today, New York's fashion industry has not fully escaped the tyranny of French design.
(20) Mourning garments were almost impossible to obtain since black cloth had to be imported from England; black armbands were introduced as a substitute. Gauze, indispensable for petticoats, aprons, and
(25) ladies' headgear, was also in short supply. There was also a taste for outlandish accessories and fanciful detailing: feathers in hats, elaborate buttons, and gaudily patterned fabrics. These excesses were called "maca-
(30) roni" and are immortalized in the song *Yankee Doodle*.

32. Which of the following is the most appropriate title for this passage?
   (A) A Revolution in Fashion
   (B) Clothing Shortages of the Revolution
   (C) Clothing Styles in Revolutionary America
   (D) Conflict in the Fashion Industry

33. The word *beau* in line 7 is closest in meaning to
   (A) male friend
   (B) husband
   (C) father
   (D) son

34. Which of the following can be inferred from the passage about people's attitudes toward fashion?
   (A) They varied according to political beliefs.
   (B) They were determined mainly by geography.
   (C) They corresponded to a person's social standing.
   (D) They were a matter of personal taste.

35. The word *loomed* in line 11 is closest in meaning to
   (A) grew bigger
   (B) wove
   (C) picked
   (D) quilted

36. What were clothes made from in rural areas?

    (A) home-made wool
    (B) imported British goods
    (C) cloth stolen from the British
    (D) gauze

37. "Fashion babies" were

    (A) dolls for children
    (B) 12-inch figures used to display clothes
    (C) life-sized models dressed in current styles
    (D) illustrations from fashion magazines

38. The word *tyranny* in line 19 is closest in meaning to

    (A) domination
    (B) bossiness
    (C) importance
    (D) evilness

39. Which of the following can best be said about the Paris fashion industry?

    (A) It has come to the forefront only recently, compared to New York.
    (B) It has long exerted a powerful influence on American fashion.
    (C) It retains its taste for gaudy, "macaroni" type excess.
    (D) It is unable to break free from New York's influence.

40. Black armbands were worn to show

    (A) the tyranny of Paris fashions
    (B) imported cloth from England
    (C) fanciful detailing
    (D) mourning

41. The word *elaborate* in line 28 is closest in meaning to

    (A) gay
    (B) vulgar
    (C) intricate
    (D) square

42. It can be inferred from the passage that "macaroni"

    (A) was so named because of its resemblance to the continent of Europe
    (B) was a very short-lived and ill-conceived fashion trend
    (C) had a more mundane application to petticoats and aprons
    (D) was not the fashion style of avowed patriots

Questions 43–50 refer to the following passage.

Sapphira and the Slave Girl was the last novel of Willa Cather's illustrious literary career. Although the story takes place in
Line 1856, well before her own birth, she drew
(5) heavily on both vivid childhood memories and tales handed down by older relatives to describe life in rural northern Virginia in the middle of the nineteenth century.

Of Cather's novels, *Sapphira and the Slave*
(10) *Girl* is the one most concerned with providing an overall picture of day-to-day life in a specific era. A number of the novel's characters, it would seem, are included in the story only because they are representative of the
(15) types of people to be found in 19th century rural Virginia; indeed, a few of them play no part whatsoever in the unfolding of the plot. For instance, we are introduced to a poor white woman, Mandy Ringer, who is
(20) portrayed as intelligent and content, despite the fact that she has no formal education and must toil constantly in the fields.

The title, however, accurately reflects that the novel is mainly about slavery. Cather's
(25) attitude toward this institution may best be summed up as somewhat ambiguous. On the one hand, she displays almost total indifference to the legal and political aspects of slavery when she misidentifies certain
(30) crucial dates in its growth and development. Nor does she ever really offer a direct condemnation of slavery. Yet the evil that was slavery gets through to us in typically subtle ways. Those characters, like Mrs. Blake,
(35) who oppose the institution are portrayed in a sympathetic light. Furthermore, the suffering of the slaves themselves and the petty, nasty and often cruel behavior of the slave owners are painted in stark terms.

43. What is the main topic of this passage?
    (A) Cather's anti-slavery stance
    (B) The backdrop of Cather's last novel
    (C) Cather's strangely titled novel
    (D) Life in the Virginia country

44. The author refers to *Sapphira and the Slave Girl* as
    (A) a heroic tale of the Civil War
    (B) a sweeping epic of the Old South
    (C) using Cather's personal recollections
    (D) a political treatise on slavery

45. The word *vivid* in line 5 most nearly means
    (A) disturbing
    (B) buried
    (C) forgotten
    (D) clear

46. What is NOT true of Mandy Ringer?
    (A) She is a slave.
    (B) She is intelligent.
    (C) She is uneducated.
    (D) She is poor.

47. In the second paragraph, the author mentions Mandy Ringer in order to emphasize which point?

    (A) The novel displays Cather's mixed feelings about slavery.
    (B) The characters are based on Cather's childhood friends.
    (C) One of the novel's purposes was to paint a portrait of life in nineteenth-century rural Virginia.
    (D) The novel's characters are shown in a positive light because Cather was a supporter of the Old South.

48. According to the author, why is Cather's attitude toward slavery somewhat ambiguous?

    (A) She was knowledgeable about the legal and political aspects of slavery.
    (B) She did not denounce slavery directly, only in indirect ways.
    (C) She identified equally with slaves and slaveholders.
    (D) She was unable to fashion a firm opinion on the issue.

49. It can be inferred that the author would probably

    (A) like Cather if the author met her
    (B) consider the character of Mandy Ringer irrelevant to the plot
    (C) oppose the academic study of Cather's other novels
    (D) have no appreciation of the novel's merits

50. Which of the following would be the best title for the passage?

    (A) *Sapphira and the Slave Girl:* Fact Versus Fiction
    (B) Willa Cather: Racist or Abolitionist?
    (C) Some Comments on the Final Novel of Willa Cather
    (D) Willa Cather's Depiction of Nineteenth-Century Virginians

END OF TEST. *Turn to Part Five, "Answer Keys and Score Conversion Chart," to find out how you did on this diagnostic test. Check the Listening Comprehension script on the pages that follow if there was anything in the Listening Comprehension section of this test that you could not understand.*

SCRIPT FOR THE LISTENING COMPREHENSION SECTION
PART A (TEST_1A.MOV)

The entire script for the Listening Comprehension section of the Diagnostic Test is provided on the following pages. If you could not understand what was said in a particular conversation or talk or why you got a particular answer wrong, look it up here.

1. **(man)** You've got a wonderful apartment.
   (woman) That's what you're saying now. But you should have seen it when we moved in.
   (narrator) What does the woman imply about the apartment?

2. **(woman)** I was calling about the job application I submitted on Monday.
   (man) Yes, well, I'm sorry. We are looking for someone with more experience.
   (narrator) What did the man say?

3. **(man)** If anyone calls for me, tell them I'm not in.
   (woman) Even if it's your mother?
   (narrator) What does the woman imply?

4. **(woman)** The soccer game was rained out today.
   (man) Well, I'm not much for watching sports anyway.
   (narrator) What does the man mean?

5. **(man)** If you want to buy beer, you'll need to prove that you're 21.
   (woman) I guess I must look younger than I am.
   (narrator) What does the woman say about her appearance?

6. **(woman)** You really can't throw very well. I don't think you can be on the team unless you improve.
   (man) I'm afraid I'm very bad at playing sports.
   (narrator) What describes the man?

7. **(man)** Look, the pond is frozen. It's perfect weather for skating. I want to go right now.
   (woman) Don't you think it's a bad idea to go alone?
   (narrator) What would the woman suggest?

8. **(woman)** Isn't this place a good value?
   (man) Unfortunately, they don't bring you your food when it's hot.
   (narrator) Where did this conversation take place?

9.   **(man)** Say, haven't I seen you somewhere before?

   (woman) Last semester, we both took European History. Don't you remember?

   (narrator) What does the woman mean?

10. **(woman)** Jeremy loves to play soccer, so I had his brother go to a store in the suburbs and get him this great soccer ball.

   (man) That's great. Do you think Jeremy will let me borrow it some time?

   (narrator) Whom is the soccer ball for?

11.   **(man)** I would have called if I had thought it would help.

   (woman) Oh well. Thanks anyway for thinking of us.

   (narrator) What does the woman say about the man's call?

12. **(woman)** Watch out for that low overpass.

   (man) I see it. We can clear it, no problem.

   (narrator) Where does this conversation probably take place?

13.   **(man)** I am so unhappy with my test results.

   (woman) Well, I'm not exactly dissatisfied with mine, and anyway, there's always next time.

   (narrator) What does the man say about his test results?

14. **(woman)** Did you see that bird fly right past us?

   (man) No, I was having enough trouble just walking down the trail.

   (narrator) Where does this conversation probably take place?

15.   **(man)** How was your trip to the state park?

   (woman) What a great place!

   (narrator) What does the woman say about her trip?

16. **(woman)** Did you find it expensive to vacation in Europe?

   (man) Not really; once you get to know it, you learn how to save money.

   (narrator) What does the man mean?

17.   **(man)** Chris has a really neat car, doesn't she?

   (woman) Are you kidding? I'd die for a car like that!

   (narrator) What does the woman mean?

18. **(woman)** I don't like it when Joe puts ketchup on his steak!

   (man) Why?

   (narrator) What does the man want to know?

19. **(man)** I got a great deal on these books.

(woman) Yes. I believe this one has been out of print for years.

(narrator) What does the woman mean?

20. **(woman)** Do you think I could borrow ten dollars until Thursday?

(man) Why not? It's no big deal.

(narrator) What does the man say about the money?

21. **(man)** These are the most extensive notes I've ever seen.

(woman) I know, I had Sally take them for me.

(narrator) What does the woman mean?

22. **(woman)** That's the best beef we've ever had in the dining hall.

(man) Isn't it, though!

(narrator) What does the man imply?

23. **(man)** That's a great sweater. Did it take you long to make it?

(woman) I can't knit a thing—I had it made for me.

(narrator) What does the woman say about the sweater?

24. **(woman)** How was your date with Kelly last night?

(man) Well, let me say I've had worse.

(narrator) What does the man think about the date?

25. **(man)** Excuse me, but why are these things just standing in the middle of the floor?

(woman) This pair of lamps goes over there, up against the wall.

(narrator) What are the man and woman discussing?

26. **(woman)** Were you finally able to get into that calculus class?

(man) Yeah, much to my regret.

(narrator) What does the man mean?

27. **(man)** I brought over a little something for you to eat.

(woman) A little something? You brought the whole farm!

(narrator) What does the woman imply?

28. **(woman)** Hey, you can't leave your car in that spot. The lot's closed.

(man) Oh, come on. How about if I pay you double?

(narrator) Where does the conversation take place?

29. **(man)** Well, to be or not to be, that's the question.

(woman) Yeah, thanks, Shakespeare.

(narrator) How does the woman feel about the man?

30. **(woman)** What's the matter with you lately? You look terrible.

(man) Oh, nothing much. I'm just a little homesick.

(narrator) What is wrong with the man?

PART B (TEST_1B.MOV)

(narrator) *Questions 31 through 34 are based on the following talk.*

(man) I'm Janie Foster's father. I got a call that she'd been in an accident. Is she all right?

(woman) Oh, yes, Mr. Foster. As I said on the phone, it's nothing serious. She was more frightened than hurt. We'd like your permission to take a couple of x rays, though, just to be absolutely sure.

(man) Of course. Can you tell me how it happened?

(woman) Apparently she was coming down that steep hill near the school. She couldn't stop her bike in time when the light changed. The driver saw her coming and stopped in the intersection, but she coasted right into his car.

(man) Great! I'll probably wind up paying for damage to the car! Can I see her now?

(woman) Surely. She's in the waiting room telling some other patients about her mishap. Come this way.

31. Whom are the man and woman talking about?

32. What injuries occurred in the accident?

33. What caused the accident?

34. Besides the girl's health, what concerns the man?

(narrator) *Questions 35 through 38 are based on the following talk.*

(woman) I really enjoyed your performance. I am a big opera fan.

(man) Oh, thank you very much. Did you see the entire opera tonight?

(woman) No, I was late because of work. But I did catch your solo.

(man) What did you think of it?

(woman) Oh, it was marvelous! I love the sound of your voice. I have to say, though, that you sounded a bit hoarse. Are you having throat trouble?

(man) Yes, I've got a bit of a cold. I didn't know it was that noticeable.

(woman) Probably only to fans like me, who've heard you over the years.

35. What is the man's occupation?

36. What is wrong with the man?

37. What did the woman think of the man's performance?

38. How much of the opera did the woman watch?

PART C (TEST_1C.MOV)

(narrator) *Questions 39 through 42 are based on the following English lecture.*

Good morning. Let's continue our talk about Harriet Beecher Stowe. Though today she is known primarily for her antislavery novel *Uncle Tom's Cabin*, she was popular in her day for other novels as well. In these books she portrayed the nineteenth century New England middle class. These novels, a number of religious poems, and articles written for housekeeping magazines form her body of work. It's enough to fill sixteen volumes, but only a small part of it is still read today.

After teaching in a school managed by her sister, Harriet moved to Cincinnati with her father. There he became head of a seminary. She was greatly influenced by her father's violent opposition to slavery. In 1852, after publishing *Uncle Tom's Cabin* in an abolitionist newspaper, she became active in the antislavery movement. Though *Uncle Tom's Cabin* was run in an abolitionist newspaper, she claimed it was not abolitionist propaganda. Harriet even claimed that the book was not directed against the South. Her most risky venture was begun after the Civil War: She bought a plantation to help the newly freed blacks. However, the farm was an economic failure. So too was her own economic life, for neither her husband's salary nor her own earnings were large enough to support a happy and comfortable existence.

39. What is Harriet Beecher Stowe most famous for today?

40. Which of the following adjectives best characterizes Harriet Beecher Stowe?

41. When did Harriet Beecher Stowe buy a plantation?

42. What claim did Harriet Beecher Stowe make about *Uncle Tom's Cabin*?

(narrator) *Questions 43 through 46 are based on the following commercial.*

There are places you can go for a pound of spaghetti for $5.95. There are also places you can go for a pound of lobster for $12.95. But in how many places can you find a pound of lobster for $5.95? Just one! That's Dan's Place on the tip of Cape Lynn right off Route 98. If you're looking for white table cloths, fancy dishes, and imported wines, you'll be happier somewhere else. But if you're looking for some really good food at really good prices, then Dan's Place is the place for you. We're not fancy, but we're a lot of fun. We carry a full range of seafood and fresh-water fish. We also offer vegetable platters for the vegetarians and pitchers of beer for the beer drinkers. What's more, we make some of the best home-made pies east of the Mississippi. So just hop into your car and don't leave the kids home. Remember, Dan's has a special junior menu with junior prices!

43. What special offer or selling point does Dan's restaurant make in its commercial?

44. What type of food does Dan's specialize in?

45. Which word best describes the atmosphere at Dan's Place?

46. What item is not found on the menu?

(**narrator**) *Questions 47 through 50 are based on the following talk.*

In 1846 Englishman William J. Thoms defined folklore as "manners, customs, observances, superstitions, ballads, proverbs, etcetera, of the olden time." But folklore doesn't happen only in the distant past. As we go about our lives, forming and participating in different groups and activities, we create modern-day folklore. The folklore of the United States can be described as a convergence of cultures and an exchange of many folk traditions. In New York City, for instance, cultures interact constantly. At the city's West Indian Day parade, celebrants dance down the avenues to the beat of reggae and soca. In many neighborhoods, Hassidic Jews walk around wearing the distinctive black hats and clothing of their ancestors, and speaking with a New York accent. At the Puerto Rican Day parade, marchers wave cardboard machetes. The machete, a large metal knife used for chopping sugar cane, symbolizes the independent spirit of farmers on the island of Puerto Rico.

47. What is the main subject of the passage?

48. In which of the following classes would this lecture most likely be given?

49. Which location is mentioned as a place where many cultures come together?

50. What does the machete symbolize for farmers in Puerto Rico?

PART THREE:

MASTERING THE TOEFL

LISTENING POWER LESSONS

The Listening Comprehension section of the TOEFL has three parts. This is true of both the paper-and-pencil TOEFL and the computer-based exam. Our Power Lessons One through Three guide you through each of these parts. Each lesson contains notes that refer to tracks on the CD-ROM that accompanies this book. Listen to these tracks when you are prompted, so that you will be able to answer the questions about the spoken conversations.

Here you will become acquainted with the kinds of questions and distractors ("TOEFL traps") that appear in each section. Also, the vocabulary at the end of each section will help you begin the vocabulary building that a truly successful TOEFL candidate must undertake. You will find Kaplan's practical approach very helpful in preparing you for the test.

Before you start to work on the Listening Power Lessons, read through "Listening Comprehension for the Computer-Based TOEFL" on the following pages. These pages will give you more details on what to expect on the Listening Comprehension section of the computer-based TOEFL.

THE BIGGER PICTURE: LISTENING BEYOND THE TOEFL

It will help your TOEFL preparation to understand why the makers of the TOEFL at ETS place such emphasis on listening skills, and why they test listening skills in the way that they do.

Remember that the TOEFL is meant to help American colleges and universities determine whether the English of a nonnative speaker of English is of a high enough level for that person to function in an American university setting.

For this reason the TOEFL tests a student's ability to understand lecture-like talks given at a natural speed. In U.S. colleges and universities, students are expected to attend and take notes in every class. Classroom lectures supplement the reading assignments; that is, they do not necessarily repeat the information in the reading homework, but rather add to it. On exams, students are expected to show that they have learned the information given in the lectures as well as the information given in the readings. Therefore, a successful international student must be able to understand his or her professors' lectures.

But successful students must be able to comprehend more than just university lectures. It is common for many American college and university classrooms to be centered around "group discussion," in which students talk about a subject at a fairly informal level. Also, you may have to ask one of your classmates to repeat an idea the professor mentioned in class, or you may have to ask a complete stranger how and where you register for a class. Finally, you will certainly want to make American friends. To accomplish these tasks, you need to understand what is often called "survival English." For this reason, the TOEFL also tests your ability to understand very short conversations about topics commonly found on an American college campus.

LISTENING COMPREHENSION FOR THE COMPUTER-BASED TOEFL

Beginning in July, 1998, the TOEFL will be administered on computer. The Listening Comprehension section includes some changes both in the way that you will experience the conversations and talks and the way that you will record your answers.

On test day, prior to taking the exam, you will have the opportunity to work through a tutorial that will guide you step-by-step on how to use a mouse, how to scroll, how to use the testing tools. In addition, before each of the four sections, you will be shown how to answer the types of questions that you will encounter in that section. Remember, the more comfortable you are with computers, the less you will have to worry about on test day!

The following are some unique features of the computer-based TOEFL:

COMPUTER ADAPTIVE

The Listening Comprehension section is "computer adaptive." This means that the difficulty of each question that you see is based on whether or not you answered the previous question correctly. Every computer adaptive section of the test will begin with a few mid-level difficulty questions. If you answer most of them correctly, then the difficulty of the question that you next receive will increase. If you answer most of the first few questions incorrectly, the questions that follow will become easier. Your goal is to answer as many questions as possible at the highest difficulty level. This is how the test determines your final score!

Because each question that you receive is based on the questions that come before it, you cannot leave any questions unanswered or skip questions to answer later.

VOLUME OF AUDIO

With the new test, *you* will be able to control the volume for the Listening Comprehension section. Before the test begins, you have an opportunity to adjust the volume. During the tutorial, you will hear a phrase repeated over and over. You will see two arrows on the screen—one pointing up and the other pointing down. The up arrow makes the volume louder; the down arrow lowers the volume. Click on the arrows until the voice is clear and at a comfortable level for you.

It is very important that you set the volume at the right level *before* the test begins! Once the Listening Comprehension section starts, you will not be able to change the volume, and the staff at the testing center will not be able to help you.

Time

In addition to being able to control the volume, you can also set the pace of the Listening Comprehension section. The time you have to take the test will vary from test taker to test taker, but it will be either 20 or 30 minutes. The actual amount of time that you are allowed to take will appear on the screen before you begin. The time that you spend listening to the conversation or talk is not counted against your total time, only the time spent answering the question. The actual amount of time you spend in front of the computer to complete the Listening Comprehension section will be up to 40 or 60 minutes.

However, unlike the paper-based exam, in which all test-takers listen to the audio at the same time and have exactly the same amount of time to answer each question, you decide when to go on to the next question. All this really means is that the Listening Comprehension section on the computer-based TOEFL is now more like the other sections in this regard.

Graphic Element

Each short conversation and long conversation will include a picture of two people talking. These pictures are there to focus your attention. They do not necessarily provide information that will help you answer the question correctly—you are being tested on your listening comprehension, not your visual comprehension.

The talks, however, will include graphic elements to which you should pay close attention. Many of these elements will simply be a word, phrase, or name that looks like it is written on a blackboard. Make a mental note of the information on this kind of graphic; you will most likely get a question based on it. Other types of graphics will include pictures or illustrations, such as a map, a technical drawing, a photograph of an animal, or a diagram, to name just a few examples.

These graphics are there to help you understand what the speaker is talking about, and are typical of the kinds of visual aids a professor in a university classroom would use. You may encounter these or similar graphics as part of the actual questions themselves.

Content of Audio

All of the items in the Listening Comprehension section of the computerized TOEFL will be set in an academic or university context.

Part A

Short conversations include a 6- to 20-second exchange between a man and a woman. The pair might be two students, a student and a professor, or a student and a university administrator. This section typically tests your ability to make inferences from word choice and tone of voice, and to understand idiomatic expressions.

Part B

Longer conversations and talks range anywhere from 30 seconds to 2 minutes and 30 seconds long. The longer conversations might be between two students, a student and a professor, or a student and a university administrator.

The talks are typical academic lectures. They can be on any number of subjects drawn from physical and natural sciences and the humanities. You need not have any prior knowledge of the topic that is discussed, however; subjects dealing with the humanities, such as history and biography, will be from American culture. In other words, you will not hear a lecture about a Japanese poet or an art movement that occurred in Russia, as these would bias the test toward test takers from those cultures.

Some of the talks include interruptions, such as a student asking a question, or the professor soliciting information from his or her students. These interruptions serve to make them more like talks that might occur in real-life classroom situations.

QUESTION FORMAT

The computer-based TOEFL has introduced some significant changes in the format of the questions. On the paper-based exam, you are given four choices, from which you pick one and fill in the corresponding oval. On the computerized test, you will record your answer directly on the screen. Unlike the paper-based exam, in which you merely hear the question, on the computer-based test you will be able to read the question on the screen after you hear the audio portion. The answer choices will not appear until after the audio has finished.

You may change your answer choice for *all* questions as often as you like until you click on Next and Confirm Answer. Once you have clicked on these boxes, you will hear the next audio clip.

Remember, you will not be permitted to leave any question unanswered, so you cannot come back to it later!

Standard Multiple-Choice

For the short and long conversations you will click on the oval next to the correct answer.

Example:

> **MAN:** Did you go to chemistry class today? When I got there, nobody was there!
>
> **WOMAN:** Didn't you remember the announcement Professor Barnes made last week? We took a field trip to the river to take water samples.
>
> **MAN:** Oh, I was sick last week, so I didn't know.

TOEFL—Listening

Why didn't the man go on the field trip?

- ⬭ He was sick.
- ⬭ He didn't remember Professor Barnes.
- ⬭ He went to a barn.
- ⬬ He was absent the week before and didn't hear about it.

For the talks, you will be asked questions in a variety of formats. Many of them will be the typical four-choice answer, as in the short and long conversation, but some will not. Other types of question formats include:

Matching

You must click on one element (a word, phrase or picture) and then click on the element to which it corresponds.

For example:

TOEFL—Listening

Match the city with its geographical location.

Click on a city. Then click on the space where it belongs. Use each city only once.

New York

San Francisco

Chicago

| West Coast | | Midwest | | East Coast |

Multiple Answer

You must click on two or more boxes to complete your answer.

TOEFL—Listening

Which of the following are American presidents?

Click on 2 answers

☒ Thomas Jefferson

☐ Andrew Mellon

☐ Charlie Parker

☒ Andrew Jackson

If you do not click on the number of choices that the question asks you to, you will not be able to proceed to the next question.

Graphic Element

You must click on a picture, or a region within a picture in order to select your answer.

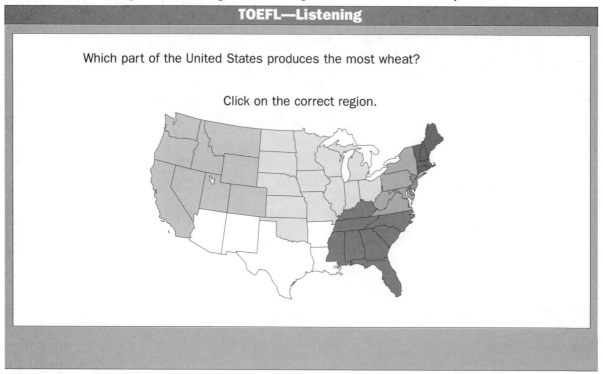

SCORING

The Listening Comprehension section of the TOEFL will be scored on a scale of 0 to 30.

SKILLS AND STRATEGIES FOR THE COMPUTER-BASED TOEFL

Specific skills that you will practice throughout this section are:

- Restatement
- Identifying the main idea
- Identifying the main topic
- Determining time and sequence
- Identifying facts
- Making inferences
- Understanding the speakers' tone

Even though the Listening Comprehension section has been adapted for the computer, the same general skill is being tested as on the paper-based exam—listening. Below we offer some strategies to help you "test your best" on the computer-based TOEFL Listening Comprehension section.

Strategies

Use the Graphics to Help You Focus

The photos of men and women talking in the short and longer conversations are there to help you focus. In the talks, the graphics are used to illustrate and clarify what the lecturer is discussing. You will always see the title of the lecture and a photo of the person lecturing. Once the lecture has begun, you will see graphics that illustrate content points in the lecture—perhaps a difficult vocabulary word or a person's name that appears to be written on a chalkboard, or pictures or charts that give an example of what the lecturer is describing—a chart, a map, a technical drawing, or an example of an artist's style, for example.

You will not receive new information in the graphic nor will you be given information that the lecturer doesn't also describe verbally. And don't worry if the voice doesn't seem to match the picture. Sometimes you will hear what sounds like a much older person's voice and see a picture of a younger adult; don't let that distract you. Remember, the Listening Comprehension section of the TOEFL is not testing your visual comprehension, it is testing your ability to make sense of what you hear.

The Kaplan EASEL Method:

(1) Engage

Engage your brain. Be ready to listen to discussions and talks that you would expect to find in a university setting.

(2) Anticipate

Think ahead. What kind of vocabulary would you expect to hear from two people talking on a campus? When the title of the talk appears, what kind of words or ideas do you think might come up?

(3) Summarize

You are not permitted to write during the TOEFL exam, but you can mentally summarize what you have already heard. Listen for pauses in the talks; this probably means that the speaker is moving on to a new thought. In your mind, note what the speaker has just finished saying. Hint: The TOEFL asks you to do this when it gives you Main Topic, Main Idea, and Restatement questions.

(4) Evaluate

What did you think of what the speaker just said? Did you agree or disagree? Was the speaker convincing? What was the tone of the speaker's voice? Hint: The TOEFL asks you to do this when it gives you Inference questions.

(5) Learn

What ideas or facts do you remember from the talk? After all, that is why you listen in the first place, isn't it? Hint: The TOEFL asks you to do this when it gives you Fact, Sequence, and Reference questions.

CHUNK!

Contemporary research shows that native speakers of a language do not learn the language word by word. Instead, they first hear and then learn language in "unanalyzed chunks." This ability to remember multi-word chunks is what produces meaningful patterns in your, the speaker's, mind. When you speak your first language, you are remembering these patterns and chunks rather than analyzing them. You probably have a repertoire of tens of thousands of these multi-word chunks in your heads which you pull from your memory storage whenever they are needed.

If you have learned English as a second language in a traditional, grammar-based way, you are probably doing something very different with the English language when you speak. You are more than likely analyzing vocabulary word for word based on rules you have learned in the past. "Do I use the preposition *of* or *at*?" "Do I use the past tense of the verb or the present?"

Chunking helps you develop a native-speakerlike intuition about the language. Americans speak in chunks and the people you will hear in the Listening Comprehension section of the TOEFL are no different. If you study in chunks, you can identify the correct response without having to analyze each individual word. For example:

> **MAN:** How are your classes this year?
> **WOMAN:** Let me tell you, it seems like this semester will never end!
> **NARRATOR:** What does the woman mean?

(A) The semester is already over.

(B) It's been her favorite year.

(C) She hopes it never ends.

(D) She's not enjoying classes.

In this exchange, you can see a couple of chunks which will help you find the answer:

- *Let me tell you* (expresses annoyance or dissatisfaction)
- *It seems like this....will never end* (expresses the feeling that an activity is difficult)

If you were studying in chunks, you would be able to figure out that the woman is not enjoying her classes (answer D) from either of the chunks above.

LISTENING POWER LESSON ONE

FOR LISTENING PART A OF THE TOEFL

This part of the TOEFL consists of a series of very short dialogues followed by a question. The student then selects one of four possible items as the best answer to the question.

For this lesson it is important to know what a *distractor* is:

> **A *distractor* is a wrong answer that looks correct. Test makers use distractors to trap you into choosing the wrong answer.**

There are seven different types of distractors found in the Listening section:

- ➤ Homophones
- ➤ Synonyms
- ➤ Negatives
- ➤ Pronouns
- ➤ Time and sequencing
- ➤ Unreal situations
- ➤ Multiple referents

Remember that the TOEFL test makers use distractors to trick you into getting the question wrong.

SESSION A: HOMOPHONE DISTRACTORS

Homophone distractors are words or phrases that sound the same as or similar to words or phrases heard in the conversation.

Here is a TOEFL question that has a homophone distractor in the answer set.

Suppose you hear:

| WOMAN: | Are you coming to the meeting tomorrow? |
| MAN: | Of course, I'll be just around the bend. |

Question: What does the man mean?
(A) He'll be close to the meeting place.
(B) He'll have to be flexible to make it to the meeting.
(C) He's just been to the meeting.
(D) The meeting will begin when he arrives.

Answer (C) contains a homophone. *Just been* is a homophone that sounds similar to *just around the bend,* which was said in the original conversation. You should not be distracted into choosing that answer simply because it sounds similar.

Both answers (B) and (D) repeat the word *meeting*. This is another common type of distractor that is related to homophones. When an answer repeats the same words that appear in the conversation, you may be tempted to choose it. However, usually the answer that sounds most like the conversation, whether because of homophones or repeated words, is wrong.

In this case (A) is the correct answer because *just around the bend* is an idiomatic expression that means *nearby*. You will also notice that (A) sounds the most different from the original conversation. Keep in mind that there is no guarantee that the correct answer on the TOEFL exam will always be the one that sounds the most different, but it is usually a complete rephrasing of the conversation.

Similar-sounding answers are often wrong.

SESSION B: SYNONYM DISTRACTORS

Synonym distractors are words and phrases that seem to mean the same thing as a word or phrase in the conversation.

Can you identify the synonym distractor in the answer set of this example?

WOMAN: What do you think of the primary race?

MAN: It's been interesting. I'll have to admit that.

Question: What is the woman asking the man?
(A) if he has been to the races
(B) what he thought of the first race
(C) if she has something on her face
(D) his opinion of the presidential primaries

Answer (B) contains a synonym distractor. *First* is substituted for *primary* in the original conversation. *Primary* and *first* are often synonyms for each other, but you have to remember that synonyms in one context may not be synonyms in another. Here you must pay special attention to the environment around the word *primary* in the conversation. A *primary race* is not the same as a *first race*, so (B) is wrong.

In fact, a presidential primary is a type of primary race, both of which refer to the special elections during which candidates for a particular political party are chosen. (D) is the correct answer.

> **Don't be fooled by answers which use the same words as in the dialogue. Read all the answer choices carefully before making your selection.**

SESSION C: NEGATIVE DISTRACTORS

> *Negative distractors* are answers in the negative that seem to mean the same as a statement in the conversation, but in reality mean the opposite.

Can you identify the negative distractor in this example?

WOMAN:	Will you be at the library tonight?
MAN:	No way! I've got tickets to the game.

Question: What does the man say?
(A) that he will not go to the game
(B) that he doesn't have a way to the game
(C) that he is going to a sporting event
(D) that he came to the library the previous night

In this question, answer choices (A) and (B) are both negative distractors. A student who is not paying careful attention might hear the negative in the man's answer—"No way!"—and incorrectly choose an answer that also contains a negative.

Answer (D) is a homonym distractor that tries to make the unwary student confuse the words *game* and *came.* But in reality the man is not going to the library because he wants to attend a game of some kind. Therefore, (C) is the correct answer.

Another variation of the negative distractor is the use of a negative tag question in the conversation. On the TOEFL, when a person responds with a negative tag question, he/she is voicing agreement.

MAN:	It's a beautiful day.
WOMAN:	Isn't it, though?

The woman's response means that she agrees with him. Take a look at how this question might look on the TOEFL below. The correct answer to the following question is (B).

MAN: Bill's quite a musician.

WOMAN: Isn't he, though?

Question: What does the woman mean?

(A) She thinks Bill is not talented.
(B) She agrees with the man.
(C) She has not heard Bill play.
(D) She did not hear his comment.

SESSION D: PRONOUN DISTRACTORS

Pronoun distractors are pronouns that either reverse the gender of the person being referred to or that confuse the interrogative pronouns *who, which,* or *what.*

Can you identify the pronoun distractor in this example?

MAN: Who gave Lucy her new bicycle?

WOMAN: Oh, it's not new. Her older brother handed it down to her.

Question: What does the woman tell the man?

(A) that he got it from her brother
(B) that she got it from her brother
(C) that Lucy's brother gave it to him
(D) that he gave it to the woman

(A), (C), and (D) are all pronoun distractors. Answers (A) and (C) contain pronouns that have the wrong gender. The man in the conversation did not receive the bike, as (A) and (C) imply. (D) also confuses the subject pronoun because the speaker (here referred to as *he*) did not give the bike to the woman.

The woman tells us that "Lucy's (*her*) older brother handed (gave) it to her." Therefore (B) is correct. Lucy (*she*) got it (the *bicycle*) from her brother.

Can you identify the interrogative pronoun distractor in this example?

WOMAN: What are you going to take this semester?

MAN: Calculus and biology, but I decided not to take composition.

Question: What does the woman ask the man?
(A) which courses he will take
(B) who he will take this semester
(C) what he will take to biology
(D) whom he will take to the prom

Answers (B), (C), and (D) all confuse the interrogative pronoun. Notice that (C) especially causes a distraction because it repeats the same interrogative question. But (C) is asking what object he will take to biology, which has a very different meaning from the question in the conversation.

"What are you taking?" is a common way of asking someone, "Which courses will you be taking?" So the correct answer is (A).

Always listen carefully to determine "who is doing what" in TOEFL dialogues.

SESSION E: TIME AND SEQUENCING DISTRACTORS

Time and Sequencing distractors offer confusing alternatives to the order of events in the conversation.

Can you identify the time/sequencing distractor in the following example?

MAN: Will you start your new job next week?

WOMAN: No, the week after that. I still have to finish up where I am.

Question: When will the woman begin her new job?
(A) in one week
(B) in two weeks
(C) She is just finishing it.
(D) She has just begun.

Answer (B) is correct. The man asks if the woman will begin her job in one week, and she replies that she will begin one week later than that. Therefore, the woman will begin her job in two weeks.

SESSION F: UNREAL SITUATION DISTRACTORS

Unreal situation distractors try to make you think that an unreal or imaginary situation truly happened.

These unreal situations may be in the future or in a conditional *if* clause. Sometimes, to answer the question correctly, the student will have to make an inference and ignore information given directly in the conversation.

Can you identify the unreal situation distractor in this example?

WOMAN: If I had bought that lampshade, I would have gotten the green one.

MAN: Well, it's not as though there was a large selection.

Question: What does the man tell the woman?
(A) He's happy with the aftershave that he bought.
(B) He's sorry that the woman bought the lampshade.
(C) He will purchase the lampshade next time.
(D) There were a limited number of lampshades.

Answer (B) is the unreal situation distractor. The woman did not buy the lampshade. When she says, "If I had bought that lampshade," she is using a conditional clause to describe an unreal situation. (See Structure Power Lesson Three, Session C for help on conditionals.) In his answer, the man justifies his choice by saying that there wasn't a large selection of lampshades. For that reason, (D) is the correct answer.

Let's take a look at another example of an unreal situation distractor. Can you find it?

WOMAN: Would you pick up some milk?

MAN: Why not? I've been sitting around all day. What kind do you want?

Question: Where does the conversation probably take place?

(A) in a supermarket
(B) at the man's home
(C) at the man's work
(D) around a table

In this example, (A) is the unreal situation distractor. A student who hears the word *milk* might think that the conversation takes place in a supermarket. Here, the phrasal verb *to pick up* means to purchase it at a store. To get this question correct, you must infer that the speakers are at home, and not be confused by the word *milk*.

SESSION G: MULTIPLE REFERENT DISTRACTORS

Multiple referent distractors occur when several people or items are mentioned and the answers then repeat all or some of the characters in an attempt to confuse you. Comparisons are often used to present this type of distractor problem.

Can you identify the multiple referent distractors in this example?

MAN: My job is harder than yours.

WOMAN: But mine is harder than John's!

Question: Who has the easiest job?
(A) the woman
(B) John
(C) the man
(D) Jan

Answer (B) is correct. If the man's job is harder than the woman's, and if the woman's job is harder than John's, then John's job is easier than the woman's and the man's. Therefore, John has the easiest job. Both (A) and (C) are multiple referent distractors. A student who is not listening carefully might select one of these as the answer.

Be careful to avoid the homophone distractor Jan [dzæn] for John [dzan] in (D).

PRACTICE #1—Homophone Distractors

Listen to Track_1.mov. Circle the letter of the answer choice that correctly answers each question.

1. (A) The faculty committee meets at one.
   (B) Most of the requests were approved.
   (C) The committee acted on one request.
   (D) Several of the requests were rejected.

2. (A) She doesn't want to eat yet.
   (B) She can't find a restaurant either.
   (C) She'd like to eat at the mall.
   (D) She found the restaurant sloppy.

3. (A) It is just before Easter.
   (B) He wants to go east with her.
   (C) The break is for two weeks.
   (D) The break is two weeks after exams.

4. (A) if the man saw a bug
   (B) how the man dug the hole
   (C) if the man wants a small hug
   (D) what size mug the man wants

5. (A) herd sheep
   (B) fry some chicken
   (C) tell a joke
   (D) lose her head

6. (A) 15
   (B) 19
   (C) 50
   (D) 90

7. (A) eat at the office
   (B) go to a restaurant for lunch
   (C) have lunch inside
   (D) look at the clock

8. (A) She has a head for science.
   (B) She may be going to the science building.
   (C) He cannot believe where she is headed.
   (D) She's near the sign for the mall.

9. (A) He's finished with the assignment.
   (B) He's going fishing tomorrow.
   (C) He's tired.
   (D) He should repeat.

10. (A) The man should take some time off.
    (B) The man should not take physical education.
    (C) The man should take her out.
    (D) The man should take a physical education course.

PRACTICE #2—Synonym Distractors

Listen to Track_2.mov. Circle the letter of the answer choice that correctly answers each question.

1. (A) She went to breakfast early.
   (B) She had a good day.
   (C) She didn't have time to eat.
   (D) She ate breakfast quickly.

2. (A) She studies the games.
   (B) The games are steamy.
   (C) Doctors can play video games.
   (D) Games help her relax.

3. (A) a large beach
   (B) the hot sun
   (C) the cold wind
   (D) the hot weather

4. (A) hostile
   (B) neutral
   (C) happy
   (D) anxious

5. (A) following the directions closely
   (B) going downstairs to ask for directions
   (C) asking someone for instructions
   (D) taking a course on how to build it

6. (A) She'll tell him what she wants.
   (B) She'd like to tell him later.
   (C) She'd really like to see the game.
   (D) Yes, the later, the better.

7. (A) He doesn't know the way.
   (B) The route to the theater is blocked.
   (C) He thinks the show will start late.
   (D) They'll be late for the performance.

8. (A) drive him to work
   (B) rush every morning
   (C) have more time to eat
   (D) eat very quickly

9. (A) He thought it was a lie.
   (B) He didn't understand the joke.
   (C) He thought it was funny.
   (D) He tried to write it down.

10. (A) a movie star
    (B) a crazy woman
    (C) a film critic
    (D) an astronomer

PRACTICE #3—Negative Distractors

Listen to Track_3.mov. Circle the letter of the answer choice that correctly answers each question.

1. (A) He doesn't want her help.
   (B) He likes talking to the woman.
   (C) He wants to fail his class.
   (D) He hasn't been able to call.

2. (A) give her a paper
   (B) call her later
   (C) speak louder
   (D) keep his voice down

3. (A) She is sure the professor is joking.
   (B) Next semester is not good for her.
   (C) It would not be of interest to her.
   (D) She'd like to become his assistant.

4. (A) She doesn't think it's hot.
   (B) She thinks yesterday was hotter.
   (C) She agrees with him.
   (D) She's sure it has been hotter.

5. (A) It was an accident.
   (B) She meant what she said.
   (C) She is mean.
   (D) She watched what she did.

6. (A) He is a good musician.
   (B) He is an excellent physician.
   (C) He isn't very talented musically.
   (D) He is an accomplished magician.

7. (A) The science quad has an excellent view.
   (B) The area is much better than before.
   (C) The science quad has done excellent work.
   (D) That there is a need still for more work.

8. (A) It is too late to protest his grade.
   (B) The economics professor won't hear his complaint.
   (C) He is happy with his quiz grade.
   (D) He doesn't want to tell the woman his score.

9. (A) He shouldn't work on the papers at night.
   (B) He should work on the papers separately.
   (C) She wonders what his plans are.
   (D) The man may have to work nonstop.

10. (A) She thinks he is correct.
    (B) There are more passes now.
    (C) It hasn't changed much.
    (D) She thinks he is funny.

PRACTICE #4—Pronoun Distractors

Listen to Track_4.mov. Circle the letter of the answer choice that correctly answers each question.

1. (A) who came by
   (B) how the man got there
   (C) what was said
   (D) where Joe is now

2. (A) why people held a certain belief
   (B) why those days are over
   (C) how the sun revolved
   (D) how did people change their beliefs

3. (A) How much did he donate?
   (B) Why is he telling her?
   (C) Is she still there?
   (D) Which woman?

4. (A) She thinks it wasn't that great.
   (B) It was free.
   (C) He thinks it was expensive.
   (D) Her friend paid for it.

5. (A) She must prove the set is broken.
   (B) It receives several channels.
   (C) He cannot receive a refund.
   (D) She must follow official policy.

6. (A) The computer might be broken.
   (B) They are driving one another crazy.
   (C) He is acting out on the computer.
   (D) He needs her help working the computer.

7. (A) His location in the office is a very good one.
   (B) His job prospects are very good.
   (C) His job is well paying.
   (D) He wants to move up.

8. (A) Go tell Sue to call him.
   (B) Tell Sue he misses her.
   (C) Tell Sue she misses her.
   (D) Tell her about him.

9. (A) an excellent television program
   (B) that she go home with them
   (C) that they see a movie
   (D) that they use her extra tickets

10. (A) what he just read
    (B) what's in his eye
    (C) what his idea is
    (D) what she just said

KAPLAN

20. The paragraph after this passage would most likely be about

    (A) the decline of the Quaker population since World War I
    (B) the similarities and differences between Quakers and Puritans
    (C) ways in which Quakers today show concern for others
    (D) social reforms enacted by Quakers during the American Revolution

21. From the passage, it can be inferred that the Puritans were

    (A) Friends
    (B) persecuted
    (C) intolerant
    (D) executed

22. The word *penchant* in line 21 most nearly means

    (A) appreciation
    (B) propensity
    (C) disinclination
    (D) proposition

23. Why did the American Quaker population surge after William Penn founded Pennsylvania?

    (A) Pennsylvania tolerated the Quaker religion.
    (B) Pennsylvania forbade religions other than Quakerism.
    (C) The Pennsylvania government tried to help escaped slaves.
    (D) Social reform was important to most Americans.

Questions 24–31 refer to the following passage.

The appearance and character of a hardened lava field depends on numerous factors. Among the key variables are the chemical
Line nature of the magma and the degree of viscos-
(5) ity of the liquid rock once it begins to flow.

Since the ultimate nature of lavas is influenced by chemical composition, it is possible to predict certain aspects of the final appearance of the field from a sample of the molten
(10) fluid. The main components of lavas are silica and various oxides, including those of potassium, iron, calcium, magnesium, sodium, and aluminum. Magnesium and iron oxides are found in high concentrations in the dark-col-
(15) ored basic basalt, while silica, soda, and potash preponderate in the lighter-colored, acidic felsite rocks.

The viscosity of the liquid rock helps to determine the appearance of the hardened
(20) field's surface. When it issues, the lava is red- or even white-hot. It soon begins to cool, and the surface darkens and crusts over. In extremely viscous flows, the underpart may yet be in motion as the surface solidifies. The crust
(25) breaks up into a mass of jagged blocks of rock that are carried as a tumbling, jostling mass on the surface of the slowly moving stream. When eventually the stream stops and hardens, the field is extremely rough and difficult to tra-
(30) verse. On the other hand, highly liquid lavas may harden with much smoother surfaces that exhibit ropy, curved, wrinkled, and wavelike forms.

PRACTICE #5—Time and Sequencing Distractors

Listen to Track_5.mov. Circle the letter of the answer choice that correctly answers each question.

1. (A) He thought the woman bought them.
   (B) He forgot to get them yesterday.
   (C) He wants the woman to get them tomorrow.
   (D) He thinks they will get them tomorrow.

2. (A) view the work she has done
   (B) go to a movie when she is finished
   (C) visit the art exhibit at school
   (D) help her protect her new work

3. (A) Don't go swimming after eating.
   (B) Think about eating.
   (C) Don't swim and eat at the same time.
   (D) Don't think while you swim.

4. (A) last night
   (B) yesterday evening
   (C) tonight
   (D) two days from now

5. (A) Friday
   (B) Saturday
   (C) Sunday
   (D) Monday

6. (A) at 10 A.M.
   (B) when the man was there
   (C) after 10 A.M.
   (D) She never went.

7. (A) has breakfast
   (B) gets dressed
   (C) brushes her hair
   (D) gets up

8. (A) The semester is already over.
   (B) It's been her favorite year.
   (C) She hopes it never ends.
   (D) She's not enjoying classes.

9. (A) Tryouts are today.
   (B) He's auditioning for it.
   (C) He's not sure he will join.
   (D) Tryouts are the same day as those for the dance club.

10. (A) They have already taken that course.
    (B) They studied together.
    (C) They have been in school a long time.
    (D) He was in a class with the woman.

PRACTICE #6—Unreal Situation Distractors

Listen to Track_6.mov. Circle the letter of the answer choice that correctly answers each question.

1. (A) ate lunch with the man
   (B) worked during lunch
   (C) passed the man his lunch
   (D) worked in the park

2. (A) He used to know Jill.
   (B) He can't accept the monitor.
   (C) He didn't know that the woman was giving the monitor away.
   (D) He is going to help Jill weigh the monitor.

3. (A) It would not be such a long vacation.
   (B) They didn't have enough money for it.
   (C) The man couldn't get time off.
   (D) They had more money than they thought.

4. (A) to take a taxicab
   (B) to go home later
   (C) to take the subway
   (D) to take him home

5. (A) at a warehouse
   (B) at a toy store
   (C) at a department store
   (D) at a florist

6. (A) He drank coffee during the drive.
   (B) He would like a cup of coffee.
   (C) He needs to fill the gas tank.
   (D) He used to drink coffee.

7. (A) in a theater
   (B) at the movies
   (C) near the ocean
   (D) at a soccer game

8. (A) Take this bus all the way to the airport.
   (B) Get off now and take the number 63 bus.
   (C) Find some other way to the airport.
   (D) Ride downtown and then get a different bus.

9. (A) missed the sale
   (B) fell down last Friday
   (C) bought several sweaters
   (D) sold her sweaters

10. (A) rain
    (B) a snowstorm
    (C) wind
    (D) thunder

PRACTICE #7—Multiple Referent Distractors

Listen to Track_7.mov. Circle the letter of the answer choice that correctly answers each question.

1. (A) Bill and Sue got them together.
   (B) Sue will get them soon.
   (C) Bill gave them to Sue.
   (D) Sue ran the errand for him.

2. (A) The woman is as beautiful as the car.
   (B) The car should have cost more.
   (C) It was a very expensive car.
   (D) The car's as shiny as a new coin.

3. (A) The picnic wasn't very well attended.
   (B) Half the people went to the theater instead.
   (C) Too many people showed up.
   (D) Only half the food actually arrived.

4. (A) that he was taking the test with her
   (B) that she wasn't very nervous
   (C) that she was not taking the test
   (D) that they were both doing the paper

5. (A) Both courses are easy.
   (B) For her, math is difficult.
   (C) She thinks physics is hard.
   (D) Both courses are difficult.

6. (A) He gets more exercise than she does.
   (B) They agree on the amount of exercise.
   (C) He worked out just the other day.
   (D) He gets the least amount of exercise.

7. (A) The woman is more worried than the man.
   (B) The woman is not as worried as the man.
   (C) The woman is as worried as the man.
   (D) The woman was worried once before.

8. (A) Larry
   (B) Larry's sister
   (C) the man's sister
   (D) the woman's sister

9. (A) the man's son
   (B) Alice and her class
   (C) Alice and the man
   (D) the woman and the man

10. (A) the man
    (B) Hugo
    (C) Eli
    (D) the woman

VOCABULARY

To hear how these words and expressions are pronounced, listen to Track_8.mov.

Just around the bend/just around the corner
In these lessons you learned that *just around the bend* means "nearby." It can also mean "close in time." Another idiomatic expression with an identical meaning and usage is *just around the corner.* Study the examples below.

> When Hoover was elected in 1928, little did he know that a major economic depression lay <u>just around the corner</u>.

> Thanksgiving is <u>just around the bend</u>.

Idioms with the word *head*
In this section you have seen three idioms with the word *head.*

To *lose one's head* means "to panic":

> Unable to escape from the burning building, he <u>lost his head</u> and ran back into the flames.

If someone was in a difficult situation but did not panic, you can say, "He kept his head."

If you are *headed somewhere,* or if you are *heading somewhere,* you are moving in the direction of that place. Sometimes these expressions are used to talk about something unpleasant. Note that the expression takes the preposition *for,* unless it is used with the word *home.*

> I <u>was heading home</u> when I ran into an old friend.

> We<u>'re headed for</u> Kansas City.

> You<u>'re heading for</u> disaster.

If you *have a head for* something, that means you are very good at it mentally.

> She <u>has a head for</u> business.

Other Vocabulary Items

Some other expressions from these lessons are:

There is no guarantee that
This means "we can't be sure that."

> There is <u>no guarantee that</u> the low inflation will continue into the next decade.

The + comparative, *the* + comparative

> <u>The sooner</u> he comes, <u>the better</u>.

> <u>The more expensive</u> the car, <u>the happier</u> he will be.

> <u>The cheaper</u>, <u>the better</u>.

> <u>The more complex</u> the characters, <u>the more interesting</u> the book.

Negative question + *though*
This is used to express strong agreement.

> Mary certainly played well in the soccer game yesterday.

> <u>Didn't she, though</u>?

To show up
This means meaning "to arrive or appear"; *to turn up* is used in the same way.

> John <u>didn't show up</u> until almost midnight.

> I went to the park, but none of my friends <u>turned up</u>.

Vocabulary Exercise

Complete the sentences below, using the given expressions. Some may be used more than once.

head	there is no guarantee that	just around the corner
are you headed	the happier I'll be	loses her head
has a head for	show up	the warmer
the more	the better	isn't it, though
later		

1. **Peggy:** I can't wait until we move to Florida.

   Dave: Just remember, _____ you'll be any happier there than you are here.

   Peggy: Oh, I'm sure I'll be happy. I need to get away from these cold Montana winters. I want to be someplace warm. _____ the climate, _____.

   Dave: Well, be patient. You know we won't _____ for Florida until we can sell our house here.

2. Tricia's management skills are remarkable. She _____ running a small company. Even when an important deadline is _____, she never _____. She remains calm, and gets the job done just as well as she would if there were no deadline at all. In fact, it seems to me that the greater the pressure she is under, _____ her work is.

3. **Sid:** Nice day, today.

   Walter: It sure is.

   Sid: It's too bad it rained all day yesterday.

   Walter: _____?

   Sid: Well, I have to be on my way.

   Walter: Where _____?

   Sid: To work. If I don't _____ by 9:30, my boss'll be upset.

   Walter: You'd better get going, then. The _____ you are, _____ upset he'll be.

Tape Script and Answers for Listening Power Lesson One

Practice #1—Homophone Distractors (Track_1.mov)

1. (woman) Has the faculty committee responded to all our requests?
   (man) Uh huh, they only rejected one.
   (narrator) What does the man mean?

2. (man) Do you think we should find a restaurant now?
   (woman) No, let's do a little more shopping.
   (narrator) What does the woman mean?

3. (woman) When do we get our spring break?
   (man) Just after Easter, two weeks after midterms.
   (narrator) What does the man say about break?

4. (man) I'd like coffee with milk, please.
   (woman) Would you like a large or small mug?
   (narrator) What does the woman ask?

5. (woman) Have you heard the story about the man with one leg?
   (man) I don't think it will amuse me, but go ahead and try.
   (narrator) What is the woman going to do?

6. (woman) I have locker number 50, right over here.
   (man) Mine's number 90. Too bad. I wish our lockers were next to each other.
   (narrator) What is the man's locker number?

7. (man) Did you want to eat lunch in the office today?
   (woman) Actually, I thought we could eat at a nice café. It's only a few blocks from the office.
   (narrator) What does the woman want to do?

8. (woman) I'm looking for Mary. Have you seen her?
   (man) I believe she's headed for the science hall.
   (narrator) What does the man say about Mary?

9. (man) We've worked all day on this assignment. Can we finish it tomorrow? I'm beat.
   (woman) Me, too.
   (narrator) What does the man mean?

10. (man) I need to take a physical education course this term. Any suggestions?
    (woman) How about taking golf?
    (narrator) What is the woman suggesting?

Practice #1 Answers

1.	B	6.	D
2.	A	7.	B
3.	D	8.	B
4.	D	9.	C
5.	C	10.	D

Practice #2—Synonym Distractors (Track_2.mov)

1. (man) How's your day gone so far?
   (woman) Right now, I'm starving. I was in such a rush I didn't get any breakfast this morning.
   (narrator) What happened to the woman?

2. (man) You know, if you spent as much time studying as you do playing video games, you'd be a doctor by now.
   (woman) That's true, but I've got to let off steam somehow.
   (narrator) What does the woman mean?

3. (woman) I enjoy the cool breeze at the beach. It makes the sun feel less hot.
   (man) I enjoy it too. But then again, I'd like the beach in any weather.
   (narrator) What does the woman like?

4. (man) I want to be a doctor so I can help people who are sick.
   (woman) But it's so easy for a doctor to make a mistake. The thought of being responsible for someone's health makes me nervous.
   (narrator) How does the woman feel about being a doctor?

5. (man) I have no idea on how to build this model.
   (woman) Won't you be able to piece it together if you follow the instructions step by step?
   (narrator) What does the woman suggest?

6. (man) Do you think you want to go to the game later?
   (woman) I'll say!
   (narrator) What does the woman mean?

7. (woman) Do you think we'll get to the theater on time?
   (man) No way.
   (narrator) What does the man mean?

8. (man) If you could drive me to work, I wouldn't have to rush through breakfast.
   (woman) That's true, but unfortunately, I don't have time this morning.
   (narrator) What would the man like the woman to do?

9.   (woman)   Wasn't Phil's joke funny?
     (man)   To tell the truth, I didn't really get it.
     (narrator)   What does the man mean?

10.   (man)   Have you read Gina Salem's review of the new movie?
     (woman)   No, but I heard she raved about it and gave it three stars.
     (narrator)   Who is Gina Salem?

Practice #2 Answers

1.	C	6.	C
2.	D	7.	D
3.	C	8.	A
4.	D	9.	B
5.	A	10.	C

Practice #3—Negative Distractors (Track_3.mov)

1.   (woman)   Don't do what you did last semester. If you're having trouble with calculus, just give me call.
     (man)   Sorry, but I would rather fail the class than ask you.
     (narrator)   What does the man mean?

2.   (man)   You're a famous rock star, aren't you? I've seen your picture in the paper.
     (woman)   Please don't speak so loudly. I don't want to call attention to myself.
     (narrator)   What does the woman ask the man to do?

3.   (man)   You wouldn't be interested in being my research assistant next semester, would you?
     (woman)   Oh, sure I would.
     (narrator)   What does the woman mean?

4.   (man)   It sure is hot out, much hotter than yesterday!
     (woman)   Isn't it though!
     (narrator)   What does the woman mean?

5.   (man)   Hey, watch where you're going.
     (woman)   I'm sorry. I didn't mean to bump into you.
     (narrator)   What does the woman tell the man?

6.   (man)   Bill's quite a musician!
     (woman)   Isn't he?
     (narrator)   What does the man say about Bill?

7.   (man)   The new landscaping really has made an improvement in the science quad.
     (woman)   Hasn't it, though!
     (narrator)   What does the woman mean?

8.   (woman)   Hey, how'd you do on the economics quiz?
     (man)   Well, I can't complain!
     (narrator)   What does the man mean?

9.   (man)   There's no way I'll be able to do both these papers by Wednesday.
     (woman)   Not unless you study night and day.
     (narrator)   What does the woman mean?

10. (man)   The game of basketball certainly has changed in the past ten years.
     (woman)   Hasn't it, though!
     (narrator)   What does the woman mean?

Practice #3 Answers

1.	A	6.	A
2.	D	7.	B
3.	D	8.	C
4.	C	9.	D
5.	A	10.	A

Practice #4—Pronoun Distractors (Track_4.mov)

1.   (woman)   A man just dropped by, looking for you and Joe.
     (man)   Who?
     (narrator)   What does the man want to know?

2.   (woman)   In the past, people thought the sun revolved around the earth.
     (man)   How come?
     (narrator)   What does the man want to know?

3.   (man)   The woman on the corner just asked me for a dollar.
     (woman)   So what?
     (narrator)   What does the woman mean?

4.   (man)   You new haircut looks great. Was it expensive?
     (woman)   Actually, it didn't cost me anything. My friend did it for me.
     (narrator)   What does the woman say about her haircut?

5.   (woman)   I'd like a refund on this TV. It's broken.
     (man)   To get your money back, you'll have to go through the proper channels.
     (narrator)   What advice does the man give?

6.   **(man)**   Oh, this computer is driving me crazy!
      (woman)   Well, let's bring it in if it's acting up.
      (narrator)   What is the problem?

7.   **(woman)**   Should we give Mr. Davis the loan?
      (man)   Yes, it would be safe. He's in a good position to find a well-paying job.
      (narrator)   What does the man say about Mr. Davis?

8.   **(man)**   If you ever see Sue, will you tell her I miss her?
      (woman)   Why not call her up and tell her yourself?
      (narrator)   What does the woman want the man to do?

9.   **(man)**   Where can I go with my parents this weekend?
      (woman)   Well, I have extra seats for the homecoming program.
      (narrator)   What does the woman suggest?

10. **(man)**   I've got a fantastic idea for my new book!
      (woman)   What?
      (narrator)   What does the woman want to know?

Practice #4 Answers

1.	A	6.	A
2.	A	7.	B
3.	B	8.	B
4.	B	9.	D
5.	D	10.	C

Practice #5—Time and Sequencing Distractors (Track_5.mov)

1.   **(woman)**   Did you get a chance to buy those history books?
      (man)   No, I thought I'd go with you and get them tomorrow.
      (narrator)   Why didn't the man get the books?

2.   **(woman)**   Well, I'm almost done with my new art project.
      (man)   Let me know when you're done. I'd like to take a look at it.
      (narrator)   What would the man like to do?

3.   **(woman)**   I often go swimming after eating.
      (man)   Don't you think that's a bad idea?
      (narrator)   What would the man probably tell the woman to do?

4.   **(man)**   Did Henry tell you that his mother is going to come over tonight?
      (woman)   Yes, he told me two days ago that she might arrive this evening.
      (narrator)   When does Henry's mother arrive?

5. (man)   Why don't we wait until tomorrow to go shopping?
    (woman)   No, let's go today. The stores are too crowded on Saturday.
    (narrator) What day is it?

6. (woman)   When I went to the store, they were all out of oranges.
    (man)   This morning at ten there were plenty.
    (narrator) When did the woman go to the store?

7. (woman)   After I get up, I take a shower, put my clothes on, and brush my hair.
    (man)   Won't you eat something too?
    (narrator) What does the woman do after she takes a shower?

8. (man)   How are your classes this year?
    (woman)   Let me tell you, it seems like this semester will never end!
    (narrator) What does the woman mean?

9. (woman)   The choir and the dance club have their auditions on Tuesday.
    (man)   So does the debating team.
    (narrator) What does the man say about the debating team?

10. (woman)   You look very familiar.
    (man)   Don't you remember? We met last semester in biology.
    (narrator) What does the man mean?

Practice #5 Answers

1.	D	6.	C
2.	A	7.	B
3.	A	8.	D
4.	C	9.	D
5.	A	10.	D

Practice #6—Unreal Situation Distractors (Track_6.mov)

1. (man)   Why didn't you eat lunch with me in the park?
    (woman)   I wanted to, but I had to catch up on some paperwork.
    (narrator) What did the woman do?

2. (woman)   I gave my 13-inch color monitor away to Jill.
    (man)   I could have used that!
    (narrator) What does the man say?

3. (man)   Don't you think it's time we took a long vacation?
    (woman)   Oh, so we've saved enough money, then?
    (narrator) What had the woman assumed about the vacation?

4. (woman)   I have to get home fast. Should I take a taxicab?
    (man)   You could, but the subway's probably your best bet.
    (narrator)   What does the man tell the woman?

5. (man)   Where would I find housewares?
    (woman)   On the eighth floor. This floor is mostly children's items.
    (narrator)   Where did the conversation probably take place?

6. (woman)   How do you feel after such a long drive?
    (man)   I could use a cup a coffee.
    (narrator)   What does the man mean?

7. (man)   Wasn't that a great play? I can't believe that man made a goal so quickly.
    (woman)   Yes, he's good. But the other team is still winning.
    (narrator)   Where does the conversation probably take place?

8. (woman)   Excuse me, but does this bus go all the way to the airport?
    (man)   No, you'll have to take this bus downtown, and then change for the number 63 bus. I'll show you where you can catch it.
    (narrator)   What does the man tell the woman to do?

9. (man)   The sale on fall sweaters ended last Friday.
    (woman)   If I had only known, I would have gone before then.
    (narrator)   What did the woman do?

10. (woman)   Did you hear the rumbling in the sky just now?
    (man)   Yes, and soon the rain will come pouring down. We're going to get soaked if we don't go inside.
    (narrator)   What are the man and the woman experiencing?

Practice #6 Answers

1.	B	6.	B
2.	C	7.	D
3.	B	8.	D
4.	C	9.	A
5.	C	10.	D

Practice #7—Multiple Referent Distractors (Track_7.mov)

1. (woman)   Bill, did you pick up these sweets at the bakery?
    (man)   No, I got Sue to do it for me.
    (narrator)   What does the man say about the sweets?

2. (woman)   John, your new car is gorgeous. I love it.
   (man)   Thanks, it ought to be nice. It cost a pretty penny.
   (narrator) What does the man mean?

3. (woman)   It must have been quite a picnic. Everyone said they were going to be there.
   (man)   Yeah, but only half the people actually showed up.
   (narrator) What does the woman mean?

4. (woman)   I'm really nervous about Professor Jones's chemistry test.
   (man)   Oh, so you're not doing the paper instead?
   (narrator) What had the man assumed?

5. (man)   I don't think math is very difficult.
   (woman)   Neither is physics.
   (narrator) What does the woman say?

6. (woman)   I try to exercise twice a week.
   (man)   Not me. I work out at least every other day.
   (narrator) What does the man say?

7. (man)   I didn't study one bit for the test. I'm worried. How about you?
   (woman)   For once, I'm not. I worked hard and learned a lot.
   (narrator) What describes the woman?

8. (man)   Please take this ribbon and give it to Larry to put on the bicycle he is giving to his sister.
   (woman)   Larry's not here. I'll give it to him later.
   (narrator) Whom is the bicycle for?

9. (woman)   Alice and her class are going to come over and look at my collection of model trains.
   (man)   I think my son would enjoy seeing the trains, too.
   (narrator) Who is going to see the trains?

10. (man)   I scored more goals than Eli, but fewer than Hugo.
   (woman)   Really? I scored more than Hugo.
   (narrator) Who scored the most goals?

Practice #7 Answers

1.	D	6.	A
2.	C	7.	B
3.	A	8.	B
4.	C	9.	B
5.	A	10.	D

Vocabulary Answers

1. there is no guarantee that; the warmer; the happier I'll be/the better; head

2. had a head for; just around the corner; loses her head; the better

3. Isn't it, though?; are you headed; show up; later; the more

LISTENING POWER LESSON TWO

FOR LISTENING PART B OF THE TOEFL

Listening Power Lesson Two will help you with Part B of the Listening Comprehension section of the TOEFL. This part of the test consists of a series of slightly longer conversations followed by several questions. Between each question there is a pause of about ten seconds. During this pause, the student selects his answer from one of four possible items, and then waits for the next question.

Although this Power Lesson is intended to help you get ready for this part of the TOEFL, keep in mind that all of the distractors you learned from the first lesson—from homophone distractors to multiple referent distractors—could show up on this part of the test, too.

As you go through the practice exercises at the end of this lesson, you will notice that many of the longer conversations are identical. Each time you hear the conversation, you will acquire a deeper understanding of it. Note, however, that even though the conversations may be the same, the questions on the conversations are different.

SESSION A: MAIN TOPIC, MAIN IDEA, AND TONE QUESTIONS FOR LONGER CONVERSATIONS

Main Topic

Main topic questions ask you to identify the general topic under discussion. When listening to the conversation, you should do the following things in order to catch the topic.

➤ Try to picture the conversation taking place.

➤ Make assumptions about who is talking.

➤ Listen to key or repeated vocabulary items.

➤ Make assumptions about where the people are talking.

It is only by gathering global knowledge of the conversation that you will be able to determine the main topic of the conversation. Main topic questions are often asked in the following ways:

"What is the main topic of the conversation?"

"What are the speakers mainly discussing?"

"What is the subject of this conversation?"

Main Idea

Main idea questions ask you to summarize the whole conversation. When listening to the conversation, you should do the following things in order to catch the main idea.

➤ Identify the topic under discussion.

➤ Make assumptions about who is talking.

➤ Listen to key or repeated vocabulary items.

➤ Make assumptions about where the people are talking.

➤ Understand the attitude of each of the speakers while they are talking.

➤ Understand how each speaker feels about the other speaker's ideas.

It is only by understanding the vocabulary and the attitude of each of the speakers that you will be able to determine the main idea of the conversation.

Main idea questions are often asked in the form of:

"What is the main idea of the conversation?"

"What best summarizes the conversation?"

Tone

Tone questions ask you to analyze the attitude of the speakers and the dynamics of their relationship during the conversation. When listening to the conversation, you should do the following things in order to catch the tone.

➤ Identify the topic under discussion.

➤ Make assumptions about who is talking.

➤ Listen to key or repeated vocabulary items.

➤ Understand the position of each of the speakers while they are talking.

➤ Understand how each speaker feels about the other speaker's ideas.

➤ Listen carefully to each speaker's intonation pattern.

➤ Listen carefully for key vocabulary and expressions that will give you the speakers' attitudes.

It is only by understanding the vocabulary and the attitude of each of the speakers that you will be able to determine the tone of the conversation.

Tone questions are often asked in the form of:

"What is the man's/woman's attitude toward the conversation?"

"How does the man/woman feel?"

"The man's/woman's feeling toward the subject can best be described as:"

SESSION B: VOCATION QUESTIONS FOR LONGER CONVERSATIONS

Vocation questions require you to identify either the profession of the speakers or the relationship of the speakers to one another. These questions occur more often in Listening Part B of the paper-based TOEFL exam than in the computer-based test. Those vocation questions that do appear in the computer-based TOEFL focus on professionals in an academic setting.

> **Vocation and location questions do not often appear in the Listening Comprehension section of the computer-based TOEFL exam. Those that do appear are set in an academic environment.**

Observe the following example. Suppose you hear:

MAN:	Terry, I'm looking for some computer disks.
WOMAN:	Well, there aren't any here. Have you tried asking someone in Supplies?
MAN:	I just did, but they said they're out of them. I really need the disks. I want to make extra copies of a few documents and reports, just in case something happens to my computer.
WOMAN:	Perhaps you should just go to an office supply shop and buy some disks yourself.
MAN:	Maybe I'll do that.

Question: What is the relationship of the speakers?
(A) lawyer and client
(B) teacher and student
(C) office mates
(D) store clerk and customer

Answer (D) is incorrect. A customer would not be likely to use the name of a store clerk. There is no vocabulary in the conversation that is typical of a legal situation, so (A) is not correct. The same can be said of (B). There are, however, some clues that the conversation took place in an office. Many offices have an area called "Supplies," where you can find items like computer disks and typing paper. Also, the man mentions documents and reports, which also suggests that they are in an office environment. They probably work together in the office. Therefore, (C) is the best answer.

In order to answer vocation and other general speaker identification questions, you should:

> ➤ Try to visualize the conversation as it takes place.
> ➤ Listen carefully to key words that will identify the speakers or their relationship.
> ➤ Listen to the intonation of the speakers to identify whether the conversation is official or familiar.

Vocation questions take the form:

"What is the person's probable vocation/job?"

"Who is the woman/man?"

While listening to a conversation in the Listening Comprehension section of the TOEFL, always try to determine the relationship between the two speakers.

SESSION C: LOCATION QUESTIONS FOR LONGER CONVERSATIONS

Location questions require you to identify where the conversation takes place. They appear relatively infrequently on the computer-based version of the TOEFL exam.

The same short conversation from Session B will serve as an example.

Example:

MAN:	Terry, I'm looking for some computer disks.
WOMAN:	Well, there aren't any here. Have you tried asking someone in Supplies?
MAN:	I just did, but they said they're out of them. I really need the disks. I want to make extra copies of a few documents and reports, just in case something happens to my computer.
WOMAN:	Perhaps you should just go to an office supply shop and buy some disks yourself.
MAN:	Maybe I'll do that.

Question: Where does this conversation probably take place?

(A) a computer store
(B) an office
(C) a department store
(D) an office supply shop

Answer (B) is correct. Again, pay attention to specific vocabulary in the dialogue that will narrow the location to a specific place. In the above conversation, the mention of "someone in Supplies" tells us that the people are in an office. Be careful not to be distracted by answer (D). Just because the exact words of an answer choice are used in the script does not mean that it is the correct answer, and often is not.

In order to best answer location questions you should:

➤ Listen for key vocabulary that gives evidence of where the speakers are.
➤ Visualize where the conversation is taking place.
➤ Listen carefully to the tone of the speakers to identify whether the conversation is friendly or official.

Location questions take the form:

"Where does the conversation probably take place?"

"Where are the man and woman talking?"

The distractors that you learned in Power Lesson One for Listening Part A of the TOEFL are very likely to show up in vocation and location questions for Listening Part B.

SESSION D: FACT-BASED AND INFERENCE QUESTIONS FOR LONGER CONVERSATIONS

Fact-Based Questions

These questions will require you to recall direct information related in the spoken text. To answer fact-based questions, you should:

➤ Listen carefully to the details of the conversation.
➤ Try to understand unfamiliar words from context.
➤ Look at the answers while the conversation is happening so that you can anticipate certain fact questions.
➤ Pay special attention to numbers and proper nouns.

Remember: Detail questions are generally asked in the same order they are presented in the conversation. So, following along with the questions while the conversation is taking place is a good way to listen for certain details. For example, if an answer set has

(A) bicycle
(B) a motorcycle
(C) a car
(D) an airplane

you know that you should listen carefully for a mode of transportation that will be mentioned in the conversation. Fact-based questions often begin with phrases like:

"According to the conversation . . ."

"What/Why/Which . . ."

> **Look at the answer choices while you are waiting for a conversation to start. This will give you a hint about what kind of information you should listen for.**

Inference Questions

Inference questions ask you to draw conclusions about specific details in the passage or to make comparisons between details. In order to answer inference questions, you should:

➤ Listen carefully to the details of the conversation.
➤ Try to understand unfamiliar words from context.
➤ Look at the answers while the conversation is happening so that you can anticipate certain inference questions.
➤ Use your knowledge about the situation to guess what sort of logical conclusions might happen.

Inference questions are usually asked in the following form:

"It can be inferred from the conversation that . . ."

"The man or woman most probably . . ."

"What will the man or woman probably do next?"

PRACTICE #1—Main Topic and Tone Questions

Listen to Track_9.mov. Circle the letter of the answer choice that correctly answers each question.

1. (A) take a walk
   (B) cook a meal
   (C) go to Chicago
   (D) read the paper with the man

2. (A) the man's friendship with Joan
   (B) the woman's desire to go for a walk
   (C) buying imported beer
   (D) growing up in Florida

3. (A) reading the paper
   (B) the cold weather in Florida
   (C) not getting a chill in the autumn weather
   (D) the chili in Chicago

4. (A) enthusiastic
   (B) dispassionate
   (C) reluctant
   (D) furious

5. (A) angry
   (B) unhappy
   (C) delighted
   (D) frustrated

6. (A) the man's move from Wisconsin
   (B) the location of the Motor Vehicles Department
   (C) transferring the man's driver's license to New York State
   (D) the expiration of the woman's license

7. (A) disinterested
   (B) enthusiastic
   (C) helpful
   (D) furious

8. (A) overwhelmed
   (B) inquisitive
   (C) confused
   (D) disinterested

9. (A) The man has a car.
   (B) The man prefers to live in Wisconsin.
   (C) The man is new to the area.
   (D) The man doesn't know the expiration date of his license.

PRACTICE #2—Location

Listen to Track_10.mov. Circle the letter of the answer choice that correctly answers each question.

1. (A) on a street corner
   (B) at a restaurant
   (C) at an office
   (D) on the phone

2. (A) near the man
   (B) in New York
   (C) close to the railway station
   (D) near the high school

3. (A) at the office
   (B) at the railway station
   (C) at the high school
   (D) at home after work

4. (A) to the high school
   (B) to his office
   (C) to New York
   (D) to the woman's house

5. (A) at home
   (B) at the high school
   (C) at the railway station
   (D) at work

6. (A) on a college campus
   (B) in the five-college area
   (C) at a hotel
   (D) at a football game

7. (A) in the five-college area
   (B) near the library
   (C) on Main Street
   (D) in the western portion of the state

8. (A) a university with a better football team
   (B) the five-college area
   (C) the woman's university
   (D) Western State

9. (A) Western State
   (B) He did not attend college.
   (C) closer to his home
   (D) in the five-college area

PRACTICE # 3—Vocation

Listen to Track_11.mov. Circle the letter of the answer choice that correctly answers each question.

1. (A) fashion designer
   (B) department store clerk
   (C) tie manufacturer
   (D) manager

2. (A) the department store
   (B) the man
   (C) the man's friend
   (D) Arturo Costanini

3. (A) fashion consultant
   (B) department store manager
   (C) we don't know
   (D) He is unemployed.

4. (A) information on current fashion designers
   (B) help choosing a tie as a gift
   (C) to know if his friend has been to see her
   (D) a new tie for his business

5. (A) policewoman
   (B) driving instructor
   (C) Motor Vehicles information officer
   (D) optometrist

6. (A) at the motor vehicles department
   (B) in Wisconsin
   (C) in the New York State professional licensing office
   (D) with the man

7. (A) driving instruction
   (B) directions to her office
   (C) an appointment
   (D) information on transferring his driver's license

8. (A) She tells him a place to register for driving instruction.
   (B) She gives him information on transferring his driver's license.
   (C) She arranges an appointment for him.
   (D) She gives him directions to the Department of Motor Vehicles.

PRACTICE #4—Fact-Based and Inference

Listen to Track_12.mov. Circle the letter of the answer choice that correctly answers each question.

1. (A) salad
   (B) chili
   (C) beer
   (D) hot soup

2. (A) Chicago
   (B) Florida
   (C) near the woman
   (D) with Joan

3. (A) her dog
   (B) some imported beer
   (C) a big salad
   (D) a Chicago newspaper

4. (A) chili con carne
   (B) salad supplies
   (C) imported beer
   (D) Joan's dog

5. (A) go shopping
   (B) read the paper
   (C) drive
   (D) stay at Joan's

6. (A) the men's department
   (B) a necktie
   (C) the woman's gift
   (D) Arturo Costanini

7. (A) the man's friend
   (B) herself
   (C) Arturo Costanini
   (D) She does not mention a designer.

8. (A) They are unfashionable.
   (B) He doesn't like them.
   (C) They are made of silk.
   (D) They are too expensive.

9. (A) He doesn't know much about the latest Japanese fashions.
   (B) He doesn't like the woman.
   (C) He is angry with his friend.
   (D) He knows Arturo Costanini.

10. (A) She is not helpful to the man.
    (B) She knows the man's friend.
    (C) She keeps up with fashion trends.
    (D) She likes expensive ties.

PRACTICE #5—Review Questions

Listen to Track_13.mov. Circle the letter of the answer choice that correctly answers each question.

1. (A) stay indoors
   (B) make lunch
   (C) read the paper
   (D) go outside

2. (A) He would rather talk on the phone.
   (B) He doesn't like the weather.
   (C) He wants to eat lunch.
   (D) He doesn't like the park.

3. (A) eat, then walk
   (B) eat supper late this evening
   (C) walk, then eat
   (D) make supper, then eat

4. (A) She likes it.
   (B) She doesn't like it.
   (C) She wants to find out what Joan thinks.
   (D) She wants to do something else.

5. (A) Wisconsin Department of Motor Vehicles
   (B) New York State Vision Services
   (C) Any state's motor vehicle department
   (D) New York's Department of Motor Vehicles

6. (A) His old license has expired.
   (B) He cannot use his Wisconsin license in New York.
   (C) His Wisconsin license will expire soon.
   (D) His New York license will expire soon.

7. (A) have his eyes tested and take a written test
   (B) have his eyes tested and take a driving test
   (C) take a written test and a driving test
   (D) take a driving test and bring his old license

8. (A) the man's company
   (B) an information service
   (C) a government agency
   (D) a driving instruction company

9. (A) husband and wife
   (B) roommates
   (C) co-workers
   (D) former classmates

10. (A) 12 P.M. on December 11th
    (B) 2 P.M. on December 11th
    (C) 2 P.M. on December 1st
    (D) 2 P.M. on December 11th

11. (A) at the train station
    (B) at the bus station
    (C) at the office
    (D) on the phone

12. (A) illegible
    (B) elegant
    (C) childish
    (D) minute

13. (A) a local business
    (B) a tour company
    (C) the local college
    (D) the college football team

14. (A) places to eat
    (B) places to see movies
    (C) bars
    (D) the five-college area

15. (A) It is quite beautiful.
    (B) His brother lived there.
    (C) His brother is going there Saturday.
    (D) It is the home of Western State.

16. (A) It is not bad.
    (B) It wins many games.
    (C) He would like to join.
    (D) It is a poor team.

17. (A) at a gas station
    (B) in a clothing store
    (C) in a grocery store
    (D) in a shoe store

18. (A) a fashionable tie
    (B) a very inexpensive present
    (C) any tie by an Italian designer
    (D) a tie by Arturo Costanini

19. (A) He hasn't kept up with fashion
        trends.
    (B) He cannot see the tie.
    (C) The woman refuses to tell him if it is.
    (D) It is an unusual type of tie.

20. (A) It is not fashionable enough.
    (B) It is too inexpensive.
    (C) It is too expensive.
    (D) It will not fit his friend.

Vocabulary

To hear how these words and expressions are pronounced, listen to Track_14.mov.

Trend/in fashion/fashionable/high fashion
In this lesson you encountered a number of expressions related to clothing styles. Look at these expressions a second time with the examples below.

Wearing a baseball cap backwards seems to be one of the latest <u>trends</u> in <u>youth fashion</u> these days. When I was young, nobody wore his baseball hat that way.

Deborah has very expensive tastes in clothes. She goes to only the <u>high fashion stores</u>.

I understand she writes for <u>a fashion magazine</u>.

He always shows up <u>very fashionably dressed</u>.

-Mate
This suffix combines with nouns that refer to a place or an activity to form a new noun that talks about a person who shares that place or activity with somebody. For example, your roommate is the person you share a room with. Below you will find some other words formed with *-mate.*

If I'm not home, leave a message with my <u>roommate</u>.

Margaret and I are <u>housemates</u>.

My <u>apartmentmate</u>, Paul, is quite messy.

Johnny does not get along well with his <u>classmates</u>, I'm afraid.

His <u>shipmates</u> gave him a solemn burial at sea.

It would be best to + **simple form of verb/***that's better than* + **gerund**
Notice that these expressions take different forms of the verb.

I think <u>it would be best to wait</u> for him.

<u>That's</u> certainly <u>better than</u> going without him and leaving him to try to get there by himself.

I can't stand + **noun or gerund**
This phrase means you hate that thing or cannot tolerate it.

> I can't stand her.

> I can't stand staying home on Friday evenings.

Inquisitive
This means "curious."

> She gave me an inquisitive look, but I refused to tell her where I had been.

Il-
The prefix *il-* combines with adjectives to mean "not."

> Her handwriting is so illegible.

> His parents are not very well educated. In fact, I believe his father is illiterate.

> I hate discussing politics with him because he's so illogical.

Quite a few
This means "many":

> We have met quite a few people who feel that there needs to be a real change in government.

VOCABULARY EXERCISE

Complete the sentences below, using the given expressions. Some may be used more than once.

fashions	it would be best	quite a few
is better than	I can't stand	inquisitive
fashionable	illegible	-mates
trends	better than	

1. **Harold:** I'm afraid I have bad news: Mark is going to meet us at the restaurant tonight.

    Maude: Oh, no! You know _____ Mark. Why did you invite him?

    Harold: I didn't invite him. But I was telling one of our other office _____ that you and I were going to Chez Jacques tonight, and Mark overheard. Then he started telling me that Chez Jacques is the most _____ restaurant in town, and that he knows the manager there, and that he could get us a free dessert if we wanted one, and the next thing I knew, he was inviting himself along.

    Maude: Well, I think in the future _____ just to be completely honest with him and tell him he's not welcome.

    Harold: I can't do that. I have to see him every day.

    Maude: Don't you think that _____ losing me?

2. **Ingrid:** _____ experts on popular culture have argued that women's _____ are influenced by the economy. They say that the higher the stock market figures, the higher the hemlines tend to get. During the stock boom of the Reagan years, short skirts became very popular.

    Chelsea: So if current economic _____ continue, we can expect hemlines to rise above the knee?

3. **Cameron:** Can you read this message? I can't make out what the phone number is.

   Aaron: Well, that number looks like a "3," but I don't know if that one is a "4" or a "7." It's very _____.

   Cameron: If there's one thing _____ , it's getting a phone message that I can't read.

4. **Marge:** My little Barry has such an _____ nature. He's only three, but he's interested in everything. If we take him to a new place, he can spend hours just studying the world around him.

   Sarah: My Jenny is exactly the same! That's so much _____ most children these days, don't you think? They're not interested in anything but watching television. At least, that all that Jenny's class _____ seem to want to do.

Tape Script and Answers for Listening Power Lesson Two

Practice #1—Main Topic, Main Idea, and Tone Questions (Track_9.mov)

Questions 1–5 refer to the following conversation between a man and a woman:

(woman)   It's such wonderful fall weather, don't you think? Let's take a walk in the park.

(man)   I can't stand the cold. Why don't we stay in and read the paper?

(woman)   I wish you weren't so worried about getting a chill. I'll just call Joan and ask her if she wants to go to the park. She can bring her dog, too.

(man)   Look, it's not my fault I grew up in Florida. I'm just not used to Chicago weather. But as long as you're going to call Joan, why don't you ask her if she wants to eat something later this afternoon. While you two go for a walk, I'll cook us supper.

(woman)   Now that's a great idea. What are you thinking of making?

(man)   Something hot. How about a nice pot of chili con carne? And a big salad.

(woman)   Yum! We can get some imported beer to go along with the meal.

1. What does the woman want to do?

2. What is the main topic of the discussion?

3. What is the man's primary concern?

4. How does the man feel about walking?

5. How does the woman feel about the man's solution?

Questions 6–9 refer to the following conversation:

(woman)   New York State Department of Motor Vehicles.

(man)   Hello. I recently moved to New York from Wisconsin. My Wisconsin driver's license expires in two months. I was wondering what I have to do to get a New York license?

(woman)   Bring your Wisconsin license to the nearest New York Motor Vehicle branch office before it expires. You will have to have your vision checked. You'll also have to take a written test on New York driving laws.

(man)   I won't have to take a driving test, will I?

(woman)   Not if you come before the expiration date of your out-of-state license. It would be best to come as soon as possible.

(man)   All right. I'll come in this week. Thank you.

6. What is the main topic of the discussion?

7. What is the woman's tone?

8. What is the man's tone?

9. What can be inferred from the preceding passage?

Practice #1 Answers

1.	A	6.	C
2.	B	7.	C
3.	C	8.	B
4.	C	9.	A
5.	C		

Practice #2—Location (Track_10.mov)

Questions 1–5 refer to the following conversation:

(man)   I am so excited to be coming to visit you in New York.

(woman)   Me too. I haven't seen you since high school. When will you arrive?

(man)   About noon on December 11th. Do you think I could meet you at work? We could have lunch.

(woman)   I don't know. I've been so busy lately I haven't been able to get out of the office. I may have to meet you at 5 P.M. Can you find my office building?

(man)   If you give me good directions. I'm coming from the railway station.

(woman)   No problem. I will write them down and mail them right away. That's better than trying to tell them to you over the phone.

(man)   Yes, but if your handwriting hasn't improved since high school, it may be a waste of time for you to send me those directions. Just tell me now.

1. Where does the conversation probably take place?

2. Where does the woman live?

3. Where will the man meet the woman?

4. Where will the man travel?

5. Where will the woman be when the man arrives?

Questions 6–9 refer to the following conversation:

(woman)   Hello, my name is Paige and I'll be your tour guide on today's tour. Please ask me any questions that you have. I want you to enjoy yourselves and I hope to see you on campus next fall.

(man)   Excuse me, I have a question.

(woman)   Sure.

(man)   I was wondering what people usually do on weekends.

(woman)	Thinking of weekends already. Spoken like a true college student. Well, if you look to your left, down the hill, you'll see Main Street. There are bars and restaurants and even a couple of movie theaters there. Also, a lot of students like to take weekend trips to the five-college area.
(man)	I think I know where that is. My brother used to go to school there. He said it was a fun town and that a lot of people from this school would drive down on Saturdays.
(woman)	That's true, the students here at Western State love to drive.
(man)	Paige, I have one more question. I've heard bad things about Western State's football team. Do you think the team will ever win another game?
(woman)	Well, nobody really knows. If we recruit guys like you, maybe not. OK. Let's go see the library.

6. Where does the conversation take place?

7. Where is the college located?

8. Where is the man interested in going to school?

9. Where did the man's brother go to school?

Practice #2 Answers

1.	D	6.	A
2.	B	7.	C
3.	A	8.	D
4.	C	9.	D
5.	D		

Practice #3—Vocation (Track_11.mov)

Questions 1–4 refer to the following conversation:

(man)	Excuse me, miss. Is this the men's department?
(woman)	Yes, sir. Is there anything I can help you find today?
(man)	Well, you see, I'm looking for a necktie, and I need some help. It's a gift for a friend of mine who's very fashionable. I want to get the best.
(woman)	You've come to the right place. Over here, in this glass case, you can see several hundred styles of silk ties. Right now we have quite a few on sale. Now, if you're looking for a well-known designer label, one of our most popular designers is Arturo Costanini. These are ties from his fall collection.
(man)	I must confess, I'm ignorant of current trends in men's clothes. Are the Costanini ties in fashion now?

(woman)	Well, sir, we keep up so you don't have to. If it's high fashion your friend wants, the Costanini ties will please him.
(man)	Yes, but I see they're a little over my price range. Do you have anything that's similar, but a bit less expensive?

1. What is the woman's job?
2. Whom does the woman probably work for?
3. What is the man's probable vocation?
4. What does the man need from the woman?

Questions 5–8 refer to the following conversation:

(woman)	New York State Department of Motor Vehicles.
(man)	Hello. I recently moved to New York from Wisconsin. My Wisconsin driver's license expires in two months. I was wondering what I have to do to get a New York license?
(woman)	Bring your Wisconsin license to the nearest New York Motor Vehicle branch office before it expires. You will have to have your vision checked. You'll also have to take a written test on New York driving laws.
(man)	I won't have to take a driving test, will I?
(woman)	Not if you come before the expiration date of your out-of-state license. It would be best to come as soon as possible.
(man)	All right. I'll come in this week. Thank you.

5. What is the woman's job?
6. Where does the woman work?
7. What does the man need from the woman?
8. What information does the woman provide for the man?

Practice #3 Answers

1. B	5. C
2. A	6. A
3. C	7. D
4. B	8. B

Practice #4—Fact-Based and Inference (Track_12.mov)

Questions 1–5 refer to the following conversation:

(woman)   It's such wonderful fall weather, don't you think? Let's take a walk in the park.

(man)   I can't stand the cold. Why don't we stay in and read the paper?

(woman)   I wish you weren't so worried about getting a chill. I'll just call Joan and ask her if she wants to go to the park. She can bring her dog too.

(man)   Look, it's not my fault I grew up in Florida. I'm just not used to Chicago weather. But as long as you're going to call Joan, why don't you ask her if she wants to eat something later this afternoon. While you two go for a walk, I'll cook us supper.

(woman)   Now that's a great idea. What are you thinking of making?

(man)   Something hot. How about a nice pot of chili con carne? And a big salad.

(woman)   Yum! We can get some imported beer to go along with the meal.

1. Which of the following is NOT mentioned as being part of the dinner plans?

2. Where did the man grow up?

3. What will Joan bring with her on the walk?

4. What does the woman intend to purchase on her walk?

5. What does the man want to do instead of walking?

Questions 6–10 refer to the following conversation:

(man)   Excuse me, miss. Is this the men's department?

(woman)   Yes, sir. Is there anything I can help you find today?

(man)   Well, you see, I'm looking for a necktie, and I need some help. It's a gift for a friend of mine who's very fashionable. I want to get the best.

(woman)   You've come to the right place. Over here, in this glass case, you can see several hundred styles of silk ties. Right now we have quite a few on sale. Now, if you're looking for a well-known designer label, one of our most popular designers is Arturo Costanini. These are ties from his fall collection.

(man)   I must confess, I'm ignorant of current trends in men's clothes. Are the Costanini ties in fashion now?

(woman)   Well, sir, we keep up so you don't have to. If it's high fashion your friend wants, the Costanini ties will please him.

(man)   Yes, but I see they're a little over my price range. Do you have anything that's similar, but a bit less expensive?

6. What is the man looking for?

7. Who is the designer the woman mentions?

8. Why does the man decide not to buy one of the ties the woman recommends?

9. What can be inferred about the man?

10. What can be inferred about the woman?

Practice #4 Answers

1.	D	6.	B
2.	B	7.	C
3.	A	8.	D
4.	C	9.	A
5.	B	10.	C

Practice #5—Review Questions (Track_13.mov)

Questions 1–4 refer to the following conversation:

(woman)   It's such wonderful fall weather, don't you think? Let's take a walk in the park.

(man)   I can't stand the cold. Why don't we stay in and read the paper?

(woman)   I wish you weren't so worried about getting a chill. I'll just call Joan and ask her if she wants to go to the park. She can bring her dog too.

(man)   Look, it's not my fault I grew up in Florida. I'm just not used to Chicago weather. But as long as you're going to call Joan, why don't you ask her if she wants to eat something later this afternoon. While you two go for a walk, I'll cook us supper.

(woman)   Now that's a great idea. What are you thinking of making?

(man)   Something hot. How about a nice pot of chili con carne? And a big salad.

(woman)   Yum! We can get some imported beer to go along with the meal.

1. What does the woman want to do?

2. Why doesn't the man want to go outside?

3. What does the man advise the woman to do?

4. How does the woman feel about the man's idea?

Questions 5–8 refer to the following conversation:

(woman)   New York State Department of Motor Vehicles.

(man)   Hello. I recently moved to New York from Wisconsin. My Wisconsin driver's license expires in two months. I was wondering what I have to do to get a New York license?

(woman)   Bring your Wisconsin license to the nearest New York Motor Vehicle branch office before it expires. You will have to have your vision checked. You'll also have to take a written test on New York driving laws.

(man)	I won't have to take a driving test, will I?
(woman)	Not if you come before the expiration date of your out-of-state license. It would be best to come as soon as possible.
(man)	All right. I'll come in this week. Thank you.

5. Which office must the man visit? (detail)

6. Why does the man want a new driver's license? (detail)

7. What must the man do to get his new driver's license next week? (detail/organization)

8. Whom does the woman work for? (vocation)

Questions 9–12 refer to the following conversation:

(man)	I am so excited to be coming to visit you in New York.
(woman)	Me too. I haven't seen you since high school. When will you arrive?
(man)	About noon on December 11th. Do you think I could meet you at work? We could have lunch.
(woman)	I don't know. I've been so busy lately I haven't been able to get out of the office. I may have to meet you at 5 P.M. Can you find my office building?
(man)	If you give me good directions. I'm coming from the railway station.
(woman)	No problem. I will write them down and mail them right away. That's better than trying to tell them to you over the phone.
(man)	Yes, but if your handwriting hasn't improved since high school, it may be a waste of time for you to send me those directions. Just tell me now.

9. What is the relationship between the man and the woman? (vocation/relationship)

10. When is the man arriving in New York? (detail)

11. Right before he goes to the woman's office, where will the man be? (detail/inference)

12. What is the best way to describe the woman's handwriting? (detail)

Questions 13–16 refer to the following conversation:

(woman)	Hello, my name is Paige and I'll be your tour guide on today's tour. Please ask me any questions that you have. I want you to enjoy yourselves and I hope to see you on campus next fall.
(man)	Excuse me, I have a question.
(woman)	Sure.
(man)	I was wondering what people usually do on weekends.
(woman)	Thinking of weekends already. Spoken like a true college student. Well, if you look to your left, down the hill, you'll see Main Street. There are bars and restaurants and

even a couple of movie theaters there. Also, a lot of students like to take weekend trips to the five-college area.

(man)   I think I know where that is. My brother used to go to school there. He said it was a fun town and that a lot of people from this school would drive down on Saturdays.

(woman)   That's true, the students here at Western State love to drive.

(man)   Paige, I have one more question. I've heard bad things about Western State's football team. Do you think the team will ever win another game?

(woman)   Well, nobody really knows. If we recruit guys like you, maybe not. OK. Let's go see the library.

13. Whom does Paige probably work for?

14. Which of the following is NOT located on Main Street?

15. What does the man say about the five-college area?

16. What does the man say about the football team?

Questions 17–20 refer to the following conversation:

(man)   Excuse me, miss. Is this the men's department?

(woman)   Yes, sir. Is there anything I can help you find today?

(man)   Well, you see, I'm looking for a necktie, and I need some help. It's a gift for a friend of mine who's very fashionable. I want to get the best.

(woman)   You've come to the right place. Over here, in this glass case, you can see several hundred styles of silk ties. Right now we have quite a few on sale. Now, if you're looking for a well-known designer label, one of our most popular designers is Arturo Costanini. These are ties from his fall collection.

(man)   I must confess, I'm ignorant of current trends in men's clothes. Are the Costanini ties in fashion now?

(woman)   Well, sir, we keep up so you don't have to. If it's high fashion your friend wants, the Costanini ties will please him.

(man)   Yes, but I see they're a little over my price range. Do you have anything that's similar, but a bit less expensive?

17. Where would this conversation probably take place?

18. What type of gift does the man want to get?

19. Why doesn't the man know if the Costanini tie is in fashion?

20. Why doesn't the man want to buy the Costanini tie?

Practice #5 Answers

1.	D	11.	A
2.	B	12.	A
3.	C	13.	C
4.	A	14.	D
5.	D	15.	B
6.	C	16.	D
7.	A	17.	B
8.	C	18.	A
9.	D	19.	A
10.	A	20.	C

Vocabulary Answers

1. I can't stand; -mates; fashionable; it would be best; is better than

2. Quite a few; fashions; trends

3. illegible; I can't stand

4. inquisitive; better than; -mates

LISTENING POWER LESSON THREE

FOR LISTENING PART C OF THE PAPER-BASED TOEFL (LISTENING PART B CONTINUED OF THE COMPUTER-BASED TOEFL)

Listening Power Lesson Three will help you with Part C of the Listening Comprehension section of the paper-based TOEFL (the same material is covered in Listening Part B of the computer-based TOEFL). This part of the TOEFL consists of talks followed by several questions. Between each question there is a pause of about ten seconds. During this pause, the student selects his or her answer from one of four possible items, and then waits for the next question.

It may be tempting for you to take notes while you are listening to the talks, but **writing while listening to the talks is considered cheating.** If you are caught, your test may be taken from you immediately.

The types of questions that you will encounter in the talks contained in Part C are of the same general type as those asked of the longer conversations in Part B, which you studied in Listening Power Lesson Two. Therefore, in this lesson you will not be learning new question types; instead, you will learn how questions on the Main Topic, the Main Idea, Tone, Location, Vocation, and Fact and Inference are asked for these talks.

As you go through the practice exercises at the end of this lesson, you will notice that many of the talks are identical. Each time you hear the talk you will acquire a deeper understanding of it. Note, however, that even though the talks may be the same, the questions on the talks are different.

> **Remember that the kinds of questions you will be asked to answer in the Listening Part C section of the paper-based TOEFL are very much like those in the Listening Part B section.**

SESSION A: MAIN TOPIC, MAIN IDEA, AND TONE QUESTIONS

Main Topic

Main topic questions ask you to identify the general topic of a talk. When listening to the talk, you should do the following things in order to catch the topic:

➤ Try to picture the talk as it is being given.
➤ Make assumptions about who is talking.
➤ Listen to key or repeated vocabulary items.
➤ Make assumptions about where the speaker is.

It is only by gathering global knowledge of the talk that you will be able to determine its main topic. Main topic questions are often asked in the following ways:

"What is the main topic of the talk?"

"What does the speaker mainly discuss?"

"What is the subject of the talk?"

Main Idea

Main idea questions ask you to summarize the whole talk. When listening to the talk, you should do the following things in order to catch the main idea.

➤ Identify the topic under discussion.
➤ Make assumptions about who is talking.
➤ Listen to key or repeated vocabulary items.
➤ Make assumptions about who the speaker is.
➤ Understand the position of the speaker while he or she is talking.
➤ Understand how the speaker feels about the ideas he or she is presenting.

It is only by understanding the vocabulary and the attitude of the speaker that you will be able to determine the main idea of the talk.

Main idea questions are often asked in the form of:

"What is the main idea of the talk?"

"What best summarizes the talk?"

Tone

Tone questions ask you to analyze the attitude of the speaker. Tone questions also ask you to comment on the relationship of the speaker to his or her audience. When listening to the talk you should do the following things in order to catch the tone.

➤ Identify the topic under discussion.
➤ Make assumptions about who is talking.
➤ Listen to key or repeated vocabulary items.
➤ Make assumptions about where the talk is being given.
➤ Understand the position of the speaker while he or she is talking.
➤ Listen carefully to each speaker's intonation pattern.
➤ Listen carefully for key vocabulary and expressions that will give you the speakers' attitude.
➤ Make assumptions about the who the audience is and how they would feel about listening to such a talk.

Understanding the attitude of the speaker will enable you to determine the tone of the talk. Tone questions are often asked in the form of:

"What is the speaker's attitude during the talk?"

"How does the woman feel about. . . ?"

"The speaker's feeling toward the subject can best be described as:"

SESSION B: LOCATION QUESTIONS FOR TALKS

Location questions require you to identify where the talk is most likely being given. In order to best answer location questions you should:

> ➤ Listen for key vocabulary that gives evidence of where the speakers are.
> ➤ Visualize where the conversation is taking place.
> ➤ Listen carefully to the tone of the speakers to identify whether the talk is friendly or official.

Location questions are usually asked in the form:

"Where is this talk most probably being given?"

"Where is the speaker during this talk?"

"In what course would this lecture most likely be given?"

SESSION C: VOCATION QUESTIONS FOR TALKS

Vocation questions require you to identify either the profession of the speaker or the identity of the audience. In order to answer vocation and other general speaker identification questions, you should:

> ➤ Try to visualize the conversation as it takes place.
> ➤ Listen carefully to key words that will identify the speakers or their relationship.
> ➤ Listen to the intonation of the speakers to identify whether the conversation is official or familiar.

Vocation questions are usually asked in the form of:

"Who is the speaker?"

"Who is the audience?"

"What is the speaker's job?"

"Whom does the speaker work for?"

Remember that most talks deal with student-related activities and sometimes with official government agencies. The more familiar you are with these topics, the better you will be able to deal with vocation questions.

SESSION D: FACT-BASED AND INFERENCE QUESTIONS FOR TALKS

Fact-Based Questions

Fact-based questions will require you to recall information revealed in the spoken text. To answer fact-based questions, you should:

➤ Listen carefully to the particulars of the talk.
➤ Try to understand unfamiliar words from their relation to the context.
➤ Look at the answers while the talk is being given so that you can anticipate certain fact questions.
➤ Pay special attention to numbers and proper nouns.

Remember that these questions are generally asked in the same order they are presented in the talk. So reading the questions while the talk is being given is a good way to listen for certain details. For example, if the first answer set has:

(A) history
(B) biology
(C) math
(D) French

then you know that you should listen carefully for some mention of a field of academic study near the beginning of the talk. Be careful, however, because in a case like this the talk will usually mention more than just one of the subjects, so you have to consider the point the speaker is making about each subject.

Inference Questions

These questions ask you to draw conclusions from specific details in the passage or to make comparisons between details. In order to answer inference questions, you should:

➤ Listen carefully to the particulars of the talk.
➤ Try to understand unfamiliar words from context.
➤ Look at the answers while the talk is being given so that you can anticipate certain inference questions.
➤ Use your knowledge about the situation to guess what logical conclusions might be true.

Inference questions are usually asked in the following form:

"It can be inferred from the conversation that . . ."

"The man or woman most probably . . ."

> **Inference questions usually ask you to make guesses about ideas not directly stated.**

Now let's see how all the different types of questions covered in this Power Lesson might come up in a talk.

Example:

MAN: I'd like to tell you about an interesting TV program that'll be shown this coming Thursday. It'll be on from 9 to 10 P.M., on Channel 4. It's part of a series called "Mysteries of Human Biology." The subject of the program is the human brain—how it functions and how it can malfunction. Topics that will be covered are dreams, memories, and depression. These topics are illustrated with outstanding computer animation that makes the explanations easy to follow. Make an effort to see this show. Since we've been studying the nervous system in class, I know you'll find it very helpful.

1. What does the speaker mainly discuss? (MAIN TOPIC)
   (A) science programs on TV
   (B) dreams, memories, and depression
   (C) requirements for the class
   (D) a television program on the human brain

The correct answer is (D). The man is talking about a particular television program whose subject is the human brain.

2. How does the speaker feel about the topic? (TONE)
   (A) enthusiastic
   (B) confused
   (C) inquisitive
   (D) embarrassed

The man uses the words *interesting, outstanding,* and *very helpful* to describe the show. Therefore we can describe his feelings about it as (A), enthusiastic.

3. What is the man's probable vocation? (VOCATION)

   (A) teacher
   (B) tour guide
   (C) television executive
   (D) physician

The correct answer is (A). The key words you must notice to answer this question correctly are, "Since we've been studying the nervous system in class . . . ."

4. What is the title of the television series which the TV program is part of? (FACT-BASED)

   (A) "History of the Human Brain"
   (B) "Biology and Computer Animation"
   (C) "Mysteries of Human Biology"
   (D) "Dreams, Memories, and Depression"

The correct answer is (C). Don't be fooled by the homophone distractor in (A) and the use of exact words from the talk in (D).

5. What is the main purpose of the program? (INFERENCE)

   (A) to demonstrate the latest use of computer graphics
   (B) to discuss the possibility of an economic depression
   (C) to explain the workings of the brain
   (D) to dramatize a famous mystery story

Answer (C) is correct. The question asks you to infer from the man's statement "The subject of the program is the human brain," and from the subsequent information given, that the purpose of the program is to explain the workings of the brain.

PRACTICE #1—Main Topic Questions

Listen to Track_15.mov. Circle the letter of the answer choice that correctly answers each question.

1. (A) a description of a bus trip
   (B) the regulations and requirements of a university trip
   (C) the registration rules for a university course
   (D) the rules for bus passengers on a vacation junket

2. (A) the requirements for a university trip to another country
   (B) the course requirements for a university class
   (C) the customs at a foreign university
   (D) immigration customs to emigres

3. (A) helpful
   (B) authoritarian
   (C) anticipatory
   (D) anxious

4. (A) ignore her advice
   (B) offer alternative regulations
   (C) abide by what she says
   (D) quit smoking

5. (A) A teacher instructs his class on the regulations of a foreign study course.
   (B) A tour guide instructs his charges on the regulations attached to a vacation package.
   (C) A student prepares for a trip.
   (D) A foreign minister instructs visitors on the customs of his country.

6. (A) the history of New York State
   (B) population statistics in New York State
   (C) the physical characteristics of New York State
   (D) Niagara Falls

7. (A) argumentative
   (B) informative
   (C) humorous
   (D) antithetical

8. (A) the physical characteristics of New York State
   (B) cities and their populations in New York State
   (C) the Adirondacks and neighboring communities in New York State
   (D) similarities among the terrains in New York State, Greece, and Vermont

9. (A) A politician argues in favor of New York State's qualities.
   (B) A teacher lectures on New York State's deficiencies.
   (C) A lecturer describes various aspects of New York State.
   (D) A tourism worker lists New York State's tourist attractions.

PRACTICE #2—Location Questions

Listen to Track_16.mov. Circle the letter of the answer that correctly answers each question.

1. (A) on a street corner
   (B) on a business lunchroom bulletin board
   (C) at a restaurant
   (D) on a tenants' notice board

2. (A) at a convenience store
   (B) at a church community center
   (C) in an apartment complex
   (D) in an office building

3. (A) in the stairwells
   (B) at the front entrance
   (C) with the doorman
   (D) at the tenant's front door

4. (A) in the public areas of the building
   (B) on the fire escape
   (C) in the tenants' apartments
   (D) in the hallways and stairways

5. (A) the front entrance
   (B) the side entrance
   (C) the rear entrance
   (D) the fire escape entrance

6. (A) at a banquet in honor of George Washington
   (B) in a classroom
   (C) on a tour of historic Alexandria
   (D) during a politician's campaign

7. (A) at a university
   (B) at a political rally
   (C) on a guided tour of an art gallery
   (D) walking through Alexandria

8. (A) nine miles
   (B) six miles
   (C) ten miles
   (D) They are located in the same place.

9. (A) in Washington, D.C.
   (B) Mount Vernon, Virginia
   (C) on the banks of the Potomac River
   (D) in Hunting Creek

10. (A) historic homes
    (B) Market Square
    (C) George Washington's townhouse
    (D) the Virginia General Assembly

PRACTICE #3—Vocation Questions

Listen to Track_17.mov. Circle the letter of the answer that correctly answers each question.

1. (A) tour guide
   (B) teacher
   (C) ambassador
   (D) immigration official

2. (A) teacher/students
   (B) politician/constituents
   (C) government official/citizens
   (D) bus driver/passengers

3. (A) passengers
   (B) tour members
   (C) students
   (D) parents of students

4. (A) information on foreign travel
   (B) a travel schedule for part two of the trip
   (C) a finalized itinerary
   (D) rules and regulations for a student foreign study trip

5. (A) tour guide
   (B) politician
   (C) university professor
   (D) historian

6. (A) students
   (B) research assistants
   (C) tourists
   (D) voters

7. (A) They are very familiar with Alexandria.
   (B) They have never been to historic Alexandria before.
   (C) They are interested in George Washington.
   (D) They have little interest in history.

8. (A) He has little knowledge of history.
   (B) He is not interested in the development of Alexandria.
   (C) He is very well trained in the history of Alexandria.
   (D) He is unhappy with his job.

PRACTICE #4—Fact-Based and Inference Questions

Listen to Track_18.mov. Circle the letter of the answer that correctly answers each question.

1. (A) There have been several break-ins in the building recently.
   (B) The tenants have been stealing from each other.
   (C) The front doors have to be repaired.
   (D) People have been loitering in the stairwells.

2. (A) They are climbing in through the fire escape.
   (B) The front entrance has been propped open.
   (C) They are breaking in.
   (D) They are being buzzed in by tenants who are helping them to steal things.

3. (A) There is no front door buzzer system.
   (B) The superintendent has little concern for building security.
   (C) It is easily burglarized.
   (D) The tenants could be more stringent about building security.

4. (A) Go to the lobby before admitting guests.
   (B) Inform the management.
   (C) Contact the police.
   (D) Lock the door.

5. (A) about the size of Vermont
   (B) about the size of Greece
   (C) Niagara Falls
   (D) the Adirondack Mountains

6. (A) around New York City
   (B) in Buffalo
   (C) outside Adirondack State Park
   (D) near Canada

7. (A) Adirondack State Park
   (B) Lake George
   (C) Buffalo
   (D) Niagara Falls

8. (A) Hiking, hunting, and fishing are illegal.
   (B) It is an urban center.
   (C) Many hikers visit it each year.
   (D) It is near Canada.

PRACTICE #5—Review Questions

Listen to Track_19.mov. Circle the letter of the answer that correctly answers each question.

1. (A) a family vacation
   (B) a school trip
   (C) a business convention
   (D) a hiking adventure

2. (A) a week
   (B) a month
   (C) 14 days
   (D) a year

3. (A) in the United States
   (B) in several foreign countries
   (C) in Washington, D.C.
   (D) in the students' town

4. (A) to pick up the itinerary
   (B) out of politeness
   (C) to receive a gift
   (D) to earn credit

5. (A) the flight arrangements
   (B) the smoking policy
   (C) punctuality
   (D) the schedule of travel

6. (A) repair of the ventilation system
   (B) pleasure
   (C) learning and pleasure
   (D) language learning

7. (A) farmer
   (B) soldier
   (C) English professor
   (D) tour guide

8. (A) 4
   (B) 9
   (C) 6
   (D) 10

9. (A) 1740
   (B) 1749
   (C) 1789
   (D) 1852

10. (A) to make it easy for ships to locate it
    (B) to appease angry Scottish and English merchants
    (C) to honor the owner of the land on which it was built
    (D) to encourage real estate investment in Virginia

11. (A) tobacco
    (B) hemp
    (C) flour
    (D) corn

12. (A) Mount Vernon
    (B) Christ Church
    (C) Market Square
    (D) District of Columbia

13. (A) to inform tenants of work being done on the building
    (B) to find out whose intercom is not working
    (C) to get tenants to lock the doors of their apartments
    (D) to get tenants' cooperation in preventing burglaries

14. (A) Several of the tenants' doors are broken.
    (B) The tenants carelessly admit strangers to the building.
    (C) The burglars entered apartments via the fire escape.
    (D) The tenants did not report seeing strangers in the building.

15. (A) refuse to pay rent
    (B) contact the management
    (C) inform the police
    (D) call a repairman immediately

16. (A) make too much noise
    (B) invite the superintendent
    (C) call the police to complain
    (D) keep the main entrance door open

17. (A) inform the superintendent
    (B) call the management
    (C) ask him what he's doing
    (D) telephone the police

18. (A) angry
    (B) fearful
    (C) celebrative
    (D) concerned

VOCABULARY

To hear how these words and expressions are pronounced, listen to Track_20.mov.

Expressions with *make*
One reason *make* and *do* cause so many problems to learners is that their usage is highly idiomatic, that is, there isn't really a reason why one is used instead of another. This means that you have to learn each expression one at a time.

Here are several expressions with *make*. For more expressions, see Structure Power Lesson 5.

>Don't make any assumptions about a person until you have met him.

>I want to make it clear that I am the boss around here.

>Let's make it perfectly clear that you are never to see her again.

>Tom makes breakfast, and his wife makes dinner.

System
The word *system* is often used when we want to talk about a device that has several parts that work together. Several organs of the body which perform a function together can also be a system.

>the ventilation system

>the buzzer system

>The computer system is shut down.

>We're studying the digestive system in my human anatomy class now.

Notices **and** *notice boards*

>We posted the notice on all the bulletin boards on campus.

>The notice boards are full of postings for used books.

Another word for *notices* is *announcement*.

>Announcements for the concert were posted all over town.

So-called
This expression is used in two ways:

(1) To show how people generally refer to something or someone.

> The rest of New York, <u>the so-called upstate portion</u>, has a much lower population.

> In this book she argues that <u>the so-called Gas Crisis</u> was intentionally caused by American oil companies.

(2) To suggest that the common name for something or someone is false.

> This historian claims that <u>the so-called American Revolution</u> was not really a revolution at all.

> I saw Sheila's <u>so-called boyfriend</u> with another woman last night.

Not under any circumstances/under any (or no) circumstances
This means "in any (or no) situation."

> Do <u>not, under any circumstances</u>, call me after 10 P.M.

> <u>Under no circumstances</u> are you to leave the country during this time.

Credit
One or more credits may be given to you if you successfully complete a university course.

> He received <u>three credits</u> for the course.

Thriving
Thriving means "prosperous."

> She lives in <u>a thriving community</u> on the east side of town.

Renowned
This word means "famous."

> This city is <u>renowned for</u> having been the home of seven U.S. senators.

Arguably

Arguably is used to describe something that is probably, but not proven to be, true.

> Ohio is <u>arguably</u> the best state in the country to live in.

Punctual

This word means "regularly on time."

> Roberta is a hard worker, but not very <u>punctual</u>.

> Professor Forsstrom places great importance on <u>punctuality</u>.

Itinerary

An *itinerary* is a plan for travel.

> According to the <u>itinerary</u>, we will be stopping in St. Louis on our way to Chicago.

Site

A *site* is a specific place.

> The town of Gettysburg was <u>the site of</u> one of the most ferocious battles of the Civil War.

Sparsely inhabited/rolling hills

Sparsely inhabited (or *sparsely populated*) and *rolling hills* are two very common expressions used when talking about the countryside.

> He avoided city life, preferring instead the <u>sparsely inhabited</u> regions.

> The state of North Dakota has <u>one of the sparsest populations</u> in the Union.

> I love <u>the rolling hills</u> of southern Missouri.

VOCABULARY EXERCISE

Complete the sentences below, using the given expressions.

punctually	itinerary	rolling hills
renowned	sparse population	thriving
arguably		

1. I am pleased to write a letter of recommendation for Margaret Winston. She is _____ the best employee I have ever had the pleasure of supervising. She always arrives _____ and works hard throughout the day, treating our customers with the utmost respect.

2. Thanks largely to its _____ _____, Canada has vast tracts of forest land. For this reason, Canada's _____ timber industry is a major competitor to U.S. timber interests.

3. From Atlanta our _____ took us north, through _____, until finally we reached the Great Smoky Mountains, _____ for their beauty and spectacular views.

Complete the sentences below, using the given expressions.

bulletin boards	notices	system
under any circumstances	make it perfectly clear	credit
sites	so-called	make assumptions

4. We left _____ all over the office telling people that the telephone _____ would be down for most of the afternoon. Unfortunately, nobody bothered to read the _____.

5. The sheer audacity of the Boston Tea Party astounded the English. The British Parliament decided that there was no choice but to _____ to the Colonies that not _____ would a similar act of rebellion be tolerated. Thus 1774 saw the passage of four punitive measures which the colonists would term the Intolerable Acts.

6. In the first part of this century, historians were quick to fault earlier archaeologists for being too quick to _____ about the location of ancient _____ based upon descriptions of those places in classical texts. Nowadays, however, historians and archaeologists agree that some the ancient texts are remarkably accurate in this respect.

7. Only on the first day of classes did I learn that French 101, a _____ introduction to the French language, was actually a five-_____ course in which you were expected to have already had at least two years of high school French.

Tape Script and Answers for Listening Power Lesson Three

Practice #1—Main Topic, Main Idea, and Tone Questions (Track_15.mov)

Questions 1–5 refer to the following talk:

Now I want to make it clear to everyone what the rules will be on this trip. First, there will be no smoking on our bus because the ventilation system isn't working well, and we don't want to deal with old smoke for two weeks. Second, you need to be punctual. We have a great deal of things to see and do, and a great number of places to visit in a short time. We can't wait for you and throw off our whole schedule. Third, you should exchange your dollars, take care of any visa or paperwork trouble, and buy gifts on your own time. Remember to give yourself plenty of time for these chores as the language difficulties can make things time consuming. Fourth, and most importantly of all, you must be present at all mandatory visits, dinners, and appointments of any kind. Otherwise this would only be a pleasure trip and you would not receive the three credits the school has approved for us. Now if there aren't any questions, I'm going to hand out our itinerary for the first week so we all know where we're headed. Part Two of the itinerary will be finalized shortly. Let's have a good trip.

1. What is the main topic of the talk?
2. What is the speaker describing?
3. What is the speaker's tone?
4. What does the speaker want her audience to do?
5. Which best summarizes the speech?

Questions 6–9 refer to the following talk:

Now let's turn our attention to the physical characteristics of New York State. The state is approximately the size of the nation of Greece. Outside of New York City, which is not the capital, the state is rather sparsely inhabited. Almost 65 percent of the people live in greater New York and Long Island, which occupies only a small percentage of the land. The rest of the state, so-called "upstate," has a few large cities, notably Buffalo, Syracuse, and Albany, the capital. Between these cities lie rolling hills, farmland, and even a thriving wine industry. The state includes portions of two of the five Great Lakes, as well as the renowned tourist areas of Lake George and Lake Champlain. Two major mountain ranges cross the state. In the south there are the Catskills, and in the north are found the Adirondacks, primarily in the 100-year-old Adirondack State Park. Hiking, hunting, and fishing are all popular in this park, which is approximately the size of the neighboring state of Vermont.

Arguably, New York's most popular tourist attraction is the majestic Niagara Falls. While not exceptionally high, the falls are extremely wide and powerful. Niagara Falls has long been a popular honeymoon destination as well as a convenient entry point into neighboring Canada.

6. What is the speaker's main concern?

7. Which of the following best characterizes the tone of the talk?

8. Which of the following would be the best title for the talk?

9. Which of the following best summarizes the talk?

Practice #1 Answers

1.	B	6.	C
2.	A	7.	B
3.	B	8.	A
4.	C	9.	C
5.	A		

Practice #2—Location (Track_16.mov)

Questions 1–5 refer to the following notice posted in an apartment building:

TO ALL TENANTS: There have been several apartment break-ins within recent months. This is a source of great concern to us, especially because there are signs that the tenants themselves may have contributed to these incidents. Therefore, we are asking all tenants to obey the following suggestions:

(1) Certain tenants prop open the main entrance door when they are giving a party or are expecting guests. This allows strangers to get to any floor of the building. Please do not leave the entrance door open under any circumstances.

(2) Certain tenants use the door buzzer system to admit people through the main entrance without bothering to find out who they are. Even if you are expecting a guest, never buzz anyone in without determining their identity. If your intercom is out of order please inform the management immediately.

(3) No strangers should ever be loitering in public areas of the building. This includes the fire escape, hallway, and stairway. If you notice someone loitering, please call the police immediately.

1. Where would this notice probably be posted?

2. Where did the break-ins take place?

3. Where should guests wait for admittance?

4. Where might strangers NOT be noticed loitering?

5. Which doorway has been left propped open?

Questions 6–10 refer to the following talk:

Hello, and welcome to historic Alexandria, Virginia. As you may know, Alexandria is located on the west bank of the Potomac River. We're now standing about six miles below Washington, D.C., and nine miles north of Mount Vernon. Much of the land near the town was devoted to tobacco farming. Scottish and English merchants who owned real estate at Cameron, a small hamlet four miles west, petitioned the Virginia General Assembly in the fall of 1748 to establish a town at West's Hunting Creek Warehouse. In the spring of 1749, this site was selected and the new town was named Alexandria in honor of its original owner, Scotsman John Alexander, who had owned the area that included the future site of Alexandria.

Alexandria became a port of entry for foreign vessels and a major export center for flour and hemp. Beautiful brick houses were constructed—many of which are still standing and which you can see about you now. In 1789, Alexandria and a portion of Fairfax County were ceded by the state of Virginia to become a part of the newly created 10-mile-square District of Columbia. Alexandria was given back to Virginia in 1847. In 1852, it acquired city status and gained a new charter.

At the time of the Revolution, Alexandria's political life and commerce were important to many local residents, especially to neighboring George Washington in Mount Vernon. Washington maintained a town house here and served as a Trustee of Alexandria.

Washington also purchased a pew in Christ Church, and had numerous social and business connections to the town. We'll soon walk by Market Square, where Washington drilled militia troops in 1754.

6. Where would the talk most probably be delivered?

7. Where are the speaker and audience?

8. How close to Alexandria is Washington, D.C.?

9. Where is historic Alexandria situated?

10. Which of the following is NOT mentioned as a site in Alexandria?

Practice #2 Answers

1.	D	6.	C
2.	C	7.	D
3.	B	8.	B
4.	C	9.	C
5.	A	10.	D

Practice #3—Vocation (Track_17.mov)

Questions 1–4 refer to the following talk:

Now I want to make it clear to everyone what the rules will be on this trip. First, there will be no smoking on our bus because the ventilation system isn't working well, and we don't want to deal with old smoke for two weeks. Second, you need to be punctual. We have a great deal of things to see and do, and a great number of places to visit in a short time. We can't wait for you and throw off our whole schedule. Third, you should exchange your dollars, take care of any visa or paperwork trouble, and buy gifts on your own time. Remember to give yourself plenty of time for these chores as the language difficulties can make things time consuming. Fourth, and most importantly of all, you must be present at all mandatory visits, dinners, and appointments of any kind. Otherwise this would only be a pleasure trip and you would not receive the three credits the school has approved for us. Now if there aren't any questions, I'm going to hand out our itinerary for the first week so we all know where we're headed. Part Two of the itinerary will be finalized shortly. Let's have a good trip.

1. What is the probable vocation of the speaker?
2. What is the relationship of the speaker to her audience?
3. Who are the probable members of the speaker's audience?
4. What information does the audience acquire from the speaker?

Questions 5–8 refer to the following passage:

Hello, and welcome to historic Alexandria, Virginia. As you may know, Alexandria is located on the west bank of the Potomac River. We're now standing about six miles below Washington, D.C., and nine miles north of Mount Vernon. Much of the land near the town was devoted to tobacco farming. Scottish and English merchants who owned real estate at Cameron, a small hamlet four miles west, petitioned the Virginia General Assembly in the fall of 1748 to establish a town at West's Hunting Creek Warehouse. In the spring of 1749, this site was selected and the new town was named Alexandria in honor of its original owner, Scotsman John Alexander, who had owned the area that included the future site of Alexandria.

Alexandria became a port of entry for foreign vessels and a major export center for flour and hemp. Beautiful brick houses were constructed—many of which are still standing and which you can see about you now. In 1789, Alexandria and a portion of Fairfax County were ceded by the state of Virginia to become a part of the newly created 10-mile-square District of Columbia. Alexandria was given back to Virginia in 1847. In 1852, it acquired city status and gained a new charter.

At the time of the Revolution, Alexandria's political life and commerce were important to many local residents, especially to neighboring George Washington in Mount Vernon. Washington maintained a town house here and served as a Trustee of Alexandria. Washington also purchased a pew in Christ Church, and had numerous social and business connections to the town. We'll soon walk by Market Square, where Washington drilled militia troops in 1754.

5. What is the speaker's job?
6. Who are the members of the speaker's audience?
7. What can be inferred about the speaker's audience?
8. What can be inferred about the speaker?

Practice #3 Answers

1.	B	5.	A
2.	A	6.	C
3.	C	7.	B
4.	D	8.	C

Practice #4—Fact-Based/Inference (Track_18.mov)

Questions 1–4 refer to the following talk:

TO ALL TENANTS: There have been several apartment break-ins within recent months. This is a source of great concern to us, especially because there are signs that the tenants themselves may have contributed to these incidents. Therefore, we are asking all tenants to obey the following suggestions:

(1) Certain tenants prop open the main entrance door when they are giving a party or are expecting guests. This allows strangers to get to any floor of the building. Please do not leave the entrance door open under any circumstances.

(2) Certain tenants use the door buzzer system to admit people through the main entrance without bothering to find out who they are. Even if you are expecting a guest, never buzz anyone in without determining their identity. If your intercom is out of order, please inform the management immediately.

(3) No strangers should ever be loitering in public areas of the building. This includes the fire escape, hallway, and stairway. If you notice someone loitering, please call the police immediately.

1. What is the reason for posting the notice?
2. Why are strangers entering the building unannounced?
3. What can be inferred about the building?
4. What should a tenant do if his or her intercom system is broken?

Questions 5–8 refer to the following talk:

Now let's turn our attention to the physical characteristics of New York State. The state is approximately the size of the nation of Greece. Outside of New York City, which is not the capital, the state is rather sparsely inhabited. Almost 65 percent of the people live in greater New York and Long Island, which occupies only a small percentage of the land. The rest of the state, so-called "upstate," has a few large cities, notably Buffalo, Syracuse, and Albany, the capital. Between these cities lie rolling hills, farmland, and even a thriving wine industry. The state includes portions of two of the five Great Lakes, as well as the renowned tourist areas of Lake George and Lake Champlain. Two major mountain ranges cross the state. In the south there are the Catskills, and in the north are found the Adirondacks, primarily in the 100-year-old Adirondack State Park. Hiking, hunting, and fishing are all popular in this park, which is approximately the size of the neighboring state of Vermont.

Arguably, New York's most popular tourist attraction is the majestic Niagara Falls. While not exceptionally high, the falls are extremely wide and powerful. Niagara Falls has long been a popular honeymoon destination as well as a convenient entry point into neighboring Canada.

5. What is the size of New York State?
6. Where is the majority of population of the state of New York concentrated?
7. Which of the following is not listed as an attraction in New York State?
8. What can be inferred about Adirondack State Park?

Practice #4 Answers

1.	A	5.	B
2.	B	6.	A
3.	D	7.	C
4.	B	8.	C

Practice #5—Review Questions (Track_19.mov)

Questions 1–6 refer to the following talk:

Now I want to make it clear to everyone what the rules will be on this trip. First, there will be no smoking on our bus because the ventilation system isn't working well, and we don't want to deal with old smoke for two weeks. Second, you need to be punctual. We have a great deal of things to see and do, and a great number of places to visit in a short time. We can't wait for you and throw off our whole schedule. Third, you should exchange your dollars, take care of any visa or paperwork trouble, and buy gifts on your own time. Remember to give yourself plenty of time for these chores as the language difficulties can make things time consuming. Fourth, and most importantly of all, you must be present at all mandatory visits, dinners, and appointments of any kind. Otherwise this would only be a pleasure trip and you could not receive the three credits the school has approved for us. Now if there aren't any questions, I'm going to hand out our itinerary for the first week so we all know where we're headed. Part Two of the itinerary will be finalized shortly. Let's have a good trip.

1. What kind of trip is described in the passage?
2. About how long is the trip?
3. Where does the trip probably take place?
4. Why is it important to attend all mandatory functions?
5. Which subject is NOT covered in the talk?
6. What is probably the purpose of the trip?

Questions 7–12 refer to the following passage:

Hello, and welcome to historic Alexandria, Virginia. As you may know, Alexandria is located on the west bank of the Potomac River. We're now standing about six miles below Washington, D.C., and nine miles north of Mount Vernon. Much of the land near the town was devoted to tobacco farming. Scottish and English merchants who owned real estate at Cameron, a small hamlet four miles west, petitioned the Virginia General Assembly in the fall of 1748 to establish a town at West's Hunting Creek Warehouse. In the spring of 1749, this site was selected and the new town was named Alexandria in honor of its original owner, Scotsman John Alexander, who had owned the area that included the future site of Alexandria.

Alexandria became a port of entry for foreign vessels and a major export center for flour and hemp. Beautiful brick houses were constructed—many of which are still standing and which you can see about you now. In 1789, Alexandria and a portion of Fairfax County were ceded by the state of Virginia to become a part of the newly created 10-mile-square District of Columbia. Alexandria was given back to Virginia in 1847. In 1852, it acquired city status and gained a new charter.

At the time of the Revolution, Alexandria's political life and commerce were important to many local residents, especially to neighboring George Washington in Mount Vernon. Washington maintained a town house here and served as a Trustee of Alexandria. Washington also purchased a pew in Christ Church, and had numerous social and business connections to the town. We'll soon walk by Market Square, where Washington drilled militia troops in 1754.

7. What is probably the occupation of the speaker?
8. How many miles is it from Alexandria to Washington, D.C.?
9. When was the town of Alexandria established?

10. Why was the new city given the name Alexandria?

11. Which of the following products is NOT mentioned as being important to commerce in Alexandria?

12. According to the passage, where did George Washington drill his troops?

Questions 13–18 refer to the following passage:

TO ALL TENANTS: There have been several apartment break-ins within recent months. This is a source of great concern to us, especially because there are signs that the tenants themselves may have contributed to these incidents. Therefore, we are asking all tenants to obey the following suggestions:

(1)   Certain tenants prop open the main entrance door when they are giving a party or are expecting guests. This allows strangers to get to any floor of the building. Please do not leave the entrance door open under any circumstances.

(2)   Certain tenants use the door buzzer system to admit people through the main entrance without bothering to find out who they are. Even if you are expecting a guest, never buzz anyone in without determining their identity. If your intercom is out of order please inform the management immediately.

(3)   No strangers should ever be loitering in public areas of the building. This includes the fire escape, hallway, and stairway. If you notice someone loitering, please call the police immediately.

13. What was the primary reason for posting the notice?

14. According to the notice, why may recent break-ins have occurred?

15. What should a tenant do if his or her intercom stops working?

16. What do some tenants do when they are giving a party?

17. What should a tenant do if he or she sees a stranger hiding in the stairwell?

18. What best describes the management's attitude in the notice?

Practice #5 Answers

1.	B	10.	C
2.	C	11.	D
3.	B	12.	C
4.	D	13.	D
5.	A	14.	B
6.	C	15.	B
7.	D	16.	D
8.	C	17.	D
9.	B	18.	D

Vocabulary Answers

1. arguably; punctually

2. sparse population; thriving

3. itinerary; rolling hills; renowned

4. notices; system; bulletin boards/notices

5. make it perfectly clear; under any circumstances

6. make assumptions; sites

7. so-called; credit

STRUCTURE POWER LESSONS

In this section you will prepare for the Structure and Written Expression section of the paper-based TOEFL and the Structure section of the computer-based TOEFL. The Structure and Written Expression section has two parts. The structure questions consist of a sentence containing a blank that can be completed correctly with only one of four answer choices. The written expression questions consist of a complete sentence with four parts underlined; the student must decide which of the four underlined parts contains an error.

Although the name of the Structure and Written Expression section has been changed to "Structure" for the computer-based TOEFL exam, the content of these two sections is virtually identical. The Structure Power Lessons provided here cover the concepts you need to know for both the paper-based and the computer-based exams.

This section of the TOEFL essentially tests English grammar. The Structure Power Lessons include, therefore, a grammar review that will give you the essential terms you need to know to do well in this section. The Grammar Review is followed by seven Structure Power Lessons, which will familiarize you with the most common types of TOEFL Structure questions. They also pinpoint the grammar points you need to know in order to do well on the test, so that you do not lose time by studying grammar points that are not tested.

Before you start to work on the Structure Power Lessons, read through "Structure for the Computer-Based TOEFL" on the following pages. These pages will give you more details on what to expect on the Structure section of the computer-based TOEFL exam.

THE BIGGER PICTURE: GRAMMAR BEYOND THE TOEFL

When American university professors are asked about the academic skills of their international students, the area of greatest concern is often these students' writing skills. Many international students who speak quite well find that their professors cannot understand what they write. When you think about it, this fact makes sense. Students *talk* about things like cafeteria food, and who is doing what over the weekend; but they write about complicated subjects, and their topics are often ideas rather than physical objects. Also, when speaking, an international student can see immediately whether the listener understands. This is not possible in writing.

In fact, it is in writing more than speaking that good grammar is essential. That is why the TOEFL tests the structure and written expression of international students.

Therefore, grammar is important, even to students who communicate very easily in spoken English. As you go through the Power Lessons, work on improving your English grammar. If there is something you do not fully understand, refer to a good book on English grammar. This book concentrates only on the grammar you will find on the TOEFL, but don't forget that there is more to English grammar than the TOEFL, and that you will certainly need more than just "TOEFL grammar" when you begin your studies in the United States.

STRUCTURE FOR THE COMPUTER-BASED TOEFL

Beginning in July, 1998, the TOEFL will be administered on computer. The Structure section includes some minor changes both in the way that you will experience the questions and in the way that you record your answers.

On test day prior to taking the exam, you will have the opportunity to work through a tutorial that will guide you step-by-step on how to use a mouse, how to scroll, and how to use the testing tools. In addition, before each of the four sections, you will be shown how to answer the types of questions that you will encounter in that section. The more comfortable you are with computers, the less you will have to worry about on test day!

The following are some unique features of the computer-based TOEFL:

COMPUTER ADAPTIVE

The Structure section is "computer adaptive." This means that the difficulty of each question that you see is based on whether or not you answered the previous question correctly. Every computer-adaptive section of the test will begin with a few mid-level difficulty questions. If you answer most of them correctly, then the level of the difficulty of the question that you next receive will increase. If you answer most of the first few questions incorrectly, the questions that follow will become easier. Your goal is to answer as many questions as possible at the highest difficulty level. This is how the test determines your final score.

Because each question that you receive is based on the questions that come before it, you cannot leave any questions unanswered or skip questions to answer later.

TIME

The time you have to take the test will vary from test taker to test taker, but will fall within a range of 15 to 20 minutes, which is a little bit less than on the paper-and-pencil test. The actual amount of time that you are allowed will appear on the screen before you begin.

QUESTION FORMAT

There is actually very little difference in the format of questions between the paper-based test and the computer-based exam. On the computer-based TOEFL, you record your answer directly on the screen rather than transposing your answer to a separate sheet of paper. In this regard, the Structure section is a little easier, and you do not run the risk of making a mistake when transferring your answer from the booklet to the answer grid.

There are two question types in the Structure section of the computerized TOEFL. The question types will be mixed together, unlike on the paper-based test, which segregates the different formats from each other.

Sentence Completion

You are given a sentence with an element missing. Beneath the question you have four choices. You should choose the word or phrase from the four choices that best completes the sentence.

TOEFL—Structure

The Human Genome Project, —, is under the supervision of the Department of Energy.

- ◯ surprised
- ◯ surprisingly
- ◯ being surprised
- ◯ will surprise

Select your answer by clicking on the oval to the left of your choice.

TOEFL—Structure

The Human Genome Project, —, is under the supervision of the Department of Energy.

○ surprised
● surprisingly
○ being surprised
○ will surprising

Error Identification

You are given a sentence that contains four underlined words. One of the four words must be changed in order to make the sentence correct.

TOEFL—Structure

Having important consequences for weather around the world, El Niño is a disrupted of the ocean-atmospheric system in the tropical Pacific.

When you select your answer by clicking on the underlined word or phrase it will darken.

TOEFL—Structure

Having important consequences for weather around the world, El Niño is a disrupted of the ocean-atmospheric system in the tropical Pacific.

You may change your answer choice as often as you like until you click on Next and Confirm Answer. Once you have clicked on these boxes, you will receive the next question.

Remember, you will not be permitted to leave any question unanswered, so you cannot come back to it later!

SCORING

The Structure section of the computer-based TOEFL will be scored on a scale of 0 to 30. This part of the test counts for 50 percent of the final score for the Structure and Writing section. At the end of the computer test, you will see an estimated score range for this section. Your final scaled score is determined after your essay has been scored by readers at ETS.

MAJOR SKILLS TESTED

The following are the major skills tested on the computer-based TOEFL:

- Clause identification
- "What is a sentence?" knowledge
- Two subjects avoidance
- Verb tense sequences
- Subject-verb agreement

- Singular and plural noun usage
- Prepositions and prepositional phrase usage
- Articles
- Active and passive voice
- Gerunds and infinitives and knowing which verbs take each
- Form and meaning of compound participles and infinitives
- Recognition of the difference between *do* and *make*
- Comparatives and superlatives
- *There* and *it* as subjects

You will practice all of these skills as you work through the Structure Power Lessons of this book. Even though the Structure section has been adapted for the computer, the same general skill is being tested as in the paper-based exam—grammar.

STRATEGIES

The following are test-taking strategies that should help you to improve your score on the Structure section of the computer-based TOEFL.

Fill-In Items

The first thing you should do is read over all of the answer choices. Sometimes you can eliminate choices right away because the grammar within the choice is incorrect. In example number 1 above, the fourth choice, "will surprising," is incorrect (to be correct, you'd need to add the word *be*).

The next step is to read through the sentence. Does the correct word automatically pop into you head? Check the answer choices to see if your guess is included in the list. Finally, mentally place each of the remaining alternatives in the blank space. Even though you may think you have imme-diately identified the correct answer, you must double-check your answer to be sure that none of the other answers are better.

Don't worry: This doesn't take as long to do as it does to read about doing it! And remember, you can't go back and check your answers later, so you have to get it right the first time.

Error Identification Items

The first thing you should do is quickly read over the entire sentence. Reread the choices. If the incorrect element is not clear to you the second time through, try clicking on each of the choices. Imagine that the darkened word or phrase is missing; then try to fill it in with your own word. Does the part of speech, verb tense, or reference fit? If not, then you may have found the incorrect element.

For example:

TOEFL—Structure

Having important consequences for weather around the world, El Niño is a disrupted of the ocean-atmospheric system in the tropical Pacific.

Both of the alternative choices are nouns; *disrupted* is a verb, so it is clear that *disrupted* is the incorrect element.

GRAMMAR REVIEW

The following review covers the minimum amount of grammatical concepts and grammatical terms necessary to use the Structure Power Lessons of this book. It is important to note that this grammar review cannot take the place of a solid understanding of English grammar. A comprehensive grammar book will be helpful if you need further information on any of the concepts outlined here.

Noun Groups

> **A *noun group* is either a noun, or a noun and a group of words that belong to it.**

The kinds of words that "belong to" a noun are usually adjectives, including determiners (see below).

In this example, the underlined words are noun groups.

> John always uses his best French when speaking on the telephone.

Conjunction

> **A *conjunction* is a word that links two equivalent parts of a sentence.**

By *equivalent* we mean a noun to a noun, an adjective to an adjective, a prepositional phrase to another prepositional phrase, etcetera.

In this example, the underlined words are conjunctions.

> John always speaks and writes in his best French or German, yet Mary doesn't seem to care that she sounds uneducated to other people.

The conjunction *and* links two verbs: speaks and writes.

The conjunction *or* joins two nouns: French or German.

The conjunction *that* links the clause *Mary doesn't seem to care* with the clause *she sounds uneducated to other people.*

The conjunction *yet* joins the first part of the sentence (*John . . . telephone*) to the second (*Mary . . . people*).

Pronouns

Pronouns can be categorized in the following way:

- ➤ subject: *I, you, he, she, it, we, they*
- ➤ object: *me, your, his, her, it, us, them*
- ➤ possessive: *mine, yours, his, hers, its, ours, theirs*
- ➤ reflexive: *myself, yourself, himself, herself, oneself, itself, ourselves, yourselves, themselves*
- ➤ demonstrative: *this, these, that, those*

Antecedents

An antecedent is a noun that a pronoun can replace.

> <u>Sharon</u> has recently accepted a new position. <u>She</u> will not be making a lot of money, but it offers <u>her</u> several career advancement opportunities.

In the above example, the noun *Sharon* is the antecedent for the pronouns *she* and *her*. In other words, *she* represents the noun *Sharon*, and *her* represents the noun *Sharon*.

Here are some more examples.

> <u>Karen</u> preferred Kevin's plan because it was more cost efficient than <u>hers</u>. (*hers = Karen's*)

> Mary wasn't satisfied with the restaurant we chose last year, but she will love <u>this</u>! (*this = the restaurant*)

Very often the demonstrative pronouns—*this, that, these,* and *those*—refer to entire ideas rather than only nouns.

> James wants to take two years off from college and tour Asia, but I am sure his parents will never approve of <u>that</u>! (*that = the idea of James's taking two years off from college and touring Europe*)

Possessive adjectives (*my, your, his, her, its, our, their*), like pronouns, have antecedents.

> <u>Annette</u> enjoys spending time with <u>her</u> grandmother. (*her = Annette's*)

Usually pronouns and possessive adjectives come after their antecedents. But sometimes they can come before their antecedents.

> When <u>she</u> thinks about her family, Annette starts to cry.

> Considering <u>her</u> size, <u>Iris</u> is very strong.

See Structure Power Lesson Six, Session B, for further information on pronoun-antecedent agreement.

Possessive Adjectives and Possessive Pronouns

Frequently the TOEFL tests a student's ability to distinguish between possessive adjectives and possessive pronouns. Students frequently confuse the two because they look so much alike.

Possessive Adjectives	Possessive Pronouns
my	mine
your	yours
his	his
her	hers
its	its
our	ours
their	theirs

However, their function in the sentence is entirely different. Possessive adjectives function as adjectives, which means that they must always go before a noun.

> <u>my</u> car
> <u>your</u> husband
> <u>our</u> problem

A possessive pronoun takes the place of another noun.

> That's not Wilma's car. <u>Hers</u> is blue. (*hers = Wilma's car*)

She is interested in the culture of the aborigines because <u>theirs</u> is a culture that looks simple on the surface, but in actuality is highly complex. (*theirs* = aboriginal culture)

Types of Nouns

Count Nouns

Count nouns are those that can be counted (for example, *one car, two cars, three cars,* etcetera).

In grammar, count nouns have a singular form and a plural form usually ending in *-s*. Count nouns also take the indefinite article *a/an*.

Noncount Nouns

Noncount nouns are those that are seen as indivisible wholes.

Unlike count nouns, they do not normally have a plural form and do not normally take the indefinite article.

Examples of noncount nouns are:

furniture	relevance	trash
information	freedom	sunlight

To measure noncount nouns, we use quantifying noun expressions.

a piece of furniture	a pile of trash
a period of freedom	a ray of sunlight

Mass Nouns

Mass nouns are a type of noncount noun. They are a little different, however, because sometimes they are used in the plural form. When they have a plural form, they mean "types of."

Cheese

NONCOUNT USAGE:	We need some <u>cheese</u> for the ravioli tonight.
COUNT USAGE:	The store carried more than a dozen <u>cheeses</u> (types of cheese).

Rice

NONCOUNT USAGE: They ate <u>rice</u> with their beans.

COUNT USAGE: The region is unique in that many <u>rices</u> (types of rice) can be grown there.

Pasta

NONCOUNT USAGE: She loves cooking <u>pasta</u>—it's so easy.

COUNT USAGE: The chef became an expert on the <u>pastas</u> (the types of pasta) of northern Italy.

Some mass nouns can be used in the plural in another way.

Customer: Give me three <u>coffees</u> and a <u>tea</u>. (COUNT USAGE)

Counter waiter: Do you want <u>sugar</u> with that? (NONCOUNT USAGE)

Customer: Yeah. Give me four <u>sugars</u>. (COUNT USAGE)

When the customer says "three coffees and a tea," he does not mean three types of coffee and one type of tea. Instead, he means three cups of coffee and one cup of tea.

In the same way, "four sugars" means four packets of sugar rather than four types of sugar.

Collective Nouns

Collective nouns are groups of individual nouns that are viewed as being a single entity. Usually collective nouns take a singular verb. Examples include *group, herd,* and *committee.*

Collective nouns are discussed in greater depth in Structure Power Lesson Six, Session B.

The difference between count, noncount, and collective nouns is important because the use of words like *much, many,* and other determiners, as well as the use of singular or plural forms of a verb, depend upon the noun in question. The TOEFL often tests a student's ability to make these kinds of judgments.

For more on subject-verb agreement, see Structure Power Lesson Six, Session B.

Transitive versus Intransitive Verbs

Verbs are categorized as *transitive* or *intransitive* depending on whether they take a direct object or not. Intransitive verbs do not take direct objects, while transitive verbs do.

Mary <u>walks</u> for 45 minutes every day. (There is no direct object, so *walks* is intransitive.)

Mary <u>bought a book</u> about the history of the United States. (*A book* is the direct object, so the verb *bought* is transitive.)

Some verbs have both a transitive and an intransitive use. For example:

John <u>read</u> during the entire flight from Los Angeles.

John <u>read a book</u> during the entire flight from Los Angeles.

Some verbs that are often intransitive are:

come	go	flow
walk	run	travel
occur	happen	

It is important to note that intransitive verbs cannot be passive. Structure Power Lesson Three, Session D, discusses this point further.

Linking Verbs

In addition to transitive and intransitive verbs, there are also linking verbs. Structurally, linking verbs look similar to transitive verbs in that they may be followed by a noun.

John <u>became</u> president of the student organization. (*become* = linking verb)

You can tell a linking verb from a transitive verb because with a linking verb the subject and the noun after the linking verb are the same thing. For example, in the sentence above, *John* and *president* are identical.

However, with a transitive verb, the subject and the noun after the verb are two different things. For example, in the sentence below, *the construction company* and *that house* are two different things.

The construction company <u>built</u> that house. (*built* = transitive verb)

Some common linking verbs are:

be	appear
become	seem

Linking verbs can also be followed by an adjective.

She seems <u>happy</u> today.

It is important to remember that linking verbs, like intransitive verbs, cannot be passive. See Structure Power Lesson Three, Session D.

Determiners

In some of the Grammar Power Lessons, there are rules that involve the concept of determiners. In this grammar, the term *determiner* refers to a specific type of adjective. Determiners are either specific or general.

Specific Determiners

Specific determiners include:

(1) the definite article

the	I didn't like <u>the</u> movie.

(2) demonstrative adjectives

this	*these*	<u>This</u> exercise seems very helpful.
that	*those*	

(3) possessive adjectives

my	*our*	
your	*your*	Please, give me <u>your</u> homework.
his/her/its	*their*	

General Determiners

General determiners include:

(1) the indefinite articles

a/an	*some*

(2) quantifiers

all	*either*	*many*	*neither*
another	*every*	*more*	*no*
both	*few*	*most*	*other*
each	*little*	*much*	*several*

<u>All</u> children should have the right to a standard education.

We saw <u>many</u> ships come and go as we sat on the beach.

I wasn't really impressed with <u>either</u> candidate.

To see how determiners are tested on the TOEFL, check Structure Power Lesson Six, Session C.

STRUCTURE POWER LESSON ONE

SESSION A: INDEPENDENT AND DEPENDENT CLAUSES

One of the most important concepts that you need to know for the Structure section of the TOEFL is what a *clause* is.

A *clause* is a group of related words with a subject and a finite verb.

A *finite verb* is a verb that, when combined with a subject, makes a complete sentence.

Look at the examples below and compare the finite verbs to the nonfinite verbs.

Finite Verbs	Nonfinite Verbs
walks	to walk
is walking	walking
has given	given

In other words, finite verb forms include the simple present, the present progressive, and the present perfect. Nonfinite verb forms include the infinitive, the present participle, and the past participle.

It is important to understand what a clause is because there are different kinds of clauses. Some combinations of clauses are grammatically correct, while other combinations are not. In English, clauses are divided into two major categories, *dependent clauses* and *independent clauses*.

> **An *independent clause* is a clause that can be a grammatical sentence by itself.**
>
> **A *dependent clause* is a clause that cannot be a sentence by itself. Therefore, a dependent clause is always connected to an independent clause.**

The following sentence contains two clauses.

<u>The President kept none of the promises</u>   <u>that he had made</u>.

The clause *The President kept none of the promises* can form a complete sentence. Therefore it is the independent clause (also called the *main clause*).

The clause *that he had made* is not a complete, grammatically correct sentence in English. Therefore, it is a dependent clause.

> **Always make sure that a sentence on the TOEFL has an independent (main) clause.**

There are three types of dependent clauses:

(1) Noun clauses, which function grammatically as nouns.

<u>Whether we are going</u> has not yet been decided.

The clause *whether we are going* functions as the subject of the verb in the main clause.

He told me <u>that he would write next week</u>.

The clause *that he would write next week* functions as the direct object of the verb.

(2) Adjective clauses, which function grammatically as adjectives.

Remember that adjectives modify ("give information about") nouns. For example, the adjective *blue* in the phrase *a blue car* tells us something about the noun *car*.

In the same way, an adjective clause gives information about a noun.

Is that the woman <u>whom you told me about</u>?

The clause *whom you told me about* gives additional information about the noun *woman*.

Please give me the letter <u>that he left in his briefcase</u>.

The clause *that he left in his briefcase* modifies the noun *letter*.

(3) Adverb clauses, which function grammatically as adverbs.

Adverbs usually answer questions like "How?," "When?," "Where?," and "Why?," or they give contrastive information. For example, *quickly* in the sentence "He walked quickly" tells us how the man walked. In the sentence "She arrived on time," the adverbial *on time* tells us when she arrived.

Here are some examples of adverb clauses:

<u>As soon as he arrives,</u> tell him to wait in the lobby.

The adverb clause *as soon as he arrives* tells when he will be told to wait.

He will not meet her <u>because she has insulted him.</u>

The adverb clause *because she has insulted him* tells why he will not meet her.

<u>Although the children had heard the story several times,</u> they always begged their grandfather to repeat it.

The adverb clause *although the children had heard the story several times* gives a contrast to the idea that the children begged their grandfather to repeat a story.

SESSION B: "WHAT IS A SENTENCE?" QUESTIONS

A very common type of question in the fill-in-the-blank section of the Structure section of the TOEFL is the "What is a sentence?" type. In such questions, the test taker must choose an answer that follows the English grammar rules of dependent and independent clauses.

A few examples of this type of question can be found below.

> Every spring, millions of American children ----- the custom of searching for Easter eggs hidden the night before by their parents.
>
> (A) enjoying
> (B) enjoys
> (C) who enjoy
> (D) enjoy

In this type of question, you will need to look at the sentence as it stands and ask, "What is missing?" At the same time, keep in mind two points:

(1) Every sentence must contain at least one independent clause.

(2) A clause is a group of words with a subject and a finite verb.

These two points help us realize that the independent clause of the sentence is missing a verb. Now that you know what the sentence is missing, you can begin your search for the correct answer. It is always a good idea also to locate the subject in the sentence before looking at the answer choices. Here the subject is *millions of American children;* it is plural.

Answer choice (A) will not work because the *-ing* form of the verb *alone* is not a finite verb. You are looking for the verb of the main clause.

Answer choice (B) could be a main verb for our sentence, but our subject, *millions of American children,* is plural and *enjoys* is singular.

Answer (C) has the *wh-* word *who,* which would create a noun or adjective clause, two types of dependent clauses. However, you are looking for a verb to serve as the independent clause verb. The verb of a dependent adjective clause cannot be the verb of an independent clause at the same time.

Answer (D) meets all of the criteria that we have established. It has a plural form and there is no subordinate conjunction like *who* which would not allow it to be the verb of the main, independent clause. (D) is the correct answer.

Always make sure that
the main clause has a finite verb.

Here is a second example of a "What is a sentence?" question.

----- of evolution involves the concept of survival of
the fittest, often called natural selection.

(A) That the theory
(B) Of the theory
(C) The theory
(D) Theories

In the above example, we look at the sentence to discover that while we have a verb, *involves*, we do not have a subject for that verb. Notice that the noun *evolution*, which does occur before the verb, cannot be the subject of *involves* because it is the object of the preposition *of*. This is an important concept:

A noun can have only one function in
a sentence.

Because of this rule, it is always safe to say that the object of a preposition can never be the subject of a verb.

Answer (A) cannot be the answer because we are looking for a subject of an independent clause, and the word *that* would create a dependent noun or adjective clause. Answer (B) does not contain a noun that could be the subject. *Theory* in (B) is the object of the preposition *of*, and therefore cannot be the subject for the same reasons discussed above. The noun *theories* in (D) is plural and our verb, *involves*, is singular. Therefore, (D) is not the correct answer.

Only (C) meets all of the requirements. It is a noun that has no function, it is not preceded by a subordinate conjunction, and it is singular. (C) is the correct answer.

Now let's practice some specific skills for this question type. Note that as we talk about independent clauses within the context of a sentence, they will be called main clauses.

PRACTICE #1—Choosing a Main Clause Subject

Circle the letter of the answer that correctly answers each question.

1. -----, regarded by archaeologists as the world's oldest continuously inhabited city, is the capital of Syria.

   (A) Damascus is
   (B) Damascus being
   (C) Damascus
   (D) That Damascus

2. -----, who died in 1953, depicted ancient man in drawings, paintings, and sculptures.

   (A) It was an artist, Charles Knight
   (B) Artist Charles Knight
   (C) Charles Knight's art
   (D) Charles Knight an artist

3. ----- of the landing of the Mayflower is a rather small, gray stone in Plymouth, Massachusetts.

   (A) The site
   (B) For the site
   (C) There is site
   (D) To the site

4. When population is not checked by artificial means, ----- increases, putting more strain on limited natural resources.

   (A) then
   (B) than
   (C) so
   (D) it

5. Although most species of fox are reddish-brown in color, ----- is often pure white.

   (A) the Arctic fox
   (B) nevertheless the Arctic fox
   (C) that the Arctic fox
   (D) but the Arctic fox

6. -----, the son of a glovemaker in Stratford-upon-Avon, went on to become the greatest playwright the English language has ever known.

   (A) William Shakespeare was
   (B) That William Shakespeare
   (C) William Shakespeare
   (D) When William Shakespeare was

7. Although Anne Tyler received a Pulitzer Prize for her novel *Breathing Lessons*, ----- has never received the broad popular acclaim of such novelists as Anne Rice.

   (A) what she
   (B) she
   (C) that she
   (D) and she

8. <u>Where</u> Anglo Saxon <u>Protestantism</u> is
     A   B

   called <u>Anglican</u> Christianity in the United
            C

   Kingdom, but the same faith in America

   is <u>referred to</u> as Episcopalianism.
         D

9. To asthma sufferers, <u>there is</u> no greater
                           A

   runner exists <u>in the annals</u> of American
                  B

   history <u>than</u> Florence Griffith Joyner, who
          C

   went on to Olympic fame <u>even though</u>
                             D

   she suffered from acute asthma herself.

10. <u>Fear of high</u> <u>cannot</u> be a <u>paralyzing</u> phobia
        A   B   C

    to <u>those</u> who enjoy bungie jumping.
       D

NOTE: Questions 1, 2, and 6 are examples of appositives, which will be treated in Structure Power Lesson Two.

PRACTICE #2—Choosing a Main Clause Verb

Circle the letter of the answer that correctly answers each question.

1. Joseph Papp ----- the New York Shakespeare Festival.

   (A) founding and directing
   (B) who founded and directed
   (C) founded and directed
   (D) in finding and directing

2. During 1977, the name "Emily" ----- for newborn girls in the United States.

   (A) was populated
   (B) most popular
   (C) was most popular
   (D) most populated

3. In the 1930s, many American plants and industries, suffering from economic hardship caused by the Great Depression, -----.

   (A) folding banks closed them
   (B) were closed by folding banks
   (C) closed folding banks
   (D) were closing by folded banks

4. A surprising amount of opposition to the D-Day landings ----- among Eisenhower's own staff.

   (A) there arose
   (B) arose
   (C) if arose
   (D) they arose

5. Northern California, in contrast to the sun-baked south, ----- a very temperate climate.

   (A) is
   (B) being
   (C) with
   (D) has

6. Upper New York State ----- some of the loveliest landscapes in the eastern part of the United States.

   (A) boasts
   (B) being
   (C) that has
   (D) with

7. Cruise ships ----- many tourists from Miami, Florida, to a number of ports in the Caribbean.

   (A) transport
   (B) transporting
   (C) transports
   (D) are transportation

8. Public defender programs, established in most American counties, ----- free legal services to needy defendants.

   (A) providing
   (B) who provide
   (C) to provide
   (D) provide

9. Today, the Bennington Memorial, a towering structure dedicated to Revolutionary War veterans, still ----- in Bennington, Vermont.

    (A) stand
    (B) standing
    (C) stands
    (D) to stand

10. The U.S. legal system ----- based upon adversarial relationships, but this is not always the case in practice.

    (A) it is
    (B) since it is
    (C) being
    (D) is

PRACTICE #3—Choosing a Main Clause Subject and Verb

Circle the letter of the answer that correctly answers each question.

1. ----- large rodents about the size of a pig that live in South America.

   (A) Capibaras
   (B) Capibaras that are
   (C) Capibaras are
   (D) Capibaras while they are

2. For several years in the 1950s, -----.

   (A) Ronald Reagan working for General Electric
   (B) that Ronald Reagan worked for General Electric
   (C) Ronald Reagan worked for General Electric
   (D) Ronald Reagan, when working for General Electric

3. ----- itinerant teachers in Greece in the fifth-century B.C. who provided instruction in the art of rhetoric.

   (A) The Sophists were
   (B) The Sophists being
   (C) The Sophists which were
   (D) For the Sophists to be

4. Every year Canada's ----- approximately one and a half million tons of fish and seafood products.

   (A) seafood industry that produces
   (B) producing seafood industry
   (C) seafood industry produces
   (D) that produces to seafood industry

5. Even in northern latitudes, -----.

   (A) to the skin the sun's ultraviolet rays can cause considerable damage
   (B) the considerable damage caused by the sun to the skin
   (C) the sun considerable damage to skin can cause
   (D) the sun's ultraviolet rays can cause considerable damage to the skin

6. ----- profitable than they used to be.

   (A) The antiques sales more
   (B) Antique sales in the United States had been more
   (C) Antique sales in the United States are more
   (D) That antique sales in the United States are more

7. Since leaving the presidency in 1980, -----.

   (A) Jimmy Carter will teaching law at Emory University in Atlanta
   (B) Jimmy Carter to teach law at Emory University in Atlanta
   (C) Jimmy Carter teaching law at Emory University in Atlanta
   (D) Jimmy Carter has taught law at Emory University in Atlanta

8. <u>When</u> pursuing the Iditerod trail, <u>many</u>
     A   B

   participants <u>that</u> are afflicted <u>by</u> serious
                  C   D

   effects of the bitter cold.

9. Before <u>running</u> for mayor, <u>Mary Smith</u> <u>to</u>
           A   B

   <u>run</u> for <u>public</u> office.
    C   D

10. <u>The</u> details of Leon Trotsky's death
     A

    <u>continuing to elude</u> the <u>most relentless</u> <u>of</u>
             B   C   D

    historians.

SESSION C: AVOIDING TWO SUBJECTS

On Section Two of the TOEFL, a grammar problem that sometimes appears is having too many subjects for a verb. It must be remembered that in English a noun must have one and only one function. For example, a noun cannot be both an object of a preposition and the subject of a verb. Nor can a noun exist in a sentence without any function at all.

> **INCORRECT:**   The Empire State Building, <u>it</u> was built in 1933.

In the above example, the subject is *the Empire State Building*. The pronoun *it* in this sentence has no function and therefore does not belong.

This kind of error may be more difficult to spot in a sentence where the subject and verb are separated, as in the example below.

> **INCORRECT:**   The Empire State Building, the largest building in New York, <u>it</u> was built in 1933.

Here, the subject is still *the Empire State Building*, but now an appositive (the largest building in New York) separates the subject from its verb.

This brings us to the next main point: A clause can have only one subject per verb. Of course, it is possible for a clause to have two subjects if they are connected by a coordinate conjunction like *and* or *or*. But if a clause has two subjects without a coordinate conjunction, it is wrong.

Here are some more examples of sentences with two subjects. Notice the difference between the correct sentences and the incorrect ones.

> **INCORRECT:**   My brothers and all my friends, <u>they</u> threw me a surprise party.
> **CORRECT:**   My brothers and all my friends threw me a surprise party.

> **INCORRECT:**   Alexander, who lives down the street, <u>he</u> doesn't have many friends.
> **CORRECT:**   Alexander, who lives down the street, doesn't have many friends.

Always make sure that there is only one subject for each clause.

PRACTICE #4—Avoiding Two Subjects

Circle the letter of the answer that correctly answers each question.

1. Woodrow Wilson, lawyer, teacher, and

    university president, he received the 1919
                        A   B
    Nobel Peace Prize for his work in founding
                        C   D
    the League of Nations.

2. Because microbes are invisible, their
    A
    existence was not confirmed until the
                                    B
    invention of microscopes, which it could
    C   D
    magnify them considerably.

3. There is increasing evidence that the
                    A
    United States it is ready to support
                    B   C
    measures to control the present chaotic
    D
    pattern of suburban growth.

4. Food it enters the digestive tract through
        A   B
    the mouth, and then proceeds to the
                C
    stomach, intestines, and finally the colon.
                            D

5. In multicellular plants and animals,

    somatic cells they contain two of each
            A   B   C
    type of chromosome.
    D

PRACTICE #5—Review Practice

Circle the letter of the answer that correctly answers each question.

1. ----- nothing quite like sleeping under the stars.

   (A) Is
   (B) Is there
   (C) There is
   (D) When there is

2. Although synthetic gemstones are similar in quality to natural stones, people ----- natural gems.

   (A) do seem prefer
   (B) to seem prefer
   (C) are seeming preferring
   (D) seem to prefer

3. ----- refers to the right to build in the space over such areas as buildings, roads, or railroad tracks.

   (A) The term *air rights*
   (B) *Air rights* term
   (C) If the term *air rights*
   (D) *Air rights* are

4. Stanislavsky ----- director of the Moscow Art Theater permanent company; he shared his title with both Vitaly Wolfe and Meyerhold.

   (A) were not only the
   (B) was not only the
   (C) was not the only
   (D) was only the

5. ----- have two sets of eyelids, an outer lid that covers the eye when the cat blinks or is asleep, and the nictitating eyelid on the inside that washes and protects the eye from the elements when the cat is awake.

   (A) Cats
   (B) That cats
   (C) For cats
   (D) A cat

6. Although he was a brilliant philosopher, much of Martin Heidegger's theory ----- into question because he was a member of Hitler's SS.

   (A) who is calling
   (B) which calls
   (C) having been calling
   (D) has been called

7. During the summer, Ann Arbor, along with Ypsilanti, Saline, and Pontiac ----- with tourists fleeing the boredom of their lives in Cincinnati and its suburbs.

   (A) flooding
   (B) is flooded
   (C) to flooded
   (D) will floods

8. ----- by members of the houses of Lancaster and York.

   (A) The Wars of the Roses fighting
   (B) Fighting the Wars of the Roses was
   (C) The Wars of the Roses were fought
   (D) To fight the Wars of the Roses were

9. Scientific research in oncology ----- the funding it deserves.

   (A) is seldom
   (B) seldom given
   (C) being given
   (D) is seldom given

10. ----- is merely speculated upon by modern clergymen and historians.

    (A) Noah's Ark exists
    (B) The existence of Noah's Ark
    (C) Noah's Ark to exist
    (D) That Noah's Ark

11. Wild animals endangering not only by
                     A
    hunting but also by predators, pollution,
           B
    and the many collectors of zoo specimens
        C   D
    who encroach on their territory.

12. Of many people believe that diamonds
       A   B
    are the costliest gems, but emeralds are
          C
    actually more valuable.
            D

13. The yearly movement of the stars
                          A
    first to notice by early travelers who used
      B   C
    the stars to guide their way across the sea.
                                        D

14. That the development of the submarine
        A
    was hindered by the lack of a power source
                    B   C
    that could propel an underwater vessel.
                       D

15. Marie Curie who won a Nobel Prize for
                  A   B
    her discoveries of radioactivity and
                       C
    radioactive elements.
       D

16. For many years, the simple pine and oak
    A   B
    furniture made in America considering to
                              C
    be a crude imitation of more elaborate
                         D
    European furniture.

17. <u>When mistletoe</u>, which is believed to
         A
    <u>have magic</u> powers, is traditionally hung
        B
    over <u>doorways</u> during <u>the Christmas</u> season.
         C   D

18. The ancient Egyptians <u>who believed</u>
                         A
    <u>that</u> cats were <u>blessed</u> and kept several
     B   C
    <u>in their homes</u> as a homage to the gods.
         D

19. <u>If the dwarf lemon</u> tree <u>is grown</u> in
          A   B
    <u>many areas</u> of <u>the world</u> and bears fruit
       C   D
    when it is less than six inches high.

20. <u>The first ten</u> amendments to the United
        A
    States Constitution <u>they</u> are <u>referred</u> to as
                  B   C
    <u>the</u> Bill of Rights.
     D

Answers for Structure
Power Lesson One

Practice #1		Practice #2		Practice #3	
1. C	6. C	1. C	6. A	1. C	6. C
2. B	7. B	2. C	7. A	2. C	7. D
3. A	8. A	3. B	8. D	3. A	8. C
4. D	9. A	4. B	9. C	4. C	9. C
5. A	10. A	5. D	10. D	5. D	10. B

Practice #4	Practice #5	
1. B	1. C	11. A
2. D	2. D	12. A
3. B	3. A	13. B
4. A	4. C	14. A
5. B	5. A	15. A
	6. D	16. C
	7. B	17. A
	8. C	18. A
	9. D	19. A
	10. B	20. B

STRUCTURE POWER LESSON TWO

SESSION A: THREE TYPES OF DEPENDENT CLAUSES

As you saw in the last lesson, there are three types of dependent clauses. They are:

➤ **Noun clauses**
➤ **Adjective clauses**
➤ **Adverb clauses**

In this lesson you will learn some more ways in which these clauses are tested on the TOEFL. The most important point to keep in mind is:

A dependent clause cannot form a sentence by itself. In a grammatically correct sentence, the dependent clause is always attached to an independent clause.

Noun Clauses

Noun clauses are dependent clauses that function as nouns. Therefore, a noun clause can occupy any position that a noun does. Below are examples of noun clause functions that are commonly found on the TOEFL. (For a brief review of grammatical functions, see the Grammar Review.)

As a subject:

> Whether he will come is still uncertain.

As a direct object:

> I don't know whether he will come.

As the subjective complement (predicate nominative):

> The question is whether he will come.

As the object of a preposition:

> We talked all night about whether he would come.

There are, of course, many noun functions that have not been illustrated above. However, for the TOEFL, the above positions are the most common.

SESSION B: THREE TYPES OF NOUN CLAUSES

There are three types of noun clauses.

(1) Some noun clauses come from statements.

> That Dolores plays the piano beautifully is a generally accepted fact.

(2) Some noun clauses come from *wh-* questions.

> I don't know what you need.

(3) Some noun clauses come from yes/no questions.

> Whether she is going to be there is not yet known.

You see from the three noun clauses above that each one is introduced by a different word: *that, what,* or *whether.* In fact, there are many more ways of introducing a noun clause. In order to know how to introduce a noun clause, you first have to know which of the three kinds of noun clauses it is.

We will discuss each of these three types in turn. Then we will consider a special type of noun clause involving the subjunctive.

Noun Clauses Derived from Statements

Sentence #1	Dolores plays the piano beautifully.
Sentence #2	This is generally accepted fact.
Combined:	<u>That Dolores plays the piano beautifully</u> is a generally accepted fact.

This type of sentence can be rephrased thus:

It is a generally accepted fact that Dolores plays the piano beautifully.

Note that when the noun clause coming from a statement is being used as the object of a verb, the connector *that* can sometimes be omitted.

Sentence #1	I believe something.
Sentence #2	The governor will fight against higher taxes.
Combined:	I believe <u>(that) the governor will fight against higher taxes</u>.

An important exception in this type of noun clause occurs when the noun clause is used as the object of a preposition. In this case, *that* is not used to introduce the noun clause. Instead, *what* is used immediately after the preposition.

Sentence #1	I am against something.
Sentence #2	You have said something.
Combined:	I am against <u>what you have said</u>.

Sentence #1	I don't want to deal with something.
Sentence #2	He deals with something every day.
Combined:	I don't want to deal with <u>what he deals with every day</u>.

The next session of this lesson will discuss another occasion when the word *what* introduces a noun clause—noun clauses derived from *wh-* questions.

Make sure that you know when to introduce a noun clause with *what*, and when to introduce one with *that*.

Noun Clauses Derived from *Wh-* Questions

A noun clause derived from a *wh-* question begins with the same *wh-* word (*who, what, where, when, why,* and *how*) that is used to make the question from which it is derived.

Sentence #1	How long is the drive?
Sentence #2	This will decide the time we leave.
Combined:	<u>How long the drive is</u> will decide the time we leave.

It is very important to observe:

In a noun clause, normal word order is used and the auxiliary *do* is not used.

Sentence #1	What do you need?
Sentence #2	I don't know this.
Combined:	I don't know <u>what you need</u>.

INCORRECT:	I don't know what do you need.
INCORRECT:	I don't know what you do need.

Noun Clauses Derived from Yes/No Questions

A noun clause derived from a yes/no question begins with the word *whether* or the word *if*.

Sentence #1	Is the president going to be on television tonight?
Sentence #2	My schedule depends on this.
Combined:	My schedule depends on <u>whether the president will be on television tonight</u>.

Or:	My schedule depends on <u>if the president will be on television tonight</u>.

Note that noun clauses derived from yes/no questions also use normal word order and do not use the auxiliary *do*.

Sentence #1	Is the telephone working?
Sentence #2	I don't know this.
Combined:	I don't know <u>if the telephone is working</u>.
	I don't know <u>whether the telephone is working</u>.
INCORRECT:	I don't know is the telephone working.

A noun clause doesn't use *do, does,* or *did* as auxiliaries, and never has its words ordered in the form of a question.

There is no difference in meaning between the use of *whether* and *if*. However, *if* is not used when the noun clause derived from a yes/no question is the subject or the object of a preposition.

Sentence #1	Did the students already finish the exam?
Sentence #2	This has not yet been reported to me.
Combined:	<u>Whether the students already finished the exam</u> has not yet been reported to me.
INCORRECT:	If the students already finish the exam has not yet been reported to me.

The Subjunctive in Noun Clauses
On the TOEFL you might encounter a fairly unusual type of noun clause in which the noun clause verb is in the simple form. The verb in this type of noun clause is in the subjunctive mode.

After expressions of desire, command, requirement and suggestion, the *that-* noun clause may take its verb in the simple form.

In this type of noun clause, the expression of command, suggestion, etcetera, may be a verb, an adjective, or in some cases, a noun.

VERB:	I <u>recommend</u> that he <u>take</u> the bus. (not *takes*)
ADJECTIVE:	It was <u>imperative</u> that John <u>call</u> at just that moment. (not *called*)
NOUN:	It is a city <u>ordinance</u> that all pet owners <u>keep</u> their animals on a leash.

Other words and expressions that can introduce this form of the subjunctive are:

Verbs	**Adjectives**	**Nouns**
suggest	important	a requirement
demand	vital	a necessity
insist	essential	a law
advise	crucial	a regulation
request	necessary	a stipulation
stipulate	propose	

Don't be fooled into thinking that a sentence like "I insist he stay at home" is incorrect because it is missing the third-person singular -s of the simple present tense.

Note that some of these expressions will be found from time to time without the simple form in the noun clause.

> The police <u>suggested</u> that the criminal was hiding in the abandoned building on Eighth Street.

The reason for not using the simple form in the above sentence is that the subject of the main clause (*police*) is not exercising force onto the subject of the noun clause (*the criminal*). Instead, the police here are simply making a guess about the location of the criminal. All of the cases in which the simple form is used in noun clauses after such expressions must include the idea of force or obligation.

PRACTICE #1—Noun Clauses

Circle the letter of the answer that correctly answers each question.

1. Ancient philosophers believed ----- around the earth.

    (A) to revolve the sun
    (B) the sun revolved
    (C) in revolving the sun
    (D) the sun revolving

2. It is a federal law ----- vaccinated before entering the first grade.

    (A) for children be
    (B) so that children will be
    (C) that children be
    (D) requires children to be

3. The National Bureau of Labor Statistics figures show that ----- are especially devastated by inflation.

    (A) the working classes
    (B) the classes working
    (C) the classes that are working
    (D) working the classes

4. Surveys of recent armed conflicts show ----- war is extremely rare between democratic nations.

    (A) where
    (B) that
    (C) there
    (D) then

5. Industrial psychologists have found that most people ----- to work even if they became very wealthy.

    (A) continuing
    (B) to continue
    (C) would continue
    (D) which would continue

6. ----- was one of the greatest discoveries in establishing Newton's theory of gravity.

    (A) The moon and the tides are linked
    (B) That the cycles of the moon and the tides are linked
    (C) Of the cycles of the moon and the tides were linked
    (D) To link the cycles of the moon and the tides

7. The reality in modern day Moscow is of
       A   B   C
   the costs of building a capitalist system are
                  D
   great.

8. What air travel would become an
   A   B
   inexpensive and efficient way of travel was
                            C
   probably not envisioned by the earliest
                            D
   aviators.

9. A recent Gallup poll <u>showed</u> <u>than</u> the
                     A   B

   senator <u>was considered</u> too old <u>to run</u> for
            C   D

   the presidency.

10. Before <u>issuing</u> its final report, the EPA will
           A

    confer with the people <u>who live</u> near the
                     B

    site in order <u>to determine that</u> the social
                   C

    impact <u>might be</u>.
          D

SESSION C: TWO TYPES OF ADJECTIVE CLAUSES

> An *adjective clause* is a dependent clause used to give information about a noun in the sentence. Another term for this kind of clause is *relative clause.*

An adjective clause has one of two functions:

(1) A *restrictive adjective clause* limits or restricts the noun so that the reader or listener does not confuse the noun in question with any other noun.

(2) A *nonrestrictive adjective clause* adds extra information to the noun that is not really essential to the message of the whole sentence.

Restrictive Adjective Clauses

A restrictive clause does not appear with commas, while a nonrestrictive clause always appears with commas.

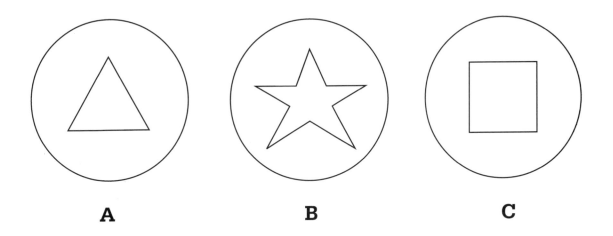

A   B   C

The circle <u>that has a star in it</u> is used in religious ceremonies.

In this restrictive clause, the adjective clause is used so that the reader or listener knows that the adjective clause is referring only to circle B and not the others. The reader needs this information in order to understand which circle is under discussion.

Note that, because it is restrictive, the clause has no commas.

Nonrestrictive Adjective Clauses

The circle, <u>which has a star in it</u>, is used for religious ceremonies.

In this nonrestrictive clause (note the use of commas), the adjective clause does restrict the noun since the noun, *the circle*, is the only possible circle under discussion.

A good rule of thumb is that if the clause describes a proper noun (the name of a person or place), it is nonrestrictive and thus uses commas. The reason for this is that a proper noun refers to a unique person, place, or thing.

Mr. Rogers, <u>who telephoned last night</u>, won't be able to come this afternoon.

Albany, <u>which is the capital of New York State</u>, is a fairly large city in the northern part of the state.

Make sure you know the difference between restrictive and nonrestrictive adjective clauses. The distinction is frequently tested on the TOEFL.

Connector Words for Adjective Clauses (Relative Pronouns)

Which is used for objects, *who* and *whom* for people, and *that* for objects and people.

Using *Which*

When the noun being described is a thing, the adjective clause begins with *which*.

The table <u>which you bought at the antique fair</u> is beautiful.

That secret, <u>which Mary told me last week,</u> has been haunting me ever since.

Using *Who* and *Whom*

When the noun being described is a person, the connector words *who* or *whom* are used.

If the noun being replaced is the subject of the verb in the adjective clause, *who* is used.

The man <u>who marries that woman</u> will be the luckiest man on Earth.

Whom is used if the noun being replaced is the object of the verb or of a preposition.

Sentence #1	The girl has been in a terrible accident.
Sentence #2	We saw the girl in the park yesterday. (The direct object of the verb is *the girl*.)
Combined:	The girl <u>whom we saw in the park yesterday</u> has been in a terrible accident.

Sentence #1	Janet Reno has served in many public offices in her successful career.
Sentence #2	President Clinton appointed Janet Reno as Attorney General. (The direct object of the verb is *Janet Reno*.)
Combined:	Janet Reno, <u>whom President Clinton appointed as Attorney General</u>, has served in many public offices in her successful career.

Note that in contemporary English *who* can replace *whom*.

The girl <u>who we saw in the park yesterday</u> has been in a terrible accident.

Using *That*

It is very common for *that* to be used for either objects or people.

The table <u>that you bought at the antique fair</u> is lovely.

She's with the same man <u>that I saw her with last week.</u>

However, the relative pronoun *that* can never be used in a nonrestrictive adjective clause.

CORRECT:	Virginia, <u>which</u> is said to be quite beautiful, is the home of many senators and representatives.
INCORRECT:	Virginia, <u>that</u> is said to be quite beautiful, is the home of many senators and representatives.

> **The relative pronoun *that* never introduces a nonrestrictive adjective clause. For this reason, you can say: If the adjective clause has commas, it can never be introduced with *that*.**

Using Prepositions in Adjective Clauses

When the relative pronoun replaces the object of a preposition, there are usually two ways of constructing the sentence. One way is to put the preposition before the relative pronoun; the other is to put the preposition at the end of the adjective clause.

Sentence #1	The man is leaving.
Sentence #2	You spoke to the man. (*The man* is the object of the preposition *to*.)
Combined:	The man <u>to whom you spoke</u> is leaving.
Or:	The man <u>whom you spoke to</u> is leaving.

For the TOEFL you should know both constructions. Often on the test you will be asked to supply a missing preposition for a relative pronoun. The example below illustrates this.

The method ----- products are recycled requires a strict separation of white and colored paper.

(A) which most paper
(B) by which most paper
(C) that most paper
(D) most paper

Examination of the sentence tells us that it consists of two finite verbs. For this reason it must contain two clauses. We can see that the sentence can be divided into two parts:

> The method requires a strict separation of white and colored paper.
> Products are recycled ----- a method.

A preposition must be inserted into the space to make the second sentence complete. Possible prepositions are *through, by,* or *in.* Looking at the choice of answers, we see that only one offers a preposition, and that this preposition fits grammatically into the original sentence of the question. (B) is the correct answer.

Omission of the Relative Pronoun

If the relative pronoun is the object of its clause, the relative pronoun can be omitted in restrictive clauses.

Sentence #1	I suggest that you read the book.
Sentence #2	I bought the book at the book fair. (*The book* is the direct object of the verb.)
Combined:	I suggest that you read the book <u>that I bought at the book fair.</u>
Or:	I suggest that you read the book <u>I bought at the book fair.</u>

If the relative pronoun is the subject of its clause, it cannot be omitted.

CORRECT:	I suggest that you read the book <u>that</u> won the Pulitzer Prize.
INCORRECT:	I suggest that you read the book won the Pulitzer Prize.

A good way to remember this point is to keep in mind that a clause is a group of related words with a subject and a finite verb. Without the word *which,* the adjective clause in the sentence above has no subject.

> ## Keep in mind that you cannot omit a relative pronoun when it functions as the subject of the clause.

Using *Where* and *When* in Adjective Clauses

Occasionally *where* and *when* are used to build adjective clauses. *Where* is used to describe a location noun and *when* is used to describe a time noun. In this case, *when* and *where* are called relative adverbs.

The city <u>where I grew up</u> is now famous for an extremely high crime rate.

She would never forget the day <u>when Sam arrived.</u>

It is very important to remember that when the relative adverbs, *where* or *when*, are used, prepositions are not necessary. Compare:

> The city <u>that</u> I grew up <u>in</u> is now famous for a high crime rate.

> The city <u>where</u> I grew up is now famous for an extremely high crime rate.

Do not use prepositions with *where* or *when* in an adjective clause.

Showing Possession in Adjective Clauses

Sometimes it is necessary to show possession in an adjective clause. The word *whose* can be used to introduce an adjective clause. It is usually used when the possessor is a person, but it can also be used for objects.

> The chairperson, <u>whose committee was so successful last year</u>, has been reelected for another term.

> The table <u>whose leg is broken</u> cannot be fixed.

A prepositional *of* phrase can also be used when the possessor is a thing. The formula for such constructions takes the form: *noun + of + which*.

Such relative constructions are usually separated by commas.

> The table, <u>the leg of which is broken</u>, cannot be fixed.

> We used the red book, <u>the title of which I cannot remember</u>.

PRACTICE #2—Adjective Clauses

Circle the letter of the answer that correctly answers each question.

1. Hugo Bart Hughes, -----, is considered the father of the modern trepanation movement.

    (A) who became a medical student in Amsterdam in the 1960s
    (B) which became a medical student in Amsterdam in the 1960s
    (C) who were a medical student in Amsterdam in the 1960s
    (D) that is a medical student in Amsterdam in the 1960s

2. The movie *The Wizard of Oz*, ----- is taken from the book of the same name, has been a children's favorite for years.

    (A) the title of which
    (B) which title
    (C) that's title
    (D) the title of that

3. The aurora borealis, ----- in the Southern Hemisphere, is not an entirely understood phenomenon.

    (A) cannot be seen
    (B) that it cannot see
    (C) it is never seen
    (D) which is never seen

4. Musical concerts, ----- popular music of various kinds, have become one of the most common forms of entertainment in the United States.

    (A) to feature
    (B) feature
    (C) which featuring
    (D) which feature

5. Some literary critics felt Pearl Buck, ----- the daughter of missionaries, allowed her upbringing to interfere with her objectivity as a writer.

    (A) who
    (B) had been
    (C) who was
    (D) being one

6. The portion of a mountain ----- trees will no longer grow is called the tree line.

    (A) there
    (B) that
    (C) so
    (D) where

7. Many cough suppressants <u>contain</u> alcohol,
                                A

   <u>whose</u> is <u>not always</u> recommended
     B   C

   <u>in treating</u> small children.
     D

8. Wine is grown in regions <u>that</u> favorable
                          A

soil and <u>climatic</u> conditions will <u>likely</u>
         B   C

<u>lead to</u> a successful harvest.
  D

9. The <u>early</u> settlers of New England were
       A

pilgrims <u>whose</u> <u>came</u> to the New World
         B   C

for <u>both</u> religious and economic freedom.
    D

10. Some psychologists have suggested <u>that</u>
                             A

people are more <u>likely</u> to hate those for
             B

<u>whose</u> they <u>have shown</u> profound affection.
 C   D

SESSION D: TYPES OF ADVERB CLAUSES

> An *adverb clause* is a dependent clause that gives information about time, place, contrast, cause, result, purpose, condition, manner, or degree.

Below is a list of common words that begin an adverb clause. The list is not complete. To get a fuller view of all of the possibilities, you should consult a good grammar of American English.

Some Common Words that Begin Adverb Clauses:

where(ever)	now that
because	as . . . as
since	in that
before	so
after	so that
until	if
although	in order that
even though	unless
whereas	in case
while	as if
as though	

The difficult task with adverb clauses on the TOEFL is choosing the correct introductory word for the meaning of the sentence. Therefore it is essential to know the exact meaning of each of the words in the above list and to know exactly how they are used.

> **Make sure you know the meanings of the subordinate conjunctions that introduce adverb clauses.**

Here are examples of some adverb clauses introduced with words that frequently give students trouble:

Boys follow her <u>wherever she goes</u>.

He has a good job <u>in that he likes the work enormously</u>.

<u>Now that the kids have left for college</u>, I can go out and look for a job.

Further practice on some troublesome words is given in the vocabulary section at the end of this lesson.

In an adverbial time clause, neither the future *will* nor the future *to be going to* is used. Instead, the present tenses are used.

<u>After the guests arrive</u>, we will have dinner.

They are going to have to work <u>until the project is finished</u>.

You should bring an umbrella <u>in case it rains tonight</u>.

Note that in standard English punctuation, a comma is used after the adverb clause when it is before the main clause. When the adverb clause follows the main clause, a comma is usually not used.

The forms will be given out <u>when the plane is in flight</u>.

<u>When the plane is in flight</u>, the forms will be given out.

PRACTICE #3—Adverb Clauses

Circle the letter of the answer that correctly answers each question.

1. ----- the polar icecaps melt, many coastal cities and small islands could be completely submerged.

   (A) For
   (B) However
   (C) If
   (D) Although

2. ----- the Chinese calendar is based on the lunar cycle, the Chinese New Year falls on a different date in the Western calendar each year.

   (A) For the reason
   (B) Because
   (C) Consequently
   (D) Due to

3. Researchers agree that violent crime tends to be the most common in areas ----- a high rate of illegal drug activity.

   (A) there is
   (B) where there is
   (C) where is
   (D) in where there is

4. A bill appears before the House of Representatives as soon as the appropriate subcommittee ----- it.

   (A) to approve
   (B) approving
   (C) approves
   (D) which approves

5. If they ----- properly maintained and regularly serviced, cars remain operational for a number of years.

   (A) are
   (B) be
   (C) being
   (D) could

6. ----- evidence of water on Mars, for years the dark lines visible on the planet were referred to as canals.

   (A) Even though
   (B) Although no
   (C) Although there is no
   (D) And even though is no

7. Building codes and fire laws prevent concert promoters from selling as many tickets ----- they possibly can.

   (A) as
   (B) if
   (C) how
   (D) that

8. Ranchers raise free range cattle just as ----- other cattle, but the free range cattle are not fed any grain.

   (A) that they raise
   (B) that raise
   (C) they raise
   (D) do they raise

9. ----- are not filed by the fifteenth of April, penalties and interest may apply to the unpaid balance.

    (A) For taxes of income
    (B) Income taxes that
    (C) With taxes of income
    (D) If income taxes

10. <u>According to</u> <u>ancient</u> myths and legends,
       A   B
vampires must <u>remain</u> inside their coffins
             C
while the <u>sun out</u>.
       D

SESSION E: REDUCED DEPENDENT CLAUSES AND APPOSITIVES

Dependent clauses can often be reduced into phrases. Here we will discuss reduced adjective clauses, reduced adverb clauses, and a related structure called appositives.

Reduced Adjective Clauses

In an adjective clause, if the subject of the adjective clause is the same as the noun being modified, it can be reduced to a phrase.

> A *phrase* is a group of related words that do not contain either a subject or a finite verb.

> The building <u>that is being destroyed</u> is located on Fifth Avenue. (ADJECTIVE CLAUSE)

> The building <u>being destroyed</u> is located on Fifth Avenue. (ADJECTIVAL PHRASE)

If the subject of the adjective clause is not the same as the noun being modified, then no reduction can take place:

> CORRECT: The building <u>that they are destroying</u> is located on Fifth Avenue. (ADJECTIVE CLAUSE)

> INCORRECT: The building <u>destroying</u> is located on Fifth Avenue.

> An adjective clause can be reduced only if the subject of the adverb clause is the same as the subject of the main clause.

Adjective Clauses with Forms of the Verb *Be*

How you reduce an adjective clause to a phrase depends upon whether the verb in the adjective clause contains a form of *be*. To reduce the clause to a phrase:

(1) Delete the relative pronoun (that is, the subject of the adjective clause);

(2) Delete the form of *be*.

> The man <u>who is standing near the tree</u> looks like a wanted criminal.

The man <u>standing near the tree</u> looks like a wanted criminal.

Adjective Clause without a Form of the Verb *Be*
The adjective clause is constructed according to the following principle:

(1) Delete the relative pronoun;

(2) Change the verb to the present participle.

The Smiths, <u>who live in the southernmost suburb</u>, must drive more than an hour to get to work. (ADJECTIVE CLAUSE)

The Smiths, <u>living in the southernmost suburb</u>, must drive more than an hour to get to work. (ADJECTIVE PHRASE)

That cat <u>that made so much noise every night</u> was probably a stray. (ADJECTIVE CLAUSE)

That cat <u>making so much noise every night</u> was probably a stray. (ADJEC-TIVE PHRASE)

Note that the restrictive versus nonrestrictive distinction exists also in the adjectival phrases, and the use of commas is the same as in the clauses:

Bill Clinton, <u>who was reelected president in 1996</u>, was formerly the governor of Arkansas. (NONRESTRICTIVE ADJECTIVE CLAUSE)

Bill Clinton, <u>reelected president in 1996</u>, was formerly the governor of Arkansas. (NONRESTRICTIVE ADJECTIVAL PHRASE)

Remember that the distinction between restrictive and nonrestrictive clauses is true of phrases as well.

Reduced Adverb Clauses

Like an adjective clause, an adverb clause can be reduced only if the subject of the adverb clause is the same as the subject of the main clause.

While I was walking in the park, I saw my old roommate. (ADVERB CLAUSE)

While walking in the park, I saw my old roommate. (ADVERB PHRASE)

After Bill moved to Mexico, he began speaking Spanish wonderfully. (ADVERB CLAUSE)

After moving to Mexico, Bill began speaking Spanish wonderfully. (ADVERB PHRASE)

The candidates went on to California after they had finished the campaign in Vermont. (ADVERB CLAUSE)

The candidates went on to California, after having finished the campaign in Vermont. (ADVERB PHRASE)

Many times the adverb phrase can be reduced even more if it is located at the beginning of the sentence. In such cases the subordinate conjunction is deleted. Note that in these cases, the implied subject of the *-ing* participle must be the same as the subject of the main clause.

Walking in the park, I saw my old roommate. (*I* did the walking.)

Having finished the campaign in Vermont, the candidates went on to California. (*The candidates* finished the campaign in Vermont.)

If the implied subject of the *-ing* participle is not the same as the subject of the main clause, you have the grammar error frequently called a *dangling modifier*.

INCORRECT: Making all kinds of noise, I watched the trucks go down the highway.

This sentence says that *I* made the noise—not *the trucks*.

Learn to recognize a dangling modifier. This kind of error appears frequently on the TOEFL.

An adverb clause with *because* can be reduced in a similar way.

Because the program is not receiving good ratings, it has been moved to another time. (ADVERB CLAUSE)

Not receiving good ratings, the program has been moved to another time. (ADVERB PHRASE)

Appositives

The *appositive* is an often-found structure on the TOEFL. In many ways it is similar to the reduced adjective clause.

An *appositive* is a noun used to give some extra information about another noun in the sentence.

An appositive may be used after any noun in a sentence, but most commonly it is found after the subject. The appositive may be a single noun, or it may be a noun group that includes articles, adjectives, and so forth.

George Washington, the first president of the United States, was born on a farm in the state of Virginia.

The big tree in front of the house, a 100-year-old oak, presents a danger since it is nearly dead.

Note that it may also be possible to have the appositive first and the subject after it.

The hottest planet in the solar system, Mercury is a mere 36,000,000 miles away from the Sun.

In the above example, *the hottest planet in the solar system* is the appositive and *Mercury* is the subject. As always, special attention should be paid to comma usage in such sentences because it is often the clue to finding the best answer on the TOEFL.

You are very likely to find some appositives on the TOEFL. Learn to use commas to quickly identify them.

PRACTICE #4—Reduced Clauses and Appositives

Circle the letter of the answer that correctly answers each question.

1. One of the most popular movies ever made is *Gone With the Wind*, -----.

    (A) besides accounting the American Civil War

    (B) to account for the American Civil War

    (C) an account of the American Civil War

    (D) in the American Civil War

2. ----- an extremely isolated and spartan existence in a land without human habitation.

    (A) Since research scientists living in the Antarctic have

    (B) Living research scientists have in the Antarctic

    (C) Research scientists living in the Antarctic have

    (D) The living in the Antarctic research scientists have

3. The war ----- is often referred to as King William's War.

    (A) to know as the Glorious Revolution

    (B) knowing as the Glorious Revolution

    (C) known as the Glorious Revolution

    (D) when known as the Glorious Revolution

4. -----, Joni Mitchell established herself as a new talent in the folk music world.

    (A) Plays the guitar and writes her own brand of music

    (B) Playing the guitar and writing her own brand of music

    (C) By play the guitar and writes her own brand of music

    (D) Who plays the guitar and writes her own music

5. Ralph Ellison, -----, is one of the most respected novelists of our time.

    (A) who writes the novel *The Invisible Man*

    (B) writing the novel *The Invisible Man*

    (C) for writing the novel *The Invisible Man*

    (D) who wrote the novel *The Invisible Man*

6. The Greater London Council, -----, was privatized in 1984 under the governance of Margaret Thatcher.

    (A) supporting by the British government

    (B) formerly supported by the British government

    (C) of former support by the British government

    (D) who was supported formerly by the British government

7. -----, the Ambassador is alleged to have misappropriated state funds.

   (A) Served as Governor of Maryland
   (B) To serve as Governor of Maryland
   (C) While serve as Governor of Maryland
   (D) While serving as Governor of Maryland

8. The name Angela, -----, is a favorite among peoples of all western nations.

   (A) meaning "girl angel"
   (B) who means "girl angel"
   (C) to mean "girl angel"
   (D) meant "girl angel"

9. J. D. Salinger's *The Catcher in the Rye,*

   <u>deals</u> with teenage alienation, has long
     A

   <u>attracted</u> the interest <u>of</u> high-school-aged
     B   C

   readers <u>in</u> America.
        D

10. <u>Offers a</u> release from tension, primal
      A

    <u>scream</u> therapy is still <u>thought of</u> as a
      B   C

    valuable therapy technique <u>by many</u>
                                    D

    practicing professionals.

PRACTICE #5—Review Questions

Circle the letter of the answer that correctly answers each question.

1. ----- is your own business.

   (A) Who you work for
   (B) Whose you work for
   (C) Who for you work
   (D) You work for who

2. My grade depends on -----.

   (A) what I master calculus
   (B) whether calculus mastered by me
   (C) whether I master calculus
   (D) when do I master calculus

3. *The Canterbury Tales,* -----, have often been interpreted into plays and films.

   (A) who are written by Geoffrey Chaucer
   (B) are written by Geoffrey Chaucer
   (C) written by Geoffrey Chaucer
   (D) which written by Geoffrey Chaucer

4. ----- has not been confirmed by the Federal government.

   (A) If the population has surpassed 230 million
   (B) The population has surpassed 230 million
   (C) That the population has surpassed 230 million
   (D) What the population has surpassed 230 million

5. As of the 1992 New Hampshire primary, Bill Clinton did not yet know -----.

   (A) which would be the presidential candidate
   (B) when would be the presidential candidate
   (C) if the presidential candidate he would be
   (D) whether he would be the presidential candidate

6. The Statue of Freedom, -----, is a likeness of a Native American woman.

   (A) finding atop the Capitol Dome
   (B) to find atop the Capitol Dome
   (C) found atop the Capitol Dome
   (D) when found atop the Capitol Dome

7. There is a reproduction of Lincoln's Gettysburg Address -----.

   (A) who is printed on the Lincoln Memorial
   (B) printed on the Lincoln Memorial
   (C) which are printed on the Lincoln Memorial
   (D) printing on the Lincoln Memorial

8. -----, Senator Ernest Hollings of South Carolina is often referred to as The Great White Father.

(A) Because he is tall
(B) Due from his height
(C) Who is height
(D) With height

9. Many health food advocates maintain -----.

(A) eggs and milk should be avoiding
(B) that eggs and milk should be avoided
(C) avoiding eggs and milk
(D) the avoided eggs and milk

10. -----, Earth is more temperate than its closer cousins.

(A) The third planet is from the Sun
(B) Third from sun
(C) The third planet from the Sun
(D) Of the third planet from the Sun

11. One can never be certain which the Moon
    A   B   C
will be full on a given day or not.
            D

12. Which was given to the United States as a
    A
gift by the country of France, the Statue of
     B   C
Liberty stands in New York Harbor.
        D

13. The South Street Seaport, what was once
                              A
a thriving merchant seaport, now houses a
  B   C
museum and several tourist attractions.
                   D

14. It has long been known which to err is
    A   B
human but to forgive is divine.
      C   D

15. That too many people inhabit the island
    A
of Manhattan it is an accepted fact
             B   C
amongst most statisticians.
D

16. Before that you have reached the city of
    A   B
Los Angeles by jet, you will see a cloud of
            C
brown smoke, known as smog, over the
                            D
city.

17. Which they are often stolen or abused by
    A
employees, office supplies are the first
           B   C
budget cut made by management trying
            D
to cut costs.

18. <u>Who</u> <u>are</u> unknown in most <u>of</u> the
    A   B

   <u>northeastern</u> United States, grits <u>are</u> a
   C   D

   Southern delicacy.

19. <u>At</u> the university <u>has long been</u> in
   A   B

   financial trouble <u>is</u> a fact none <u>of us</u> can
               C   D

   continue to deny.

20. Most scholars <u>agree</u> <u>when</u> <u>*Plutarch's Lives*</u>
              A   B   C

   <u>was</u> the source for William Shakespeare's
   D

   Roman plays.

Answers for Structure
Power Lesson Two

Practice #1

1.	B	6.	B
2.	C	7.	C
3.	A	8.	A
4.	B	9.	B
5.	C	10.	C

Practice #2

1.	A	6.	D
2.	A	7.	B
3.	D	8.	A
4.	D	9.	B
5.	C	10.	C

Practice #3

1.	C	6.	C
2.	B	7.	A
3.	B	8.	C
4.	C	9.	D
5.	A	10.	D

Practice #4

1.	C	6.	B
2.	C	7.	D
3.	C	8.	A
4.	B	9.	A
5.	D	10.	A

Practice #5

1.	A	11.	C
2.	C	12.	A
3.	C	13.	A
4.	C	14.	B
5.	D	15.	B
6.	C	16.	B
7.	B	17.	A
8.	A	18.	A
9.	B	19.	A
10.	C	20.	B

STRUCTURE POWER LESSON THREE

SESSION A: VERB TENSE SEQUENCES

Though the TOEFL often tests verb forms, it generally does not test verb tenses. Occasionally, however, it will test the past perfect or the sequencing of tenses between two verbs in a sentence.

The Past Perfect and the Simple Past

The past perfect should only be used when the action expressed in the past perfect verb happens before another past event in the sentence. This other past event may be expressed by another verb in the sentence, as the example below shows:

Before we <u>ate</u>, we <u>had finished</u> all of our work.
2ND EVENT   1ST EVENT

Or the other past event may be expressed by an adverbial expression in the sentence.

Before <u>1929</u>, no one <u>had believed</u> that the U.S. economy could ever crash.
2ND EVENT   1ST EVENT

The word *ago* is never used with the past perfect. It can be used only with the simple past.

I last went to Thailand three years <u>ago</u>.

If you want to speak about an event that took place before a more recent second event, use the word *before* and the past perfect.

He remembered that he had last been to Thailand <u>three years before</u>.

Other Troublesome Verb Sequences

The term *verb sequences* means the use of different verb tenses together. Sometimes mixing verb tenses is perfectly grammatical, but it can lead to problems at other times. When a sentence has two verbs, make sure that the relationship between the two verbs is correct.

I <u>live</u> in New York now, but I <u>lived</u> in Chicago before.
CURRENT EVENT   FORMER EVENT

In the above example, the first verb has a present time reference, while the second verb has past time reference. Since the two verbs logically refer to separate points in time, the mix of tenses is correct. But look at the sentence below.

INCORRECT: While she <u>has been addressing the committee</u>, she <u>kept</u> repeating the main points of her speech.

This sentence is ungrammatical because the two actions in the sentence occur at the same time. The first verb, in the present perfect progressive, refers to a present time frame, whereas the second verb, in the simple past, refers to the past. To express this idea correctly, we would use the past progressive:

While she <u>was addressing</u> the committee, she <u>kept</u> repeating the main points of her speech.

In the error identification part of the Structure section, the TOEFL will often give you sentences in which the sequence of tense is wrong. Here is an example:

While she <u>has been addressing</u> <u>the committee</u>, she
                    A   B

kept <u>repeating</u> the main <u>points</u> of her speech.
    C   D

For such a question the student would choose (A), since it is the element in the sentence that needs to be changed in order to form a correct sentence.

PRACTICE #1—Checking Verb Tenses

Circle the letter of the answer that correctly answers each question.

1. During his formative years, Ronald Reagan ----- on a farm in Illinois.

    (A) has lived
    (B) lived
    (C) living
    (D) had living

2. In most American cities, computers are
   A

   now far more prevalent than they are only
   BC

   a few years ago.
   D

3. The collapse of the Thai economy
   A

   starts a domino effect on other
   B$$C

   Pacific countries during 1998.
   D

4. For the last 100 years Carnegie Hall
   A

   is playing host to the world's greatest
   BC$$D

   musicians.

5. In the early 1900s, the versatile Jim
   A$$B

   Thorpe played professional football

   and participate in the Olympic Games.
   CD

6. The earliest automobiles were started
   A

   with a crank that the driver has to turn
   B$$C

   manually before getting into the driver's
   D

   seat.

7. While gasoline prices continued to rise,
   A$$B

   people complain that the oil companies
   C

   were creating a fictitious gas shortage.
   D

8. In 1990, a play by Beckett has been selected
   AB

   to represent the Irish contribution to
   C

   avant-garde theater at the international

   theater festival in Paris.
   D

9. The workers <u>viewed</u> the work-sharing
            A

plan with hostility <u>out of fear</u> that
                B

<u>it will undermine</u> the seniority system and
    C

<u>negatively affect</u> retirement benefits.
    D

10. According to <u>some experts</u>, grammar books
           A

<u>have originally been</u> compiled in the 16th
      B

Century <u>in an effort</u> to protect the
        C

English language from <u>change</u>.
               D

SESSION B: INCORRECT VERB FORMS

Here is a list of rules that you should learn to avoid some impossible compound verb forms.

The auxiliary verb *have* is followed by the past participle, whether it is used as:
(1) Part of a finite verb

> We <u>have seen</u> that movie three times.

(2) A participle

> <u>Having seen</u> the movie three times, we really didn't want to see it again.

(3) An infinitive

> He was glad to <u>have seen</u> the movie so that he could follow the discussion on it.

Remember that the auxiliary *have* is always followed by a past participle.

The verb *be* is followed by:
(1) A present participle in the progressive tenses

> Kate has <u>been writing</u> her book for the last five years.

> John will <u>be joining</u> us for lunch tomorrow.

(2) A past participle in the passive

> The books <u>were given</u> to the students on the first day of class.

> All accidents must <u>be reported</u> to the medical offices immediately.

(3) An infinitive with the meaning of must, or the meaning of an unreal present conditional (See Session C):

> Students <u>are to report</u> to the foreign student advisor as soon as they arrive in the country.

If we <u>were to leave</u> at five, we would get there on time.

A modal verb is always followed by the simple form of the verb without the word *to.*

Citizens <u>should play</u> an active role in the election of their political leaders.

We <u>might have</u> been living in that house at the time, but I honestly don't remember.

An apparent exception to this is the modal *ought to.*

You <u>ought to pay</u> more attention to pedestrians when you drive.

PRACTICE #2—Identifying Incorrect Verb Forms

Circle the letter of the answer that correctly answers each question.

1. Archaeologists believe that the calendar ----- by the Aztecs centuries before it appeared in Europe or the Middle East.

   (A) were inventing
   (B) have been invented
   (C) had been invented
   (D) being invented

2. Water safety experts feel we should ----- at as young an age as possible.

   (A) begin to teach children to swim
   (B) begins taught children to swim
   (C) beginning to teach children to swim
   (D) began to teach children to swim

3. The U.S. legislative system ----- based upon a multiparty system, but historically, the serious candidates have come from only two parties.

   (A) it is
   (B) since it is
   (C) being
   (D) is

4. Many businesses, <u>having been</u> taxed heavily
                        A
   for <u>a long time</u>, were finally <u>to be obliged</u>
          B   C
   to leave the state and <u>relocate</u> elsewhere.
                                D

5. Some psychiatrists feel that adult problems may <u>came from</u> unresolved
                                                        A
   childhood fears of <u>separation</u>, <u>rivalry, or</u>
                            B   C
   <u>loneliness</u>.
       D

6. The Cy Young Award is <u>give</u> <u>each year</u> to
                              A   B
   an <u>outstanding</u> pitcher in <u>major</u> league
          C   D
   baseball.

7. Betsy Ross <u>known</u> for her work <u>on</u> the
                   A   B
   original flag <u>of</u> the newly <u>independent</u>
                     C   D
   United States.

8. Despite <u>much</u> public criticism, history has
               A
   <u>prove</u> Jimmy Carter <u>to have been</u> <u>more</u>
       B   C   D
   politically astute than many other past

   U.S. presidents.

9. <u>Depending</u> on the wind <u>currents</u>, ash
    A   B

from a volcano can be <u>distribute</u> hundreds
                     C

<u>of</u> miles from the eruption.
D

10. The commission <u>has been studying</u> urban
                    A

problems <u>for several months</u> and is
          B

<u>recommend</u> some possible <u>long-range</u>
    C   D

solutions.

SESSION C: CONDITIONALS

Conditional verb forms present special problems for TOEFL takers because of the complexity of the verbs and because of the contrary-to-fact information often contained in the sentences.

There are four types of conditional sentences:

➤ Real present
➤ Real future
➤ Unreal present/future
➤ Unreal past

In referring to conditional sentences, we will refer to the *if* clause and the result clause, that is the main clause of the sentence.

I <u>would have met you at the airport</u>   <u>if I had known you were coming</u>.
RESULT CLAUSE   *IF* CLAUSE

The order of the *if* clause and the result clause is interchangeable. If the result clause is first, there is no comma between the clauses; but if the *if* clause is first, a comma comes before the result clause.

<u>If I had known you were coming</u>,   <u>I would have met you at the airport</u>.
IF CLAUSE   RESULT CLAUSE

Real Conditionals

Real conditionals are used when the *if* clause expresses an idea that is probably true, or at least very possible.

Real Present Conditional Sentences

A *real present* condition is one in which the situation is true in the habitual present time. This form is usually used to express general truths.

If it <u>rains</u>, we <u>carry</u> our umbrellas.

Water <u>boils</u> if it <u>is heated</u> to 212 degrees Fahrenheit.

In the real present condition (like in the examples above), a present tense is used in the *if* clause and a present tense is used in the result clause. In these examples, the simple present is used, but, depending on the intended meaning, we could also see the present progressive, a present modal, or even the present perfect, as the following examples illustrate.

If it <u>is raining</u>, we <u>may carry</u> our umbrellas.

Water <u>boils</u> if it <u>has been heated</u> to 212 degrees Fahrenheit.

Real Future Conditional Sentences
A *real future* condition is one in which the situation will most probably be true in the future.

If it <u>rains</u> tomorrow, we <u>will carry</u> our umbrellas.

In a real future condition, we use present tense (any present tense) in the *if* clause, and a future tense (any future tense) in the result clause. Imperative verb forms are also possible in the result clause.

If the sun <u>is shining</u> tomorrow, he <u>will have already gone</u> to the beach by the time we get to his house.

<u>Tell</u> me if you <u>see</u> anything strange.

Real future conditions can also be formed with the modal *should*. This conveys the impression that the action in the *if* clause is a little less likely (though still far more likely than it would be if the unreal present or future were used). It is also fairly formal.

If I <u>see</u> her, I will tell her. (It is very likely that I will see her.)

If I <u>should see</u> her, I will tell her. (It is a little less likely that I will see her.)

Note that the modal *will* is almost never used in an *if* clause.

Unreal Conditions

We use unreal conditions when the idea expressed in the *if* clause is impossible or unlikely.

Unreal Present/Future Conditional Sentences
The *unreal present/future condition* is one in which the action is impossible or highly doubtful in the opinion of the speaker.

If I <u>called</u> the president, he probably <u>wouldn't speak</u> to me. (But I'm not going to call the president.)

If the United States <u>won</u> the next World Cup Games, the entire world would be shocked. (But it is unlikely that the United States will win the Games.)

The time reference in this type of conditional is either to a repeated, habitual event in the present:

If you <u>studied</u> harder, I'm sure you <u>would do</u> better in school.

Or to a specific point in the future:

If I <u>called</u> the president, he probably <u>wouldn't speak</u> to me.

Note that the verb in the *if* clause is identical in form to the past and the verb form in the result clause begins with the modal *would* plus the simple form of the main verb. In reality, either the simple past or the past progressive could all be used in the *if* clause. And *would, could,* or *might* could be used in the result clause.

The following formula summarizes these different possibilities:

***IF* + simple past/past progressive, subject + *would/could/might* + simple form of the verb**

The formula is illustrated in these examples.

If the United States <u>won</u> the next World Cup Games, the entire world <u>would be</u> shocked. (It is unlikely that the United States will win the games.)

If they <u>were playing</u> instead of sleeping, their mother <u>might be</u> very angry. (But they aren't playing. They are sleeping.)

A past tense verb in an *if* clause refers to the unreal present and not the past.

Progressive forms are possible in the result clause:

If their mother <u>were working</u> now, the children <u>would probably be playing</u>. (But their mother isn't working now.)

Pay attention to the verb *be*. In the unreal present/future, it always appears in the form *were* in the *if* clause. Although in colloquial English native speakers often use *was* in the unreal present/future unreal with the first and third person, it is not considered standard for the TOEFL.

FORMAL/TOEFL: If he <u>were</u> here, I <u>would tell</u> him exactly how I feel.

FORMAL/TOEFL: I hate to think what John <u>would do</u> if he <u>were</u> president of the company.

INFORMAL: If I <u>was</u> rich, I would buy a new car.

Were + infinitive can replace an unreal present verb.

> If I <u>were to call</u> the president, he probably wouldn't speak to me.

Unreal Past Conditional Sentences

An *unreal past condition* is one in which the situation did not occur in the past. In such sentences, the speaker is imagining the past as different from the way it happened. The speaker is talking about "the way things could have been" under a different set of conditions.

> If there <u>had been</u> more time, we <u>would have finished</u> the project. (But, in reality, we didn't have more time, and we didn't finish the project.)

> My sister <u>would never have seen</u> South America if she <u>hadn't met</u> that young man from Bolivia. (But she did meet that man from Bolivia, so she has seen South America.)

In the unreal past, the verb in the *if* clause is identical in form to the past perfect (or past perfect progressive) and the verb in the result clause contains the modal *would, might,* or *could* plus the perfect auxiliary *have* plus the past participle of the main verb.

The following formula might be helpful:

***IF* + past perfect/past perfect progressive, subject + *WOULD/MIGHT/COULD* + *HAVE* + past participle.**

> If she <u>hadn't been dancing</u>, she <u>would never have broken</u> her leg.

> If we <u>had seen</u> you at the party, we <u>might have stayed</u> longer.

As with the unreal present, the result clause may contain a progressive form:

> If I <u>had taken</u> that job with so little money, I <u>would have been watching</u> every penny I spent.

Mixed Conditionals

It is possible to mix certain conditions. It is quite common, for example, to mix an unreal past *if* clause and an unreal present result clause.

> If you <u>had been born</u> in Japan, you <u>would speak</u> Japanese.

If I <u>hadn't gotten</u> into that car accident last week, I <u>would be swimming</u> in the Caribbean right now.

Omitting the Word *If*

Sometimes the word *if* can be omitted from a conditional sentence. *If* can be omitted:

> ➤ **In an unreal past condition**
> ➤ **In an unreal present condition if the main verb or auxiliary verb is *be* (*were*)**
> ➤ **In a real future condition that contains the modal *should***

If the word *if* is omitted, the subject and the auxiliary are reversed, and the sentence begins with a verb.

If <u>he had called</u> me, I would not have been so angry.
<u>Had he called</u> me, I would not have been so angry.

If <u>it were</u> sunny today, I would gladly volunteer to go.
<u>Were it</u> sunny today, I would gladly volunteer to go.

If <u>you should need</u> help, don't hesitate to call.
<u>Should you need</u> help, don't hesitate to call.

If the word *if* is omitted from a clause in the negative, the word *not* is separated from the auxiliary and placed before the main verb. In this case, it cannot be contracted.

If <u>she hadn't called</u> me, I would never have heard the news.
<u>Had she not called me</u>, I would never have heard the news.

If <u>it weren't</u> such a long drive, I would have gone.
<u>Were it not</u> such a long drive, I would have gone.

If <u>you shouldn't manage</u> to find her, please let me know.
<u>Should you not manage</u> to find her, please let me know.

PRACTICE #3—Checking Conditional Forms and Meanings

Circle the letter of the answer that correctly answers each question.

1. If the primary candidates ----- more on the issues, the results of the election would have been quite different.

    (A) have focused
    (B) had focused
    (C) focused
    (D) were focused

2. Unless a public official ----- with the regulations, he can be removed from office at any time.

    (A) will comply
    (B) had complied
    (C) complies
    (D) complied

3. Lately, several linguists have come to the conclusion that if we ----- to model cognitive processes for language in a manner different from other mental functions, we would not have an adequate theory of language.

    (A) are
    (B) had been
    (C) will be
    (D) were

4. Several businesses would stand to lose a great deal of money if open trade agreements ----- followed.

    (A) have not been
    (B) had not being
    (C) are not being
    (D) were not being

5. Many writers ----- it very difficult to produce a coherent essay if they haven't prepared a detailed outline first.

    (A) finding
    (B) had found
    (C) find
    (D) found

6. If in fact the Warren Commission

    should have concluded that the assassination
            A
    of John Kennedy was not the result of one
                B
    man, some Americans would not have
                    C
    been surprised in the least.
         D

7. If civil rights are to benefit all Americans,
           A   B
    petty arguments and long-standing

    prejudices would have to be put aside.
           C   D

8. The NAFTA agreement <u>could</u> have been
                       A
   more far-reaching if more <u>politicians</u>
                              B
   <u>were convincing</u> of <u>its</u> worth.
        C   D

9. Had the American colonies <u>chosen</u> a
                             A
   working language <u>based</u> on population
                    B
   figures, they probably <u>would choose</u>
                          C
   German <u>as a language</u> rather than English.
          D

10. <u>Should</u> a foreign student <u>needing</u> <u>help</u>,
       A   B   C
    she <u>must</u> see the foreign student
        D
    advisor.

SESSION D: ACTIVE AND PASSIVE VOICE

In an active sentence the subject is the doer of the action and the direct object is the receiver of the action. In a passive sentence, the subject is the receiver of the action. You can get a strong idea of the structure and meaning of the passive by comparing it to an active counterpart.

ACTIVE:	*doer*	*action*	*receiver*
	John	bought	the book.
	subject	*verb*	*direct object*

PASSIVE:	*receiver*	*action*	*doer*
	The book	was bought	by John.
	subject	*verb*	*prepositional byphrase*

In this way you can see that in an active sentence, the direct object of the active counterpart has become the subject. This leads to one of the most important points to remember when dealing with the TOEFL:

A passive verb cannot have a direct object.

There is an exception to this rule. Some active verbs that take a direct object (DO) and an indirect object (IO), like *give* and *send,* may actually keep a direct object if the indirect object becomes the subject of the passive.

ACTIVE:	Mary gave <u>John</u> <u>the book</u>.
	(IO) (DO)

PASSIVE:	John was given <u>the book</u>.
	(DO)

But this is rare on the TOEFL, and the best advice to follow is the above assertion that a passive verb does not have a direct object.

The following is a list of passive forms for the various English verb tenses. The tenses in which the passive is not possible are not included.

Tense	Passive Verb Form
past perfect	had been loved
simple past	was loved
past progressive	was being loved
present progressive	has been loved
simple present	is loved
present progressive	is being loved
future perfect (will)	will have been loved
simple future (will)	will be loved
future perfect (to be going to)	is going to have been loved
simple future (to be going to)	is going to be loved

Not all verbs can be in the passive voice. Only transitive verbs (verbs that take a direct object) can be passive. Therefore, an intransitive verb must be in the active voice. (See the Grammar Review for a discussion of transitive and intransitive verbs).

There are several verbs that often cause trouble for the student learning English. *Happen, occur, seem,* and *appear* present special problems for students and can cost points on the TOEFL. It should be remembered that these verbs are never passive in form, and that some verbs are always passive, like *be born.*

An accident <u>occurred</u> on Main Street early this morning.

That man <u>appears</u> to be quite ill.

She <u>was born</u> on a cold night in January, 1889.

The verbs *happen, occur, seem,* and *appear* are always in the active voice.

PRACTICE #4—Active and Passive Voice

Circle the letter of the answer that correctly answers each question.

1. Spanish culture ----- the New World by sixteenth-century conquistadors.

    (A) was brought to
    (B) be brought to
    (C) brought to
    (D) brought

2. By the end of the year, the speed limit in many states ----- 55 miles per hour.

    (A) was reducing
    (B) had reduced to
    (C) had been reduced to
    (D) was being

3. The MPAA <u>sets</u> ratings for movies
           A
   <u>based of</u> the <u>degree</u> of violence and sexual
      B   C
   <u>explicitness</u> portrayed.
         D

4. Spending programs that <u>initiate</u>
                              A
   economic expansion <u>are typically embrace</u>
                            B
   by conservatives, <u>even</u> if these programs
                        C
   lead <u>to</u> inflation.
        D

5. Coffee <u>often drank</u> <u>from</u> a mug
            A   B
   <u>rather than</u> a cup, because a mug <u>holds</u>
        C   D
   more.

6. A <u>person's</u> sense <u>of</u> taste <u>deadens</u> by excessive
       A   B   C
   <u>seasoning</u>.
        D

7. <u>That</u> dolphins <u>were</u> once land animals
      A   B
   <u>can see</u> <u>by examining</u> their skeletal structure.
      C   D

8. The Battle of Little Bighorn also
   <u>has called</u> Custer's Last Stand and is
      A
   <u>commemorated by</u> a monument at <u>its</u>
         B   C
   Montana <u>site</u>.
           D

9. The <u>agricultural</u> <u>center</u> of the United
         A   B

States, often <u>called</u> the "breadbasket,"
           C

<u>locates</u> in Kansas and Nebraska.
   D

10. Officers of protocol in the Chinese

government <u>made</u> sure that the silverware
         A

<u>lay out</u> properly <u>at</u> the banquet <u>held</u>
   B   C   D

in honor of President Nixon.

11. <u>The course of</u> history <u>over the</u> last 50
        A   B

years <u>is being demonstrated</u> the aptness of
            C

<u>the saying</u>, "The only thing necessary for
   D

the triumph of evil is for good men to do

nothing."

P R A C T I C E   #5—Recognizing Intransitive Verbs

Circle the letter of the answer that correctly answers each question.

1. Although <u>the various cultures</u> in Africa
   A
   <u>have traditions</u> that <u>reach back</u> for
   B   C
   centuries, the names of the political states

   <u>are seemed</u> to change yearly.
   D

2. Whenever <u>elections are occurred</u> in this
   A
   country, there <u>is often</u> a candidate, as well
   B
   as a few media broadcasters, <u>who becomes</u>
   C
   an immortalized figure on <u>the landscape</u>
   D
   of American history.

3. Even though my grandparents <u>have not born</u>
   A
   in this country, <u>they feel</u> <u>more American</u>
   B   C
   than <u>many of their</u> American neighbors.
   D

4. <u>Many</u> baby boomers <u>feel that</u> a terrible
   A   B
   thing <u>is happened to</u> the moral fiber
   C
   <u>of this country</u>.
   D

5. Where he <u>was seemed to be</u> is a
   A
   question for <u>the courts</u> to determine, <u>not</u>
   B   C
   television jurors <u>like</u> you and me.
   D

Answers for Structure
Power Lesson Three

Practice #1

1.	B	6.	C
2.	C	7.	C
3.	A	8.	B
4.	B	9.	C
5.	D	10.	B

Practice #2

1.	C	6.	A
2.	A	7.	A
3.	D	8.	B
4.	C	9.	C
5.	A	10.	C

Practice #3

1.	B	6.	A
2.	C	7.	C
3.	D	8.	C
4.	D	9.	C
5.	C	10.	B

Practice #4

1.	A	7.	C
2.	C	8.	A
3.	A	9.	D
4.	B	10.	B
5.	A	11.	C
6.	C		

Practice #5

1.	D	4.	C
2.	A	5.	A
3.	A		

STRUCTURE POWER LESSON FOUR

SESSION A: USING GERUNDS AND INFINITIVES IN SENTENCES

A *gerund* is an *-ing* participle that is used as a noun.

Skydiving is dangerous, but fun.

An *infinitive* consists of *to* followed by the simple form of the verb.

But, Mom, I don't want to visit Uncle Clark!

The topic of gerunds and infinitives is very important in the study of English grammar. Listed below are some quick facts about gerunds and infinitives that will help you on the TOEFL.

Gerunds

Indicating the "Subject" of a Gerund

The gerund is formed from a verb, so very often there is a subject, or doer, of the action.

You can indicate the doer of the action with a possessive adjective or with the possessive form of a noun.

> I understand <u>your</u> wanting to leave us for a better-paying job elsewhere.

> <u>My brother's</u> losing his job meant that the family now had no source of regular income.

> Mr. Thomas justified <u>his client's</u> breaking the law to the jury.

Although it is not "TOEFL English," you should be aware that, less formally, native speakers might use simply the object pronoun or the noun to express the subject of a gerund.

> INFORMAL: I miss <u>you</u> calling me up every night.

> INFORMAL: I enjoyed <u>John</u> passing by to visit every once in a while.

With intransitive verbs, the subject may be expressed after the gerund in an *of-* phrase. This usually happens when the definite article precedes the gerund. Therefore, you may see both forms:

> <u>The children's screaming</u> was heard by everyone.

> <u>The screaming of the children</u> was heard by everyone.

Indicating the "Object" of a Gerund

The object, or receiver, of a gerund's action can follow the gerund like a direct object:

> <u>Posting notices</u> on the street is strictly forbidden.

You can also indicate the receiver of an an action with the structure:

A/the + gerund + *of* + noun

> <u>The posting of notices</u> on the street is strictly forbidden.

We saw Westminster Abbey and <u>the changing of the guards</u> at Buckingham Palace when we were in London last year.

Therefore, we may see both of the following sentence structures:

<u>Signing a contract</u> is a big step for someone as young as you.

<u>The signing of a contract</u> legally requires the presence of a witness.

You will not be tested on the difference in meaning among the various ways of expressing subjects and objects of gerunds on the TOEFL. What is important is that you be familiar with the different ways of expressing subjects and objects of gerunds, and be able to recognize correct and incorrect combinations.

Infinitives

Indicating the "Subject" of Infinitives
To show the subject, or doer, of an infinitive, we use the preposition *for* and the object case of the noun or pronoun before the infinitive.

It will be necessary <u>for him</u> to sign these papers.

I am going to pay <u>for Martha</u> to go to college.

The infinitive after certain verbs, however, does not need to be preceded by *for*. Many of these verbs are provided in List 3 of Session B of this lesson. An example of the use of such a verb is:

I asked <u>him to meet me</u> there at noon.

Indicating the "Object" of Infinitives
Objects, or receivers, of the action of an infinitive are generally expressed by placing the noun or pronoun directly after the infinitive.

I don't intend to study <u>economics</u> beyond the required 3 credits.

I challenge you to find <u>anything wrong</u> with my thesis statement.

Problems with Gerunds and Infinitives on the TOEFL

The following is a discussion of troublesome areas on the TOEFL regarding gerunds and infinitives.

Using Infinitives to Express Purpose

The TOEFL often tests the use of infinitives to express purpose. A typical question might look like the following:

> We came here ----- the beautiful beaches.
>
> (A) for visit
> (B) visiting
> (C) to visit
> (D) for visiting

The correct answer is (C), which completes the sentence with the meaning of "in order to visit." Be careful not to fall for the distractors in (A) and (D).

You can recognize an infinitive of purpose by placing *in order* in front of the word *to*. If the new sentence still "sounds good," it is an infinitive of purpose.

> Melissa hurried <u>to get</u> there on time.

> Melissa hurried <u>in order to get</u> there on time.

Other examples of the use of an infinitive to express purpose can be found in the sentences below.

> He stayed up all night <u>to study</u> for his exams.

> We worked hard <u>to finish</u> by midnight.

Using Gerunds after Prepositions

An infinitive never follows a preposition, while a gerund may.

> Try to leave quietly, <u>without waking</u> everybody in the house up.

CORRECT: I am <u>against your going</u> to Florida for spring break.
INCORRECT: I am against you to go to Florida for spring break.

See Structure Power Lesson Seven, Session A for more on prepositions.

To + Gerund

Do not be fooled by sentences where a gerund follows the preposition *to*. Many students avoid sentences such as:

He is addicted <u>to gambling.</u>

because they are more accustomed to using the simple form of a verb after the word *to*.

You should be aware that in a sentence like:

He is used <u>to living</u> in a small town.

the word *to* is a preposition, while in a sentence like:

He used <u>to live</u> in a small town.

the word *to* is part of the infinitive *to live*.

The most difficult point about gerunds and infinitives for the TOEFL is knowing which verbs take a gerund object and which verbs take an infinitive object. Session B on the following pages is dedicated to this topic.

SESSION B: LEARNING WHICH VERBS TAKE GERUND OBJECTS AND WHICH VERBS TAKE INFINITIVE OBJECTS

Deciding whether a verb requires a gerund object or an infinitive object is a special problem for students. Although it is possible to acquire native-speakerlike intuition on this grammar point, the fastest and most direct method of mastering it for the TOEFL is simply through memorization. The following lists classify many verbs according to whether they take a gerund or an infinitive. The most common verbs are boldfaced.

The lists classify verbs in four ways:

> ➤ Verbs that take a gerund
> ➤ Verbs that are followed directly by an infinitive
> ➤ Verbs that are followed by a direct object + infinitive
> ➤ **Verbs whose meaning changes depending on whether a gerund or an infinitive is used**

Some verbs take either a gerund or an infinitive, but without a significant change in meaning. These verbs are listed twice.

Learning when to use an infinitive and when to use a gerund is hard work. If you have little time before you take the TOEFL, study the boldfaced verbs in these lists instead of trying to memorize them all.

List 1: Verbs That Take a Gerund

abhor	defer	**finish**	**postpone**	**risk**
acknowledge	**delay**	**give up**	**practice**	sanction
admit	**deny**	**imagine**	**prevent**	**suggest**
advocate	detest	**involve**	**put off**	tolerate
anticipate	dread	justify	**quit**	understand
appreciate	**enjoy**	**keep**	**recommend**	urge
avoid	entail	**keep on**	relish	withhold
cannot help	escape	leave off	renounce	
commence	evade	mention	report	
consider	facilitate	**miss**	**resent**	
contemplate	fancy	necessitate	**resist**	

Here are some examples of the verbs in List 1. Note the use of the possessive adjective to indicate the subject of the gerund.

After years of marriage, <u>I've given up trying</u> to understand my husband.

The defendant <u>admitted being</u> at the scene of the crime.

The professor <u>resented his students' wearing</u> baseball caps in the classroom.

She <u>recommended our visiting</u> the campus before we enrolled there.

List 2: Verbs That Are Followed Directly by an Infinitive

arrange	condescend	**hate**	prepare	swear
ask	consent	hesitate	pretend	**tend**
attempt	**continue**	**hope**	proceed	threaten
beg	**decide**	**intend**	profess	undertake
begin	decline	**learn**	**promise**	venture
bother	**deserve**	**like**	propose	volunteer
cannot afford	desire	**love**	**refuse**	**want**
cannot bear	determine	**manage**	resolve	wish
cannot stand	dislike	**mean**	seek	
care	endeavor	neglect	**start**	
choose	**expect**	**plan**	strive	
claim	fail	**prefer**	struggle	

Here are some examples of the verbs in List 2:

> She <u>can't afford to buy</u> a new car.

> I <u>didn't mean to hurt</u> him!

> We <u>managed not to wake</u> the baby up.

Compare these examples to the verbs below from List 3, which require a direct object to come between the main verb and the infinitive.

> I <u>caution</u> you to <u>listen</u> carefully.

> We <u>got</u> John <u>to do</u> the dishes.

> The Great Depression <u>caused</u> the nation <u>to reevaluate</u> its treatment of its least fortunate citizens.

List 3: Verbs That Are Followed by a Noun + Infinitive

advise	**convince**	forbid	oblige	**tell**
allow	**dare**	**force**	**order**	tempt
ask	defy	**get**	permit	urge
beg	desire	impel	**persuade**	**want**
cause	direct	implore	prepare	warn
caution	empower	incite	**promise**	wish
challenge	enable	induce	provoke	would like
coerce	**encourage**	instruct	**remind**	would love
command	entitle	**invite**	request	
compel	entreat	motivate	**require**	
condemn	**expect**	obligate	**teach**	

The material in this session is important. You are almost certainly going to see some exercises testing the use of gerunds and infinitives on the TOEFL.

List 4: Verbs Whose Meaning Changes Depending on Whether a Gerund or an Infinitive Is Used

forget	regret	remember	stop	try

Let's deal with these five on a verb-by-verb basis.

Forget
Forget + infinitive is used when we fail to do something.

> John <u>forgot to call</u> his mother on her birthday. (John did not call his mother.)

Forget + gerund is used when we can no longer remember something that happened. This structure is not very common and is almost always in a negative or question form.

> I'll never <u>forget reading</u> *For Whom the Bell Tolls* for the first time.

Regret
Regret + infinitive is usually used with a reporting verb in the infinitive position.

I <u>regret to inform</u> you that your son has passed away.

He is, <u>I regret to say</u>, one of the most disobedient students I have ever encountered.

Regret + gerund is used when we wish something in the past hadn't happened.

Now, of course, I <u>regret not inviting</u> Larry to the party.

Even in jail, she <u>did not regret having</u> told Mary the truth.

Remember

Remember + infinitive can be said to be the opposite of *forget* + infinitive.

John forgot to call his mother on her 53rd birthday, but he <u>remembered to</u> call her on her 54th birthday.

Remember + gerund is used when we recall something that happened in the past.

As the car pulled out of the driveway, she looked back and <u>remembered arriving</u> at the house for the very first time.

Stop

Stop + infinitive expresses purpose.

On the way home, he <u>stopped to get</u> some groceries.

Stop + gerund is used when an action ends.

The traffic light changed and the cars temporarily <u>stopped making</u> so much noise.

Jimmy, <u>stop hitting</u> your sister!

Try

Try + infinitive is used when our ultimate goal is to perform the action in the infinitive position.

I <u>tried to exercise</u> more frequently, but I just didn't have the time.

I'll <u>try to do</u> better in the future.

Try + gerund is used when the action in the infinitive position is one way of reaching a different goal.

> Melanie <u>is trying to find</u> the right career for herself. She <u>has tried working</u> in an office, she<u>'s tried teaching</u>, and she<u>'s even tried managing</u> a pizza parlor. She's thinking about <u>trying to get</u> an M.B.A.

In the example above, Melanie's goal is to find a suitable career, so *try* + infinitive is used. On the other hand, she hoped to accomplish this goal by working in an office, by teaching, and by managing a pizza parlor. She is considering an M.B.A. as another way of reaching her goal. Since these actions are ways of reaching her goal, and not the goal itself, *try* + gerund is used.

PRACTICE #1—Choosing a Gerund and Infinitive Object

Circle the letter of the answer that correctly answers each question.

1. The primary symptoms of tinnitus are intermittent headaches and -----.

   (A) to ring in the ears
   (B) a ringing in the ears
   (C) in the ears ring
   (D) the ringings in ear

2. Every few years, changes in the legal profession force the American Bar Association ----- its curriculum guidelines.

   (A) rewriting
   (B) to rewrite
   (C) rewrite of
   (D) for to rewrite

3. In 1892, Dr. James Naismith invented the game of basketball ----- college students with exercise during the winter months.

   (A) provide
   (B) for providing
   (C) to have provided
   (D) to provide

4. ----- steel, iron must be alloyed with a small amount of carbon.

   (A) Forming
   (B) To form
   (C) It forms
   (D) To be formed

5. During polio epidemics, quarantines and travel restrictions were often imposed because people were terrified of ----- the disease.

   (A) to contract
   (B) contracting
   (C) contracted
   (D) having contract

6. -----, many long distance swimmers coat their bodies with an insulating layer of grease.

   (A) Against hypothermia
   (B) To guard against hypothermia
   (C) Guard against hypothermia
   (D) Guarding hypothermia against

7. During a fire, ----- may help prevent injury due to smoke inhalation.

   (A) to keep low ground
   (B) keeping low to the ground
   (C) low to the ground keeping
   (D) keeping low to the ground, that

8. Liberal politicians are very <u>dissatisfied with</u>
                                            A
   economic programs <u>that</u> control inflation
                        B
   <u>by increasing</u> unemployment so as <u>causing</u>
       C   D
   recession.

9. The IRS is understanding <u>when it comes</u>
                                A

to inadvertent errors on tax returns, but

<u>discrepancies such as</u> <u>to claim fictitious</u>
        B   C

deductions often result in indictments

<u>for tax fraud</u>.
   D

10. <u>Established by</u> California <u>for house</u> its
        A   B

<u>most</u> dangerous prisoners, Alcatraz Prison
  C

<u>was considered</u> escape-proof.
     D

SESSION C: THE FORM AND MEANING OF COMPOUND PARTICIPLES AND INFINITIVES

Students are most familiar with simple infinitives and simple participles.

He loves <u>to watch</u> a good baseball game.

He loves <u>eating</u> popcorn when he watches a baseball game.

However, in written and formal forms of English you will frequently find several compound forms of the infinitive and the participle. These forms often appear on the TOEFL.

Here is a list of all the forms of the infinitive and participle in English. A discussion of the meaning of the forms follows.

Forms of the Infinitive:

	Active	**Passive**
(simple)	to love	to be loved
(progressive)	to be loving	-----
(perfect)	to have loved	to have been loved
(perf. progressive)	to have been loving	-----

Forms of the Participle:

	Active	**Passive**
(simple)	writing	written
(progressive)	------	being written
(perfect)	having written	having been written
(perf. progressive)	having been writing	-----

Notice that there are several "missing" forms in the above charts. This is an indication that the forms do not exist, or are so extremely rare that they never appear on the TOEFL.

Compound Participles

(1) Progressive participles and infinitives indicate a continuous action.

Mario seems <u>to be sleeping</u>, so I don't want to disturb him.

The action of the progressive infinitive, *sleeping*, is happening at the same time as the action of the main verb.

(2) Passive participles and infinitives indicate a passive meaning.

> <u>Being told</u> that he would no longer receive government money, the researcher had to look for another source of support. (The researcher was told that he would no longer receive government money.)

> He loves <u>to be watched</u> when he plays baseball. (He loves it when he is watched by other people.)

(3) Perfect participles and infinitives indicate a completed action.

> <u>Having finished</u> my homework, I met my friends downtown. (First I finished my homework, then I met my friends.)

> I want <u>to have completed</u> this project when the conference begins. (I want to complete the project before the conference begins.)

You don't need to know the names of all the possible participles and infinitives, but you should be familiar with how they are formed and what they mean.

Participles and Infinitives at the Beginning of a Sentence

It is important to note that when a participle or infinitive occurs at the beginning of a sentence, it must modify the subject of the sentence.

> <u>Being used daily</u>, the telephone book next to the dictionary began to look rather old and torn up. (The telephone book—not the dictionary—was being used daily, because the telephone book is the subject of the verb *began*.)

We have already seen in Structure Power Lesson Two, Session E, that this kind of mistake is called a *dangling modifier.*

Participles or infinitives that aren't at the beginning of a sentence come after the nouns they modify.

You should give this book to the boy <u>sitting over there</u>. (The participle phrase *sitting over there* refers to the noun *boy*.)

Of course, a participle that is not part of a phrase usually comes before the noun it modifies.

I looked at the <u>dancing</u> couples.

The <u>bored</u> cat stretched himself out on the carpet and yawned.

PRACTICE #2—Checking Compound Participles and Infinitives

Circle the letter of the answer that correctly answers each question.

1. Anarchists believe that political institutions are not necessary ----- people.

   (A) to have governing
   (B) that govern
   (C) governing
   (D) to govern

2. The spacecraft, ----- by the high surface temperature of Venus, stopped transmitting radio signals.

   (A) to be melted
   (B) having been melted
   (C) having melted
   (D) to melt

3. <u>Having been decay</u> in a damp attic for
             A
   years, the Van Gogh <u>painting</u> requires
                            B
   <u>extensive</u> restoration before it can be
      C
   <u>exhibited</u>.
      D

4. <u>The phonograph</u> was hailed as one of the
      A
   greatest inventions, <u>having make</u> it possible
                            B
   <u>to enjoy</u> a recording <u>for</u> a lifetime.
      C   D

5. Until the <u>invention of</u> the telephone,
                A
   <u>skyscrapers</u> were not <u>consider</u> very
      B   C
   <u>practical.</u>
      D

6. The essay <u>is</u> a flexible literary form
                A
   <u>being allowed</u> writers freedom in <u>their</u>
      B   C
   choice of subject, <u>composition</u> and style.
                            D

7. For those plants to <u>withstood</u> <u>their</u> dry
                            A   B
   environment, <u>they</u> <u>must</u> have conserved
                   C   D
   water incredibly efficiently.

8. In 1903, Orville and Wilbur Wright
   finally <u>constructed</u> an <u>airplane</u>
                A   B
   <u>having based</u> on calculations they had
      C
   been <u>making</u> for years.
           D

9. To have <u>clear</u> all the snow <u>from</u> the streets,
          A   B

   additional snowplow drivers must have

   <u>been hired</u> by the sanitation <u>department</u>.
      C   D

10. The fans will be <u>thrilled</u> to <u>see</u> the rock
                   A   B

    concert, although not to <u>be stand</u>
                           C

    outdoors in <u>the cold</u>.
               D

SESSION D: THE DIFFERENCE BETWEEN DO AND MAKE

Do and *make* must be carefully distinguished for the TOEFL.

Generally speaking, *make* means to create something new:

> The chef <u>made</u> a wonderful salad from romaine lettuce.

Do generally means to manipulate something that is already created:

> The children <u>did</u> the exercise with little difficulty.

Usually, this distinction is quite subtle and difficult for the nonnative speaker to grasp. There are also several obvious exceptions. For these reasons, it may be best to learn phrases with *do* or *make* individually.

Some of the most common phrasal verbs and expressions with *do* or *make* can be found in the following lists. A good dictionary will give you still more examples of these usages, as well as provide you with even more phrasal verbs and expressions that are not included on these lists.

Idiomatic Expressions with *Make:*

Example	Meaning
Her story <u>made me</u> sad.	I felt sad after I heard her story.
He always <u>makes us</u> laugh.	We always laugh when we are with him.
He promised to <u>make her</u> a star.	He promised that she would become a movie star because of his effort.
Am I <u>making myself understood</u>?	Am I speaking clearly (OR understandably)?
Bob <u>made $100,000</u> last year.	Bob earned over $100,000 last year.
I need to <u>make some money</u>.	I need to earn some money.
He <u>makes friends</u> very easily.	He finds new friends easily.
This house <u>is made of</u> brick.	This house was built with brick.
Do you want me to <u>make some coffee</u>?	Do you want me to prepare some coffee?
Don't <u>make a mistake</u> by acting too quickly.	It might be a mistake if you act too quickly.

He'll <u>make a good</u> father someday.

He will be a good father someday.

Can you <u>make it to</u> the party?

Can you come to the party?

<u>I finally made it!</u>

It wasn't easy (OR there was some problem), but I've arrived!

<u>Make believe that</u> you are alone on a desert island.

Imagine that you are alone on a desert island.

We'll just have to <u>make do with</u> what we have.

We'll have to manage (OR live our lives) with the few things that we have.

Phrasal Verbs with *Make:*

Example

He <u>made for</u> the door.

Meaning

He went to the door in a hurry.

What do you <u>make of</u> her story?

What is your opinion of her story?

The tall man <u>made off with</u> the diamonds.

The tall man stole the diamonds and took them with him.

I couldn't <u>make out</u> what they were saying.

I couldn't understand what they were saying.

She looked, but in the darkness she couldn't <u>make out</u> where her brother was hiding.

She looked, but in the darkness she couldn't see where her brother was hiding.

Women <u>make up</u> only 13 percent of the executive staff.

Only 13 percent of the executive staff are women.

He <u>made</u> that story <u>up</u>.

He invented that story.

Can we <u>make up</u> for lost time?

Can we do something to regain the time that we have lost?

We finally <u>made up</u> after three years.

We finally became friends again after the quarrel we had three years ago.

I promise I will <u>make it up to you</u> somehow.	I promise I will repay you for the favor you have done for me (OR repay you for the problem I have caused you).
<u>Make up your mind</u>!	Make a decision!

Idiomatic Expressions with *Do:*

Example	**Meaning**
I couldn't <u>get</u> any work <u>done</u> today.	I didn't complete much work today.
They refused to <u>do anything about</u> his problem.	They refused to help him with his problem.
It'll <u>do you a lot of good</u> to rest.	You badly need to rest.
You don't realize what liquor <u>does to</u> you.	You don't realize how badly you behave when you drink. (OR: You don't realize how much liquor is hurting you.)
<u>What do you do</u>?	What's your job?
<u>How do you do</u>?	It's nice to meet you. (A formal way of saying "hello" when you meet someone for the first time.)
What did you <u>do with</u> my book?	I can't find my book, and I think you put it someplace.
Okay, <u>that will do</u>!	That's enough!
She <u>did well for herself</u>.	Her life was (OR is) very successful.
<u>What do you think you're doing</u>?	I don't like what you are doing.
He has to have a Porsche. No other car <u>will do</u>.	He has to have a Porsche. No other car will satisfy him.
<u>That won't do</u>.	That is not satisfactory.
<u>Just do it</u>!	Don't hesitate, don't think—take action!

Phrasal Verbs with *Do:*

Example	**Meaning**
We must <u>do away with</u> racism.	We must eliminate racism.
She <u>did away with</u> her husband.	She killed her husband.
His work was so bad that I had to ask him to <u>do it over</u>.	His work was so bad that I had to ask him to redo it (OR ask him to do it again).
If I had the chance to <u>do it over</u>, I never would have taken that job in the first place.	If I could relive that moment (OR live that moment again), I never would have taken that job in the first place.
You'll just have to <u>do without</u> a brand new computer.	You will have to manage (OR survive) with out a brand new computer.
What does this <u>have to do with</u> you?	How does this concern (OR relate to) you?
But what you're saying <u>has nothing to do with</u> the issue.	But what you're saying is not related to the issue.

PRACTICE #3—Choosing Between *Do* and *Make*

Circle the letter of the answer that correctly answers each question.

1. ----- an aerobic exercise for 20 minutes a day will strengthen your heart and get rid of excess fat.

   (A) Do
   (B) Make
   (C) Making
   (D) Doing

2. Betsy Ross was certainly a seamstress, but she may or may not ----- the first American flag.

   (A) making
   (B) have made
   (C) done
   (D) have done

3. The capacity to recognize syntax and
                     A

   to do words into intelligible sentences
    B   C

   seems to be a genetic trait that exists

   only in humans.
       D

4. Alexis de Tocqueville did many trips to
                    A

   the United States, during which he wrote
                B   C

   essays on the state of American democracy.
                 D

5. According to many scientists, the release
     A   B   C

   of man-made chemicals into the atmosphere

   has made much damage to the fragile
    D

   ozone layer.

6. Lip reading is a skill in which a person ----- words just by observing the movement of a speaker's mouth.

   (A) does with
   (B) does out
   (C) makes out
   (D) makes with

7. Unless we can find a better solution for ----- with nuclear waste, scientists fear that future generations on this planet will have difficulty finding clean drinking water.

   (A) making up
   (B) doing away
   (C) make up
   (D) do away

8. For students who have trouble making out
     A   B

   their mind about a major in college, most

   schools have an undergraduate classification
              C

   simply called "undecided."
         D

9. A person <u>which</u> kidneys have failed
　　　　　　A
cannot <u>do without</u> the medical <u>treatment</u>
　　　　　B　　　　　　　　　　C
<u>known</u> as dialysis.
　D

10. A publishing formatter's job is <u>to do</u> a
　　　　　　　　　　　　　　　　　A
clear design so that the layout <u>of a page</u>
　　　　　　　　　　　　　　　　B
supports <u>the development</u> <u>and</u> purpose of
　　　　　　　　C　　　　　　　D
a text.

Answers for Structure
Power Lesson Four

Practice #1		Practice #2		Practice #3	
1. B	6. B	1. D	6. B	1. D	6. C
2. B	7. B	2. B	7. A	2. B	7. B
3. D	8. D	3. A	8. C	3. B	8. B
4. B	9. C	4. B	9. A	4. A	9. A
5. B	10. B	5. D	10. C	5. D	10. A

STRUCTURE POWER LESSON FIVE

SESSION A: INVERSION AFTER INITIAL NEGATIVES AND OTHER STRUCTURES

Normally the words in an English sentence appear in subject-verb-object order. Beginning learners of English quickly learn that this pattern changes to verb-subject-object for most questions. More advanced learners must learn that there are other times when the usual word order changes to verb-subject-object or even object-verb-subject. This change of word order is called *inversion*. In addition to questions, inversion can take place when a sentence begins with any of the following:

> ➤ Some negative expressions
> ➤ Some near-negative expressions
> ➤ *Only, such,* and *so*
> ➤ *Here* and *there*
> ➤ Some other expressions of location

Inversion after Negatives and Near-Negatives

In formal or written English, a negative or a near-negative expression may be placed at the beginning of a sentence. Doing this requires subject-auxiliary inversion.

Negative expressions include:

no	not
never	none

Near-negative expressions include:

barely	hardly	seldom
rarely	little	scarcely
almost never		

Look at the following examples. The first sentence of each pair has the negative expression in its normal position in the sentence. The second sentence shows the negative expression moved to the first or initial position of the sentence.

> <u>He had</u> never gone there alone before.
> Never <u>had he</u> gone there alone before.

> <u>They could</u> not see a single ship.
> Not a single ship <u>could they</u> see.

Note that in the first pair the subject *he* and the auxiliary *had* have changed positions, while the main verb *gone* does not move. In the second pair the subject *they* and the auxiliary *could* (a modal verb) reverse positions.

The example below shows that forms of the verb *be* change in exactly the same way.

> <u>They were</u> scarcely able to hear the music.
> Scarcely <u>were they</u> able to hear the music.

If there is no auxiliary verb, then *do, does* or *did* is placed before the subject and the verb is used in the simple form. This resembles the way a question is constructed in English.

<u>The enemy had</u> no chance of winning the battle.
No chance <u>did the enemy have</u> of winning the battle.

<u>They know</u> little about their son's affairs.
Little <u>do they know</u> about their son's affairs.

It is important to remember that inversion is used only when the negative or near-negative refers to a part of the sentence other than the subject.

<u>Not a single ship</u> did they see. (*A single ship* is the direct object.)

<u>Never</u> had he gone there alone before. (*Never* is an adverb.)

<u>Little</u> do they know about their son's affairs. (Here, *little* functions as an adverb.)

Compare these sentences to the following sentences, in which the negative or near-negative refers to the subject of the sentence, so that no inversion is used.

<u>Little water</u> can be found in the desert.

<u>Not a single ship</u> was found.

<u>No human being</u> can learn in that kind of situation.

Inversion after *Only, Such,* and *So*

When an expression containing *only, such,* or *so* is placed at the beginning of a clause, the normal subject-verb order is changed in exactly the same way as in sentences beginning with negatives and near-negatives.

<u>I have</u> been to Argentina only once.
Only once <u>have I</u> been to Argentina.

<u>He was</u> so hungry that he ate nonstop for three whole hours.
So hungry <u>was he</u> that he ate nonstop for three whole hours.

> The falling pots made such a clamor that the noise woke the sleeping baby.
> Such a clamor did the falling pots make that the noise woke the sleeping baby.

Note that, again, when the expression refers to the subject of the sentence, no inversion takes place.

> Only John was awake.

> So many people came to the party that we ran out of food.

Inversion after *Here* and *There*

In both formal and informal English, if a sentence begins with *here* or *there,* the subject and object are inverted. The rules of this type of inversion are different from those of the type of inversion you have seen so far, however. After *here* and *there,* the entire verb—not just the auxiliary—changes positions with the subject.

Usually this kind of structure is limited to the verbs *be, go,* and *come.* In literary English, other verbs are possible.

> There are your books.

> Here comes Mary.

> There goes Thomas.

> Here lies Wilfred B. Owen (an expression used on gravestones).

If a pronoun is used instead of a noun, no inversion occurs.

> There they are.

> Here she comes.

> There he goes.

Inversion after Other Expressions of Location

Inversion can also take place after prepositional phrases which express location. There are two cases: when inversion is optional, and when inversion is necessary.

When Inversion Is Optional

The verbs usually used in this type of structure are: *be located, be situated, hang, lie* (in the sense of "to lie in bed"), *rise,* and *stand.* In this case, the entire verb—not simply the auxiliary—changes position with the subject.

Over the top of the hill <u>stands the oldest house</u> in the entire area.

On the top of the mountain <u>is located the cabin</u> where my father was born.

In the closet <u>hung a number of dresses</u> from the 1920s.

Across the front yard <u>lay the old oak tree.</u>

Unlike the other structures that use inversion, this structure is usually optional. That is, inversion is usually not necessary.

In the closet <u>a number of dresses</u> were hung.

Across the front yard <u>the old oak tree lay.</u>

When Inversion Is Necessary

Sometimes inversion is necessary with the verb *be.* Inversion is necessary when the prepositional phrase is needed to make the sentence complete.

A golden pen was on his desk.

In this sentence, the prepositional phrase *on his desk* is needed. In other words, *a golden pen was* is not a complete sentence. Therefore, if you want to begin the sentence with the prepositional phrase, you must use inversion.

On his desk <u>was a golden pen.</u>

In the next sentence, however, the prepositional phrase is not needed.

The grass is always greener on the other side of the fence.

The grass is always greener forms a complete sentence by itself. In this case, inversion cannot be used if the sentence starts with the prepositional phrase.

CORRECT: On the other side of the fence, <u>the grass is</u> always greener.

INCORRECT: On the other side of the fence is the grass always greener.

PRACTICE #1—Inversion after Initial Negatives and Other Structures

Circle the letter of the answer that correctly answers each question.

1. ----- that climbers can only take a couple of steps per minute as they near the summit.
   - (A) The height Mount Everest is
   - (B) How high Mount Everest is
   - (C) Mount Everest is high
   - (D) So high is Mount Everest

2. Off the coast of North Carolina -----, a popular summer resort area.
   - (A) lie the Barrier Islands
   - (B) the Barrier Islands lie there
   - (C) around the Barrier Islands
   - (D) there lie the Barrier Islands

3. Not until a frog develops lungs ----- the water and live on the land.
   - (A) that it leaves
   - (B) it leaves
   - (C) leaves it
   - (D) does it leave

4. Only after they are identified as nontoxic ----- be eaten.
   - (A) should wild mushrooms
   - (B) wild mushrooms should
   - (C) when wild mushrooms should
   - (D) then should wild mushrooms

5. ----- Mary Ann Shadd famous for helping escaped slaves, she was also the first African Canadian woman to establish a newspaper.
   - (A) Was only not
   - (B) Not only was
   - (C) Was not only
   - (D) Not only

6. Such a <u>weak case</u> the Warren Commission

　　　　　　A
   <u>did</u> make that <u>many still believe</u> in a

B　　　　　　　　C
   government conspiracy <u>in the assassination of</u>

　　　　　　　　　　　　　D
   President Kennedy.

7. Down the street <u>did live</u> the man and his

　　　　　　　A
   wife <u>without</u> anyone suspecting that

　　　B
   <u>they were really</u> spies <u>for a foreign power</u>.

　　C　　　　　　　　D

8. Hardly ever <u>there have</u> been so many

　　　　　　A
   choices <u>for young</u> people <u>entering</u> the

　　　　B　　　　　　C
   work force <u>as there are</u> today.

　　　　　D

9. Rarely <u>did he speak</u> a word <u>about</u> the
          A   B
young <u>woman lives</u> in a hospital in the
          C
<u>state's capital</u>.
    D

10. <u>Through</u> the highway <u>stood</u> the <u>elderly</u>
     A   B   C
couple <u>for many</u> hours.
      D

SESSION B: WORD ORDER IN DEPENDENT CLAUSES BEGINNING WITH *WH*- WORDS

Dependent clauses that begin with a *wh-* word (*who, what, where, when, how, why*) present a special problem. These clauses begin with question words, but they do not have the question word order. They also differ from questions in that they do not use the auxiliaries *do, does,* and *did.*

The examples below illustrate this fundamental difference between *wh-* clauses and questions.

QUESTION: What   <u>is</u>   <u>your name?</u>
                              VERB   SUBJECT

DEPENDENT   I asked you what   <u>your name</u>   <u>is.</u>
CLAUSE: SUBJECT   VERB

QUESTION: Whom   <u>did</u>   <u>you</u>   <u>speak</u>   to at the party?
                              AUX.   SUBJECT   MAIN VERB
                              VERB

DEPENDENT   He insisted on knowing whom   <u>you</u>   <u>spoke</u>   to.
CLAUSE: SUBJECT   VERB

QUESTION: Whom   <u>did</u>   <u>you</u>   <u>see?</u>
                              AUX.   SUBJECT   MAIN VERB
                              VERB

DEPENDENT   The man whom   <u>you</u>   <u>saw</u>   is my father.
CLAUSE: SUBJECT VERB

> **The presence or absence of a question mark can tell you whether a sentence is a true question or whether it is really a dependent clause beginning with a question word.**

PRACTICE #2—Word Order in Dependent Clauses Beginning with *Wh-* Words

Circle the letter of the answer that correctly answers each question.

1. Public transportation vehicles are what ----- as a chief cause of the deterioration of the ozone.

    (A) have identified many ecologists
    (B) have many ecologists identified
    (C) many ecologists have identified
    (D) have many identified ecologists

2. The number of Hispanic children enrolled in the New York Public School System in the year 2000 depends on whether ----- to rise.

    (A) will the immigration rate continue
    (B) continue the immigration rate
    (C) the immigration rate will continue
    (D) will continue the immigration rate

3. What ----- look like when they are children can be radically different from the way they look as adults.

    (A) people
    (B) do people
    (C) people did
    (D) do

4. George Burns was a comedian whom many Americans ----- first on television in the 1950s.

    (A) watching
    (B) did watch
    (C) watched
    (D) watch

5. To the foreign observer, it was never actually clear ----- the power in many governments of the old Eastern Block.

    (A) whom had
    (B) who had
    (C) who did have
    (D) who do have

6. The Democratic Party has guaranteed the
                                        A
   U.S. military that it will continue to
                  B   C
   receive whatever funds it does need.
                                   D

7. The world community is shocked by what
                   A   B
   has been happening in America
       C   D
   Midwest.

8. George Washington doubted <u>whether should</u>
                                              A
   any man <u>serve more</u> <u>than</u> one
                    B   C
   term <u>as president</u>.
              D

9. How <u>does a person get</u> money matters
                A
   <u>as much as</u> the quantity <u>of money</u> he <u>gets</u>.
        B   C   D

10. Jacqueline Kennedy Onassis, <u>whom</u>
                                          A
    <u>did America love</u> very much, <u>was most</u>
              B   C
    famous for her regal demeanor and rigid

    allegiance <u>to</u> a private family life.
                   D

SESSION C: PARALLEL STRUCTURE

Parallel structure is probably one of the most easily recognized and therefore most easily avoided mistakes on the TOEFL. The rule of parallel structure states that coordinate conjunctions must join structures of the same type.

Using Coordinate Conjunctions (*and, but, or,* and *yet*)

Look at the following example:

> The issue is too <u>large</u> and <u>complicated</u> to be solved in one meeting.

In the example above, you can see that the adjective *large* is on one side of the conjunction *and*. Another adjective, *complicated,* is on the other side. The adjectives are therefore parallel structures.

INCORRECT: On the weekend, I like playing tennis, hiking, and to take my dog for walks.

This sentence is not considered grammatically correct because the three structures linked by the word and are not of the same type: *playing* and *hiking* are gerunds, whereas *to take* is an infinitive. To make the sentence correct, change either the gerunds to infinitives, or the infinitive to a gerund.

The coordinate conjunctions that involve parallel structure are: *and, but* and *or.* These conjunctions can link any part of speech as well as phrases and even entire clauses. See the examples below.

VERBS LINKED: I would like to <u>visit</u> but not <u>live in</u> New York City.

Notice that the word *to* precedes both *visit* and *live in,* so they are parallel structures. The following sentence is also correct:

> I would like <u>to visit</u> but not <u>to live in</u> New York City.

ADVERBS LINKED: You can travel <u>comfortably</u>, <u>quickly</u>, or <u>safely</u>, but never all three at the same time.

PREPOSITIONAL
PHRASES LINKED: You can get there by driving <u>around the tunnel</u> or <u>over the mountain</u>.

NOUN CLAUSES
LINKED: I know that <u>he loves her</u> but <u>she doesn't love him</u>.

Using Correlative Conjunctions

English also has a set of paired conjunctions that are called correlative conjunctions. They are *either . . . or, neither . . . nor*, and *both . . . and.* Correlative conjunctions add emphasis when they are used.

Like coordinate conjunctions, structures linked by correlative conjunctions must be in parallel structure.

NOUNS LINKED:	Both <u>mother</u> and <u>daughter</u> have beautiful black hair.
VERBS LINKED:	One can either <u>see</u> or <u>hear</u> if there is a problem with the car.
ADJECTIVES LINKED:	The speech is neither <u>too long</u> nor <u>too boring</u>.

In the last example above, the word *too* comes before both adjectives. If only one *too* were used, the structures would no longer be parallel, and therefore the sentence would be incorrect.

Using *Than* and *Not*

Note also that *than* and sometimes *not* also follow the rule of parallel structure:

VERBS LINKED:	I would rather <u>die</u> than <u>hurt</u> a single hair on her head.
NOUNS LINKED:	It was the <u>roller coaster</u>, not <u>the popcorn</u>, that made me sick!

The TOEFL often tests parallel structure in the following way:

The <u>presidential</u> committee will both recommend
     A
<u>the new</u> proposal <u>or</u> make improvements in the
  B   C
<u>existing</u> one.
   D

Naturally, (C) is the correct choice here because the correlative conjunction is made up of *both . . . and,* never *both . . . or.* The correlatives, in the pairs given above, are the only possible combinations.

PRACTICE #3—Parallel Structure

Circle the letter of the answer that correctly answers each question.

1. This operating system has become popular because it gives the user the ability to multitask and ----- the computer in a more intuitive way.

   (A) operating
   (B) to operate
   (C) the operation of
   (D) to the operation of

2. For centuries scientists have sought to discover when the universe was created and -----.

   (A) if began the evolutionary process
   (B) beginning with the evolutionary process
   (C) have begun with evolutionary process
   (D) what began the evolutionary process

3. A successful triathlete must be a strong swimmer, -----, and an excellent cyclist.

   (A) long distance runner very capable
   (B) running very capably long distance
   (C) a very capable long distance runner
   (D) a runner very capable long distance

4. Jared Ingersoll was a candidate for vice president in 1812, signed the Constitution, and twice ----- in the Continental Congress.

   (A) to serve
   (B) served
   (C) a member
   (D) serving

5. In short bursts, both a cheetah or a jaguar
                                                     A
   can run 60 miles an hour, much faster
                        B
   than any other land animal.
          C   D

6. A poem written in iambic pentameter
       A   B
   must have both a particular stress pattern
      C
   or the proper number of syllables per line.
   D

7. An ordinary household oven may be used
               A   B
   to broil, bake, fried, or roast many types
            C   D
   of food.

8. The kangaroo has <u>been called</u> an
                         A
   overgrown rabbit that <u>walks on</u> <u>two feet</u>
                            B   C
   and <u>raising</u> its young in a pocket.
        D

9. <u>Either the English novelist</u> George Eliot
                  A
   and the French novelist George Sand

   <u>are</u> <u>celebrated women</u> of the 19th century
    B   C
   <u>who</u> used male pseudonyms.
    D

Session D: Comparative and Superlative Adverbs and Adjectives

Comparatives and superlatives are tested on the TOEFL in two ways: first, according to whether the form is correct, and, second, according to whether the comparative or the superlative is used correctly.

For this reason, Session D concentrates on the form and usage of comparatives and superlatives. Remember, an adjective is used to describe a noun, while an adverb is used to describe a verb, an adjective, or another adverb.

> **When a comparison is made between two things, the adjective or adverb takes an -er ending or has the word *more* preceding it.**

Forms of the Comparative

-Er **is used for:**

(1) adjectives of one syllable (that are not past participles—see below):

big	bigger	white	whiter

(2) one-syllable adverbs that do not end in *-ly:*

hard	harder	fast	faster

(3) two-syllable adjectives ending in *-y* or *-ple*:

sunny	sunnier	simple	simpler

(4) a few other common adjectives:

stupid	stupider/more stupid
quiet	quieter/more quiet
handsome	handsomer/more handsome

Either *-er* or *more* is used for:

(1) two-syllable adjectives ending in *-ly, -er,* or *-ow:*

friendly	friendlier/more friendly
clever	cleverer/more clever
narrow	narrower/more narrow

More **is used for:**

(1) other adjectives that have two or more syllables:

useful	more useful
loathsome	more loathsome
interesting	more interesting

(2) participles used as adjectives:

bored	more bored
tired	more tired

(3) adverbs ending in *-ly:*

quickly	more quickly
happily	more happily
softly	more softly

Irregular comparative forms:

good	better (adjective)
well	better (adverb)
far	farther (adjective and adverb)
bad	worse (adjective and adverb)

As you will see, the rules for forming the comparative are the same as the rules for forming the superlative. Therefore, making the effort to learn them will pay off in two ways.

Usage of the Comparative

The comparative form is used to compare two things. It is often followed by the word *than*.

Allen writes <u>faster than</u> I write.

He has seen that movie <u>more often than</u> they have seen it.

Note that after the word *than,* a clause is used. If the verb and complement are the same in both clauses of the sentence, the *than*-clause can be reduced in two ways.

(1) The verb and complement can be reduced to an auxiliary.

Allen writes faster than I <u>do</u>.

He has seen that movie more often than they <u>have</u>.

(2) The verb can be completely omitted so that only the subject is used. In this case, one should be sure to use the subject form of the pronoun.

Allen writes faster than <u>I</u>.

He has seen that movie more times than <u>they</u>.

Forms of the Superlative

When a comparison is made of three or more things, the adjective or adverb takes an *-est* ending or has the word *most* preceding it.

Generally, *-est* is used in the superlative wherever *-er* is used in the comparative.

big	bigger	biggest
sunny	sunnier	sunniest
fast	faster	fastest
clever	cleverer	cleverest

The word *most* precedes the adjective wherever *more* is used in the comparative.

interesting	more interesting	most interesting
quickly	more quickly	most quickly
bored	more bored	most bored

Adjectives and adverbs that are irregular in the comparative are also irregular in the superlative.

good	better	best
well	better	best
far	farther	farthest
bad	worse	worst

Usage of the Superlative

The superlative is used to compare three or more things. It is almost always preceded by the definite article *the*.

> The Cadillac is <u>the biggest</u> car that we have.

> He was talking to <u>the most gorgeous</u> woman I have ever seen.

Equal Comparisons

To say that things are equal in terms of a certain adjectival or adverbial quality, English uses this formula:

As + adjective/adverb + *as*

> **ADJECTIVE:**   Marcia is <u>as</u> lucky <u>as</u> I am lucky.

> **ADVERB:**   Few authors today write as well as Graham Greene did.

Note that after the second *as*, a clause is used. If the verb and complement are the same after the word *as*, this clause can be reduced in two ways.

(1) The verb can be reduced to an auxiliary.

> Marcia is as lucky as I <u>am</u>.

> Bill Rogers drives as fast as his wife <u>does</u>.

> My family has visited that area as often as yours <u>has</u>.

(2) The verb can be completely omitted so that only the subject is used. In this case, one should be sure to use the subject form of the pronoun.

Marcia is as lucky as <u>I</u>.

Bill Rogers drives as fast as <u>his wife.</u>

My family has visited that area as often as <u>yours</u>.

PRACTICE #4—Comparatives, Superlative Adverbs, and Adjectives

Circle the letter of the answer that correctly answers each question.

1. Eight ounces of skim milk contains ----- the same volume of regular milk.

   (A) more than protein as
   (B) more protein than
   (C) more protein as
   (D) as more protein

2. The mass of insects on Earth is ----- all other land animals combined.

   (A) greater than that of
   (B) as large as
   (C) more greater
   (D) broader than the one of

3. Everest being the highest, K2 is ----- mountain peak in the world.

   (A) the second of the
   (B) of the second highest
   (C) the second highest of the level
   (D) the second highest

4. ----- on an airplane's wings, the less the resistance on the craft and the greater its fuel efficiency.

   (A) The smaller the amount drag
   (B) The smaller drag
   (C) If the smaller the amount of drag
   (D) The smaller the amount of drag

5. Humans reach physical maturity more slowly than -----.

   (A) most other large mammals were
   (B) most other large mammals
   (C) does most other large mammals
   (D) the most other large mammals

6. Though they travel ----- Central America, the swallows always make a punctual return to the mission in Capistrano.

   (A) far away as
   (B) far as away
   (C) as far away as
   (D) away as far

7. The largest and powerfulest member of
   <u>A</u>   <u>B</u>
   the cat family is the tiger.
                  C   D

8. Small amounts of some minerals are just
   <u>A</u>   <u>B</u>
   so important to the human system
   C
   as vitamins are.
   D

9. <u>Fluorescent lighting</u> usually <u>does</u> not
      A   B
   provide plants with <u>too</u> much light
                        C
   <u>as they need</u>.
        D

10. <u>Of the three</u> metals, aluminium, iron, and
       A
   steel, aluminium <u>is</u> the <u>stronger</u> even
                     B   C
   though it has less <u>density</u> than the other
                         D
   two.

SESSION E: THE PARTS OF SPEECH

The TOEFL often requires you to identify an incorrect form of the word in a sentence. The mistake will often be based on the fact that the word in question is in the wrong part of speech for its grammatical use in the sentence.

To answer this type of question correctly, you need to know:

(1) What part of speech should be used in various grammatical functions
(2) What sorts of expressions are used in English

The second type of knowledge is more difficult to acquire than the first, as this example may show:

<u>Too many</u> political posters <u>litter</u> the streets <u>during</u>
   A   B   C

an <u>elective</u> year.
    D

A student who has only the first type of knowledge listed above might think that the word *elective* is correct because he or she might believe that the adjectival form of the word *election* is needed to modify the noun *year*. Sometimes this kind of reasoning will be sufficient to identify the incorrect part of the sentence.

Unfortunately, such reasoning doesn't work in this case. In English, the compound noun *election year* is always used to refer to the year in which an election is held. The expression *elective year* does not exist in this sense. Therefore, (D) is the answer.

Remember to be flexible about learning grammar. Fixed expressions, like idioms and collocations such as *election year*, are often tested on the TOEFL, but they don't always seem to follow the rules of grammar.

> **The only way to learn fixed expressions is one at a time. The vocabulary sections at the end of each lesson introduce you to many fixed expressions.**

PRACTICE #5—The Parts of Speech

Circle the letter of the answer that correctly answers each question.

1. Vermont is ----- maple syrup in the United States.

    (A) the leading producer of
    (B) the leading production of
    (C) producing leader
    (D) the produce to leader

2. Oliver Sacks, <u>author</u> of *Awakenings,*
                      A
   is <u>a</u> <u>renowned</u> brain <u>research</u>.
      B   C   D

3. <u>It</u> is only a matter of time before the
   A
   <u>population</u> of the <u>global</u> <u>doubles</u>.
        B   C   D

4. <u>Evidently</u>, scientists <u>have no yet</u> proved
        A   B
   <u>conclusively</u> that the universe <u>began with</u>
        C   D
   the Big Bang.

5. <u>Most</u> species of fish move <u>slow</u> <u>through</u>
      A   B   C
   water, <u>compared</u> to dolphins.
              D

6. A proficient <u>lecture</u> is one who can <u>both</u>
                    A   B
   stimulate <u>and</u> maintain an <u>audience's</u>
                C   D
   attention.

7. Whales, the largest <u>of all</u> <u>life</u> things,
                          A   B
   <u>require</u> an <u>enormous</u> amount of food.
      C   D

8. The ostrich, though unable to fly, is the

   <u>largest of the</u> birds, <u>sometimes</u> <u>reaching</u>
        A   B   C
   almost seven feet in <u>high</u>.
                            D

9. <u>Creator</u> of the <u>private eye</u> Philip Marlowe,
      A   B
   author Raymond Chandler <u>was</u> for several
                              C
   years an <u>employing</u> of an oil company.
                D

10. The light, <u>transportable</u> homes <u>favored by</u>
                   A   B
    the Sioux Indians arose from <u>theirs</u> need
                                    C
    to move with the <u>seasons</u> and the herds.
                        D

SESSION F: *THERE* AND *IT* AS SUBJECTS

Often in English, *there* and *it* occupy the subject position of a sentence while the real subject appears elsewhere in the sentence after the verb.

Using *There*

There is used when a noun is being introduced for the first time.

Waiter, <u>there</u> is a fly in my soup.

In this case, the waiter does not know yet that a fly is in the customer's soup. The customer is pointing out the fly to the waiter. The sentence could be rephrased in this way: "A fly exists in my soup."

It is important to remember that the word *there*, as used in this example, does not mean the same as the word *there* when used to indicate a place.

Finally, remember that the noun following the *there is/there are* construction determines whether the verb is singular or plural in form.

There <u>are five bottles</u> on the table.

There <u>has</u> been <u>a problem</u> with this car since we first bought it.

Using *It*

It is used as the subject when the subject is a long clause or phrase.

It is important <u>that all students report to the main office.</u>

In this example, the real subject is the *that* clause. In such a sentence the *it* has no meaning by itself, but simply fills in the subject spot for the real subject. The form of the verb in such sentences is always singular. Sometimes the real subject is an infinitive phrase, as in the example below:

It seems foolish <u>to complain about such things.</u>

Not just the verb *be,* but also *seem, appear,* and *take* are often used with *it.*

It seems obvious <u>that we will be late.</u>

It appears <u>that you have missed the point.</u>

It takes <u>two hours to get there.</u>

PRACTICE #6—Recognizing *There* and *It* as Subjects

Circle the letter of the answer that correctly answers each question.

1. ----- in Central Park every year to com-
   memorate John Lennon's death and to
   argue for stricter gun laws.

   (A) Huge crowds there are
   (B) There are huge crowds
   (C) That there are huge clouds
   (D) Are there huge crowds

2. In the cells of the common garden pea
   ----- seven pairs of chromosomes.

   (A) it is
   (B) they are
   (C) there are
   (D) there is

3. ----- many technological advances that
   have affected twentieth-century life, but
   the most far-reaching has been the introduction of the computer.

   (A) Being that there are
   (B) There being
   (C) There have been
   (D) They have been

4. Atlanta, Georgia is a city where -----
   recently.

   (A) there a lot of media attention
   (B) there a lot of media attention has
   (C) there has been a lot of media atten-
       tion
   (D) there a lot of media attention has
       been

5. Although ----- more than 40 presidents in
   the United States over the last 200 years,
   Americans can seldom remember more
   than 15 at any given time.

   (A) there have been
   (B) there has been
   (C) has been
   (D) have been

6. ----- scandalous that in spite of the clear
   evidence, the destruction of the world's
   rain forests continues.

   (A) They are
   (B) There are
   (C) It is
   (D) There is

7. There are recent studies indicating that the
        A
   average height of Americans, which has
                                      B
   been increasing for decades, may be reaching
                                    C
   its maximal.
        D

8. They are necessary to have a solid plan
        A   B
   and financial backing before launching
                 C   D
   any private business.

9. <u>Over the past</u> several decades, <u>there have</u>
      A   B

been a steady and recurrent cycle

<u>in the predominant</u> economic <u>forecast</u> for
          C   D

first world countries.

10. <u>Despite</u> all of the research, <u>it is</u> still
     A   B

<u>not certain</u> that we will <u>never</u> have an
    C   D

AIDS vaccine.

11. <u>There are no</u> argument or proof
     A

<u>that will convince</u> most Americans that
        B

<u>paying higher</u> taxes will result in a higher
   C

standard of living <u>for everyone</u>.
                   D

Answers for Structure
Power Lesson Five

Practice #1

1. D   6. B
2. A   7. A
3. D   8. A
4. A   9. C
5. B   10. A

Practice #2

1. C   6. D
2. C   7. D
3. A   8. A
4. C   9. A
5. B   10. B

Practice #3

1. B   6. D
2. D   7. D
3. C   8. D
4. B   9. A
5. A

Practice #4

1. B   6. C
2. A   7. B
3. D   8. C
4. D   9. C
5. B   10. C

Practice #5

1. A   6. A
2. D   7. B
3. C   8. D
4. B   9. D
5. B   10. C

Practice #6

1. B   7. D
2. C   8. A
3. C   9. B
4. C   10. D
5. A   11. A
6. C

STRUCTURE POWER LESSON SIX

SESSION A: SUBJECT-VERB AGREEMENT

Singular/plural or "number" agreement is an important aspect of the English language. English is often said to be a very "redundant" language for this reason.

The <u>two</u> smartest <u>girls</u> in the class <u>were</u> chosen to win the award.

In this example sentence, there are three ways in which the subject (*girls*) is shown to be plural: (1) the adjective *two;* (2) the plural marker *-s* at the end of the noun; and (3) the verb *to be* in its plural form (*were*). In English grammar, the adjective, subject, and verb *agree* if they all indicate either a singular or plural number.

A common type of TOEFL question tests your ability to recognize agreement errors. Below is a list of some of the confusing areas in subject-verb agreement that occur on the TOEFL.

When a Subject Is Separated from the Verb by a Prepositional Phrase

When trying to determine whether a verb should be in the singular or plural form, find the subject and ignore all other words coming after it in the sentence. If the subject is singular, then the verb is singular. If the subject is plural, then the verb is plural.

The <u>problems</u> with the student <u>have</u> not yet been resolved.

The <u>cat</u> lying in the midst of hundreds of papers <u>is</u> content to doze in the afternoon sun.

The word *problems* is the subject of the first sentence, so the verb is in the plural form; the subject of the second sentence is *cat,* so the verb is in the singular form.

Using *All, Most, Some,* and *Any* + a Plural Count Noun

When these words are followed by a plural count noun, the verb is plural. This rule does not change if *of the* comes between the word and the noun.

<u>All men</u>   <u>are</u> created equal.

<u>Most</u> of the <u>notebooks</u>   <u>were</u> completed last week.

<u>Some</u> of the <u>students</u>   <u>have</u> finished.

<u>Any members of that group</u>   <u>are</u> permitted to enter the museum for free.

Using *All, Most, Some,* and *Any* + a Noncount Noun

When these words are followed by a noncount noun, the verb is singular. This rule does not change if *of the* comes between the word and the noun.

<u>All</u> of the <u>cake</u>   <u>has</u> been eaten.

<u>Some fat</u>   <u>is</u> good for you.

<u>Most car exhaust</u>   <u>contains</u> pollutants that threaten all living things.

If <u>any</u> of the <u>sugar</u>   <u>is</u> lost, you will be responsible.

For more information on noncount nouns, see the "Types of Nouns" section in the Grammar Review.

Using *None* and *Neither*

In "TOEFL English," *none* and *neither* always take a singular verb, whether followed by a plural or a noncount noun.

<u>None</u> of the dogs <u>belongs</u> to me.

<u>Neither</u> of the women <u>is</u> the one who spoke to me yesterday.

<u>None</u> of the boys <u>wants</u> to go on the field trip with the girls.

<u>Neither</u> computer <u>has</u> enough memory to run this software.

<u>None</u> of the tea in this store <u>is</u> fresh.

Note that the rule for *neither* alone is not the same for *neither . . . nor*, as the next grammar point makes clear.

> In "TOEFL English," *none* and *neither* always take singular verbs.

Using *Either . . . Or* and *Neither . . . Nor*

With these expressions, the noun that is closest to the verb determines whether the verb is singular or plural.

Neither the children nor <u>their mother</u>   <u>wants</u> to leave.

Either you or <u>I</u>   <u>am</u> going to call an end to this charade.

In the first sentence above, *their mother* is closer to the verb than *the children,* so the verb takes the third-person singular form, *wants.* In the second sentence, *I* is closer to the verb than *you,* so the verb takes the first-person singular form, *am.*

Notice the same logic in the sentences below:

Neither Eve nor <u>her children</u>   <u>want</u> to leave.

Either I or <u>you</u>   <u>are</u> going to call the police.

Note that *both . . . and* is always plural.

<u>Both my brother and I</u>   <u>are</u> interested in joining the team.

Using *Every*

Although it does not seem logical, nouns following *every* are singular, and they take singular verbs. This includes the nouns *everyone, everybody,* and *everything.*

<u>Everybody</u>   <u>is</u> going to be there!

Every man, woman, and child   has been rescued.

Every watch in the store   is on sale.

Every is always followed by a singular noun and a singular verb.

Using Singular Nouns that End in -s

There are a few nouns that end in -s that take a singular verb. These nouns often refer to countries, fields of study, activities, and diseases.

Countries: *the United States, the Philippines, the Netherlands, Wales*

The United States   doesn't have a centralized governing body for educational affairs.

Fields of study: *mathematics, classics, economics, genetics, linguistics, physics, electronics, statistics* (*Statistics,* when not referring to a field of study, is plural.)

Mathematics   was not my favorite subject in school.

The statistics   do not seem correct.

Activities: *aerobics, politics, athletics*

The politics of even a small town   is often very complicated.

Diseases: *measles, mumps, diabetes, rabies*

Measles   is a serious childhood disease if not treated properly.

Other common nouns ending in -s taking singular verbs: *news, series*

The news   was interesting.

That television series   is broadcast on Thursday nights.

> Make sure you learn the singular nouns ending in *-s* that are listed in this session. It is easy to lose points on the TOEFL because of this grammar point.

Using Collective Nouns

A noun is considered collective when it refers to a group of individuals. Most collective nouns take the singular form of the verb because the group is seen as a united whole.

The <u>committee</u>	<u>doesn't</u> have to come up with a solution until next week.
The <u>crowd</u>	<u>has</u> been standing in front of the building for almost two hours already.

Some common collective nouns are: *army, military, audience, committee, press, public, team, jury, government,* and *family.*

Remember, however, that the nouns *people* and *police* are considered plural, so they take plural verbs.

The <u>people</u>	<u>were</u> happy to see the return of their king.
The <u>police</u>	<u>are</u> here to serve and protect.

Using Expressions of Time, Distance, and Money in the Plural Form

Expressions of time, distance, and money are often seen as collective items and so take a singular verb.

<u>Two miles</u>	<u>is</u> too far to walk in this blistering sun.
<u>Sixty dollars</u>	<u>is</u> a fair price for such an old painting.
<u>Five hours</u>	<u>has</u> already passed since his surgery ended.
<u>Three days</u>	<u>is</u> too long for them to wait.

Using *the* + an Adjective as a Subject

The + an adjective takes a plural verb because it refers to a whole group of people.

The rich	are not respected by the blue-collar constituency of this area.
The educated	are at an advantage when looking for a job.
The sick	were be taken to the hospital immediately.
The unemployed	do not have to work on the weekends.

Using Adjective Clauses

The verb inside a relative clause agrees with the subject of the clause. If the subject is a relative pronoun (*who, which,* or *that*), the verb agrees with the antecedent of the pronoun.

The woman who lives there is my mother.

The subject of the verb *lives* is *who*. *Who* is singular because its antecedent—*woman*—is singular.

If the antecedent for a relative pronoun is plural, then the verb form in the adjective clause is also plural:

The women who live there are my aunts.

PRACTICE #1—Subject-Verb Agreement

Circle the letter of the answer that correctly answers each question.

1. It is natural that baby eagles ----- to their mother.

    (A) while still in the nest do submits
    (B) while still in the nest are submitted
    (C) while still in the nest submit
    (D) while still in the nest submits

2. No Supreme Court decision ------, who meet in private, have conferred on the case in question.

    (A) are ever given until the justices
    (B) are ever give until the justices
    (C) is ever given until the justices
    (D) ever gives until the justices

3. Public discussion of our international and domestic problems ----- by congressmen who are actually interested only in re-election.

    (A) is being overpoliticized
    (B) are being overpoliticized
    (C) to be overpoliticized
    (D) overly politicizes

4. The traffic laws of each state
                                A
   varies with regards to speed limit and
    B   C
   minimum driving age.
    D

5. Several strains of rice is bred
            A   B
   specifically for resistance to pests.
                 C   D

6. The Iowa Caucus, the first primary

   election in the race for the American
    A
   presidency, has traditionally been an

   accurate forecasts of who will be the
    B   C
   major parties' nominees.
              D

7. In an American presidential election, the

   most important vote come from the
        A   B
   Electoral College, not from the popular
                      C   D
   vote.

8. Popular method of treating colds include
            A   B
   taking extra vitamins, getting a lot of
          C
   sleep, and drinking plenty of liquids.
                                   D

9. The maximum recorded height <u>of the</u>
                                    A

   giant sequoia <u>of</u> Northern California, the
                B

   largest tree <u>in</u> the world, <u>reach</u> more than
           C   D

   330 feet.

10. Citrus fruits that <u>has</u> been exposed to
                A

   <u>cool temperatures</u> during maturation <u>are</u>
      B   C

   sweeter and more tender <u>than those</u> that
                       D

   have not.

11. The term *track and field* <u>refer</u> to athletic
                        A

   events that include foot <u>races</u> <u>and</u> jumping
                    B   C

   and <u>throwing events</u>.
        D

12. In spite of its <u>historical significance</u>, the
                A

   <u>library's</u> exhibit of rare books <u>are attracting</u>
     B   C

   <u>little attention</u>.
      D

13. A <u>member of</u> the citrus <u>family</u>,
      A   B

   <u>pineapple fruits</u> has an abundance of
         C

   magnesium, but <u>surprisingly</u> little vitamin C.
                 D

14. The Bering Strait, <u>which</u> <u>separate</u> the land
               A   B

   masses of Asia and North America,

   <u>was once</u> <u>probably</u> crossed by wandering
      C   D

   hunters.

15. <u>Generally</u>, a <u>perennial</u> weed is one that
      A   B

   <u>live</u> longer than two years and <u>is</u> often
   C   D

   very difficult to kill.

SESSION B: PRONOUN-ANTECEDENT AGREEMENT

The *antecedent* of a pronoun is the noun that the pronoun refers to. Possessive adjectives also have antecedents.

Here are some examples of pronouns and possessive adjectives and their antecedents.

<u>Christopher Columbus</u> first sailed to the new world in 1492, when <u>he</u> was trying to find a new route to India.

All <u>citizens</u> have the responsibility of voting in order to preserve <u>their</u> freedom through the democratic process.

For more information on pronouns, possessive adjectives, and antecedents, see the Grammar Review.

Pronouns and possessive adjectives must agree with their antecedents. This means making sure that all pronouns are correctly singular or plural depending on their antecedents. Pronouns must also agree with the gender (the sex) of their antecedents.

As mentioned in Session A, collective nouns (*family*, *committee*, etcetera) are considered singular in American English. *People* and *police* are generally plural. Pronouns and possessive adjectives referring to these nouns should agree with them according to number and gender.

A <u>family</u> will always feel a duty to protect <u>its</u> members.

The <u>committee</u> worked late into the night reviewing its policy and procedure manual.

The <u>police</u> are eager to improve <u>their</u> image in the eyes of the public.

Certain pronouns, while commonly used in the plural in informal speech, are considered singular in the more formal style of English which the TOEFL tests. For example, *everybody, everyone,* and the like are often referred to with the possessive adjective *their.* While this is acceptable for speaking, it should be avoided in more formal English and therefore, avoided on the TOEFL.

FORMAL/TOEFL: <u>Everybody</u> has to live <u>his</u> own life.
INFORMAL: <u>Everybody</u> has to live <u>their</u> own life.

Although usually the antecedent of a pronoun is introduced first and the pronoun second, in adverb clauses and phrases that occur at the beginning of a sentence, the pronoun is given before the noun to which it refers.

> During <u>his</u> eight years as president, <u>Ronald Reagan</u> held the admiration of the American people.

PRACTICE #2—Checking for Pronoun-Antecedent Agreement

Circle the letter of the answer that correctly answers each question.

1. ----- in many colleges and universities, Latin is no longer spoken as an everyday tongue.

   (A) Although they are still studied
   (B) Although he is still studied
   (C) Although this still studies
   (D) Although it is still studied

2. Most labor unions provide insurance benefits -----.

   (A) at your members
   (B) in they members
   (C) for their members
   (D) for its members

3. Many people are uncertain of ----- in difficult times.

   (A) themselves
   (B) theirselves
   (C) himself
   (D) ourselves

4. Even though the World Health Organization <u>was constituted</u> to promote
   A
   health on a <u>global</u> scale, <u>their</u> <u>efforts</u> have
   B   C   D
   remained uneven, essentially restricted by

   a lack of funding.

5. The <u>Lewis and Clark</u> expedition lost
   A
   <u>their way</u> many <u>times</u> on <u>its</u> journey across
   B   C   D
   the mountains.

6. The property insurance industry has

   <u>flourished</u> because people do not want
   A
   <u>to expose</u> <u>itself</u> to the <u>risk of</u> catastrophic
   B   C   D
   loss.

7. In <u>his</u> naturally <u>occurring</u> pure forms,
   A   B
   carbon <u>appears</u> as <u>either</u> diamond,
   C   D
   graphite, or amorphous carbon.

8. The Loch Ness monster came

   <u>into recorded history</u> <u>around</u> A.D. 565,
   A   B
   <u>when</u> Saint Columba is said to
   C
   <u>have seen itself</u> rise from the lake.
   D

9. <u>Most of</u> us are <u>unable to</u> remember the
       A   B
   <u>first few</u> years of <u>his lives</u>.
     C   D

10. A married man <u>with two</u> children
                    A
    <u>may take</u> two exemptions on <u>their</u> income
      B   C
    tax: one for <u>himself and</u> one for his wife.
             D

11. <u>Many</u> new facts about the <u>origin of man</u>
      A   B
    came to light through the <u>investigations</u>
                        C
    of Mr. Louis Leakey and <u>her wife,</u> Mary.
                     D

12. Each element <u>produces</u> <u>differently colored</u>
               A   B
    flames when <u>they are</u> exposed <u>to</u> fire.
             C   D

13. The <u>city of</u> Syracuse, New York, <u>takes</u> <u>his</u>
        A   B C
    name from an <u>ancient</u> community in
              D
    Greece.

14. A DNA molecule <u>consists of</u> <u>phosphate</u>,
                 A   B
    deoxyribose, and four different bases,
    <u>both</u> of <u>which</u> are necessary to complete a
     C   D
    DNA ladder.

15. A tug-of-war <u>pits</u> the <u>combined</u> strength
               A   B
    of one team <u>against</u> that of <u>other</u>.
             C   D

SESSION C: SINGULAR AND PLURAL NOUN USAGE

The TOEFL often tests a student's ability to recognize whether a noun should be in singular or plural form. The following rules will help you avoid some of the most common mistakes on the TOEFL.

Using *Another*

The word *another* is always followed by a singular count noun.

> <u>Another topic</u> that we will cover is the forced migration of the Cherokee from the East toward Oklahoma.

> We don't need <u>another boss</u>; we need someone who will do the work.

Keep in mind that *another* can never be preceded by a determiner (*the, a/an, this, that, my, your, his,* etcetera). See the Grammar Review for a more complete list of determiners.

Using *Few* and *a Few*

Few and *a few* are always followed by a plural.

> <u>Few people</u> have seen the Northern Lights.

> The army is looking for <u>a few</u> good <u>men</u>.

Using *Less, Much, Fewer,* and *Many*

Less and *much* are used before noncount nouns while *fewer* and *many* are used before plural-count nouns.

> There is <u>less food</u> than I thought there would be.

> We don't have <u>much work</u>, so I can meet you at 5:00.

> How <u>much gasoline</u> can I get for a dollar?

> I wish you would make <u>fewer mistakes.</u>

> There are <u>many ways</u> to deal with this challenge.

> How <u>many amoebas</u> can fit on a microscope slide?

Note also that *a lot of* can be followed by either a plural-count or a noncount noun.

<u>A lot of people</u> say he would make a great politician.

I take <u>a lot of sugar</u> in my tea.

Using *Some* and *Most*

Some and *most* are always followed by a noncount noun or a plural count noun.

<u>Some children</u> never learn to read.

If you're thirsty, drink <u>some water</u>.

<u>Most people</u> are nice, once you get to know them.

Nowadays, <u>most petroleum</u> is found deep beneath the surface of the earth.

Some of and *most of* are always followed by *the* + a noncount noun or *the* + a plural-count noun.

<u>Most of the men</u> have received their orders.

<u>Some of the food</u> has been eaten.

Using *the Majority Of*

The majority of is usually followed by a plural noun, but is sometimes found preceding a noncount noun.

<u>The majority of the pens</u> were blue.

<u>The majority of oxygen molecules</u> consist of two atoms combined.

The pesticides destroyed <u>the majority of the groundwater</u>.

Using *Every*

Every is always followed by a singular-count noun.

<u>Every book</u> was too old to read easily.

We looked at <u>every house</u> for sale in the area.

Using Numbers

The words *hundred, thousand, million,* etcetera do not have a plural *-s* when preceded by numbers greater than one (a definite number).

These words do take an *-s* when they refer to an indefinite number. In such cases the number is always followed by an *of-* phrase with a plural noun.

> I have three <u>hundred</u> CDs at home. (= exactly 300)

> The university had <u>thousands of</u> international students. (indefinite—between a thousand and ten thousand)

Using *Both*

Both, used as an adjective or a pronoun, always refers to exactly two things, so *both* is always followed by a plural noun.

> <u>Both men</u> were happy to be rescued.

Using *Between* and *Among*

Between always refers to two things. *Among* always refers to three or more things. Therefore, they always have plural nouns as their objects.

> <u>Between</u> the <u>trees</u>, there are many beautiful flowers. (two trees)

> <u>Among</u> the <u>trees</u>, there are many beautiful flowers. (three or more trees)

Every singular noncount noun must be modified by a determiner (that is, a word like *the, a/an, my, his, this, that,* and *another*). Note that this rule may be broken in certain idiomatic expressions.

PRACTICE #3—Checking for Singular and Plural Noun Usage

Circle the letter of the answer that correctly answers each question.

1. Scientists have discovered a similarity between ----- chocolate and love affect one's body chemistry.

   (A) the way
   (B) a way which
   (C) which way
   (D) the ways that

2. Real estate prices in New York, like those of many other major cities, have declined -----.

   (A) over the few years
   (B) over the past few years
   (C) over less years
   (D) over the past few year

3. ----- have amphibious attributes, although not all are amphibians.

   (A) Much quadrupeds
   (B) More quadrupeds
   (C) Many quadrupeds
   (D) A quadruped

4. The <u>development</u> of the plow was
        A
   <u>more important</u> to agriculture than
        B
   <u>any another</u> <u>technological</u> advance.
        C   D

5. <u>Less</u> tornadoes <u>have occurred</u> in Alaska
      A   B
   and Rhode Island than in <u>any other</u> <u>state</u>.
                              C   D

6. <u>The</u> Swahili language <u>is only one</u> of about
      A   B
   two <u>thousands</u> that <u>are</u> spoken on the
        C   D
   African continent.

7. Niels   Bohr,   Ernest   Rutherford,

   <u>and another</u> experimental physicists were
        A
   <u>responsible for</u> the development of
        B
   quantum <u>physics</u> <u>in</u> the early twentieth
              C   D
   century.

8. Many children <u>dislike</u> certain <u>variety of</u>
                    A   B
   vegetables <u>such as</u> peas, lima beans, and
                 C
   <u>even</u> corn.
     D

9. The most <u>renowned</u> of the <u>large</u> carnivorous
             A   B

dinosaurs, the *Tyrannosaurus rex* walked

on two <u>foot</u> and had two <u>small</u>, stunted
        C   D

arms.

10. After <u>getting</u> nominated, most candidates
       A

<u>spend</u> the rest of the election season
 B

<u>looking for</u> endorsements and making
   C

<u>speech</u>.
  D

11. <u>In some</u> <u>area</u> of the country, <u>particularly</u>
   A   B   C
New England, Lyme disease is an important

health <u>concern</u>.
      D

12. <u>Underneath</u> <u>thousands of years</u> of earth
    A   B
and dirt, undiscovered <u>treasure</u> of the <u>past</u>
                  C   D

are hidden.

13. The <u>large</u> majority of <u>Canadian</u> will
     A   B
<u>change</u> careers several times in <u>their</u> lives.
  C   D

14. Before watches <u>were</u> commonplace,
               A

<u>another</u> devices, <u>like</u> sundials and water
  B   C
clocks, were <u>used to</u> tell time.
             D

15. <u>Much</u> American Indians in California
   A
<u>lived</u> in small villages and ate <u>primarily</u>
  B   C
wild <u>plants</u>, seeds, and nuts.
    D

PRACTICE #4—Review Questions

Circle the letter of the answer that correctly answers each question.

1. Until he was president, Abraham Lincoln never admitted the power of -----.

    (A) his persuasive speaking capacity to herself
    (B) his persuasive speaking capacity to him
    (C) their persuasive speaking capacity to himself
    (D) his persuasive speaking capacity to himself

2. Although alone and undistracted in the African jungle for several years, Dian Fossey ----- her studies of the great apes.

    (A) were never completed
    (B) was never able to complete
    (C) were never able to complete
    (D) is never completing

3. What an exceptionally enduring story Mary Shelley's *Frankenstein* -----.

    (A) is turned out to be
    (B) were
    (C) have turned out to have be
    (D) has turned out to be

4. Never in his life ----- have a single day of doubt about his purpose.

    (A) did Thomas Edison
    (B) do Thomas Edison
    (C) was Thomas Edison
    (D) does Thomas Edison

5. Those who have experienced its power ----- light of the sighting of a tornado.

    (A) never makes
    (B) never making
    (C) never would make
    (D) never make

6. Drawing from ----- and unpublished work, the Noam Chomsky Readers' Series has been enormously successful.

    (A) their published
    (B) his published
    (C) published
    (D) it published

7. Pantheon Books ----- to making previously unpublished Soviet writings available to U.S. audiences.

    (A) is a publisher dedicated
    (B) is publishing dedicated
    (C) is published dedicating
    (D) it publishes dedicated

8. Stephen Hawking, along with his university professor, who ----- not teaching at the time, published his first version of chaos theory early in his career.

    (A) was
    (B) were
    (C) did
    (D) would

9. Everything that lives ----- some source of energy.

    (A) need
    (B) needs
    (C) will be needs
    (D) needing

10. The factors in vocal control beyond conscious control ----- the act of respiration.

    (A) includes
    (B) including
    (C) include
    (D) was included

11. Subject to partial or involuntary control is
    A   B   C
    the responses we call respiration,
                   D
    heartbeat, and reflex.

12. Capitalism have been inherent in Western
                  A   B
    society from ancient Egypt on.
           C   D

13. Efforts to motivate New Yorkers to recycle
    A   B
    their plastic and glass products has shown
    C   D
    great progress in recent years.

14. Of the millions of loans administered by
                              A
    the federal government, student loans to
                           B   C
    Harvard University is the most unsuccessful
                       D
    in terms of repayment.

15. .The American Indians living on the open
                         A
    plain has seen the decimation of
          B   C
    the buffalo.
    D

16. Much governments use gold as the
    A   B
    standard of their currency; other countries
             C
    differ from that in their use of silver.
                        D

17. The ghost of Ichabod Crane ride on
            A   B
    horseback with his head under his arm,
              C
    according to The Legend of Sleepy
              D
    Hollow.

18. <u>Authors</u> Mark Twain <u>was born</u> Samuel
   A   B
    Langhorne   Clemens <u>prior</u> <u>to</u> the
                          C   D
    beginning of the American Civil War.

19. <u>The development</u> of submarines <u>were</u>
         A   B
    hindered by the lack of a <u>power source</u>
                              C
    that could propel <u>an underwater</u> vessel.
                      D

20. Mistletoe, which <u>are</u> believed to
                   A
    have magic powers, <u>is</u> traditionally hung
                      B
    over <u>doorways</u> during <u>the Christmas</u> season.
         C   D

Answers for Structure
Power Lesson Six

Practice #1

1.	C	9.	D
2.	C	10.	A
3.	A	11.	A
4.	B	12.	C
5.	B	13.	C
6.	C	14.	B
7.	B	15.	C
8.	A		

Practice #2

1.	D	9.	D
2.	C	10.	C
3.	A	11.	D
4.	C	12.	C
5.	B	13.	C
6.	C	14.	C
7.	A	15.	D
8.	D		

Practice #3

1.	D	9.	C
2.	B	10.	D
3.	C	11.	B
4.	C	12.	C
5.	A	13.	B
6.	C	14.	B
7.	A	15.	A
8.	B		

Practice #4

1.	D	11.	C
2.	B	12.	A
3.	D	13.	D
4.	A	14.	D
5.	D	15.	B
6.	B	16.	A
7.	A	17.	B
8.	A	18.	A
9.	B	19.	B
10.	C	20.	A

STRUCTURE POWER LESSON SEVEN

SESSION A: PREPOSITIONS

Correct use of English prepositions can be very difficult for nonnative speakers of English. One reason for this is that, although there are sometimes rules for the use or prepositions, many prepositional phrases fall under the category of idiomatic expressions. This means that there is often no easily identifiable reason why one preposition is correct while another preposition is wrong.

Native speakers usually learn prepositions in association with other words (often a verb or an adjective). We recommend that you learn these in the same way—in *verb + preposition* or *adjective + preposition* combinations.

In this session, you will first review some rules for the use of prepositions with expressions of time. Then you will learn some verb + preposition and adjective + preposition combinations. Finally, you will learn a list of adverb clause conjunctions and prepositions that are similar in meaning but used in different ways.

Prepositions Used with Expressions of Time

Use *at* for specific times of the day:

> Sheila got up <u>at</u> 6:30. She ate lunch <u>at</u> noon.

Use *on* for days:

He'll arrive <u>on</u> June 4th.

His job forces him to travel all the time. <u>On</u> Christmas Day he was in Houston, and <u>on</u> New Year's Eve he traveled to Phoenix.

Use *in* for weeks, months, seasons, years, and centuries:

I hope to have it finished <u>in</u> the second week of September.

She was born and died <u>in</u> the same month.

What do farmers do <u>in</u> the winter?

We moved to Portugal <u>in</u> 1986.

<u>In</u> the 1700s, the horse offered the fastest means of transportation.

In English, people say *in the morning, in the afternoon,* and *in the evening,* but for the words *day* and *night, by day* and *at night* are used.

I work <u>in the morning</u> and study <u>in the afternoon</u>. <u>In the evening</u> I watch TV.

A nocturnal animal is one that does most of its activity <u>at night</u>. An animal that does most of its activity <u>by day</u> is said to be diurnal.

Some Verb + Preposition Combinations

Some verbs can take more than one preposition, but with a change in meaning. For example, *speak* and *talk* can be followed by *to* or *with* + the person being addressed, and *about* + the topic being discussed.

He spoke <u>to</u> Marilyn. He spoke <u>about</u> literature.

Sally talked <u>with</u> Howard <u>about</u> what movie they would watch.

The verbs *argue* and *quarrel* take *with* + the person being disagreed with, and *about* or *over* + the issue causing the disagreement.

My sister argued <u>with</u> my brother. She argued <u>with</u> him <u>about</u> (or <u>over</u>) politics.

The left and right wings of the party quarreled <u>with</u> each other <u>over</u> (or <u>about</u>) which side would get the most cabinet positions.

The verb *agree* takes *with* + a person, and *on* + the topic of agreement.

Terri agreed <u>with</u> Lawrence <u>on</u> where they should look for a house.

Almost all other verbs take only one preposition. A few may take more than one preposition, but have the same meaning with either one. Here are some of the verb + preposition combinations you might find on the TOEFL. As you study the list, note that some of the verbs are transitive (that is, they take a direct object), whereas others are intransitive (they have no direct object). For example:

TRANSITIVE: I <u>thanked Alfred</u> for his help.

INTRANSITIVE: Lori <u>prayed for</u> a major snowstorm on the day of the exam.

For more on transitive and intransitive verbs, see the Grammar Review.

> **As you learn verbs other than the verbs in this list, learn the preposition or prepositions that usually go with them. That will make your learning easier. You will find a good English dictionary indispensible for this task.**

Verb + Preposition Combinations:

against
react against

at
stare at
hint at

for
apologize for
blame for
excuse for
fight for
hope for
pay for
pray for
substitute for
thank for
vote for

from
distinguish from
emerge from
escape from
hide from
obtain from
prevent from
prohibit from
recover from
rescue from
stop from
suffer from

in
believe in
excel in
invest in
participate in
result in
succeed in

of
accuse of
think of

on
bet on
insist on

to
belong to
contribute to
lead to
object to
respond to

with
associate with
cover with
provide with
sympathize with

Verbs That Can Take More Than One Preposition without a Change in Meaning:

care about/care for
compare to/compare with
complain of/complain about
contribute to/contribute towards
count on/count upon
decide on/decide upon

depend on/depend upon
dream of/dream about
end in/end with
improve on/improve upon
insist on/insist upon
rely on/rely upon

There is no complete list of TOEFL verb + preposition, or adjective + preposition, combinations. As you read in English, or listen to English-language movies or television, you can improve your TOEFL score by making your own lists of combinations that are not in this session.

Some Adjective + Preposition Combinations

Like some verbs, many adjectives are usually followed by a single preposition. Here are some adjective + preposition combinations you might find on the TOEFL.

about
concerned about
confused about
excited about
worried about

against
discriminated against

for
known for
prepared for
qualified for
remembered for
responsible for

from
absent from
different from

in
dressed in
interested in
involved in

of
afraid of
aware of
capable of
composed of
conscious of
envious of
fond of
guilty of
innocent of
jealous of
proud of
scared of
terrified of
tired of

to
able to
accustomed to
addicted to
committed to
connected to
confined to
dedicated to
engaged to
equal to
exposed to
faithful to

inferior to
limited to
opposed to
polite to
related to
similar to
superior to
unrelated to
used to

with
acquainted with
annoyed with
associated with
bored with
content with
displeased with
dissatisfied with
done with
familiar with
filled with
finished with
furnished with
patient with
pleased with
satisfied with
upset with

Adjectives That Can Take More Than One Preposition without a Change in Meaning:

angry at/angry with
based on/based upon
disappointed in/disappointed with
friendly to/friendly with

made of/made from
puzzled at/puzzled by
surprised by/surprised at

As discussed in Structure Power Lesson Four, Session B, if a verb comes after a preposition, it must be in the form of a gerund. Thus:

> We're afraid of an airplane crash.
> We're afraid of <u>dying</u> in an airplane crash.

> I am annoyed with Peter.
> I am annoyed with Peter's <u>leaving</u> early.

Prepositions that Resemble Adverb Clause Subordinate Conjunctions

A few prepositions resemble or are identical in form and meaning to subordinate conjunctions that introduce adverb clauses. These deserve special attention. Column A consists of a list of subordinate adverb clause conjunctions, while Column B consists of a list of prepositions. This means that the words in Column A should be followed by a clause (subject and verb) and the words in Column B should be followed by a noun.

Subordinate Conjunctions	Prepositions
because	because of
while	during
despite the fact that	despite
in spite of the fact that	in spite of
until	until
since	since
after	after
before	before

Examples:

> <u>Because it rained</u>, the game was cancelled.
> <u>Because of rain</u>, the game was cancelled.

> <u>While he was in class</u>, he fell asleep.
> <u>During class</u>, he fell asleep.

> <u>Despite the fact that they lost money</u>, they still have hope for the future.
> <u>Despite losing money</u>, they still have hope for the future.

> <u>Since he arrived yesterday</u>, he has done nothing but complain.
> <u>Since yesterday</u>, he has done nothing but complain.

PRACTICE #1—Prepositions

Circle the letter of the answer that correctly answers each question.

1. To many old-time boxing fans, Joe Louis is still the standard ----- fighters are judged.
   - (A) on which all modern
   - (B) to which all modern
   - (C) in which all modern
   - (D) by which all modern

2. Gelatin is a protein ----- the skin, tendons, and bones of animals.
   - (A) obtained by
   - (B) obtained from
   - (C) obtained in
   - (D) obtained of

3. Actor Paul Newman received an Academy Award for Lifetime Achievement ----- dozens of popular movies over several decades.
   - (A) because acting in
   - (B) for acting in
   - (C) with acting in
   - (D) in his acting in

4. Young animals depend <u>more on</u> <u>their</u>
                                   A   B
   mother than <u>for</u> any other member <u>of</u>
                    C   D
   their family.

5. <u>Every year</u> <u>on</u> April, the nation's high
       A   B
   school seniors eagerly <u>await</u> the <u>results of</u>
                             C   D
   their college applications.

6. The fluctuation <u>of</u> the prime interest rate
                     A
   depends <u>from</u> <u>an</u> array of factors, according
                B   C
   <u>to</u> the Federal Reserve Board.
   D

7. Stephen Spielberg <u>is known</u> <u>throughout</u>
                            A   B
   the world <u>of</u> his highly successful family
                  C
   <u>films</u>.
   D

8. <u>Although</u> synthetic gemstones are superior
      A
   <u>in quality</u> <u>from</u> natural stones, people
        B   C
   seem <u>to</u> prefer natural gems.
          D

9. A carpet, as <u>opposed from</u> a rug,
                  A

   <u>completely</u> <u>covers</u> <u>a</u> floor and
        B   C

   <u>is tacked down</u>.
        D

10. <u>A</u> picture taken <u>with</u> a 35mm camera is
    A   B

    <u>very</u> different <u>of one</u> taken with a pocket
    C   D

    camera.

11. The extent <u>of which</u> the stock market
              A

    <u>is affected</u> by the <u>day-to-day</u> pronouncements
       B   C

    of the president of the United States

    <u>is astonishing</u>.
       D

12. <u>Many</u> <u>homeowners</u> <u>feel that</u> the Queen
    A   B   C

    Anne style <u>reflects of</u> the grace and beauty
                    D

    of a long-forgotten era.

13. For many years, the four-minute mile was

    <u>thought on</u> <u>as an</u> <u>unreachable</u> goal for
       A   B   C

    human <u>track</u> athletes.
              D

14. <u>A baseball</u> is <u>the oldest</u> and <u>one of</u> the
    A   B   C

    most popular <u>of</u> American professional
                     D

    sports.

15. To achieve the two-thirds majority

    <u>required to</u> override a presidential veto,
       A

    support is <u>usually</u> necessary from both
                   B

    <u>sides</u> the political <u>aisle</u>.
    C   D

SESSION B: PATTERNS WITH *LIKE* AND *ALIKE*

Most of the questions that test *like, alike, unlike,* and *not alike* on the TOEFL are based on the ability to recognize patterns in which these words appear. Although the word pairs have very similar meanings, they are used in different and very specific sentence patterns.

Like (Preposition) and *Alike* (Adjective/Adverb)

Like and *alike* both convey the idea of "the same." The difference is that *like* is a preposition, so is always followed by a noun. On the other hand, *alike* is either a predicate adjective or an adverb, which means that it always comes after the verb of the clause it is in.

Like is used in the first four sentence patterns below, and *alike* is used only in the fourth.

Like X, Y . . .

> <u>Like</u> Kate, Vicky stays out all night.

> <u>Like</u> oranges and grapefruits, lemons contain vitamin C.

X, like Y, . . .

> Kate, <u>like</u> Vicky, stays out all night.

X . . . like Y

> I don't stay out all night <u>like</u> Kate and Vicky.

> Kate is <u>like</u> Vicky.

X and Y are like each other

> Kate and Vicky are <u>like</u> each other in that both stay out all night.

X and Y . . . alike

> Kate and Vicky talk very much <u>alike</u>.

> Insofar as they both contain vitamin C, lemons and oranges are <u>alike</u>.

Like and *alike* are related in exactly the same way that *unlike* and *not alike/unalike* are related. If you understand the difference between the first pair, you understand the difference between the second.

Unlike (Preposition) and *Not Alike/Unalike* (Adjective/Adverb)

In a way similar to *like* and *alike, unlike* and *not alike* convey similar meanings but use different patterns.

Unlike X, Y . . .

> Unlike Millie, Vicky stays out all night.

> Unlike oranges and grapefruits, apples contain no vitamin C.

X, unlike Y, . . .

> Vicky, unlike Millie, stays out all night.

X . . . unlike Y

> I prefer to read at home on Friday nights, unlike Kate and Vicky.

> Oranges and grapefruits are very much unlike broccoli.

> Oranges and broccoli are unlike each other.

X and Y . . . not . . . alike/
X and Y . . . unalike

> Kate and Vicky do not look much alike.

> Lemons and broccoli are not at all alike.

> Kate and Vicky look very much unalike.

> Lemons and broccoli are completely unalike.

PRACTICE #2—Patterns with *Like* and *Alike*

Circle the letter of the answer that correctly answers each question.

1. Although similar in appearance, the tangerine and the clementine are ----- each other in taste.

   (A) not alike
   (B) unlike
   (C) like
   (D) alike

2. Early in his political career, Richard Nixon realized that the world of politics was ----- his nurturing childhood home among the Quakers.

   (A) unlike
   (B) like
   (C) not alike
   (D) alike

3. The American and the Soviet space exploration programs, even though they are reputedly opposites, are very much ----- in their empirical goals.

   (A) unlike
   (B) alike
   (C) not alike
   (D) like

4. A long-time leader in fine clockworks, Seth Thomas manufactures products that are far superior and not at all ----- its competitors' products.

   (A) unlike
   (B) like
   (C) alike
   (D) not alike

5. As she grows older, Liza Minelli looks more and more ----- her mother, Judy Garland.

   (A) alike
   (B) not alike
   (C) like
   (D) not unlike

6. <u>The accidental</u> discovery of <u>plastic</u> was
         A   B
   <u>alike</u> the accidental discovery of America
    C
   by Christopher Columbus in that both

   <u>experimenter</u> and explorer set off on one
          D
   trail and ended up in a much more

   profitable place.

7. The story <u>of</u> Christ and <u>the Tale of</u>
          A   B
Genji are <u>surprising</u> very much <u>alike</u>.
          C   D

8. <u>In his experience</u> and success <u>with</u> foreign
         A   B
policy, Jimmy Carter has <u>proven</u> to be
                        C
<u>not alike</u> Richard Nixon before him.
   D

9. <u>Because they</u> use the <u>same wire</u> services,
     A   B
UPI, AP, and Knight Ridder, <u>many</u> U.S.
                        C
newspapers run stories that are <u>like</u>.
                   D

10. <u>The reign</u> of Elizabeth I and <u>this of</u> James
      A   B
I were <u>unalike</u> even though they were
         C
<u>successive</u>.
  D

Session C: Identifying the Missing Word

On the error identification part of the TOEFL Structure Section, a word that is necessary for the grammatical correctness of a sentence is often left out.

This type of error actually requires you to use your knowledge of many other grammar points learned in this book. For example, a missing word could affect whether an adjective clause has been constructed correctly or not.

> They had <u>difficulty</u> identifying the man <u>committed</u>
>   A   B
> the crime <u>because of</u> the poor <u>lighting</u> along the
>   C   D
> street.

In the above sentence, (B) is the incorrect part of the sentence because the relative pronoun *who* is missing after *the man,* which would serve as the subject for the verb *committed.* It is your knowledge of adjective clauses that will tell you whether this is correct or not. Specifically, you will need to be able to recognize that the relative pronoun cannot be omitted in an adjective clause if it is the subject of that clause. (See Structure Power Lesson Two, Session C, where adjective clauses are discussed.)

Look at another example:

> As the surgeon <u>operated</u> the patient there <u>were</u> a
>   A   B
> number of specialists who <u>looked on</u> from the
>   C
> viewing room in order to learn <u>how to do</u> the new
>   D
> procedure.

In the above example, (A) is the incorrect part of the sentence. Your being able to recognize this really comes from your knowledge about which verbs are transitive and therefore take a direct object, and which verbs are intransitive and therefore require a preposition. (See Session A of this lesson).

Specifically, *operate* is an intransitive verb and therefore cannot take a direct object; we need the preposition *on* between the verb *operate* and the noun *the patient.* Therefore, the answer is (A).

On the error-identification part of the TOEFL, remember to look not just for a word or expression that is wrong—you must also look for underlined parts of the sentence that might be missing a word.

PRACTICE #3—Discovering Missing Words on the TOEFL

Circle the letter of the answer that correctly answers each question.

1. When we <u>are infants,</u> <u>we</u> must <u>depend</u> our
        A   B   C

   parents <u>for</u> everything.
        D

2. <u>There seldom</u> a <u>more</u> spectacular sight
       A   B

   <u>than</u> the Fourth of July fireworks <u>over</u> the
     C   D

   Statue of Liberty.

3. <u>Left</u> their own in the wild, <u>many domesticated</u>
    A   B

   animals <u>will begin</u> to behave <u>like</u> their
          C   D

   undomesticated cousins.

4. <u>The pleasures</u> of <u>life are</u> diminished <u>not</u>
       A   B   C

   shared <u>with</u> a friend.
        D

5. Robert Pirsig's *Zen and the Art of*

   Motorcycle Maintenance <u>has</u> been <u>cult</u>
                          A   B

   classic <u>now</u> <u>for more</u> than 20 years.
         C   D

6. <u>With the</u> advent of Microsoft Windows,
    A

   <u>many other software</u> makers were
            B

   <u>forced upgrade</u> their <u>own</u> products.
       C   D

7. <u>When</u> a cat, large or small, <u>raises its</u> tail,
    A   B

   <u>it is</u> normally a <u>sign greeting</u>.
    C   D

8. <u>World</u>, although once perceived <u>to be</u>
    A   B

   limitless, <u>is beginning</u> to reach <u>its</u> capacity.
         C   D

9. <u>American</u> idioms and <u>British</u> idioms
    A   B
frequently differ, <u>since two</u> languages have
                    C
<u>been evolving</u> separately for more than
    D
three hundred years.

10. <u>Once considered</u> pastime <u>of college</u>
       A   B
students, ultimate Frisbee <u>has attained</u>
                               C
worldwide <u>recognition</u> as a potential
            D
professional sport.

SESSION D: ARTICLES

The rules for the correct use of articles (*a, an, the*) in English are difficult to master, but very interesting to learn. The reason that the article system (and there really is a system) is so hard for a nonnative speaker of English to understand fully is that the correct use of articles is very closely connected to subtle differences in meaning that English speakers are trying to convey.

Fortunately, the TOEFL usually does not try to test these subtle differences in meaning. Usually the TOEFL tests articles in only a few ways. The rules in this section will help you avoid the common mistakes in article usage that the TOEFL tests.

Rule 1: All singular count nouns must be modified by a determiner.

The articles *a, an,* and *the* are determiners. Other determiners are words like *this, that, my, your, his,* and *her.* For more information on determiners, see the Grammar Review.

What this rule tells you is that a singular count word—for example, *pen*—cannot be used in a sentence without a determiner.

> This pen is red.

> Where is the pen?

> That's a strange pen.

> Someone has chewed on my favorite pen.

Keep Rule 1 in mind as you take the TOEFL—it can save you a lot of easy points.

Rule 2: *A* and *an* are used only with singular nouns.

Rule 3: An expression of a definite quantity in the singular is usually preceded by *a/an.*
Expressions of a definite quantity include *a mile, a quart, a pound, a dozen,* and *a ton.*

Rule 4: No article is used in English with noncount nouns when they refer to general concepts of the noun.

> Freedom is our most important possession.

Gold makes a wonderful gift for a person you love.

Sugar costs 50 cents a pound.

If the noncount noun is followed by a descriptive adjective clause or phrase, we use the article *the*.

The freedom that Thomas Jefferson envisioned is very different from the kind of freedom we have today.

He could buy a car with all the gold in his teeth.

The sugar that he had bought the previous day was covered with ants.

Rule 5: *The* is used with certain proper noun names of rivers, lakes, mountains, etcetera.

the Mississippi River
the Nile River
the Rocky Mountains
the Pacific Ocean
the Hawaiian Islands
the Caribbean Sea
the Amazon Jungle

But note this isn't true with the words *lake* and *mount,* which precede the name.

Mount Kilimanjaro
Lake Michigan

Rule 6: When a proper noun is used as a modifier for another noun, *the* always precedes the proper noun.

the Smiths' house
the Egyptian pharaohs
the European Community

Rule 7: Articles are usually not used with parts of the body or clothing when the owner of the parts of the body or clothing is known.

In these cases a possessive adjective is usually used.

Julia cut <u>her</u> hair.

I wore <u>my</u> best pants.

If the owner of the body part or item of clothing is not known, an article may be used.

In the barn I found <u>an</u> old T-shirt.

One of David Lynch's films begins with the discovery of <u>a</u> human ear.

Rule 8: *The* always precedes *same*.

This story is almost exactly <u>the</u> <u>same</u> as a story I read last year by a different author.

PRACTICE #4—Articles

Circle the letter of the answer that correctly answers each question.

1. Bill Gates is as ----- he can be.

    (A) a business as
    (B) as the happy businessman
    (C) happy a businessman as
    (D) happy a businessman since

2. There is nothing quite ----- sleeping under the stars.

    (A) the same as
    (B) as the same
    (C) different than the
    (D) as same a

3. If Sharon lived in that house, she would -----.

    (A) have been more the lucky than I am
    (B) be a more luckier
    (C) be luckier than I am
    (D) have more the luck than I do

4. Wild animals are endangered not only by ----- by predators, pollution, and the many collectors of zoo specimens who encroach on their territory.

    (A) a hunting but also
    (B) a hunted but also
    (C) hunting but also
    (D) an hunt but also

5. Although <u>most people</u> believe <u>that</u>
              A   B
    diamonds <u>are costliest</u> gems, emeralds are
              C
    actually <u>the more</u> valuable.
             D

6. The yearly movement of <u>a stars</u> was first
                      A
    noticed by <u>early</u> travelers <u>who</u> used them
               B   C
    to guide their way across <u>the sea.</u>
                     D

7. <u>The development</u> of the submarine was
      A
    hindered by <u>the lack</u> of <u>power source</u> that
              B   C
    could propel <u>an underwater</u> vessel.
              D

8. Marie Curie <u>won</u> <u>a Nobel</u> Prizes for her
              A   B
    discoveries of <u>radioactivity</u> and <u>radioactive</u>
              C   D
    elements.

9. Eggs, which are symbols of rebirth, are
   A   B
   traditionally painted with bright colors

   and displayed during Easter season.
   C   D

10. The ancient Egyptians believed that
                          A
    the cats were blessed and kept several
    B   C
    in their homes as an homage to the gods.
    D

11. In many parts of a world, the grass called
                       A   B
    vetiver is known for its fragrant oil as well
            C
    as its ability to prevent soil erosion.
                              D

12. It can sometimes take more a ton of
                           A   B
    ore to produce one ounce of pure gold.
           C   D

13. While our parents' generation looked
          A
    upon separation as a last-resort solution,
                        B
    many of today's young couples consider
              C
    the divorce an easy alternative.
    D

14. Many people take classes in art of self-
                   A   B
    defense; the stretching, strengthening,

    and tumbling involved are excellent exercise.
        C   D

15. Income tax evasion rather than murder
                A
    or illegal alcohol trafficking led to arrest of
                                    B
    the infamous Prohibition-era gangster Al
        C   D
    Capone.

PRACTICE #5—Review Questions

Circle the letter of the answer that correctly answers each question.

1. In accordance -----, American tax returns are used every ten years to provide population statistics for the United States.

   (A) to Census Bureau guidelines
   (B) with Census Bureau guidelines
   (C) Census Bureau guidelines to
   (D) Census Bureau guidelines with

2. When the book was published, the style of prose ----- *To the Lighthouse* stunned fellow writers and readers alike.

   (A) used to Virginia Woolf's
   (B) used at Virginia Woolf's
   (C) used in Virginia Woolf's
   (D) used on Virginia Woolf's

3. Never to be outdone by his peers, Christopher Marlowe was once known as -----.

   (A) scourge of Elizabeth's England
   (B) scourge of the Elizabeth's England
   (C) the scourge of Elizabeth's England
   (D) Elizabeth's scourge of the England

4. Generally, a dog makes a better house pet than -----.

   (A) snake does
   (B) the snake do
   (C) a snake does
   (D) snakes does

5. A ----- is a secret meeting between courting lovers, often during the afternoon.

   (A) tryst
   (B) trysts
   (C) the tryst
   (D) to tryst

6. There will never be two snowflakes that are exactly -----.

   (A) like
   (B) unlike
   (C) alike
   (D) liking

7. When the weather is pleasant in New York, it is ----- on Earth.

   (A) finest place
   (B) the finer place
   (C) the finest place
   (D) finer place

8. It would be impossible to say that Spanish ------ Japanese.

   (A) is like to
   (B) is exactly like
   (C) likes
   (D) is not alike

9. Some of Charles Dickens's novels were originally published -----.

   (A) in magazines
   (B) on magazines
   (C) at magazines
   (D) as is magazines

10. Low-fat yogurt contains ----- in order to keep the number of calories from fat to a minimum.

    (A) the skimmed milk
    (B) a skimmed milk
    (C) skimmed milk
    (D) skimming milk

11. Kirsch <u>is</u> <u>a</u> German liqueur <u>that</u> is
       A B   C
    <u>made to</u> cherries.
       D

12. <u>Alfred Hitchcock placed</u> <u>all</u> his passion <u>to</u>
       A   B   C
    his films to make <u>a</u> perfect product.
                       D

13. Tragicomedy <u>refers to</u> a form of play,
                   A
    novel, <u>or</u> film that <u>follows neither</u> the
            B   C
    rules of comedy nor <u>those on</u> tragedy
                          D
    exactly.

14. "The Boy Who Cried Wolf" refers to <u>a</u> story
                                        A
    <u>in which a</u> young man <u>often called</u>
       B   C
    attention <u>for</u> himself when nothing was
               D
    wrong.

15. Locust bean <u>gum used</u> <u>in</u> ice cream and
                   A   B
    yogurt <u>to</u> help give <u>the</u> products body.
            C   D

16. <u>When attending one's</u> first golf tournament,
       A   B
    <u>following on</u> the ball with the eye can be
       C
    <u>quite a challenge</u>.
       D

17. <u>In</u> the U.S.A., film stars <u>are often called</u>
    A   B
    American royalty <u>because their</u> <u>immense</u>
                       C   D
    popularity.

18. <u>Although the</u> strawberries <u>are</u> a spring and
       A   B
    summer fruit, they <u>can be</u> purchased from
                         C
    southern farmers <u>in</u> the winter.
                       D

19. Cartoonist Charles Schultz is famous <u>for</u>
                                          A
    his creation <u>on</u> <u>the</u> *Peanuts* <u>comic</u>
                 B   C   D
    strip.

20. <u>The</u> Federal Reserve vault <u>below</u> Wall
    A   B
    Street houses the gold <u>with</u> <u>many</u> different
                           C   D
    countries.

Answers for Structure
Power Lesson Seven

Practice #1			Practice #2			Practice #3	
1. D	9. A		1. B	6. C		1. C	6. C
2. B	10. D		2. A	7. C		2. A	7. D
3. B	11. A		3. B	8. D		3. A	8. A
4. C	12. D		4. B	9. D		4. C	9. C
5. B	13. A		5. C	10. B		5. B	10. A
6. B	14. A						
7. C	15. C						
8. C							

Practice #4			Practice #5	
1. C	9. D		1. B	11. D
2. A	10. B		2. C	12. C
3. C	11. A		3. C	13. D
4. C	12. B		4. C	14. D
5. C	13. D		5. A	15. A
6. A	14. B		6. C	16. C
7. C	15. C		7. C	17. C
8. B			8. B	18. A
			9. A	19. B
			10. C	20. C

READING POWER LESSONS

The Reading Power Lessons in this book will prepare you for the several different kinds of questions you should expect on the reading passages in both the computer-based and the paper-based TOEFL exams. The lessons contain many practice reading passages, and the vocabulary sections at the end of each lesson provide you with useful vocabulary items. By the time you finish this section of the book, your readiness for the test will have improved enormously.

However, to do really well on this section of the TOEFL, you will have to do a great deal of outside reading on many different topics. The TOEFL does not test test-taking skills—it tests language proficiency. There is a limit to how much test-taking skills will improve your TOEFL score. The point is this: to do really well on the Reading Comprehension section of the TOEFL, you must do a lot of reading in English. So . . . get started! In the meantime, you can work through this book's Reading Power Lessons.

Before you start to work on the Reading Power Lessons, read through "Reading Comprehension for the Computer-Based TOEFL" on the following pages. These pages will give you more details on what to expect on the Reading Comprehension section of the computer-based TOEFL exam.

THE BIGGER PICTURE: READING BEYOND THE TOEFL

Depending on the major, American college students typically have to read 50 to 400 pages a week. Graduate students may have to read even more. Even students majoring in the sciences (which generally require less reading than the humanities) will spend the first two years of their academic careers taking courses outside of their major. In other words, a student in the American system cannot avoid courses in literature, philosophy, or psychology—which ask students to read a great deal.

This is why the TOEFL places such importance on students' reading skills. It is also why the passages in the TOEFL's Reading Comprehension section are about so many different topics; every student going through an American college or university—whether American or not—will have to do a lot of reading on many different topics.

Now that you know why the TOEFL tests reading skills, you can begin your study of how you can prepare yourself for this section of the test as well as possible.

Reading Comprehension for the Computer-Based TOEFL

Since July, 1998, the TOEFL has been administered on computer. The Reading Comprehension section of the new computer-based TOEFL includes some changes both in the way that you will experience reading the passage and the way that you will record your answers.

On test day, prior to taking the exam, you will have the opportunity to work through a tutorial, which will guide you step-by-step on how to use a mouse, how to scroll, and how to use the testing tools. In addition, before each of the four sections, you will be shown how to answer the types of questions that you will encounter in that section. The more comfortable you are with computers, the less you will have to worry about on test day!

In the following pages, we will discuss some unique features of the computer-based TOEFL.

Computer Linear

The Reading Comprehension section is "computer linear." This means that you will receive a predetermined set of questions. You will get either 44 or 60 questions and the time allotted for the Reading Comprehension section will appear on the "Directions" screen prior to the actual test section. Your Reading Comprehension section will be either 70 or 90 minutes long.

Because the Reading Comprehension section is linear and not computer adaptive, you may skip questions and return to them later. However, we do not recommend skipping around; unlike the paper-and-pencil exam, you will not be able to see at a glance which questions you have skipped, and you are likely to become confused. It is better to work through the exam passage by passage.

Content

The Reading Comprehension section tests a person's ability to read and understand passages written in a style that students at a North American university would typically encounter. The passages that appear on the computer-based TOEFL are similar in content to those on the paper-and-pencil exam. The one difference is that they may be somewhat longer. However, the topic areas, such as physical and natural science and humanities, remain the same. Passages that discuss humanities topics, such as history, biography, and the arts, will focus on aspects of American culture. You will not be presented with passages on a historical figure from Sweden, a national holiday in Korea, or a musical style that is indigenous to South America, for example.

PASSAGE FORMAT

The passage will appear on the screen rather than printed on paper. You must practice reading off a computer screen to get comfortable with this way of reading. If you have access to the Internet, you should practice reading English texts on the Web (if you do not have a computer at home, check the local public library—many now have free Internet access).

All of the passages will require that you scroll in order to read them in their entirety. The best way to scroll is to click on the grey bar located to the right of the passage. Clicking on the grey bar will advance the text one full screen. If you try to scroll by moving the little scroll box or by clicking on the arrow at the top or bottom, you may lose your place. Be sure to practice scrolling in a word-processing program or on the Internet.

QUESTION FORMAT

Some significant changes have been made in the format of the questions on the computer-based TOEFL. On the paper-and-pencil exam, you are given four choices, from which you pick one and fill in the corresponding oval. On the computerized test, you will record your answer directly on the screen. Overall, Kaplan students who have taken both the paper-based and the computer-based test tend to agree that the Reading Comprehension section is now much easier, because you no longer have to hunt around for the correct line, sentence, or paragraph since it is either marked with an arrow or highlighted in bold print.

All question type examples refer to this passage:

During the late 1880s, some failing farms were bought up and turned into resorts. Originally they were designed for Eastern
Line European Jewish families who wanted to
(5) escape the overcrowded, polluted Lower East Side ghettos of New York City (this is how the region attained its nickname, "the Borscht Belt," so named for the Eastern European soup made from beets).
(10) Kuchaleyns, Yiddish for "cook-alones," were inexpensive bungalows where the guests supplied their own linens and did their own cooking. Usually ten families would share a single kitchen.

(15) The Kuchaleyns served another purpose besides providing an opportunity to breathe fresh air. Marriage-minded young Jews (or more likely their anxious parents) saw these vacation days as a chance to meet other eligi-
(20) ble young people and to get to know each other outside of the constraints of their neighborhood. The resort owners hoped to capitalize on the idea of courtship, bragging about matches made at their resorts.

(25) Over time, these Kuchaleyns evolved to become more luxurious. Clients no longer had to cook for themselves and sheets were provided for the beds. Even so, the clientele

continued to come from the New York City Jewish community and the social function of the resorts remained pretty much the same. Resort owners continued to take a direct role in match-making in a couple of ways. For one, they would spread rumors about what a "good catch" this or that one was. They also liked to present a view of overabundance of eligible young men. One owner, David Katz, would hire future doctors, dentists and lawyers to be his dining-room staff. Once a week he would call meetings to remind them that they were not hired for their ability to balance dishes. They were there because they were clean-looking and single. They were encouraged to "romance" the girls, but to be discreet.

As time wore on into the sixties, Jewish families that could afford to go to the grand Catskill resorts could also afford to go abroad for vacations. Eventually, the resorts were either taken over by larger chains with a more diverse clientele, or they were torn down completely.

Standard Multiple-Choice

You will click on the oval next to the correct answer choice.

Example:

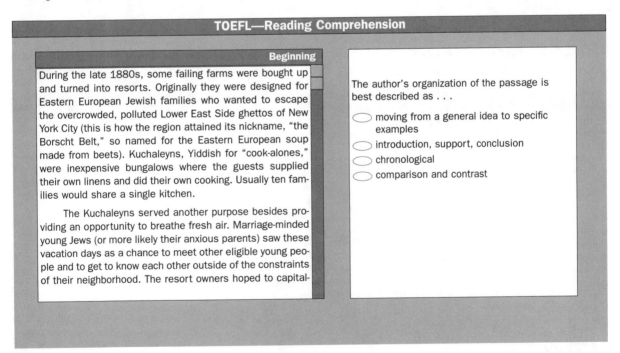

Click on Reference

You will be given a vocabulary word or pronoun and asked to click on the word in a particular paragraph or section (identified by bold text) to which it refers. An example can be found on the following page:

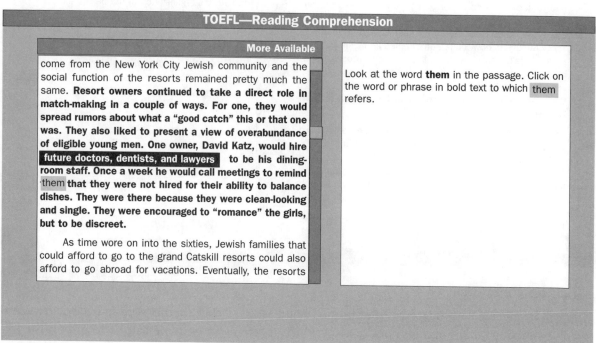

TOEFL—Reading Comprehension

More Available

come from the New York City Jewish community and the social function of the resorts remained pretty much the same. **Resort owners continued to take a direct role in match-making in a couple of ways. For one, they would spread rumors about what a "good catch" this or that one was. They also liked to present a view of overabundance of eligible young men. One owner, David Katz, would hire future doctors, dentists and lawyers to be his dining-room staff. Once a week he would call meetings to remind** them **that they were not hired for their ability to balance dishes. They were there because they were clean-looking and single. They were encouraged to "romance" the girls, but to be discreet.**

As time wore on into the sixties, Jewish families that could afford to go to the grand Catskill resorts could also afford to go abroad for vacations. Eventually, the resorts

Look at the word **them** in the passage. Click on the word or phrase in bold text to which them refers.

To answer, you can click on any part of the word or phrase in the passage. Your choice will darken to show which word you have chosen.

TOEFL—Reading Comprehension

More Available

come from the New York City Jewish community and the social function of the resorts remained pretty much the same. **Resort owners continued to take a direct role in match-making in a couple of ways. For one, they would spread rumors about what a "good catch" this or that one was. They also liked to present a view of overabundance of eligible young men. One owner, David Katz, would hire** future doctors, dentists, and lawyers **to be his dining-room staff. Once a week he would call meetings to remind** them **that they were not hired for their ability to balance dishes. They were there because they were clean-looking and single. They were encouraged to "romance" the girls, but to be discreet.**

As time wore on into the sixties, Jewish families that could afford to go to the grand Catskill resorts could also afford to go abroad for vacations. Eventually, the resorts

Look at the word **them** in the passage. Click on the word or phrase in bold text to which them refers.

Click on Sentence or Paragraph

You will be given a question and asked to click on the sentence or paragraph in which the answer can be found.

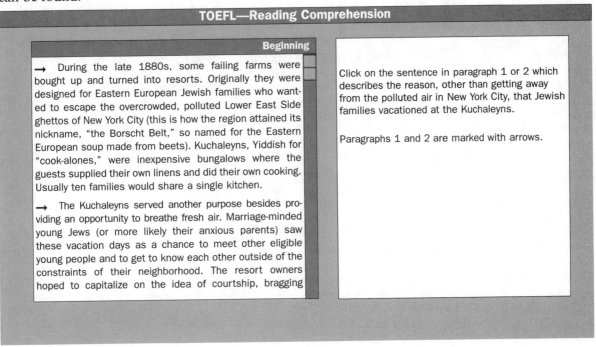

You can click on any part of the sentence in the paragraphs. The sentence will darken to show which answer you have chosen. The correct answer is darkened in the passage below.

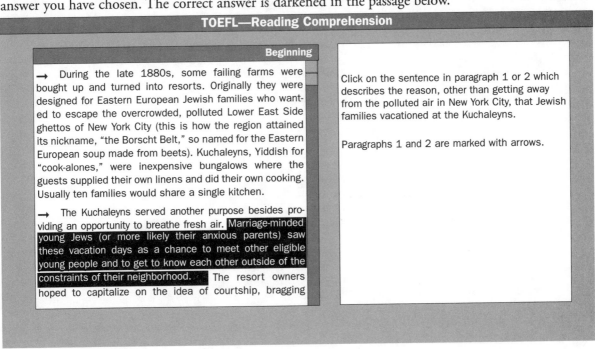

Insert Sentence

You will click on a square to add a sentence to the passage for this type of question.

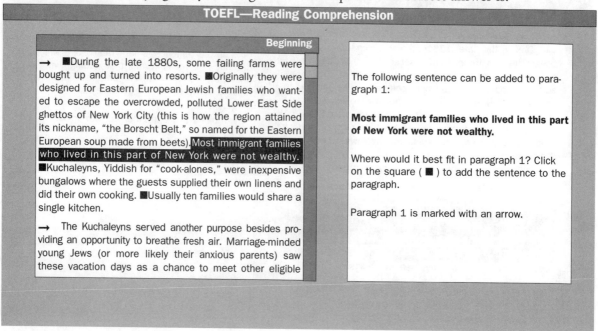

Click on a square and the sentence will appear in the passage at that point. When the sentence is added, it will be shown in a dark box. You should read the passage to see if it makes sense with the new sentence. If not, try again by clicking on another square. The correct answer is:

SCORING

The Reading Comprehension section of the computer-based TOEFL is scored on a scale of 0 to 30.

SKILLS AND STRATEGIES

Skills Tested on the Computer-Based TOEFL

Specific skills that you will practice throughout this section are:

- Reading for facts
- Reading for main ideas
- Reading for organization
- Reading for usage
- Reading for inference
- Answering negative fact questions
- Identifying references

Even though the Reading Comprehension section has been adapted for the computer, the same general skill is being tested as in the past—reading.

Strategies

Some tips for doing your best on the Reading Comprehension section are:

(1) Immediately scroll to the bottom of the passage in order to advance to the first question for each passage.

In order to see the first question, you have to scroll to the bottom of the screen. Once you have scrolled all the way through the text, you will see a box that says Proceed. Click on this box and you will advance to the first question. The reading passage is included with every question.

(2) Budget your time.

Do not spend too much time reading a passage. Nor should you waste time on any particular question. Once you know how much total time you have, you can figure out about how much time you can spend on each question. Generally, it is estimated that you will have about 2 minutes to answer each question (approximately 10 minutes to read the passage and answer five questions).

(3) Don't panic if there are a lot of words you don't recognize.

You do not need to know every word in a reading passage to answer the questions correctly. If you stay calm and make educated guesses, you can answer questions correctly even if you don't understand every word in the question. Part of being able to read in any language is the ability to figure out the meaning of new words from context.

(4) Click on the grey bar to advance through the text.
If you use the scroll bar, you may lose your place. If you click on the grey area above or below the scroll bar, the passage will advance or go back one whole screen.

(5) Avoid skipping questions.
Even though you are able to skip questions and return to them on this part of the test, you should avoid doing so. Unlike paper-and-pencil tests in which you can see immediately which questions you missed, in the computer version, you will have to click through all of the screens in between in order to find the question that you did not answer. If you find that there are a couple of questions in one section that are too difficult, you should skip the entire passage and come back to it later. It is easier to find a whole section of questions than just one or two.

(6) Answer all questions for a passage before moving on.
Answer every question for a reading passage before going on to the next passage. One thing you do not want to do on this section of the TOEFL is reread a passage—you simply do not have the time. If you leave a question unanswered in Passage 2, for example, and go on to Passage 3, you will forget what Passage 2 is about. You will have to reread Passage 2 before you can answer the question you left unanswered.

As on the paper-based test, you should skim and scan:

(7) Skim for organization and tone.
Don't read every individual word, one at a time. Group words together and look for key transitional words to get an overall feel for how the passage is organized and what the author thinks about what he or she is saying.

(8) Scan for facts and references.
You can find the information you are looking for by quickly scanning the passage for key words. Read the question, then look at the answer choices and look for words that correspond (don't get tricked, though; sometimes the TOEFL will throw in distractors!) One advantage to doing the Reading Comprehension section on the computer-based TOEFL is that you no longer have to search and count to find "the word *you* in line 17." On the computer, if the question asks you to analyze a particular word, phrase, sentence or paragraph, it will be clearly marked with either bolding, highlighting, or an arrow.

READING POWER LESSON ONE

SESSION A: READING FOR THE MAIN IDEA

Main idea questions require you to summarize the basic topic of the passage as well as the purpose of the passage.

Main idea questions often take the form:

"What is the main topic of this passage?"

"The best title for the passage is . . ."

"The main topic for this passage is . . ."

The following suggestions will help you answer main idea questions accurately.

When you read the reading passage for the first time, you should:

(1) Note the topic sentence.
(2) Note the general tone of the passage.

After you have found a main idea question, you should:

(3) Scan the passage for key vocabulary that might indicate the author's attitude toward the topic.
(4) Read this part of the passage carefully to answer the question.

Remember that the topic sentence alone will not contain the main idea. The main idea can only be generalized from the entire passage. It is only by following the entire passage from beginning to end and following the author's position that you will be able to determine the main topic of the passage.

> **The steps recommended in this lesson work for many students. After trying our suggestions on the practice questions, if you find that you prefer to adapt them to suit your own style of test taking—go ahead!**

SESSION B: DISCERNING THE MAIN TOPIC FROM THE MAIN IDEA

The TOEFL asks two types of questions related to the major focus of the passage, topic questions and main idea questions. Though they are similar, they do not mean the same thing.

Main Topic Questions

The *topic* is the subject being discussed in the reading passage. It is not necessarily the same as the argument or the point the author is making.

For example, in a reading passage in which the author is trying to persuade the reader that the 55-mile-per-hour speed limit should be changed:

> ➤ The topic is the 55-miles-per-hour speed limit.
> ➤ The author's point is that the 55-mile-per-hour speed limit should be changed.

Main topic questions are almost always asked in the form:

"What is the main topic of the passage?"

To answer main topic questions, you should:

(1) Read the first and last sentences carefully.
(2) Locate the topic sentence.
(3) If you are still not certain, scan the passage for repeated vocabulary. Repeated vocabulary often indicates the main topic of a reading passage.

Main Idea Questions

Main idea questions, first examined in Session A, differ from topic questions because they include the author's main point. In other words the *main idea* takes into account what the author is saying about the topic. Again, main idea questions take the form:

"What does the author mainly discuss?"

"The best title for the passage is . . ."

"The main idea of this passage is . . ."

The main topic is the subject that the passage discusses. The main idea includes the main topic along with the point or position of the author.

Listed below is an example of the difference between the two categories, main idea and main topic.

Read the following passage for its main idea and its main topic.

Each country has several favorite customary cookies. Most often they are made with the land's most common and plentiful foods. *Line* Oats are popular in Scottish cookies, for (5) example. Because Scotland's climate is not receptive to wheat growing, oats have dominated as a primary crop. In the same way, because the date palm is bountiful in North Africa and many Middle Eastern countries, (10) dates are a common ingredient in cookies from those areas.

> QUESTION: What is the main topic of the passage?
> QUESTION: What is the main idea of the passage?

The *topic* of the passage is: The ingredients in cookies from various geographical areas.

The *main idea* is: Ingredients in cookies differ from region to region, depending on the country's most fundamental and abundant agricultural products.

Note that the main topic can usually be expressed with just a noun (for example, *cookies*). The main idea usually requires a sentence (subject + verb).

SESSION C: ANSWERING FACT QUESTIONS

The most common type of reading question on the TOEFL is the fact question. Fact questions require you to answer very specific information questions about the passage.

Here are some of the different ways that fact questions can be asked. Each statement would be followed by the four answer choices, only one of which would complete the statement correctly according to the passage.

> Nimbostratus clouds are . . .
>
> According to the article, nimbostratus clouds . . .
>
> The passage states that all chimpanzees . . .
>
> The author indicates that when nimbostratus clouds are visible, the weather . . .

Note the way each question is structured as well as the vocabulary it uses. You will often see words like *according to, states,* and *indicates* on this section of the TOEFL.

To answer fact questions, you should:

(1) Select from the question a key word or phrase.
(2) Scan the reading passage for this key word or phrase, or for words related to this key word or phrase.
(3) When you have found the key word or phrase in the passage, read this part of the passage carefully to answer the question.

Fact questions are almost always asked in the same order that they appear in the passage. Therefore, the first fact question about any reading will be located closer to the beginning of a passage than the last fact question. Knowing this will help you scan the passage faster because if you are answering question 1, you will know to look at the beginning of the passage. On the other hand, if answering question 5, you will know to look toward the end of the passage.

SESSION D: ANSWERING NEGATIVE FACT QUESTIONS

Negative fact questions offer three incorrect statements and one correct statement. Therefore, you are required to recognize the three correct statements about the passage and choose the one answer that is not true about the passage.

Negative fact questions usually take the form of one of the following statements:

According to the passage, all of the following are true EXCEPT . . .

The author mentions all of the following EXCEPT . . .

To answer negative fact questions, you should:

(1) Read the question carefully to determine the information you have to locate in the passage.
(2) Scan the passage to locate the answers that are true about the passage.
(3) Mark the answer that is not true about the passage.

This type of question usually takes longer to answer due to the need to find three correct statements in the passage. Slower readers may want to skip these questions until they have answered all of the easier types.

Remember, however, that for the Reading Comprehension section of the TOEFL, you should make your best guess for all the questions belonging to one reading passage before going on to the next passage. If you move on to a new passage before completing your first passage, you will forget what you have read in this passage. When you return to the question about it, you will have to read the entire passage a second time—a very time-consuming process.

P R A C T I C E #1—Reading Practice

Circle the letter of the answer that correctly answers each question.

San Francisco, America's romantic city by the bay, has always been a haven for the artists, writers, and lovers who have left at
Line least part of their hearts there. One of the
(5) great American romantics who wrote in San Francisco was Jack Kerouac. Kerouac rewrote the history of an entire postwar generation of youth, forcing them out of their postwar confines and leading them out "on
(10) the road."

Born on March 12, 1922 in Lowell, Massachusetts, to a working-class Catholic, French-Canadian family, Kerouac had a typically all-American childhood. He played
(15) sandlot baseball, read pulp fiction, and became a high school football star. He entered Columbia University on a football scholarship, but when a leg injury put him out of action on the gridiron, he chose the
(20) literary field of work. American literature would never be the same. His romanticized autobiographical novels and wayward travels, which were often the basis of his work, made him the unquestioned king of the Beat
(25) Generation writers.

Before becoming the father of the San Francisco–based Beat Generation, Kerouac was writing in the bars and basement apartments of New York City's Lower East and
(30) Lower West sides. Here he met and worked with William S. Burroughs and Allen Ginsberg before they all took their restless spirits west and started a literary and cultural revolution.
(35) Kerouac first landed in the San Francisco Bay Area in 1947, hoping to get a berth on a merchant marine ship. Here he soon met his kindred spirit, Neal Cassady, whose frenetic letters and cross-country travels
(40) spurred Jack to write *On the Road,* perhaps his preeminent work, in one long paragraph during the month of April 1951.

Since the book was written as a simple personal testament "in search of his writing
(45) soul," Kerouac had no idea that *On the Road* would spur a generation onto the highways and into the tumultuous activism of the Vietnam era a decade later.

Almost overnight, Kerouac became a
(50) media superstar and even a mythical figure himself. But in the end, he could not live with the myth he created. He split from the ranks of his fellow beat writers, like Ginsberg, and actually voiced support for
(55) America's war effort in Vietnam. Later in his life, he moved back in with his mother, drank too much, and became more and more reactionary. His later years were an ironic turn on the life of freedom he wrote
(60) about and lived to a great extent. Still, the stories he created live on within the souls of American youth, the lingering American romantics.

1. Jack Kerouac was born
   (A) to a working-class family in Massachusetts
   (B) to a Canadian family
   (C) to Irish Catholic parents
   (D) in a sandlot

2. Jack Kerouac relocated to San Francisco in

   (A) 1922
   (B) 1951
   (C) 1947
   (D) the midst of the Vietnam War

3. Kerouac met Neal Cassady in

   (A) French-Canadian Massachusetts
   (B) San Francisco
   (C) New York
   (D) Vietnam

4. *On the Road* was

   (A) not important to the youth of America
   (B) one long paragraph
   (C) Alan Ginsberg's poem
   (D) Kerouac's autobiography

5. Which of the following is NOT mentioned about Kerouac's life?

   (A) his support for the U.S. war effort in Vietnam
   (B) his French-Canadian upbringing
   (C) his leading role in the beat generation
   (D) his unsuccessful marriage

6. The best title for this passage would be

   (A) Postwar Literature and a New Beginning
   (B) Kerouac: King of the Beats Opens a New Road
   (C) San Francisco Writers
   (D) Vietnam Protests: The Early Years

PRACTICE #2—Reading Practice

Circle the letter of the answer that correctly answers each question.

Rock, or rock-and-roll, is a form of music that was invented in the United States in the 1950s. It has become popular in the United *Line* States, Europe, and many other parts of the (5) world. African American performers like Little Richard, Fats Domino, Ray Charles, and Big Joe Turner were among the first people to come out with true rock-and-roll, a combination of various elements from coun-(10) try and western, gospel, rhythm and blues, and jazz. The influences of early performers like bluesman Muddy Waters, gospel performer Ruth Brown, and jazz musician Louis Jordan on rock-and-roll are still felt today. (15) For example, the songs of early country legend Hank Williams affected musicians from early rock star Buddy Holly to '80s rocker Bruce Springsteen.

In the segregated 1950s, African American (20) musical forms were not considered appropriate for white audiences. Much of the U.S. population had not been exposed to them. All that changed, when, in 1953, Cleveland disc jockey Alan Freed began to play rhythm (25) and blues to a largely non–African American audience. Freed was successful, and a lot of records were sold. The music spread, and the term that Freed had adopted for the music— rock-and-roll—began to spread as well.

(30) Teenagers, and the money they were willing to spend on records, provided an impetus for rock-and-roll. On their way to becoming rock stars, many performers copied songs from the original artists. For (35) instance, Pat Boone scored a hit with a toned-down version of Little Richard's song,

"Tutti Frutti," prompting Little Richard to comment, "He goes and outsells me with my song that I wrote." In 1955–56, Chuck (40) Berry, Bill Haley and the Comets, and particularly Elvis Presley became famous for their version of traditional rhythm and blues. Elvis Presley's first television appearance in January 1956 marked rock-and-roll's (45) ascendancy into the world of pop music.

1. What is the main topic of this passage?
   (A) American popular music
   (B) the careers of successful rock musicians
   (C) the musical elements that distinguish pop from classical music
   (D) the origins of the music that came to be called "rock-and-roll"

2. Who is NOT mentioned as an African American performer who was among the first to come out with rock-and-roll?
   (A) Fats Domino
   (B) Little Richard
   (C) Elvis Presley
   (D) Ray Charles

3. According to the passage, true rock-and-roll is characterized by a combination of which of the following?

    (A) the music of Bruce Springsteen and Hank Williams
    (B) musical influences from Europe and Asia
    (C) forms of music heard on most radio stations in the early 1950s
    (D) country and western, gospel, rhythm and blues, and jazz

4. In the 1950s rock-and-roll

    (A) was invented
    (B) was not considered appropriate for white audiences
    (C) sold few records
    (D) was the property of Buddy Holly

5. Many performers copied songs from

    (A) classical music
    (B) Pat Boone
    (C) original artists
    (D) "Tutti Frutti"

6. Which of the following is NOT mentioned in the passage as being a factor in the commercial success of early rock-and-roll?

    (A) the purchasing power of early rock enthusiasts
    (B) the charismatic personality of disc jockey Alan Freed
    (C) the exposure of a non–African American audience to African American musical forms
    (D) rock's popularity with teenage audiences

PRACTICE #3—Reading Practice

Circle the letter of the answer that correctly answers each question.

Primitive mammals called monotremes are the only living representatives of the subclass *Prototheria*. This makes them the most like-
Line ly living representatives of creatures that
(5) were part of the evolutionary transition from reptiles to mammals. They share some qualities with reptiles and birds, but are nevertheless true mammals. Like birds and reptiles, monotremes lay eggs rather than
(10) giving birth to live young. But, like other mammals, they have hair, large brains, and mammary glands that produce milk to nourish their offspring.

Their primitive organization and close
(15) relation to reptiles is manifested in their uncomplicated brain structure, egg-laying habits, and cloaca. (A cloaca is found in amphibians, reptiles, birds, certain fish, and monotremes, but not in placental mammals
(20) or most bony fishes. The animal's intestinal, urinary, and genital tracts open into this common cavity, which also functions as an outlet.)

Another feature that indicates they may be
(25) related to reptiles is their egg-laying behavior. Monotremes lay shelled eggs, which are predominantly yolk, like those of reptiles and birds. The young are born in a relatively early stage of development and remain
(30) dependent upon the parent. The females have no teats; the milk that they secrete from their mammary glands passes directly through their skin.

There are only three types of monotremes
(35) in existence: the duck-billed platypus and two species of spiny echidna, or anteater. The platypus has webbed feet, a flat tail, and a "bill" like a duck's. The short- and the long-nosed echidnas have spines and tube-
(40) like noses. The female echidna lays one egg at a time into a pouch that she develops on her abdomen. Her young will hatch in it and develop for several months.

1. The passage focuses on which of the following aspects of monotremes?
   (A) the food they eat and their behavior in the wild
   (B) the times of day when they are most active
   (C) their relationship to both reptiles and mammals
   (D) their mating behavior and reproductive organs

2. Which of the following is NOT mentioned as a quality that monotremes share with other mammals?
   (A) hair on the body
   (B) development of mammary glands
   (C) egg-laying
   (D) a large brain

3. The passage states that monotremes are
   (A) extinct
   (B) reptiles and birds
   (C) egg-laying mammals that are related to reptiles and birds
   (D) highly intelligent

4. Monotreme babies are born

   (A) in the early stages of development and must rely on their mothers
   (B) fully developed and quickly become independent
   (C) live like the babies of other mammals
   (D) without mammary glands

5. The duck-billed platypus is

   (A) the tubelike nose of a monotreme
   (B) a subspecies of anteater
   (C) a portion of the monotreme reproductive system
   (D) one of a few surviving species of monotremes

6. According to the passage, where do young echidnas live right after they are hatched?

   (A) in a pouch on their mother's abdomen
   (B) in their mothers' cloaca
   (C) in amphibians, birds, reptiles, and certain fish
   (D) in an egg that has a shell and that is predominantly yolk

PRACTICE #4—Reading Practice

Circle the letter of the answer that correctly answers each question.

Asteroids are rocky, metallic objects that orbit the Sun but are too small to be considered planets. The largest known asteroid, Ceres, has a diameter of about 1,000 kilo-
(5) meters. The smallest asteroids are the size of pebbles. Millions are the size of boulders. Most are irregularly shaped—only a few are large enough for gravity to have made them into spheres. About 250 asteroids in the solar
(10) system are 100 kilometers in diameter, and at least sixteen have a diameter of 240 kilometers or greater. Their orbits lie in an area that stretches from Earth's orbit to beyond Saturn's orbit. Tens of thousands of asteroids
(15) exist in a belt between the orbits of Mars and Jupiter. An asteroid that hits Earth's atmosphere is called a meteor or shooting star, because it burns and gives off a bright flash of light. Whatever does not completely burn
(20) falls to Earth as a meteorite. Between 1,000 and 10,000 tons of this material fall to Earth daily. Much is in the form of small grains of dust, but about 1,000 metallic or rocky bits fall to Earth each year.
(25) There has been much speculation about large meteors hitting Earth. A large asteroid or comet is thought to have landed in Mexico about 65 million years ago. The impact may have led to the extinction of
(30) many species, including the dinosaurs, by throwing dust into the atmosphere, blocking the sunlight, and causing a climate change. The period of time between such large meteor impacts is probably in the millions of
(35) years, but smaller meteors, such as the one that caused the Meteor Crater in Arizona (about 1.2 kilometers in diameter), may hit the earth every 50,000 to 100,000 years. There's no historical record of a person being
(40) killed by a meteorite. The only reported injury occurred on November 30, 1954, when an Alabama woman was bruised by an eight-pound meteorite that fell through her roof.

1. Which of the following assumptions about asteroids is expressed in the passage?
   (A) They rarely become meteorites.
   (B) Most are relatively small.
   (C) Many exist, but few actually fall to Earth.
   (D) They are a major cause of death in some regions.

2. The majority of asteroids are
   (A) the size of boulders
   (B) symmetrical
   (C) about 1,000 kilometers in diameter
   (D) irregular in shape

3. Which of the following explains why a meteor is called a shooting star?
   (A) It may have caused the extinction of the dinosaurs.
   (B) No one is known to have been killed by one.
   (C) It burns in a flash of light.
   (D) It can be rocky or metallic.

4. In line 36, why does the author mention the Meteor Crater in Arizona?

    (A) to give an example of a smaller meteor impact

    (B) to increase interest in astronomy

    (C) to close the passage on an interesting note

    (D) to show how meteors can wipe out animal species

5. The Alabama woman in line 42 is mentioned to

    (A) show that meteorites can kill

    (B) illustrate the only documented injury of a human by a meteorite

    (C) show that meteorites can damage homes

    (D) summarize the historical records

PRACTICE #5—Reading Practice

Circle the letter of the answer that correctly answers each question.

A highly acclaimed motion picture of 1979 concerned a nearly disastrous accident at a nuclear power plant. Within a few weeks *Line* of the film's release, in a chilling coincidence, (5) a real-life accident startlingly similar to the fictitious one occurred at the Three Mile Island plant near Harrisburg, Pennsylvania. The two incidents even corresponded in certain details; for instance, both in the film (10) and in real life, one cause of the mishap was a false meter reading caused by a jammed needle.

Such similarities led many to wonder whether the fictional movie plot had been (15) prophetic in other ways. The movie depicted officials of the power industry as seriously corrupt, willing to lie, bribe, and even kill to conceal their culpability in the accident. Did a similar coverup occur in the Three Mile (20) Island accident? Perhaps we will never know. We do know that, despite the endeavors of reporters and citizen groups to uncover the causes of the accident, many of the facts remain unknown. Although they declare (25) that the public is entitled to the truth, many of the power industry leaders responsible have been reluctant to cooperate with independent, impartial investigators.

1. The nuclear accident described in the movie
   (A) was successfully concealed by power industry leaders and officials
   (B) was caused by a series of coincidences
   (C) was a surprisingly accurate foreshadowing of actual events
   (D) took place at the Three Mile Island

2. Officials of the nuclear power industry
   (A) have committed murders to make possible a cover-up of the incident at Harrisburg
   (B) had predicted that nuclear accidents were likely to occur
   (C) have been reluctant to reveal the full story about the Three Mile Island incident
   (D) have tried to make all the facts freely accessible to those concerned

3. According to the passage, public concern over the accident near Harrisburg
   (A) had no effect on the subsequent investigation
   (B) was lessened by the quick response of industry leaders and officials
   (C) prompted widespread panic throughout Pennsylvania
   (D) persisted as many questions were left unanswered

4. Reporters looking into the accident at Three Mile Island

   (A) uncovered more facts than did citizen groups

   (B) did not succeed in uncovering all the facts about the cause of the accident

   (C) cooperated closely with power industry officials

   (D) kept documented information from the public

5. All of the following are true EXCEPT

   (A) The movie about a nuclear accident has been praised.

   (B) The press has sought fuller information about the Three Mile Island mishap.

   (C) A mechanical breakdown was a partial cause of the Harrisburg accident.

   (D) The release of the movie came only weeks after the Three Mile Island accident.

PRACTICE #6—Reading Practice

Circle the letter of the answer that correctly answers each question.

At one time in North America, wolves ranged from coast to coast and from Canada to Mexico—the greatest natural range of any
Line mammal except humans. Unfortunately, in
(5) industrialized human society, wolves seem to have met their match. Gray wolves began declining in the American West around 1870 as westward-moving settlers depleted the bison, deer, and elk that wolves preyed
(10) on. Wolves then turned to the sheep and cattle as their prey. Settlers and government trappers responded with intensive campaigns to wipe out the wolf. Approximately 1.5 million wolves were killed in various bounty-
(15) hunting campaigns carried out between 1850 and 1900. As late as 1965, hunters were offered $20 to $50 for every wolf they could kill.

Human incursions on their habitat, and
(20) purposeful extermination campaigns, had a devastating effect. Except for a small number of wolves in Minnesota, wolves were gone from the 48 states of the continental U.S. by the late 1920s. Wolves were listed as endan-
(25) gered in 1973, and remain so today, meaning that they are in danger of becoming extinct in all or part of their natural habitat.

However, there are some hopeful signs of a recovery in the wolf population. In the
(30) 1980s, wolves began appearing in Montana, apparently having migrated from Canada. There are currently about 65 wolves in northwestern Montana. The work of the U.S. Forest Service in augmenting the wolf
(35) population in the continental U.S. with wolves from Canada could speed the recovery process. Recently, Forest Service employ-

ees released eight Canadian gray wolves in Yellowstone National Park and four in cen-
(40) tral Idaho. The goal is to have ten breeding pairs and their young—about 100 wolves— in each of three recovery areas (northwest Montana, central Idaho, and the Yellowstone National Park area) by 2002. If this goal is
(45) reached, the gray wolf would no longer be considered endangered.

1. What is the main purpose of the passage?
   (A) to explain why early American settlers had such hatred for wolves
   (B) to describe the decline and possible recovery of the North American wolf population
   (C) to describe the U.S. Forest Service and its mission
   (D) to outline several alternatives for reviving the once-large North American wolf population

2. With the depletion of their natural food source, wolves began turning for food to
   (A) human beings
   (B) each other
   (C) farm animals
   (D) plants and shrubs

3. Wolves began to vanish largely because of

   (A) human intrusion and hunting
   (B) laws against them in 48 states
   (C) other animals assuming their habitats
   (D) extreme weather conditions

4. The author mentions all of the following as designated recovery areas for the wolf population, EXCEPT

   (A) central Idaho
   (B) northwest Montana
   (C) Yellowstone National Park
   (D) Canada

5. The passage supports which of the following conclusions?

   (A) The wolf population of the continental United States may be making a comeback as early as the year 2002.
   (B) The wolf population of North America is almost certainly headed for extinction.
   (C) The Canadian Forest Service must stimulate a recovery of the Canadian wolf population.
   (D) It's unclear how many species are in danger of extinction.

6. Forest Service employees have done which of the following to aid the recovery of the wolf population in the United States?

   (A) begun breeding wolves in zoos
   (B) created recovery centers for injured wolves
   (C) released wolves into protected areas
   (D) begun researching wolves' breeding patterns

PRACTICE #7—Reading Practice

Circle the letter of the answer that correctly answers each question.

For a jazz musician in New York City in the early 1940s, the most interesting place to spend the hours between midnight and
Line dawn was probably a Harlem nightclub
(5) called Minton's. After finishing their jobs at other clubs, young musicians like Charlie Parker, Dizzy Gillespie, Kenny Clarke, and Thelonious Monk would gather at Minton's and play jam sessions—informal perfor-
(10) mances featuring lengthy group and solo improvisations. The all-night sessions result-ed in the birth of modern jazz. Working together, these African American artists forged a new sound, known as "bebop."

(15) Unlike swing, the enormously popular jazz played in the 1930s, bebop was not dance music. It was often blindingly fast, incorpo-rating tricky, irregular rhythms and discor-dant sounds that jazz audiences had never
(20) heard before. Earlier jazz, like practically all of Western music up to that time, used an eight-note scale. Bebop, in contrast, was based on a twelve-note scale, thereby open-ing up vast new harmonic opportunities for
(25) musicians. The musicians who pioneered bebop shared two common elements—a vision of the new music's possibilities, and astonishing improvisational skill, the ability to play or compose a musical line on the spur
(30) of the moment. Improvisation within the context of a group setting is, after all, the essence of jazz, which has been described as the musical experience of the passing moment.

(35) Like many revolutions, unfortunately, the bebop movement encountered heavy resis-tance. Opposition came from older jazz musicians originally, but later and more last-ingly from a general public alienated by the
(40) music's complexity. Furthermore, due to the government ban on recording that was in effect during the early years of World War II, the creative ferment that first produced bebop remains largely undocumented today.

1. Which of the following is the most like-ly title for this passage?
   (A) Jazz Greats of the 1940s
   (B) Bebop's Evolution into Jazz
   (C) The Genius of the Twelve-Note Scale
   (D) A Short History of Bebop

2. The passage is primarily concerned with
   (A) an art form involving live perfor-mance and innovation
   (B) an artistic revolution that attained great commercial success
   (C) public resistance to the work of creative artists
   (D) the difficulty of putting emotion into a live performance

3. According to the passage, which of the following best characterizes bebop?

   (A) lengthy group and solo improvisations

   (B) jam sessions

   (C) informal performances

   (D) tricky, irregular rhythms and discordant sounds

4. How was bebop received by contemporary audiences?

   (A) It was welcomed.

   (B) It was well liked.

   (C) It was not liked.

   (D) It was commercially successful.

5. Which of the following is NOT mentioned as a characteristic of the musicians who pioneered bebop?

   (A) a vision of the new music's possibilities

   (B) improvisational skill

   (C) a background in classical music

   (D) the ability to play or compose a musical line on a moment's notice

PRACTICE #8—Reading Practice

Circle the letter of the answer that correctly answers each question.

Emma Goldman was an activist, writer, and orator who became well known for her advocacy of anarchism in the United States. Anarchists oppose all forms of government and advocate voluntary cooperation between individuals and groups.

Goldman was born in Kovno, Russia in 1869. As a schoolgirl, she met and was influenced by radical students. She also saw a peasant being cruelly beaten, which had a lasting effect on her. At the age of 17, Emma Goldman emigrated to the United States, and found work in a Rochester, New York clothing factory. Rochester had a long history of progressive activity, as a center of Abolitionist activity, and Goldman attended German socialist meetings there. However, the oppressive factory work and a bad marriage made her decide to move.

She arrived in New York in 1889, and was by this time an anarchist. She used her speaking skills to advocate for anarchism, and grew close to Russian anarchist Alexander Berkman. With Margaret Sanger, Goldman fought for the right to birth control, and women's rights. In 1893, Goldman was imprisoned for inciting a riot in New York City. In 1917, Goldman and Berkman were sentenced to two years in prison for obstructing the military draft, and when they were released, they were deported to Russia.

Emma Goldman later lived in England, Canada, and Spain. She wrote a great number of articles, traveled widely on behalf of the anarchist movement, and was sometimes imprisoned for her work. Her contemporaries remarked on her unbounded energy, magnetic personality, and enthusiasm for her cause. She is the author of *Anarchism and Other Essays, The Social Significance of the Modern Drama, My Disillusionment in Russia,* and *Living My Life.*

1. What is the main purpose of the passage?

    (A) to describe the life and times of Alexander Berkman
    (B) to give a history of early American anarchism
    (C) to describe the writings of Emma Goldman
    (D) to relate important facts about the life of Emma Goldman

2. Which of the following statements can best be inferred from the passage?

    (A) Goldman began to describe herself as an anarchist while in Rochester.
    (B) Emma Goldman was not on very good terms with Alexander Berkman.
    (C) Emma Goldman was politically opposed to all wars.
    (D) Emma Goldman should not have been imprisoned in 1893.

3. Emma Goldman was an activist primarily in the field of

    (A) animal rights
    (B) government advocacy
    (C) oration
    (D) antigovernment activity

4. According to the passage, Margaret Sanger fought with Goldman for what cause?

    (A) the abolition of slavery
    (B) factory workers
    (C) birth control and women's rights
    (D) obstruction of the military draft

5. When Emma Goldman was released from prison, she

    (A) fought the military draft
    (B) was deported to Russia
    (C) married Alexander Berkman
    (D) incited a riot in New York City

P RACTICE #9—Reading Practice

Circle the letter of the answer that correctly answers each question.

When a ray of light hits the surface of an object, one or a combination of the following three things happens: the light may be thrown back towards the source of the light (reflection), it may be passed through the object (refraction), or it may be absorbed into the object. Different materials and substances have unique patterns in the way light behaves when it falls upon them. This pattern gives objects their special appearance and color. If an object allows light to pass directly through it, as does a totally clear sheet of glass, it is said to be transparent. If it scatters and diffuses the light, in a manner similar to a frosted pane of glass, it is translucent. Finally, if it obstructs the passage of light it is deemed opaque.

When light is shined upon a reflecting object, it makes a certain angle with an imaginary line that is at right angles, or normal, with that object. This angle is called the angle of incidence. The ray that is reflected from the object also makes an angle with the normal line. This is termed the angle of reflection. The law of reflection dictates that the angle of incidence is always equal to the angle of reflection. In a reflecting object with a smooth surface, like a mirror, the light reflects back without spreading out; however, if the object is rough, the light does spread out. This explains why light reflected from a mirror forms such a sharp image while that from a piece of cloth forms no image at all. The law of reflection holds true in any case.

When light is refracted, it slows down as it passes through the substance. If it enters the object at other than a right angle, this slowing down causes the light to bend at the surface of the substance. This accounts for the well-known example of a pencil appearing to bend if it is placed in a glass of water.

When a material absorbs light, the light either raises the energy level of the material's atoms, or the light may be converted into heat energy. The most common example of the latter is that objects left in sunshine tend to heat up from the absorption of light.

Line (5)

(10)

(15)

(20)

(25)

(30)

(35)

(40)

(45)

1. The primary purpose of the passage is to
    (A) explain the consequences of light hitting an object
    (B) discuss the process of light reflection
    (C) predict the color and appearance of an object
    (D) determine which of the three theories is best

2. The pattern of a substance does which of the following?
    (A) It absorbs the rays of light that strike it.
    (B) It affects the appearance and color we perceive in an object.
    (C) It alters the shape of an object.
    (D) It causes the object to behave differently.

3. According to the passage, the law of reflection

    (A) effects a piece of cloth
    (B) has no continuity
    (C) changes under no circumstances
    (D) has been radically changed in recent years

4. Which of the following is true of refracted light?

    (A) It decelerates as it passes through a substance.
    (B) It is unaffected by substances it strikes.
    (C) It is reflected back from the surface it strikes.
    (D) It bends the surface of the substance.

5. Which of the following is NOT true of a material when it absorbs light?

    (A) The light lowers the energy of the material's atoms.
    (B) The light can be converted into heat energy.
    (C) The light can boost the energy of the material's matter.
    (D) The material may become hotter.

PRACTICE #10—Reading Practice

Circle the letter of the answer that correctly answers each question.

Dinosaurs lived in New Mexico for about 154 million years, between 220 and 66 million years ago. In geologists' terms, this time
Line span covers the Late Triassic Period and the
(5) entire Jurassic and Cretaceous periods. Dinosaur fossils and other remains have been found throughout New Mexico. One of the most important remains in New Mexico are the footprints found at Clayton
(10) Lake, in the northeastern corner of the state. After studying the hundreds of footprints at Clayton Lake, scientists identified a period in dinosaur evolution known as the Sauropod hiatus.

(15) Sauropods are classified as "lizard-hipped" dinosaurs, and are distinguished from the "bird-hipped" Orthiniscan dinosaurs. They are quadrupedal, herbivorous animals with a relatively simple body—a long neck and tail,
(20) a fairly small skull and brain, and erect limbs similar to those of elephants. Numerous Sauropod footprints from the Early Cretaceous period—100 million years ago and earlier—exist in Texas, Oklahoma, and
(25) Arkansas. But, at Clayton Lake, northeastern New Mexico, Oklahoma, and Colorado, footprints from the same time period clearly show that no Sauropods were present, and that Orthiniscans predominated.

(30) From the fossil record, it seems that the Sauropods disappeared in many parts of North America between 70 million and 100 million years ago. Scientists think the last North American Sauropod was a creature
(35) discovered in the San Juan Basin of northwestern New Mexico and named Alamosaurus. Alamosaurus closely resembles Sauropods from South America, which were quite numerous even as their North
(40) American cousins died out. Alamosaurus must have come to New Mexico from South America near the end of the Cretaceous.

1. What does the passage mainly discuss?
   (A) the Sauropod hiatus, and the evidence supporting it
   (B) the physical attributes of the Sauropods
   (C) the fossil record of dinosaurs in North America
   (D) geologists' method of searching for fossils at Clayton Lake

2. *Lizard-hipped* in line 15 most likely refers to
   (A) a species
   (B) the dinosaur's physical makeup
   (C) a derogatory nickname for the Sauropod
   (D) the geological era in which the Sauropod lived

3. According to the passage, Clayton Lake is home to
   (A) thousands of dinosaurs
   (B) fossilized footprints of several dinosaurs
   (C) only a few fossils
   (D) a scientific hiatus

4. Which of the following is NOT used in the passage to describe the characteristics of Sauropods?

(A) quadruped
(B) erect
(C) herbivorous
(D) carnivorous

5. When did the Sauropod disappear from North America?

(A) in the 70th century B.C.
(B) over the course of about 30 million years
(C) 200 million years ago
(D) before the Orthiniscans

VOCABULARY

To hear how these words and expressions are pronounced, listen to Track_21.mov.

To segregate/to integrate
To segregate means to keep two groups of people or things physically separate. Groups of people are often segregated from each other on the basis of race, sex, or religion. *Segregation* is the act of segregating, and usually refers to a separation of people based on race.

> Many societies practice <u>racial segregation</u>, though it is not always written into the legal code.

> Most U.S. cities remain <u>segregated according to race</u>, with white, black, Asian, and Hispanic Americans frequently living in separate neighborhoods.

To integrate means to bring different groups of people or things physically together. An integrated school or neighborhood is one in which different groups of people study or live together—usually the term refers to groups differentiated according to race.

> In certain parts of the world where racial or religious enmity is great, it may be a mistake to try to force people from different backgrounds <u>to integrate</u>. <u>Integrated</u> city districts, for example, may result only in violence and unrest.

> <u>The integration of</u> our education system has been much resisted and is still not complete.

> It is important for both the immigrant and the society that immigrants <u>integrate themselves into</u> the community as a whole.

To cover something up
This phrasal verb has two related meanings:

(1) You *cover something* up when you try to protect it or hide it by putting something else on top of it.

> The spy entered enemy territory by <u>covering himself</u> up in a wagon full of hay.

(2) You *cover something up* when you hide its existence from other people.

> Government officials were successful in <u>covering up</u> the election fraud.

The noun *cover-up* usually has a political connotation.

The government's real error lay not in the crime itself—which most people did not care about—but in the <u>cover-up</u> that followed.

To exterminate/to wipe out

These words are used when all of a group of people or animals in a particular location are killed. The words are fairly synonymous, though *wipe out* is a little more informal.

It is difficult to <u>exterminate</u> termites without professional help.

A couple of hundred years ago, bears were plentiful throughout North America. Now they <u>have been exterminated</u> from all but a few regions, mostly in protected areas.

Many animal species become extinct not due to their intentional <u>extermination</u> by humans, but because of the side-effects of human intrusion into their habitat.

Diseases brought from Europe <u>wiped out</u> many Native American tribes.

On the spur of the moment

You do something on the spur of the moment when you do it suddenly and without planning to do it.

Originally we were going to drive to Atlanta, but <u>on the spur of the moment</u> we decided to fly.

Carnivorous/herbivorous/omnivorous

These three terms refer to the eating habits of animals. A *carnivorous* animal eats only meat. A *herbivorous* animal largely eats grasses and other plants. An *omnivorous* animal eats both. The nouns are *carnivore, herbivore,* and *omnivore.*

Although it might look ferocious, the bison is a gentle, <u>herbivorous</u> grazing animal different from the sheep only in its size.

Tigers are <u>carnivores</u> that do most of their hunting at night.

It is not clear when or how man's primate ancestors made the transition from <u>herbivore</u> to <u>omnivore</u>.

VOCABULARY EXERCISE

Complete the sentences with the expressions given. Some may be used more than once.

segregated	omnivores	to integrate
cover	carnivorous	extermination
segregated according	cover up	wipe
on the spur of the moment	integrated	

1. In the recent past, a number of countries have had policies designed to _____ out one or more of its minority populations. When the outside world catches wind of these policies, voicing protest against practices resulting in the mass _____ of thousands of people, the countries typically _____ the crimes and deny any wrong-doing.

2. Until the Supreme Court decision on *Brown v. Board of Education of Topeka*, it was common practice in the United States for schools to be _____ to race. Prior to this decision, public facilities were permitted to be "separate but equal," that is, racially _____ yet, in theory, at least, providing equal services to whites and African Americans. In *Brown v. Board of Education*, however, the justices of the Court unanimously declared that separate educational systems were by their very nature unequal.

   After the Supreme Court decision, busing—transporting children from one school district to another in order _____ the two systems—became common practice. Though technically limited to the public schools, the Supreme Court decision further implied that other public facilities—including swimming pools and community centers—must also be _____ .

3. Many animals commonly thought to be _____ are actually omnivorous: foxes, for example, frequently feed on berries and fruit. Likewise, many animals that are generally believed to be herbivores are actually _____, among them some species of mice whose diet at certain times of the year may depend primarily on insects.

4. When Bob asked her if she would like to go out with him that Friday night, _____ Patricia told him that she already had plans. How embarrassing it was, when, the very next day, Leslie and Wendy invited her to a party on Friday and Bob overheard her accept the invitation. "I thought you said you had to go to a nephew's birthday party," he said to her, in an indifferent tone that nonetheless revealed his feelings were hurt. Lamely she tried to _____ up her lie by saying that the birthday party had been put off until the next day. He seemed to believe her, but she never felt comfortable around him after that.

Answers for Reading Power Lesson One

Practice #1

1. A   4. B
2. C   5. D
3. B   6. B

Practice #2

1. D   4. A
2. C   5. C
3. D   6. B

Practice #3

1. C   4. A
2. C   5. D
3. C   6. A

Practice #4

1. B   4. A
2. D   5. B
3. C

Practice #5

1. C   4. B
2. C   5. D
3. D

Practice #6

1. B   4. D
2. C   5. A
3. A   6. C

Practice #7

1. D   4. C
2. A   5. C
3. D

Practice #8

1. D   4. C
2. A   5. B
3. D

Practice #9

1. A   4. A
2. B   5. A
3. C

Practice #10

1. A   4. D
2. B   5. B
3. B

Vocabulary Exercise

1. wipe; extermination; cover up

2. segregated according; segregated; integrate; integrated

3. carnivorous; omnivores

4. on the spur of the moment; cover

READING POWER
LESSON TWO

SESSION A: READING FOR INFERENCE

> An *inference* is a conclusion based on information you
> have.

On the TOEFL, inference questions ask you to draw conclusions that are not explicitly given in the reading passage.

Below are two examples of inferences based on facts.

FACT: All children acquire their first language before the age of four.

INFERENCE: All six-year-old children speak a language.

FACT: AT&T used to have a monopoly on telephone services in the United
                  States.

INFERENCE: There is currently more than one telephone company. (*Used to* means that
                  something was true in the past, but no longer is.)

Inference type questions usually take the form:

From the passage, it can be inferred that . . .

The author implies that . . .

To answer inference questions, you should:

(1) Read the question carefully.
(2) Read the answers to see what kind of answers you have available.
(3) Scan the passage to find where the information related to the inference can be found.
(4) Make assumptions about the information using what the passage says directly and what you already know about the topic.
(5) Select the best answer.

A good reader makes inferences while reading a text. You can improve your ability to answer inference questions by making inferences when you read the passage for the first time.

Inference questions require a high level of reading skills. Previous knowledge of a topic (called *background knowledge*) will also help with inference-type questions. For example, a student with little knowledge of science will probably have difficulty trying to infer information from reading passages about science. For this reason, it is smart to learn a little about a lot of different topics by reading a wide variety of materials. This will give you background knowledge as well as a wide vocabulary.

SESSION B: READING FOR REFERENCE

Reference questions require you to identify the specific meaning or use of some word in the passage. The two main types of reference questions are vocabulary questions and questions about pronoun/possessive adjective reference.

A vocabulary question usually takes the form:

The term *anaplasty* in line 12 is closest in meaning to . . .

In line 17, *King William's War* is referring to . . .

A question about pronoun or possessive adjective reference takes the form:

She in line 5 refers to . . .

The word *their* in line 16 refers to . . .

To answer reference questions you should:

(1) Use the line numbers given at the side of the passage to find the word or words mentioned in the question.
(2) Read the context of the word or words carefully.
(3) Select the best answer.

Look at the following two examples of reference questions:

There is a crisis in faith among Americans today regarding their political system. This has heavily affected the last two election *Line* cycles. Candidates are addressing the integrity (5) of the system and the importance of Democracy more and more frequently in what appears to be an effort to restore voters' trust in "politics as usual."

The word *this* in line 2 refers to:

(A) a crisis in American political institutions
(B) doubts among U.S. citizens about the political system
(C) the American political system
(D) a campaign cycle

Although answer (A) contains the word *crisis,* which may distract you, answer (B) is correct. The crisis in faith mentioned in line 1 is not within the political institutions themselves, but concerns doubts held by citizens about the system.

The word *integrity* in line 4 is closest in meaning to

(A) character
(B) honesty
(C) deceit
(D) cunning

Here the correct answer is (B), *honesty*. Notice that the answer set gives two synonyms of integrity, *character* and *honesty*. Only one of these is correct in the context of the word in the reading passage. The TOEFL often presents this kind of distractor to the the test taker.

Don't answer vocabulary questions too quickly. Sometimes the obvious synonym is a distractor—not the correct answer. Always check the answer you choose by seeing how the word is used in the reading passage.

SESSION C: READING FOR ORGANIZATION

Organization questions require you to understand the overall organization of the passage so that you can answer one of several types of questions.

Organization questions are sometimes the most difficult kind of TOEFL reading question. For this reason, you may want to select your answer by eliminating the wrong answers first.

There are four types of organization questions. They are discussed separately below.

Basic Organization Questions

An organization question typically takes the form:

"The author's organization of the passage is best described as . . ."

(A) moving from a general idea to specific examples
(B) introduction, support, and conclusion
(C) chronological
(D) comparison and contrast

You should answer basic organization questions by:

(1) Determining what exactly the question requires you to answer.

(2) Reading the first and last paragraphs of the passage carefully, and identifying the topic sentence of the passage.

(3) Paying special attention to "linking words," such as *next, secondly, in conclusion,* etcetera.

(4) Eliminating the wrong answer choices until you have the best answer.

The Location of Specific Facts in the Passage

A location question typically takes the form:

"Where in the passage does the author discuss the aging of neural transmitters?"

(A) lines 1–3
(B) line 7
(C) lines 8–9
(D) lines 12–14

You should answer specific-fact location questions by:

(1) Identifying a key word or words in the questions.

(2) Read the lines in the reading passage given in the answer choice, looking for the key word or its synonym.

(3) Eliminating the wrong answer choices until you have the best answer.

Questions About Paragraphs That Precede or Follow a Passage

This type of question typically takes the form:

"The paragraph after this passage would most likely be about . . ."

"The paragraph preceding this passage would most likely concern . . ."

You should answer this type of organization question by:

(1) Going to the first paragraph of the reading passage if the question is about the preceding paragraph, or to the last paragraph of the reading passage if the question concerns the following paragraph, and reading that paragraph carefully.

(2) Keeping in mind the main idea of the passage as a whole, eliminating the wrong answer choices until you have the best answer.

Questions About the Kind of Larger Work in Which the Passage Would Be Found

This type of question typically takes the form:

"Where would this reading passage most likely be found?"

(A) in an introductory textbook
(B) in a newspaper
(C) in a personal letter to a friend
(D) in a company memo

You should answer this type of organization question by:

(1) Reading the answer choices carefully.
(2) Skimming through the reading passage, noting characteristics such as tone, style, and main idea.
(3) Eliminating the wrong answer choices until you have the best answer.

In order to answer organization questions, it will be necessary for you to draw conclusions about ideas not explicitly given in the text. In this way, organization questions are very similar to inference type questions.

If possible, you may want to leave organization questions until you have answered all the other types of questions for a reading passage. As you answer the other questions, you may come across the information needed to answer the organization questions. This is easier to do on the paper-based exam on the computer-based exam, as we have discussed.

SESSION D: READING FOR TONE

Your ability to judge the author's tone is sometimes tested on the TOEFL. In essence, this question is not very different from the tone questions used in the Listening Comprehension section (see Listening Power Lessons Two and Three).

Tone questions frequently take the form:

"The author's tone can best be described as . . ."

You should answer a tone question by:

(1) Reading the answer choices carefully.
(2) Skimming through the reading passage, looking for words and ideas that indicate how the author feels about the topic or about the audience.
(3) Eliminating the wrong answer choices until you have the best answer.

PRACTICE #1—Reading Practice

Circle the letter of the answer that correctly answers each question.

Combustion is the scientific name for burning. Although there are many different types of combustion, the basic process is the same: Oxygen from the air combines with a material that can burn. Heat is then produced from this reaction. If the process occurs very quickly, flames or an explosion can result. When combustion occurs under controlled conditions, it can produce useful energy. Such controlled combustion is what drives the engines that power our cars.

Gasoline is burned within each cylinder of an engine in a controlled fashion. The role of the engine is to convert chemical energy stored in the gasoline into work. This controlled combustion results in a great force which acts on a piston. The piston then turns a crankshaft which, using a rotary motion, is then used to propel the car. The combustion process in the piston occurs over a four-stroke cycle. This cycle includes two up and two down movements of the piston during the combustion of a single introduction of fuel. These four strokes are: intake, compression, power, and exhaust.

As the intake stroke begins, a valve opens at the top of the cylinder, which allows an air-fuel mixture to fill the expanding chamber. When the piston reaches the bottom of the intake stroke, the valve closes, trapping the air-fuel mixture inside. The upward stroke that immediately follows compresses the mixture to about ten percent of its original volume. The downward power stroke is the result of the explosion that occurs when the spark plug releases up to 30,000 volts of electricity. The force which drives the piston

downward can equal up to three tons. Finally, the cycle is completed with the upward exhaust stroke. When the piston has reached the bottom during the power stroke, the exhaust valve opens. As the piston rises in the chamber, it forces out the remaining combustion gases. When the piston again reaches the top of the chamber, it is ready to start the four-stroke cycle all over again.

The ideal air-to-fuel ratio for gasoline engines in automobiles is 15:1 (fifteen parts of air to one part of fuel). A "rich" mixture has less air and more fuel, and thus a lower ratio (10:1). A "lean" mixture has a higher ratio (20:1). The only time a mixture richer than 15:1 is required is when starting a cold engine. When the engine is cold, the gasoline is not vaporizing readily. By manipulating the choke, air intake is reduced. At such times, closing the choke on the carburetor provides the necessary rich mixture. To help a cold engine start easily, gasoline manufacturers also produce a blend of gasoline that contains special hydrocarbons that vaporize at low temperatures. But at normal operating temperatures, a rich mixture wastes fuel, fouls the spark plugs, and causes pollution. A lean mixture can be even more costly in the long run, since it can cause the valves and pistons to burn, warp, and even crack.

1. This passage primarily describes

    (A) how automobile engines waste fuel
    (B) how combustion powers an automobile engine
    (C) the proper proportion of air to fuel in a car engine
    (D) why lean mixtures save money

2. An air-to-fuel ratio of 15:1 is

    (A) required at all times
    (B) required when starting a cold engine
    (C) less expensive over time than a leaner mixture
    (D) undesirable at any time

3. It can be inferred from the passage that a lean mixture

    (A) contains an air to fuel ratio greater than or equal to 20:1
    (B) has approximately one part of air to 20 parts of fuel
    (C) has exactly 20 parts of air to one part of fuel
    (D) is always more efficient than a richer one

4. Over a car's lifetime, the most important reason for setting the proper air-to-fuel ratio is that

    (A) a lean mixture can cause expensive damage to the car
    (B) the choke cannot be used when the engine is warm
    (C) a lean mixture wastes fuel
    (D) a rich mixture must be avoided in cold climates

5. The word *exhaust* in line 42 means

    (A) use up
    (B) waste gases
    (C) tire out
    (D) fume

6. The word *it* in line 45 refers to

    (A) the stroke
    (B) gasoline
    (C) the chamber
    (D) the piston

PRACTICE #2—Reading Practice

Circle the letter of the answer that correctly answers each question.

One of the major achievements of modern science is the determination of the approximate age of the earth, now reckoned at 4.6 billion years. This makes the earth far older than was formerly imagined. Indeed, one eighteenth-century religious and scientific authority circulated the widely accepted view that the planet was only some four thousand years old. To modern scientists, however, geologic time begins with the formation of the earth's solid crust sometime earlier than the age of the oldest known rock. Geologists divide this vast expanse of time into four eras—the Precambrian, the Paleozoic, the Mesozoic, and the Cenozoic, which takes us to the present. Thus, the almost five billion years of planetary history and the 100,000 or so years of human existence are encapsulated in a mere four categories. Obviously, to aid in the discussion of such vast periods of time, further division and specification becomes necessary. Accordingly, the last three eras are further divided into 12 periods and more than 40 epochs, each division being determined by characteristic types of rock and plant and animal fossils. Since the Precambrian era alone is more than four billion years long, is structurally complex, and has few fossils, it has been divided roughly in half for convenience of discussion. Scientists are working hard to discover clues about the earth's most distant past, but there still is a startling lack of detail about both portions of the planet's Precambrian era.

Line (5) (10) (15) (20) (25) (30) (35)

1. It can be inferred from the passage that
   (A) the Mesozoic period predates the Paleozoic
   (B) the Precambrian period predates the Cenozoic
   (C) the four eras are of approximately equal duration
   (D) the Precambrian period is divided into periods and epochs

2. The paragraph following the passage would most likely address
   (A) the Mesozoic era
   (B) the Cenozoic era
   (C) what is known about the Precambrian era
   (D) continuing scientific research into the Precambrian era

3. The word *This* in line 4 refers to
   (A) the achievements of modern science
   (B) a scientific discovery
   (C) the determination of Earth's age
   (D) geologic time

4. According to the passage, what can be inferred about the Precambrian era?
   (A) Its duration is brief.
   (B) It is impossible to study.
   (C) Division of the era was necessary for more focussed discussion.
   (D) It had a plenitude of fossils.

PRACTICE #3—Reading Practice

Circle the letter of the answer that correctly answers each question.

Until recently, it has been merely an unexplained observation that, in disk-shaped galaxies, certain bright, intensely hot, young
Line stars known to astronomers as O-stars are
(5) concentrated along spiral arms radiating from the galactic center. The recent discovery of vast clouds of interstellar gas in our own galaxy, and their subsequent study, indicate both a solution for this puzzle and a mecha-
(10) nism that may, in part, explain how stars are generated out of interstellar gas and dust.

The spiral arms are now thought to have been formed from density waves in the galaxy, induced by gravitational fluctuations
(15) that arise at the galactic center. These waves appear to cause scattered clouds of interstellar gas to collect and coalesce into clumps of relatively high concentration.

These gas concentrations, or molecular-
(20) cloud complexes, are now thought to consist of about 99 percent molecular, or diatomic, hydrogen, and have been mapped by radio telescope. Molecular hydrogen itself is invisible to radio telescopes. But astronomers
(25) have been able to use carbon monoxide as a reliable tracer of hydrogen, since the asymmetric molecule of that gas emits specific electromagnetic wave bands as it rotates.

Extensive mapping has established a clear
(30) correlation between the cloud complexes and the O-stars on the spiral arms—a coincidence too striking, in view of the expanse of "unpopulated space" even within galaxies, to be the result of chance. It is now theorized
(35) that pressure waves generated by the O-stars themselves may condense the gases of these clouds to initiate the formation of new stars.

1. In line 7, *interstellar* most nearly means
   (A) starlike
   (B) terrestrial
   (C) between stars
   (D) astronomical

2. It can be inferred that, in the mapping of molecular cloud complexes, carbon monoxide plays a role that is
   (A) invisible
   (B) highly useful
   (C) unnecessary
   (D) ineffective

3. In line 12, the word *arms* is closest in meaning to
   (A) hands
   (B) appendages
   (C) departments
   (D) estuaries

4. In line 33, *unpopulated space* probably means:
   (A) the countryside
   (B) galaxies outside our own
   (C) the empty part of space
   (D) galaxies peopled with other races

5. The paragraph following this passage would probably go on to address
   (A) the destruction of O-stars
   (B) theories on the O-stars' immediate role in the formation of new stars
   (C) molecular cloud gas constitution
   (D) pressure waves and their role in the formation of galaxies

PRACTICE #4—Reading Practice

Circle the letter of the answer that correctly answers each question.

New York successfully averted bankruptcy in the mid-1970s through the creation of the Municipal Assistance Corporation, which
Line issued nearly $2 billion in special bonds to
(5) help finance city spending, and through a loan program offered by the federal government later in 1975. But the essential problems of the city are still present and continue to play a role in how the city is
(10) managed, even today. In the 1970s, income from taxation was limited by the shrinking of New York's middle-class population, which resulted in revenues inadequate for supporting the vast, expensive city govern-
(15) ment. A number of major businesses left the city, taking with them jobs, income, and more tax revenues. The wealth of New York, during this financial crisis, slowly dwindled.

Realizing that the remarkable prosperity of
(20) the 1950s and 1960s had faded, New York's leaders had to closely reexamine the city's financial position. As a first step, the city's wasteful practices had to be halted, for only a new era of thrifty and efficient government
(25) could enable New York to retain its position as the economic, social, and cultural capital of the United States.

1. In line 13, *revenues* most nearly means
   (A) number of inhabitants
   (B) salaries
   (C) individual assets
   (D) income from taxes

2. Which of the following would best replace the word *dwindled* in line 18?
   (A) augmented
   (B) diminished
   (C) increased
   (D) outshone

3. The passage implies that New York
   (A) has lost its pre-eminent place in American society
   (B) has permanently escaped the threat of bankruptcy
   (C) has managed to avoid asking the national government for assistance
   (D) enjoyed a period of unusual economic strength prior to 1970

4. The word *faded* in line 20 is closest in meaning to
   (A) lightened
   (B) bleached
   (C) passed
   (D) deteriorated

5. The paragraph preceding the passage most likely talked about
   (A) the economic climate of New York in the 1950s and 1960s
   (B) the economic decline of New York in the 1970s
   (C) the economic history of New York in the nineteenth century
   (D) New York's financial troubles in the 1920s and 1930s

PRACTICE #5—Reading Practice

Circle the letter of the answer that correctly answers each question.

The eighteenth century "slave-poet" Phillis Wheatley is considered the first important black woman poet in the United States. Her
Line life and work is notable for what it shows us
(5) about black Americans during Colonial times, and one human being's determination to express herself.

Learning for slaves was not prohibited by law, as it would be later on in the South.
(10) Still, colonial slavemasters did not generally approve of educating slaves. Wheatley was treated differently; she was allowed to read, write, and publish her work. Wheatley, born in Senegal, arrived in Boston Harbor in
(15) 1761. At dockside, she was sold to the family of the merchant John Wheatley to be made into a house-servant. At the age of 12, she began to learn Latin, and to translate the Latin poet Ovid. At 14, she published her
(20) first poems. Her first published work, "An Elegiac Poem on the Death of the Celebrated Divine . . . George Whitefield," was widely read. The Countess of Huntingdon published Wheatley's *Poems on*
(25) *Various Subjects, Religious and Moral* in England in 1773, and Wheatley's fame grew in Europe as well as America.

Not fully included in slave or white society, Phillis was often isolated and treated as
(30) an object of curiosity. Still, she continued to successfully write and publish. Fame left Phillis as quickly as it had come, however. After the American Revolution broke out, the Wheatley family fell upon hard times
(35) and set Phillis free to fend for herself. Hard labor as a servant, the only work Wheatley could find, weakened her already frail body. She died in poverty in her early 30s, and was buried in an unmarked grave.

1. The words *slave-poet* in line 1 could best be replaced by:
   (A) incarcerated artist
   (B) quashed creator
   (C) prisoner of verse
   (D) servant-writer

2. According to the passage, education of a slave in eighteenth-century America was
   (A) commonplace
   (B) forbidden by law
   (C) unusual
   (D) required by state government

3. The passage mentions the Countess of Huntingdon as someone who helped Phillis Wheatley by
   (A) employing her as a servant
   (B) teaching her to read and write
   (C) introducing her to important people
   (D) publishing her book

4. In line 31, the word *left* is closest in meaning to

 (A) maintained
 (B) remained
 (C) fled from
 (D) consumed

5. In line 34, the term *fell upon* could best be replaced with which of the following?

 (A) leaned on
 (B) frowned at
 (C) maneuvered around
 (D) began to experience

PRACTICE #6—Reading Practice

Circle the letter of the answer that correctly answers each question.

The phylum Cnidaria is diverse, composed of some 9,000 species. They may be polyps—attached to the bottom of the ocean
Line like sea anemones—or medusas (free-float-
(5) ing jellyfish). In the class Hydrozoa, the polyp phase is dominant, and the medusa phase is either absent or very small. In the class Scyphozoa, that includes large jellyfish, the polyp stage is small. In both classes the
(10) polyp stage produces new medusas asexually, and the medusas reproduce sexually, making an egg that becomes a polyp. Many Cnidarian polyps form colonies which get very large, as in the case of some huge coral
(15) reefs. Other Cnidarians are important as predators in the open ocean.

Jellyfish are essentially bags made of two cell layers. The ectoderm, or outer layer, contains the cnidocysts, the stinging cells that
(20) are characteristic of the phylum. The inner endoderm, or gastrodermis, lines the gut. Between the two there is a firm, gelatinous middle layer (mesoglea), which may be thin or thick. Jellyfish are shaped like a bell or
(25) upside-down bag. Their mouth is at the end of a projection called the manubrium, which hangs down within the center of the bell, and is often surrounded by a ring of tenta-cles. Jellyfish range in size, from tiny, trans-
(30) parent forms a few millimeters across, to huge undersea creatures 6 feet in diameter with 100-foot-long tentacles.

Jellyfish prey upon tiny plankton, fish, or other jellyfish, which they capture with
(35) nematocysts, small stingers on their tenta-cles. Jellyfish move by contracting the outer lip of their "bell," and expelling the water

within it. Some jellyfish move swiftly, while others tend to drift.

1. In line 17, the word *essentially* means
   (A) nearly
   (B) officially
   (C) dangerously
   (D) basically

2. *Gelatinous* in line 22 could best be replaced by which of the following?
   (A) semiliquid
   (B) icy
   (C) curved
   (D) milky

3. *Prey* in line 33 is closest in meaning to which of the following?
   (A) hunt
   (B) game
   (C) dirt
   (D) capitalize on

4. Where in the passage does the author mention the size of jellyfish?
   (A) lines 2–5
   (B) lines 14–15
   (C) lines 29–32
   (D) lines 34–35

5. According to the passage, what is characteristic of all creatures in the phylum Cnidaria?
   (A) lack of movement
   (B) resistance to cold
   (C) stinging cells
   (D) small size

PRACTICE #7—Reading Practice

Circle the letter of the answer that correctly answers each question.

The human liver is composed of the right lobe (the largest), the left lobe, and two small lobes that are located behind the right
Line lobe. Each lobe is composed of small, multi-
(5) sided units called lobules. Most livers have between 50,000 and 100,000 lobules. The essential work in each lobule is performed by a bundle of liver cells that surround the central vein found in each lobule. These
(10) bundles, often called sheets, are separated by cavities known as sinusoids. It is the presence of these sinusoids that accounts for the liver's somewhat spongy texture and its ability to absorb large amounts of blood.
(15)   Each lobule also contains structures called bile capillaries. These very small tubes carry the bile that is continuously secreted by the liver cells, even in the absence of digestion in the small intestine. The bile capillaries come
(20) together to form bile ducts, which function to remove the bile from the liver. Finally, these ducts, after leaving the liver, come together to form the hepatic duct. Excess bile goes to the gall bladder, where it is
(25) stored for later use.

1. According to the passage, the human liver is composed of how many lobes?

   (A) 2
   (B) 4
   (C) 5
   (D) 50,000 to 100,000

2. According to the passage, the most important work within a lobule is

   (A) performed by a central vein
   (B) inside the sinusoids
   (C) the work done by the lobes
   (D) done by the sheets

3. Which of the following words is closest in meaning to *cavities* as used in line 11?

   (A) infections
   (B) holes
   (C) blood cells
   (D) mounds

4. It can be inferred that without the sinusoids, the liver would

   (A) include many more bundles
   (B) lose its unique texture
   (C) increase bile flow into the gall bladder
   (D) absorb even more blood

5. Which is probably the largest structure?

   (A) a liver cell
   (B) a bile capillary
   (C) a bile duct
   (D) the hepatic duct

PRACTICE #8—Reading Practice

Circle the letter of the answer that correctly answers each question.

Scientists speculate that prehistoric peoples first obtained iron from the remains of ancient meteorites. They used this iron to
Line fashion tools, weapons, ornaments, and a
(5) variety of other items. Some credibility is given to the claims of these scientists by the fact that in several old languages, the word for iron is roughly translated as "metal from the sky." Scientists have documented the
(10) earliest use of iron as occurring around 4000 B.C., but they are uncertain when iron was first produced by smelting iron ore.

The Hittites of ancient Turkey were the first society known to make extensive use of
(15) the iron they created. By 1400 B.C., they were manufacturing large quantities of hardened iron for tools and weapons. By 1000 B.C., civilizations in India and China also acquired the ability to produce iron; the so-
(20) called Iron Age was well under way. Initially, the furnaces used to produce iron were shallow, bowl-shaped hearths where iron ore and charcoal were heated. When heated in this way for several hours, the iron ore would
(25) release its oxygen into the surrounding hot carbon. Shiny iron would remain. However, usable, hardened iron this was not. A repeated process of hammering and reheating had to be applied to the iron to remove weak-
(30) nesses and impurities. Only then was the iron of sufficient quality. Later, furnaces were improved by blowing air into them. This increased the maximum temperature of the furnace and allowed for a higher quality
(35) of iron.

Eventually, bellows were developed to replace the more primitive method of tuy-

eres that was first used to inject air into the furnace. By A.D. 700, ironworkers in what is
(40) now modern Spain invented a furnace where air was forced by water power. This led to large increases in efficiency. A single furnace could now produce over 350 pounds of wrought iron in a five-hour period.
(45) Subsequent developments in furnaces included the shaft furnace of the Middle Ages, and the blast furnace, which was really just a shaft furnace made with molten iron, that was frequently used after 1300.

1. According to most scientists, when was iron ore first smelted?
   (A) 4000 B.C.
   (B) 1400 B.C.
   (C) 1000 B.C.
   (D) It has not been determined.

2. Why did the iron have to be repeatedly hammered in the early days of hearths?
   (A) to prevent the in-take of air
   (B) to release its oxygen content
   (C) because it contained impurities
   (D) to increase its temperature

3. In line 34, the word *allowed* is closest in meaning to
   (A) granted
   (B) yielded
   (C) differed
   (D) confessed

4. In lines 39–40, the phrase *what is now* alerts the reader to the fact that

    (A) modern Spain was formed in A.D. 700
    (B) Spain was once a much larger country
    (C) Spain was not then in existence
    (D) this development revolutionized Spanish industry

5. Which of the following would likely be the most efficient method of iron production?

    (A) the shaft furnace
    (B) shallow bowl-shaped hearths
    (C) the method of ancient India
    (D) the tuyere furnace

PRACTICE #9—Reading Practice

Circle the letter of the answer that correctly answers each question.

When glaciers covered large areas of the United States, their movement cut deep, sharp valleys into the landscape. When the
Line climate warmed, the melting water of a
(5) glacier often remained to fill a valley. This is the most common vehicle of lake formation in the United States, and it explains why there are more lakes in the northern states than in the southern ones. Lakes can also be
(10) formed because of the presence of underlying beds of limestone, as in many of the over one thousand lakes in Lake County, Florida. This foundation of limestone gradually dissolves as it comes into contact with slightly
(15) acidic rainwater. Eventually, this erosion of the limestone results in the formation of a number of underground streams that function to carry off the rainwater. When the top of one of these subterranean passages col-
(20) lapses, a sinkhole is formed. With the proper climactic conditions this sinkhole may fill with subsequent rainfall and become a lake. The long-term collection of rainwater in the craters of extinct volcanoes can also form
(25) lakes, as can a naturally occurring deposit of silt that backs up a river at its natural outlet to the sea. Finally, the construction of dams in the United States and worldwide has resulted in the creation of great artificial
(30) lakes.

1. Because there are more lakes in the northern United States than in the southern United States, it can be inferred that
   (A) the valleys cut by southern glaciers were less sharp
   (B) glaciers were once less common in the south than in the north
   (C) the south generally lacks adequate limestone layers
   (D) the southern glaciers have yet to melt

2. *Beds* as used in line 11 most likely means
   (A) cots
   (B) deposits
   (C) bunks
   (D) cribs

3. Given a proper bed of limestone, it can be inferred that sinkholes would develop
   (A) in the craters of old volcanoes
   (B) only under Floridalike conditions
   (C) more slowly if the rain was highly acidic
   (D) quickly in areas with high precipitation

4. Which of the following best describes the passage's organization?

   (A) by method of formation
   (B) historical
   (C) literary
   (D) chronological

5. In line 19, *subterranean* most nearly means which of the following?

   (A) underwater
   (B) less visible
   (C) earthly
   (D) underground

PRACTICE #10—Reading Practice

Circle the letter of the answer that correctly answers each question.

Traditional nineteenth century education is usually associated with the image of a stern teacher standing in front of a blackboard in
Line a one room schoolhouse, teaching only the
(5) three *R's* of reading, writing, and arithmetic, and demanding rote learning in an atmosphere of silence and restraint.

Accurate or not, that image conflicts sharply with the modern reality. Today, the
(10) typical public school offers students a diversity of subject areas, a plethora of educational materials, and a variety of activities from creative dramatics to journalism. The modern school complex contains an array of
(15) educational facilities. Within the classroom setting, students are encouraged to speak up and engage in guided discussion. In fact, articulate speech and debate are desired skills. Children are encouraged to interrelate
(20) on class projects that are independent of the teacher. Teachers may certainly demand quiet when necessary, but they in turn are expected to be flexible about individual student needs.

(25) Contemporary schools reflect the thrust of a progressive educational philosophy whose main proponent was the pragmatic philosopher John Dewey. Dewey believed that education must serve the whole child to fully
(30) prepare him or her for an active role in society. To that end, the school curriculum was to include both academic and utilitarian courses. He posited that children have innate curiosity and talents which will be
(35) stimulated by an environment varied enough to call forth these qualities and provide an outlet for their expression.

Following the precepts of progressive educational philosophy, the Gary, Indiana
(40) school system initiated the Gary Plan between 1908 and 1915. The plan was later embraced by schools throughout the country. In addition to classroom space, the Gary Plan provided room for recreational activi-
(45) ties, a theater, science laboratories, and craft shops. The actual merit of progressive philosophy is still a very controversial issue, especially in light of figures that indicate a high degree of illiteracy among high school
(50) graduates in the past two decades. However, Dewey's progressive philosophy continues to exert a strong influence on the American education scene.

1. How does the author feel about the stereotypical image of nineteenth-century education?

   (A) It is valid.
   (B) It is not accurate.
   (C) Its accuracy is not important.
   (D) It is accurate, but only to a point.

2. In line 11, *plethora* most nearly means which of the following?

   (A) lack
   (B) multitude
   (C) supply
   (D) group

3. It can be inferred that in the stereotypical nineteenth-century classroom, active student involvement

   (A) was a primary educational goal
   (B) consisted of crafts and skills
   (C) occurred in one subject area only
   (D) was not actively encouraged

4. In line 32, *utilitarian* is closest in meaning to which of the following?

   (A) useless
   (B) practical
   (C) organized
   (D) recreational

5. The paragraph following this passage would most likely go on to address

   (A) Dewey's life after his involvement in education
   (B) the effects of progressive philosophy on the nineteenth-century classroom
   (C) modern ramifications of Dewey's work in education
   (D) The differences between modern education and nineteenth-century education

VOCABULARY

To hear how these words and expressions are pronounced, listen to Track_22.mov.

To lead to
This expression means "to cause." It is often, but not always, used when the result of the action is an unpleasant situation.

> Research shows that too much stress <u>leads to</u> irritability, headache and greater vulnerability to disease.

> Your first cigarette <u>can lead to</u> an addiction for life.

> A better-designed cover <u>will certainly lead to</u> increased sales.

Often the connection between the first action and the second action is not direct. In the second example above, many things must happen between the first cigarette and addiction.

This usage generally requires a gerund if an action is to be used in place of the noun.

> Your first cigarette <u>can lead to your being</u> addicted for life.

> You'll never believe it, but a car accident <u>led to my getting</u> a raise today.

As a whole
This may be defined as "generally" or "entirely."

> Although there were some voices who opposed further incursion into Indian territory, the European settlers <u>as a whole</u> behaved as though the land was already theirs.

> In ancient Egypt, the god favored by the strongest region of the time enjoyed the worship of the nation <u>as a whole</u>.

Subsequent
This is a formal word meaning "following in time."

> The rise of ancient Rome and its <u>subsequent</u> fall make for some fascinating reading.

Carol Livingstone was appointed chair of the committee in 1989, and she <u>subsequently</u> used the position as a stepping-stone to higher positions elsewhere.

Awe-inspiring
This means "amazing" or "remarkable."

From a certain point at the canyon's northern rim you get an <u>awe-inspiring</u> view of the sun as it sets.

To account for
This expression can also mean "to cause."

The city's dependence on heavy manufacturing <u>accounted for</u> its terrible air pollution in the early part of the century.

While talent <u>may have accounted for</u> some of her popularity, there was more to the devotion Marilyn's fans paid her than mere acting ability.

Wide/wider/widely
Probably you are familiar with the literal meaning of these words. But you may not be familiar with their frequent figurative or metaphorical use.

Wide, and its derivatives *wider* and *widely,* can mean "completely":

When I looked into her room, she was <u>wide</u> awake and her mouth was <u>wide</u> open.

Wide can mean "great" or "covering a large range." Here it is synonymous with a certain meaning of the word *broad.*

In her early twenties she traveled <u>widely</u> throughout Asia.

This bookstore has <u>a wide variety</u> of magazines and journals.

Although Michael's knowledge may not be as deep as Walter's, he has <u>a wider range</u> of interests.

Prey and *predator*

An animal that hunts other animals is a *predator*. The plural is *predators*. Animals that are hunted are *prey*. The noun *prey* is noncount, which means it has no plural form. But, unlike other non-count nouns, it is used like a plural count noun (like the word *people*). This means that it takes a verb in the plural form, and is modified by quantifiers used for plural nouns like *few* and *many*.

> Lions have many <u>prey</u>, from insects to antelopes, but they have only one <u>predator</u>: Man.

> Mice are <u>prey</u> to many <u>predators</u>, including foxes and owls.

Prey can also be a verb, and takes *on* or *upon* as a preposition.

> Eagles <u>prey on</u> rodents and other small mammals.

To play a role in

This expression means "to be involved in."

> Robert Burkhoff <u>played a role</u> in the opening of diplomatic relations between China and the United States.

Robert Burkhoff was not the only cause of the opening of diplomatic relations, and he may not even have been the most important. If you want to emphasize the importance of the subject, use *to play a major role in*.

> Exposure to direct sunlight <u>plays a major role in</u> the development of melanoma, or skin cancer.

VOCABULARY EXERCISE

Complete the sentences with the expressions given. Some may be used more than once.

accounts for

awe-inspiring

preying

as a whole

prey

play a role in

leads to

predators

subsequent

widely

1. It is obvious that a predator depends on its _____ for survival, but it is less obvious that the prey depend on their _____. For example, in many states deer populations would suffer if hunting were banned because their numbers would grow to the point that they would quickly exhaust their food supply. The _____ decline in the population would be greater than the number of deer that are killed by hunters today. In this way, we can say that hunters actually _____ the species' survival. Deer did not need this kind of "harvesting" by humans in the past because, formerly, they had natural _____ in mountain lions, which once roamed _____ across the continent, and which made the deer herds stronger by _____ on the slowest, the weakest, or the sick members of the population.

2. **Kyle:** Jim! I haven't seen you in weeks. What have you been up to?

    Jim: Well, I just got back from a vacation in the Sahara.

    Kyle: In the Sahara! Well, that _____ your tan.

    Jim: Actually, I got my tan after that, on the beach. In the desert I kept my body protected from the sun at all times. Our guides wouldn't even let us take off our hats. They said that exposing yourself to the hot desert sun _____ dehydration, which—in the desert—means death.

    Kyle: So, was it a good trip?

Answers for Reading
Power Lesson Two

Practice #1

1. B   4. A
2. C   5. B
3. A   6. D

Practice #2

1. B   3. C
2. C   4. C

Practice #3

1. C   4. C
2. B   5. B
3. B

Practice #4

1. D   4. C
2. B   5. A
3. D

Practice #5

1. D   4. C
2. C   5. D
3. D

Practice #6

1. D   4. C
2. A   5. C
3. A

Practice #7

1. B   4. B
2. D   5. D
3. B

Practice #8

1. D   4. C
2. C   5. A
3. B

Practice #9

1. B   4. A
2. B   5. D
3. D

Practice #10

1. C   4. B
2. B   5. C
3. D

Vocabulary Exercise

1. prey; predators; subsequent; play a role in; predators; widely; preying

2. accounts for; leads to; awe-inspiring; As a whole

WRITING POWER LESSONS

AT A GLANCE:

SESSION A: AN OVERVIEW OF THE ESSAY TEST

The first and most frequently asked question by ESL students who are confronting the TOEFL essay is: "What exactly is an essay?" This is a very good question, as essay organization and formation may vary greatly from one country to another. Quite simply, an essay is a written composition based on a particular topic. In the following writing sections, we will describe the kind of essay that the TOEFL examiners are looking for as well as provide you with the background you'll need to feel confident when you are faced with writing your TOEFL essay on the day of the exam.

Essay writing is a required part of every computer-based TOEFL exam (as of July 1998). The essay will, however, continue to be optional for the paper-based TOEFL. Your essay score will be combined with the score from the Structure section to form one Structure/Writing score. On the day of the exam, you will be given one topic on which to base your essay and allowed 30 minutes to write your essay. Unlike with the rest of the new TOEFL, you will be able to choose whether you wish to write your essay on the computer or by hand.

The range for your score of the essay component is from 0 (lowest score) to 6 (highest score); your final Structure/Writing score will range from 0 to 30. The readers of your essay are English or ESL specialists and work under the direct supervision of a "reading manager." These scorers will rate your essay independently of each other. That is, neither will know the rating of the other, and your final grade will be an average of the two scores. If there is a difference of more than one point between the two, a third reader will also rate your essay. Your final score could be a 6.0, 5.5, 5.0, 4.5, 4.0, 3.5, 3.0, 2.5, 2.0, 1.5, 1.0 or 0 (for a paper that is blank or written in a language other than English, or one which in no way addresses the topic).

To help you prepare for the essay component, you should study the "Writing Topics" provided to you by ETS (Educational Testing Service) in its *Information Bulletin for Computer-Based Testing*. By practicing essay writing prior to the day of the TOEFL, especially within the 30-minute time frame, you can greatly enhance your chances of doing well on this section of the test. There is a typing test included in the CD-ROM that will help you decide whether to use the keyboard or write your essay by hand (see the "User's Guide" in the beginning of this book for more details).

While becoming a proficient English writer may seem like a daunting task at first, there is no way to get around one very simple and basic truth: The only way to become a writer is to write and read as much and as often as you can. This may sound trite, but it is the fundamental key to improving your writing skills. Whereas it is important that you read and study examples of "good writing," unless you are willing to put in time and effort to write yourself, you will never become a competent writer of English. Great writers of English certainly did not become that way overnight; it obviously took a great deal of commitment, diligence, and time to perfect their craft. Thus, you—as an English as a Second Language writer and speaker—will need to be willing to invest an even greater effort into perfecting your English writing.

In the writing sections of this book, we will take you through steps that will help you learn how to organize your ideas, form an outline and develop organization, write a draft, and finally edit/proofread your essay. And yes, by the day of the test, you will need to know how to accomplish all of this in the 30-minute time frame that the TOEFL essay allows! But don't be discouraged. With dedication and perseverance, you will no doubt see results.

Your final essay must achieve the following in order for you to achieve the highest score possible:

(1) Your essay must effectively discuss the topic you have been asked to address.
It is vital that you read the assigned topic very carefully and not add or delete anything. This is one of the most common mistakes in writing an essay—by adding a few words, or conversely ignoring

one or two significant ones, a test-taker can easily digress from the assigned topic. Of course, the end result is failure to address the topic.

(2) Your essay must be well organized.
You must have an introduction (with a thesis statement), a body (with supporting details for your thesis), and a conclusion. Because essay organization is very important, this will be dealt with in greater detail later in this chapter.

(3) You must show consistent ease in your use of the English language.
This includes using correct grammar as well as the appropriate use of idiomatic language. Remember, you are trying to prove that your English skills are advanced enough for you to do as well as native-English speakers in an American university class.

(4) You must prove to your readers that you possess a wide range of vocabulary and know how to use terms in an appropriate fashion.
In other words, be very careful with the words you choose and avoid redundancy of both words and ideas. You want to be conservative so that you can show how much vocabulary and how many different word forms you know.

You must be able to paraphrase some or all of the question asked or the quotation given. This shows that you have a broad vocabulary, that your reading comprehension is adequate, and that you can avoid redundancy in your writing. You will also need to be able to paraphrase your thesis in your conclusion to remind your readers of your main idea.

SESSION B: STANDARD ESSAY FORM

In general, an essay is made up of three basic components: an introduction, a body, and a conclusion. The length of an essay may vary greatly, but because you only have 30 minutes in which to prepare, write, and proofread your TOEFL essay, you should aim for an essay containing a maximum of four to five paragraphs (unless you are a highly accomplished English writer). Your first paragraph, the introduction, will introduce the main topic of your essay to your reader, and it typically ends with your thesis statement (the most important sentence in your essay). The next part of your essay is the body. The body provides detailed support to prove your thesis. The body will be made up of the main subpoints of your thesis, each with its own paragraph. Thus, your body will most likely consist of 2–3 paragraphs. Your final paragraph is your conclusion. These three basic parts are outlined below and discussed in greater detail in subsequent lessons.

I. Introduction

    A. Hook (to capture your reader's attention)

    B. General information on assigned topic (no details)

    C. Thesis (one-sentence statement of main idea plus viewpoint)

II. Body

    A. Sub-Point One

        1. Topic sentence

        2. Details supporting topic sentence

    B. Sub-Point Two

        1. Topic sentence

        2. Details supporting topic sentence

    C. (Possible) Sub-Point Three

        1. Topic sentence

        2. Details supporting topic sentence

III. Conclusion

    A. Paraphrase of thesis

    B. Summary of viewpoint

    C. (Possible) General final statement/comment

SESSION C: TIME DIVISION FOR A 30-MINUTE ESSAY EXAM

One of the biggest dilemmas students face with essay examinations is how to make the best use of their time during the test. Certainly, the amount of time each student will need to make an outline, write the essay, and proofread will vary. However, all of these steps are necessary to produce a clear, organized essay with few grammatical errors. Below is a suggested way to divide the limited time you are given:

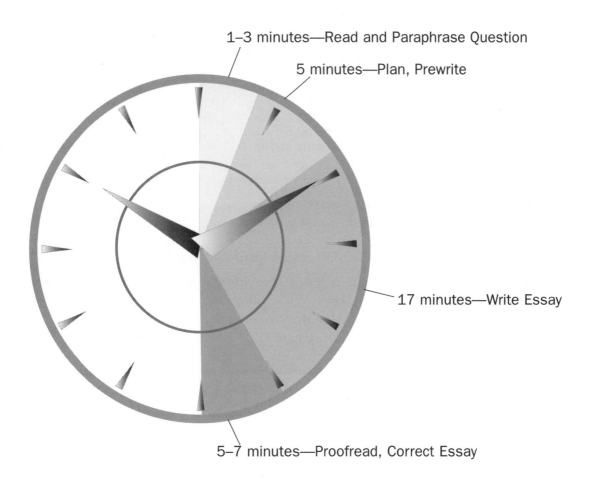

1–3 minutes—Read and Paraphrase Question

5 minutes—Plan, Prewrite

17 minutes—Write Essay

5–7 minutes—Proofread, Correct Essay

SESSION D: TYPES OF ESSAYS

The list below contains the most common types of essays found in an essay examination. After you have read your essay question and interpreted it, the next step is for you to decide what kind of essay you will need to organize and write. Determining the type of essay will help you write your thesis statement, decide how many body paragraphs are needed, know which transitions are appropriate to use, and much more.

Compare and Contrast Essay

This is one of the most typical forms of essay examinations. A comparison tells the ways in which a person, place, thing, event and so on are similar. A contrast points out differences. There are two common methods of organizing compare/contrast essays. Let's use the topic of "urban life vs. rural life" as an example:

(1) Body
      A. Similarities between urban and rural life
      B. Dissimilarities between urban and rural life

(2) Body
      A. Urban life: advantages and disadvantages
      B. Rural life: advantages and disadvantages

Persuasive Essay (Also Known as Personal Opinion Essay)

In the persuasive essay, you are trying to convince your reader to agree with a particular position or viewpoint you have expressed in your thesis. While adjectives and adverbs may sway your reader, the most effective way to bring your reader over to your side is through facts, detailed examples, and/or personal knowledge. Be sure to incorporate some aspects of the latter in the body of your persuasive essay.

This type of essay may be written in the first person and include: *in my opinion, it seems to me,* or *in my view.* However, even if you use the third person (and this is often more convincing), you can make your stand clear to your reader.

Descriptive Essay

The purpose of a descriptive essay is to present a detailed picture of a person, place, object, event, etcetera. To make the image as real as possible, you can use words or linguistic devices known as "imagery." These may be words which appeal directly to the reader's senses. That is, you can help your reader see, hear, taste, smell, or feel what it is you are describing by choosing vivid vocabulary. Avoid vague, general words such as *good, nice,* and *bad,* and replace these with more descriptive, specific terms. Metaphors (comparisons of two unlike items) are also often used in descriptions. Try to imagine that your reader has never experienced the object that you are describing; it is your job to bring this subject to life.

Cause and Effect Essay

To "cause" an action means to make something happen; the result or consequence of that action is the "effect." For example: "What are the chief causes of divorce, and how does it affect the children of the couple?" Typical transitions for this type of essay are: *as a result, as a consequence, consequently, therefore,* and *thus.*

Conditional sentence-type essay questions are sometimes classified as "cause and effect" as well. For example: "If you won a million dollars in the lottery, how would you spend the money? Describe in detail how your think your life would change as a result of your new-found wealth."

Interpretation/Analysis Essay

In the interpretation-type essay, you are given a short quotation (usually 1–3 sentences in length). You are asked to interpret the saying (i.e., paraphrase the author's message); then, either analyze or form your own opinion about the original quotation.

This kind of essay is rapidly growing in popularity, especially for essay entrance examinations to American university campuses and for many standardized tests. The time given for the essay test may vary from 15 minutes to two hours, depending on the school and/or standardized test. Therefore, when you practice writing this type of exam, you should try several different time frames.

Illustrative Essay

Another type of essay is the one that is based on examples or illustrations to support the writer's thesis. For example: "What were the best classes you ever took? Give examples of at least two classes which you found outstanding, and explain why you chose these." Illustration may also be used to provide clarification of a point made earlier.

Process Essay

Process writing, generally speaking, provides instructions or details a process: that is, it tells the reader how to operate a VCR, apply to a school, build a bookshelf, learn a foreign language, etcetera. Therefore, while this writing style is quite common, it is not typically tested in an essay examination. On the other hand, it is not uncommon to be given this type of essay as an at-home assignment.

SESSION E: THE INTRODUCTION TO THE ESSAY

Like all first impressions, the introductory paragraph of your essay will leave a lasting imprint. Therefore, it is extremely important that it be well written. To favorably impress your readers, your introduction should contain the following:

Hook

How is a hook used in fishing? It dangles in front of its target (the fish) and tries to lure or captivate it. In much the same way, the "hook" in an essay is used to catch the attention of your audience. To accomplish this, begin your essay with an interesting, thought-provoking idea about the topic you have been assigned. Avoid asserting the obvious; that is, merely stating a fact that everyone knows is true. For example, "Learning a new language is difficult" is a fact known to be true by almost everyone, and, therefore, serves no useful purpose. Sometimes a quotation (or proverb) works well as a hook if it is particularly relevant to the thesis.

General Statements Regarding the Assigned Topic

Your introduction should only introduce the main ideas of your essay. This is not the place for you to provide supporting details, such as specific names, places, and dates. Save these for the body of your essay.

Thesis

The thesis is the most significant statement in your essay. It consists of one sentence only and is usually the last sentence of your introduction. A thesis must be a complete sentence (unlike a title). It should also be narrow enough for you to be able to discuss it within the short time frame allowed on the TOEFL and within a two- or three-paragraph body. Yet it must also be general enough for you to be able to write two to three sub-points on this topic.

Unlike some countries, in the United States, we do not state directly what we plan to do or say in our essay; for example, "I will write about . . . " is unacceptable in an American essay. If your essay is well written, your intentions should be obvious to your reader without your having to explicitly state them.

The thesis serves two basic functions. First, it states the main topic of your essay. Secondly, it provides a viewpoint or position that you, the writer, holds about this topic.

For example, this is not a thesis: "Smoking in restaurants in New York is illegal." It merely states a fact, but provides no position or opinion concerning this fact.

This is a thesis: "That smoking in restaurants in New York is illegal is highly unfair to the smoker and unjustified for the nonsmoker." Here we are given both a topic (i.e., smoking in restaurants in

New York is illegal) plus an opinion about this topic. Because this thesis states two positions regarding the topic, it will also help the writer to be able to quickly and effectively set up the organization for the body of his/her essay. That is, the two sub-points have been clearly laid out in the introduction for both the reader's and the writer's ease and comprehension.

Often students feel that there must be a "right" or "wrong" position that they should take on a given topic. Remember: You are always entitled to your own opinion. The readers are only interested in whether you have logically, clearly, and effectively supported the position which you have taken.

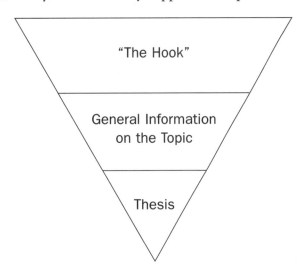

Practice One

Which of the following sentences is a thesis? If the sentence is a thesis, put a "T" in the space provided next to it. If it is not a thesis, put in "NT" in the space provided. Be prepared to discuss the reasons for your choices.

1. _____ Washington, D.C., is the capital of the United States.

2. _____ There are two basic reasons for the decline of divorce in America: the lack of communication skills and financial problems.

3. _____ Divorce is not legal in my country. Some people think it should be.

4. _____ Walking is the best exercise: it is good for one's health, and it doesn't cost anything!

5. _____ Traveling for fun and education.

6. _____ Because I wanted to learn how to speak English fluently, I felt it essential that I move to an English-speaking country.

7. _____ Financial woes and the lack of free time are the major causes of stress.

8. _____ The Beatles sold over a million records in the 1960s.

9. _____ The Beatles and the Rolling Stones were far more talented than the popular rock bands of today.

10. _____ Now, I am going to write about the reasons I moved to the United States.

To check your responses above, be sure the thesis statement:

- Contains one, and only one, complete sentence
- Provides a clearly defined main topic
- Takes a clearly stated position on the topic (instead of merely stating a fact)
- Doesn't explicitly state what you plan to do/say

Answers

1.	NT	6.	T
2.	T	7.	T
3.	T	8.	NT
4.	T	9.	T
5.	NT	10.	NT

Practice Two

Take the following topics and questions, and turn them into theses. Remember that each thesis must be a complete sentence that clearly states your main idea and takes a position on this topic. Ideally, it will also set up the organization for the body of your essay.

EXAMPLE: **Topic/Question:** In many countries, the government practices censorship of television programs. Do you support this practice or not? Support your answer with specific examples.

Possible Thesis: The censorship of television programs is an undemocratic and fiscally wasteful step taken by the government.

1. **Topic/Question:** If you had a choice, would you like to live forever? Explain why this does or does not appeal to you.

   Thesis:

   _____

   _____

2. **Topic:** Students attend a university or college for a variety or reasons. In your opinion, what should be the chief goal(s) of a university education?

   Thesis:

   _____

   _____

   _____

   _____

3. **Topic:** When many people think of the United States, words such as "independent" and "free-spirited" come to mind. If you had to describe your country by its personality, what trait(s) would best describe it?

   Thesis:

   _____

   _____

   _____

   _____

4. **Topic:** Most people experience at least some degree of culture shock when they are getting accustomed to a new culture. What advice would you give to a friend of yours to help him get over culture shock?

Thesis:

_____

_____

_____

_____

5. **Topic:** It is necessary to be a competitive person in order to succeed in life. Do you agree with this statement? Why or why not?

Thesis:

_____

_____

_____

_____

Practice Three

Choose one of the questions from the above list (1–5) and write an introduction. Be sure to follow the steps laid out in the inverted pyramid diagram, and watch the time. Remember, on the actual test you will only have a very short time in which to compose your introduction.

SESSION F: THE BODY OF THE ESSAY

The main purpose of the body of your essay is to give support to your thesis (usually the last sentence of your introduction). To give sufficient support, you need to provide a minimum of two or three paragraphs in your body for an essay examination. However, a take-home essay generally has several body paragraphs.

All body paragraphs begin with a topic sentence. The topic sentence states the main idea of the body paragraph, a main sub-point of your thesis. For this reason, it may be said that after your thesis, topic sentences are the most important part of your essay.

Immediately following the topic sentence, you should provide clear, specific details to lend credence to the argument of your paper; specifically, to the topic sentence of that paragraph. To accomplish this, you should use specific dates, people, places, and/or events. You will most likely need more than one sentence to provide sufficient details for each point. Use transitions to introduce your examples (see list in appendix).

Generally speaking, the body paragraphs are longer than the introduction and conclusion. However, be sure that each body paragraph contains only one main sub-point. All the ideas included in each paragraph must fall under the broader topic sentence. That is, every new idea requires a new paragraph. Think of each sentence after the topic sentence ("the set") as a sub-set of it.

While you will want to use transitions within your body paragraphs, you also need to use them to connect one body paragraph to another. This is necessary to make your paper smooth and coherent. For example, if you are writing a compare/contrast essay, you may want to begin your second body paragraph with a transition phrase such as *on the other hand* or *in contrast*. Study the list of transition terms at the end of this chapter to determine which one(s) would be appropriate for the type of essay you are writing.

Practice One: Possible Body Divisions for an Essay

Read the following sample essay body divisions, and think of possible topics for these divisions.

1. I.   Introduction
   II.   Body
      A. Past
      B. Present
      C. Future
   III.   Conclusion

2. I. Introduction
    II. Body
        A. Infant
        B. Child
        C. Adult
        D. Old Age
    III. Conclusion

3. I. Introduction
    II. Body
        A. Emotional
        B. Mental
        C. Physical
    III. Conclusion

4. I. Introduction
    II. Body
        A. Urban
        B. Small Town
        C. Countryside
    III. Conclusion

5. I. Introduction
    II. Body
        A. Home
        B. Work
        C. School
    III. Conclusion

Practice Two

In the exercises below, take the topic provided and, together with a partner, create your own sub-topics.

EXAMPLE: **Topic:** Best uses of home computers
                    II. Body
                         A. School work
                         B. Entertainment
                         C. Pay bills

1. **Topic:** The most practical college majors
   II. Body
       A.
       B.
       C.

2. **Topic:** Advantages to living in a foreign country
   II. Body
       A.
       B.
       C.

3. **Topic:** What a person must do to have a successful life
   II. Body
       A.
       B.
       C.

Practice Three

Choose one of the topics above, and write a 3-paragraph essay body on it. You have 20 minutes in which to write the body. You may choose either two or three sub-points (body paragraphs).

SESSION G: THE CONCLUSION OF THE ESSAY

The conclusion of the essay is often neglected. One reason for this is that students often run out of time during the essay examination and never get beyond the body of their papers. Another factor is that students often do not know how or when to end their essay. Yet failure to end your essay is analogous to not finishing the final chapter of a book. Your reader is left with unanswered questions; you must put these to rest before you finish your paper. However, if you have gone through the recommended organization steps laid out in our earlier sections and practiced timed writing on your own, finishing your essay should have become an easier task.

The following guidelines can help you improve your concluding paragraph:

- Before writing your conclusion, reread your introduction (paying special attention to your thesis) and your topic sentences. This will refresh your memory as to the main idea and main subpoints of your paper.
- Begin your conclusion with a paraphrase of your thesis. It is vital that you not repeat your thesis verbatim. Doing so is redundant and boring, and you miss the opportunity to show your readers the breadth of your vocabulary.
- Follow with general statements. These should be a summary or evaluation of previously-mentioned main thoughts.
- Your last sentence should provide a final thought or comment concerning your main topic.

The following should be avoided in a conclusion:

- New information does not belong in a conclusion. You have neither the time nor the space to develop it further (this is what the body paragraphs are for).
- Avoid detailed information in support of your thesis. This, too, should be found in the body of the essay, after your topic sentences.
- Don't begin your conclusion with "to conclude" or "in conclusion." It is clear to your reader that this is your final paragraph and is obviously your conclusion. (You may, however, begin your conclusion with transitions like *therefore, thus, to sum up,* or *in summary.*)
- A conclusion should not be lengthy. In general, three or four sentences will suffice. This is especially true of a 30-minute essay examination conclusion.

Diagram of a Typical Essay Conclusion

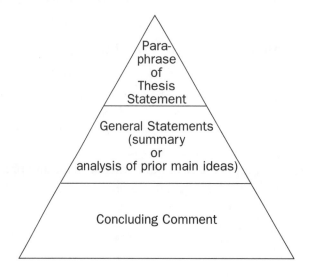

Practice One

Take the following thesis statements and paraphrase them so that they would fit into a conclusion. Remember that a paraphrase keeps the same ideas of the original statement, but uses your own words. When paraphrasing a thesis, it is often helpful to underline the key words in the original sentence. Be sure to use synonyms for these where possible. Also, be sure to include all of these main ideas in your rewrite. For example:

| THESIS: | Getting married and having children is not key to one's happiness. |
| PARAPHRASED THESIS: | A person may find contentment in life even if (s)he never marries or has children. |

1. **Thesis:** "If you want to live a long and productive life, you must exercise regularly and eat healthy foods."

   Paraphrased thesis:

   _____

   _____

   _____

2. **Thesis:** "Because of the conveniences and the cultural opportunities available in the city, living there is superior to living in the countryside."

   Paraphrased thesis:

   _____

   _____

   _____

   _____

3. **Thesis:** "The only ways to become a proficient writer are to read as much as possible and write whenever you can."

Paraphrased thesis:

_____

_____

_____

_____

_____

WRITING ASSIGNMENTS

The following writing topics cover a variety of essay types (*compare and contrast, agree vs. disagree, interpretation, descriptive,* etcetera). These assignments may be done in class or as a homework assignment, but they should always be done within a 30-minute time allotment.

1. What do you think is the most important invention of the 20th century? Choose only one. Provide specific details to support your choice.

2. Smokers should have the right to smoke whenever and wherever they please, without any government restrictions. Do you agree or disagree with this statement?

3. Your university requires that you declare both a major and a minor. What would you choose for your major field, and what would you select for your minor? Explain your reasons for making these selections.

4. If you had a child who was not a native English speaker, would you prefer that she learn English through a bilingual education program, an English as a Second Language program, or regular English classes with native speakers? Choose one of these three methods, and explain why you would choose this method for your child.

5. Which is better: life in a big city or in a small town? Compare and contrast the advantages and disadvantages of these two.

6. What is the most important advice your parents gave you when you were growing up? Include what they taught you, how you learned this "lesson," and why it is important to you today.

7. "The death penalty should be abolished." Do you agree or disagree with this statement? Be specific in your supporting arguments.

8. You have been given a choice by your university to live in an on-campus dormitory or to live in your own apartment off campus. Which of the two would you choose and why?

9. *Success* is a very subjective term. How do you define success? In your essay, include both your definition and a description of a person whom you find to be *successful*.

10. Many American universities today have done away with grades. Do you think that grades are necessary? Why or why not?

11. Often, newcomers to a foreign country find it difficult to make friends with people who are natives of the country. Explain a process for making new friends in a foreign country.

12. What makes a great boss? Describe your ideal employer or boss.

13. Do you think physical education courses should be required for university students? Take a position, and write a persuasive essay supporting your stand.

14. "Life seems to me like a Japanese picture which our imagination does not allow to end with the margin. We aim at the infinite and when our arrow falls to earth it is in flames."
    —*Oliver Wendell Holmes, 1932*

    Interpret the above quotation by Holmes and explain whether you agree or disagree with his metaphors on a person's life.

15. Is the American family structure similar to that in your country? Compare and contrast: What are the similarities? What are the dissimilarities? Be specific.

16. There are many environmental problems facing the world today. Some are primarily the responsibility of corporations and government. However, there are several steps an individual can take to help save the environment. Describe the steps that we can all can take to help improve the environment.

17. Interpret the following statement: "Unbridled freedom will ultimately abolish the very democracy it wishes to protect." What does this mean? Do you agree or disagree with the author of this quotation?

18. Describe the best teacher you ever had. What characteristics make this teacher stand out so strongly in your mind? Support your answer by including specific traits and anecdotes.

19. If you inherited $10 million, what would you do with the money? Limit your response to the two major ways you would spend or invest the money.

20. Do you think the national age for drinking alcohol should be lowered from 21 years of age to 18? Why or why not? Provide specific examples to support your response.

PUNCTUATION GUIDELINES

The following is a general list of punctuation rules, beginning with the two most common types of punctuation: the period and the comma. It is important that you correctly use all of the types of punctuation; however, refrain from overuse of the types that are less frequently used in American English (such as the semicolon, colon, and dash).

Period

The period ends a complete sentence that is a statement.

> Classes will begin next week.

Comma

The comma has several functions and is very common. It is used:

(1) To separate clauses and phrases; especially after an initial dependent clause or a long prepositional phrase.

> If I were you, I would call her.

> At the beginning of next year, I'll be starting graduate school.

(2) To separate items.

> I shopped, watched videos, called friends, and took a nap on my day off.

(3) To introduce a direct quotation.

> He said, "I hope we can get tickets to the Yankees game."

(4) To separate appositives or nonrestrictive clauses.

> Ms. Jones, my physics professor, is on sabbatical.

(5) To separate two independent clauses joined by a conjunction.

> Bill was really exhausted, but he still managed to meet the deadline of the project.

Question Mark

Obviously, this is used at the end of the question.

> What time is it?

Exclamation Point

This may be used to end a sentence statement, but it is rarely used because its purpose is to make a very strong point or to indicate great surprise.

> Wow! That's amazing!

Semicolon

(1) This is used to separate two independent clauses, especially if one or both are short and if they are closely related ideas.

> Jill runs ten miles a day; she's ready for the marathon.

(2) This separates groups of words when there are smaller groups within them set off by commas.

> We visited Kyoto, a beautiful city; Seoul, also an interesting place; Honolulu, Hawaii; and several cities on the West Coast.

Colon

(1) This provides further explanation.

> There are several reasons for my moving here: good job opportunities, a rich cultural life, and the chance to meet people from a variety of backgrounds.

(2) It can introduce a direct quotation (you may also use a comma in this situation).

> The police shouted: "Stop, and put your hands up."

Dash

In general, this should be restricted to informal writing, and avoided on an essay examination. It is usually used to separate thoughts (often two short independent clauses).

> Tell me what you want now—or I'll go ahead and decide without your input.

Apostrophe

(1) The apostrophe shows ownership or possession.

> That is Kate's book.

(2) It also shows a contraction of two words.

> That's her book; it's not mine.

Quotation Marks

(1) These are used to set off a direct quotation.

> He said, "I'm a graduate student here." (Note that the period is inside the quotation mark.)

(2) In a few cases, these are used to indicate that a word or phrase is used in a way different from its traditional use or meaning or is slang.

> He thought the idea was "far out."

(3) Quotation marks also indicate titles of chapters in a book, articles in a newspaper or magazine, or foreign words when you do not have access to italics.

Hyphen

(1) The hyphen indicates that a word will resume on the following line when you have run out of space at the end of the line (words should always be separated by syllables).

(2) It also separates compound words (most common in compound adjectives and compound nouns).

> I have a two-year-old son.

TRANSITION TERMS

The word *transit* means to move or pass from one place to another. Thus, the words and phrases we use to move smoothly from one idea to another one in an essay are called transitions. To create a coherent, smooth essay, you must use these terms, and use them correctly.

While not every sentence in an essay requires a transition, you must disperse a variety of them throughout the essay to link sentences and paragraphs to each other. The chart below states the purpose of the transition and provides you with a variety of similar ones to use. Avoid redundancy in your essay by choosing several different ones. In other words, don't use "however" every time you want to show contrast; instead, select as many different phrases as needed that serve the same function. Use commas to separate transitions from the rest of your sentence.

Purpose of Transition	Possible Transition Terms
to show likeness or add information	*also, too, in addition, furthermore, moreover*
to show contrast	*however, but, on the other hand, conversely, yet, though, in contrast, nevertheless*
to introduce examples	*for example, such as, e.g., to illustrate, for instance*
to explain	*that is, in other words, i.e.*
to emphasize	*in fact, indeed, certainly, clearly, of course*
to generalize	*generally speaking, in general, overall, for the most part, usually, typically*
to conclude or show result	*therefore, thus, consequently, as a result, as a consequence*
to indicate sequence or show order	*first, second, next, then, finally, lastly*

RECURRING TOEFL TOPICS AND RELATED VOCABULARY

The paper-based and the computer-based TOEFL exams tend to cover a limited number of topics in both the Reading Comprehension and Structure sections. This is good for you because you can focus your energy on learning important vocabulary and concepts about these topics. The more familiar you are with the vocabulary related to these topics, the better you will do on the TOEFL.

In this part of the book, we provide short texts on some of these recurring topics. They are meant to introduce you to some of the vocabulary typically used to talk about these topics. We don't pretend to give you all the words you need concerning these important TOEFL topics. Rather, the purpose of the texts is to get you started on your task of building your vocabulary in these areas yourself. In other words, you should view this part of the book as a beginning. The vocabulary items given here are not complete, and you should continue to collect vocabulary concerning these topics yourself.

For each style, you should:

(1) Study the text. Note new vocabulary, including expressions consisting of two or more words.
(2) Complete the sentences in the exercise with the given words. These are just some of the important words used in the texts, not all of them.
(3) Build on this vocabulary base with outside reading.

HEALTH AND MEDICINE
Text

There is an interesting story about the British King George the III. Most Americans know this king because he was the English monarch at the time of America's independence from England. His fame in England is actually due to his contracting a disease. In the years following the American Revolutionary War, King George started to exhibit bizarre behavior such that many members of Parliament thought that he was mentally ill. The practice of medicine was, of course, very rudimentary in those days, so doctors could not pinpoint the exact nature of his disease. They tried a number of cures, but in the end all they could do was administer narcotics to keep him sedated and speculate on the cause of this health concern of international significance. Finally, when his condition became acute, the decision was made to remove him from power and let his son assume the crown. However, at the last minute King George suddenly recovered from the disease, which enabled him to remain the Sovereign until his death.

Exercise
Complete the sentences with the words given.

cure	health concern	narcotics
acute	contracted	mental illness

In the past, people thought physical and _____ were very similar. Basically, it was thought that a person _____ a mental illness in the same way that he or she acquired a physical disease. Because there weren't any other treatments available, doctors often administered strong _____ to sufferers of mental illness. This was often considered a _____ since the heavily sedated patients no longer posed a danger to themselves or others. Much has changed, and now it is realized that mental illness is not one thing but several different types of disorders. The symptoms and effects of these disorders may be mild, where the patient needs minimal care, to _____, where hospitalization is necessary. Since the mid-1970s, mental illness has been treated seriously and professionally in the United States as a major _____.

Answers
mental illness; contracted; narcotics; cure; acute; health concern

BIOLOGY

The words used here relate to zoology—the biology of animals. You should also try to become familiar with some of the vocabulary typically used in botany—the study of plants.

Text

It is interesting to compare the order of mammals to the five other orders within the animal phylum Chordata—birds, fish, reptiles, amphibians, and tunicates. Mammals are the only order whose adults give milk to their young. Also, except for a few species whose reproductive systems differ slightly, mammals bear their young live. Consider this in contrast to a bird, which lays eggs, and after a given period of incubation within the egg, the young bird hatches out. Mammals, like reptiles, birds, and adult amphibians, also breathe oxygen directly out of the air. Consider this in contrast to fish, which have gills that filter oxygen out of the water. Although it may seem strange because they are undersea creatures, dolphins and whales are more closely related to humans than they are to fish. They possess more mammalian characteristics than the characteristics of their undersea companions, the fish, including the fact that they are warm-blooded and must surface to the top of the water from time to time so that they can breathe.

It is also interesting to note that the evolutionary kinship between fish and mammals is made evident by the fact that mammals in an early stage of development—in fact, when still inside of the mother's womb—have gills through which amniotic fluid passes and delivers oxygen to the unborn fetus.

Exercise

Complete the sentences with the words given.

young	gills	warm-blooded
characteristics	lay eggs	their development
characteristic	cold-blooded	lungs
mammals	creatures	related

Here we will summarize the main _____ of the six orders of the phylum Chordata. _____ are characterized chiefly by the existence of mammary glands in the female. They are _____ creatures that breathe through _____ and, generally, possess hair. *Birds* are also warm-blooded and lung-breathing, but instead of hair they have feathers.

They are bipedal, the front limbs being adapted for wings, though it is true that some birds are flightless. Finally, birds are characterized by egg laying in the female. *Amphibians,* on the other hand, are cold-blooded. They spend the first stages of _____ in fresh water. After their body undergoes a change (called metamorphosis), they move to land as adults, returning to the water to _____. Like amphibians, *reptiles* are _____, but unlike them they lay their eggs on land. Another differentiating _____ is the fact that young reptiles are fully formed when they are born. *Fish* are the only order discussed so far that use _____ to obtain oxygen from the fresh or sea water that they live in. They are cold-blooded, and may either lay eggs or give birth to live young. The order of fish consists of two superclasses that are not closely _____: the jawed fishes and the jawless fishes. Finally, *tunicates,* the phylum's least-known group of animals, are sack-shaped _____ whose size may vary from a tenth of an inch to 12 inches in length. The _____ are free swimming, whereas the adults attach themselves to rocks, obtaining food by filtering water that enters through one duct and leaves through another.

Answers

characteristics; Mammals; warm-blooded; lungs; their development; lay eggs; cold-blooded; characteristic; gills; related; creatures; young

THE PHYSICAL SCIENCES

The text presented here concerns astronomy, only one field of the huge area of study called the physical sciences, which include chemistry, physics, and geology. To be prepared for the TOEFL, you should do some reading in, and vocabulary-collecting from, all of these fields.

Text

One of the biggest questions these days among research scientists working in the field of astronomy is how the universe came into existence. The leading theory, known as the Big Bang Theory, is based on the idea that the universe was originally a super-dense area of matter, smaller than a pea in size, and hotter than 10^{25} degrees C in temperature. This compact matter is believed to have undergone an explosion that scattered it outward at a tremendous velocity; this would explain the fact that our universe still seems to be expanding. Most versions of the theory argue that, due in part to gravitational forces, some of this matter remained closer together than other parts. These parts began rotating, eventually evolving into galaxies and giving rise to other celestial bodies like stars—which orbit around the center of a galaxy—and planets, that revolve around stars.

Scientists do not agree why or how long ago the Big Bang occurred, though estimates on the latter range from 10 to 20 billion years. One of the big questions that the theory, if true, poses is whether the universe will continue to expand, or eventually reach a point at which it stops expanding and eventually contracts back into itself under the force of gravity.

Exercise

Complete the sentences with the words given.

due largely	orbit	gravity
based on	research	galaxies
stars	planet's	revolving around

To learn more about the universe, many scientists have helped launch extensive space exploration programs, the realization of which is _____ to the financial support of national governments. These programs usually involve the use of space probes, a very important _____ tool in astronomy. Some probes are sent out to obtain data about other planets by _____ them, while others are supposed to obtain information merely by passing by, without getting caught in the planet's _____. Pioneer 10 was the first probe to leave the solar system, in 1983; in 1992 it was more than 4 billion miles from the sun and was still transmitting information about the light of _____ back to Earth.

Satellite telescopes, which _____ the earth, provide other important data about the universe. From their position in outer space, these telescopes can detect types of radiation that cannot pass through our _____ atmosphere, yet provide a great deal of information about the life cycle of stars and _____. Much of what we know about the universe outside our solar system is _____ satellite telescopes.

Answers

due largely; research; revolving around; gravity; stars; orbit; planet's; galaxies; based on

COLLEGE LIFE

The college life topic is a little different from other topics covered in this section, primarily because the vocabulary will be far more useful in the Listening Comprehension section of the TOEFL than in the Reading Comprehension section. In fact, it would be very surprising if a text in the Reading Comprehension section employed the kind of vocabulary you will find here. On the other hand, you should expect to find this kind of language in the Listening Comprehension section, especially in Part A, Short Conversations.

Because of this, the TOEFL vocabulary concerning college life is distinctly more informal than the vocabulary used for the other topics. Logically enough, the Listening Comprehension section of the TOEFL tends to use spoken rather than written English.

For this reason, to illustrate the vocabulary we will here use shorter texts that might be spoken rather than longer reading texts.

Texts

1. Susan needs just 20 credits to graduate in May, so she's taking a lot of courses this semester. Since she's majoring in comparative literature, all her courses have huge reading lists. And, to top it all off, she's hoping for straight A's. She thinks she has a chance to be selected as class valedictorian for the commencement ceremony.

2. After our classes are over for the day, my roommate and I head over to the cafeteria for dinner. We usually take our books with us so we can go straight to the library to study afterward. We can't study in the dormitories because our friends keep coming by to visit. The library is the only place on campus where we can study in peace and quiet.

3. **Claude:** Hey, where are you going for spring break?
   Boris: A couple of friends and I are driving down to Florida. What are your plans?
   Claude: Unfortunately, I have to write a term paper for a course I took last semester. So I'll be stuck in the dorms during the break.
   Boris: Last semester? Why do you have to do a paper for a course from last semester?
   Claude: I didn't finish the work, so the professor gave me an incomplete. Now I wish I'd dropped the course when I had a chance.

4. To register for your classes, first you have to meet with your academic advisor. When he or she signs your registration form, you can proceed to Tully Hall, Room 109. There you can pay your tuition.

5. Your final grades will be based on your grades for the weekly assignments and for the two exams—the midterm and the final. Exams will cover the lectures, any handouts I give in class, and the assigned reading.

Exercise

Complete the sentences with the words given.

break	Biology 101	graduate
course	credits	an incomplete
advisor	term paper	classes
dorms	semesters	majoring
tuition		

1. **Patty:** Hey, Tom, didn't I see you in Umrath Hall yesterday?

    Tom: Yeah. I was waiting to meet with my _____. Why didn't you say "hi"?

    Patty: Well, to be honest, I walked right by you, but you didn't even notice. You seemed kind of down.

    Tom: Yeah, I was. I had to ask my advisor to sign a drop-add form. I decided to drop _____.

    Patty: But you can't drop that course! You're _____ in biology! That's a prerequisite for all the other courses.

    Tom: I've given up on the idea of a bio major. The courses are too difficult. I would fail half of them if I stayed with the major. I can't afford an additional semester's _____ and I certainly can't afford an additional semester of living in the _____.

2. **Suzanne:** How many courses are you taking, Mickey?

    Mickey: Five. I know that doesn't sound like much, but actually this is going to be one of my hardest _____. One of my courses is worth five _____, and two others are four-credit labs.

Suzanne: So you have a total of how many credits?

Mickey: Nineteen. Plus, two of my _____ require a ten-to-fifteen-page _____. I don't know how I'm going to make it.

Suzanne: Maybe you should drop a _____.

Mickey: I can't. I want to _____ in two semesters. But I could take _____ for a course, and do the paper during the winter _____.

Answers
1. advisor; Biology 101; majoring; tuition; dorms
2. semesters; credits; classes; term paper; course; graduate; an incomplete; break

PART FOUR:

PRACTICE TEST TWO

DIRECTIONS FOR PRACTICE TEST TWO

Practice Test Two is designed to give you further practice in TOEFL test-taking. You should take this test after trying your luck at the Diagnostic Test (Practice Test One) and after working through some or all of the Power Lessons. If you are taking the paper-based TOEFL exam, you should make it a priority to take this test.

Although this test is paper-based, keep in mind that it covers the same basic content that is covered in the computer-based TOEFL exam. Therefore, even if you plan to take the computer-based version of the exam, Practice Test Two will give you a good indication of the kinds of questions you can expect and will also let you know if there is a content area in which you still need more practice.

As with Practice Test One, take Practice Test Two as much like a real TOEFL test as possible. This means that you must find a space of about two-and-a-half hours during which you can take the practice test completely uninterrupted. Do not take breaks between the three sections of the practice test; you are not allowed breaks during the real TOEFL, so you need to build up your mental stamina. Particularly if you are taking the paper-based TOEFL, it is strongly recommended that you use the answer grid provided, as you would have to use a similar grid if you took the real paper-based exam.

Before you take the practice test, you should also reread the section of this book entitled "TOEFL Test Strategies." Then, as you take the test, try to give yourself practice using these strategies as well. They can really improve your score.

As you take Practice Test Two, give yourself only the allotted time for each section of the test. Stop when your time is up. Then use the answer key and conversion chart at the back of the book to give yourself a TOEFL score. (Don't forget to check the Listening Comprehension script immediately following the test if you don't understand why you got a particular Listening Comprehension answer wrong.) Finally, use this practice test to guide your TOEFL preparation by following the suggestions in the "TOEFL Study Plan" in the introduction.

Directions and examples are provided at the beginning of each section of this practice test. Turn to the directions for the Diagnostic Test (Practice Test One) earlier in this book for an example of the general instructions that you might receive if you were to take the actual paper-based TOEFL exam.

Answer Grid for Practice Test Two

1 | LAST NAME | FIRST NAME | MI

SECTION 1

1 Ⓐ Ⓑ Ⓒ Ⓓ
2 Ⓐ Ⓑ Ⓒ Ⓓ
3 Ⓐ Ⓑ Ⓒ Ⓓ
4 Ⓐ Ⓑ Ⓒ Ⓓ
5 Ⓐ Ⓑ Ⓒ Ⓓ
6 Ⓐ Ⓑ Ⓒ Ⓓ
7 Ⓐ Ⓑ Ⓒ Ⓓ
8 Ⓐ Ⓑ Ⓒ Ⓓ
9 Ⓐ Ⓑ Ⓒ Ⓓ
10 Ⓐ Ⓑ Ⓒ Ⓓ
11 Ⓐ Ⓑ Ⓒ Ⓓ
12 Ⓐ Ⓑ Ⓒ Ⓓ
13 Ⓐ Ⓑ Ⓒ Ⓓ
14 Ⓐ Ⓑ Ⓒ Ⓓ
15 Ⓐ Ⓑ Ⓒ Ⓓ
16 Ⓐ Ⓑ Ⓒ Ⓓ
17 Ⓐ Ⓑ Ⓒ Ⓓ
18 Ⓐ Ⓑ Ⓒ Ⓓ
19 Ⓐ Ⓑ Ⓒ Ⓓ
20 Ⓐ Ⓑ Ⓒ Ⓓ
21 Ⓐ Ⓑ Ⓒ Ⓓ
22 Ⓐ Ⓑ Ⓒ Ⓓ
23 Ⓐ Ⓑ Ⓒ Ⓓ
24 Ⓐ Ⓑ Ⓒ Ⓓ
25 Ⓐ Ⓑ Ⓒ Ⓓ
26 Ⓐ Ⓑ Ⓒ Ⓓ
27 Ⓐ Ⓑ Ⓒ Ⓓ
28 Ⓐ Ⓑ Ⓒ Ⓓ
29 Ⓐ Ⓑ Ⓒ Ⓓ
30 Ⓐ Ⓑ Ⓒ Ⓓ
31 Ⓐ Ⓑ Ⓒ Ⓓ
32 Ⓐ Ⓑ Ⓒ Ⓓ
33 Ⓐ Ⓑ Ⓒ Ⓓ
34 Ⓐ Ⓑ Ⓒ Ⓓ
35 Ⓐ Ⓑ Ⓒ Ⓓ
36 Ⓐ Ⓑ Ⓒ Ⓓ
37 Ⓐ Ⓑ Ⓒ Ⓓ
38 Ⓐ Ⓑ Ⓒ Ⓓ
39 Ⓐ Ⓑ Ⓒ Ⓓ
40 Ⓐ Ⓑ Ⓒ Ⓓ
41 Ⓐ Ⓑ Ⓒ Ⓓ
42 Ⓐ Ⓑ Ⓒ Ⓓ
43 Ⓐ Ⓑ Ⓒ Ⓓ
44 Ⓐ Ⓑ Ⓒ Ⓓ
45 Ⓐ Ⓑ Ⓒ Ⓓ
46 Ⓐ Ⓑ Ⓒ Ⓓ
47 Ⓐ Ⓑ Ⓒ Ⓓ
48 Ⓐ Ⓑ Ⓒ Ⓓ
49 Ⓐ Ⓑ Ⓒ Ⓓ
50 Ⓐ Ⓑ Ⓒ Ⓓ

SECTION 2

1 Ⓐ Ⓑ Ⓒ Ⓓ
2 Ⓐ Ⓑ Ⓒ Ⓓ
3 Ⓐ Ⓑ Ⓒ Ⓓ
4 Ⓐ Ⓑ Ⓒ Ⓓ
5 Ⓐ Ⓑ Ⓒ Ⓓ
6 Ⓐ Ⓑ Ⓒ Ⓓ
7 Ⓐ Ⓑ Ⓒ Ⓓ
8 Ⓐ Ⓑ Ⓒ Ⓓ
9 Ⓐ Ⓑ Ⓒ Ⓓ
10 Ⓐ Ⓑ Ⓒ Ⓓ
11 Ⓐ Ⓑ Ⓒ Ⓓ
12 Ⓐ Ⓑ Ⓒ Ⓓ
13 Ⓐ Ⓑ Ⓒ Ⓓ
14 Ⓐ Ⓑ Ⓒ Ⓓ
15 Ⓐ Ⓑ Ⓒ Ⓓ
16 Ⓐ Ⓑ Ⓒ Ⓓ
17 Ⓐ Ⓑ Ⓒ Ⓓ
18 Ⓐ Ⓑ Ⓒ Ⓓ
19 Ⓐ Ⓑ Ⓒ Ⓓ
20 Ⓐ Ⓑ Ⓒ Ⓓ
21 Ⓐ Ⓑ Ⓒ Ⓓ
22 Ⓐ Ⓑ Ⓒ Ⓓ
23 Ⓐ Ⓑ Ⓒ Ⓓ
24 Ⓐ Ⓑ Ⓒ Ⓓ
25 Ⓐ Ⓑ Ⓒ Ⓓ
26 Ⓐ Ⓑ Ⓒ Ⓓ
27 Ⓐ Ⓑ Ⓒ Ⓓ
28 Ⓐ Ⓑ Ⓒ Ⓓ
29 Ⓐ Ⓑ Ⓒ Ⓓ
30 Ⓐ Ⓑ Ⓒ Ⓓ
31 Ⓐ Ⓑ Ⓒ Ⓓ
32 Ⓐ Ⓑ Ⓒ Ⓓ
33 Ⓐ Ⓑ Ⓒ Ⓓ
34 Ⓐ Ⓑ Ⓒ Ⓓ
35 Ⓐ Ⓑ Ⓒ Ⓓ
36 Ⓐ Ⓑ Ⓒ Ⓓ
37 Ⓐ Ⓑ Ⓒ Ⓓ
38 Ⓐ Ⓑ Ⓒ Ⓓ
39 Ⓐ Ⓑ Ⓒ Ⓓ
40 Ⓐ Ⓑ Ⓒ Ⓓ
41 Ⓐ Ⓑ Ⓒ Ⓓ
42 Ⓐ Ⓑ Ⓒ Ⓓ
43 Ⓐ Ⓑ Ⓒ Ⓓ
44 Ⓐ Ⓑ Ⓒ Ⓓ
45 Ⓐ Ⓑ Ⓒ Ⓓ
46 Ⓐ Ⓑ Ⓒ Ⓓ
47 Ⓐ Ⓑ Ⓒ Ⓓ
48 Ⓐ Ⓑ Ⓒ Ⓓ
49 Ⓐ Ⓑ Ⓒ Ⓓ
50 Ⓐ Ⓑ Ⓒ Ⓓ

SECTION 3

1 Ⓐ Ⓑ Ⓒ Ⓓ
2 Ⓐ Ⓑ Ⓒ Ⓓ
3 Ⓐ Ⓑ Ⓒ Ⓓ
4 Ⓐ Ⓑ Ⓒ Ⓓ
5 Ⓐ Ⓑ Ⓒ Ⓓ
6 Ⓐ Ⓑ Ⓒ Ⓓ
7 Ⓐ Ⓑ Ⓒ Ⓓ
8 Ⓐ Ⓑ Ⓒ Ⓓ
9 Ⓐ Ⓑ Ⓒ Ⓓ
10 Ⓐ Ⓑ Ⓒ Ⓓ
11 Ⓐ Ⓑ Ⓒ Ⓓ
12 Ⓐ Ⓑ Ⓒ Ⓓ
13 Ⓐ Ⓑ Ⓒ Ⓓ
14 Ⓐ Ⓑ Ⓒ Ⓓ
15 Ⓐ Ⓑ Ⓒ Ⓓ
16 Ⓐ Ⓑ Ⓒ Ⓓ
17 Ⓐ Ⓑ Ⓒ Ⓓ
18 Ⓐ Ⓑ Ⓒ Ⓓ
19 Ⓐ Ⓑ Ⓒ Ⓓ
20 Ⓐ Ⓑ Ⓒ Ⓓ
21 Ⓐ Ⓑ Ⓒ Ⓓ
22 Ⓐ Ⓑ Ⓒ Ⓓ
23 Ⓐ Ⓑ Ⓒ Ⓓ
24 Ⓐ Ⓑ Ⓒ Ⓓ
25 Ⓐ Ⓑ Ⓒ Ⓓ
26 Ⓐ Ⓑ Ⓒ Ⓓ
27 Ⓐ Ⓑ Ⓒ Ⓓ
28 Ⓐ Ⓑ Ⓒ Ⓓ
29 Ⓐ Ⓑ Ⓒ Ⓓ
30 Ⓐ Ⓑ Ⓒ Ⓓ
31 Ⓐ Ⓑ Ⓒ Ⓓ
32 Ⓐ Ⓑ Ⓒ Ⓓ
33 Ⓐ Ⓑ Ⓒ Ⓓ
34 Ⓐ Ⓑ Ⓒ Ⓓ
35 Ⓐ Ⓑ Ⓒ Ⓓ
36 Ⓐ Ⓑ Ⓒ Ⓓ
37 Ⓐ Ⓑ Ⓒ Ⓓ
38 Ⓐ Ⓑ Ⓒ Ⓓ
39 Ⓐ Ⓑ Ⓒ Ⓓ
40 Ⓐ Ⓑ Ⓒ Ⓓ
41 Ⓐ Ⓑ Ⓒ Ⓓ
42 Ⓐ Ⓑ Ⓒ Ⓓ
43 Ⓐ Ⓑ Ⓒ Ⓓ
44 Ⓐ Ⓑ Ⓒ Ⓓ
45 Ⓐ Ⓑ Ⓒ Ⓓ
46 Ⓐ Ⓑ Ⓒ Ⓓ
47 Ⓐ Ⓑ Ⓒ Ⓓ
48 Ⓐ Ⓑ Ⓒ Ⓓ
49 Ⓐ Ⓑ Ⓒ Ⓓ
50 Ⓐ Ⓑ Ⓒ Ⓓ

IMPORTANT INFORMATION

USE ONLY A NO. 2 OR HB PENCIL TO COMPLETE THIS ANSWER SHEET. DO NOT USE INK.

MARK ONE AND ONLY ONE ANSWER TO EACH QUESTION.

BE SURE TO FILL IN COMPLETELY THE SPACE FOR YOUR INTENDED ANSWER CHOICE.

IF YOU ERASE, DO SO COMPLETELY.

MAKE NO STRAY MARKS.

RIGHT MARK: ●

WRONG MARK: ⊘ ⊗ ◉

LISTENING COMPREHENSION

Directions: Listening Comprehension Section

In this section of the test, you will demonstrate your ability to understand conversations and talks in English. You will find the audio tracks for this section on the CD-ROM included with this book. There are three parts to this section, with different directions for each part. Answer all the questions according to what the speakers say or imply. When you take the actual TOEFL test, you will not be allowed to take notes or write in your test book. Try to work on this sample test in the same way.

PART A

Test_2A.mov

Directions: In Part A, you will hear two people having short conversations. After each conversation, you will hear a question. The conversations and questions will not be repeated. After you hear a question, read the four possible answers and choose the best answer. Then, on one of the answer sheets at the back of this book, find the number of the question and fill in the space that corresponds to the letter of the answer you have chosen.

Listen to an example.

> **On the recording, you hear:**
> **Now listen to a sample question.**
>
> **In your book, you read:**
>
> (A) He is too tired to walk in the park.
> (B) He agrees to go walking in the park with her.
> (C) He is not Jim. His name is Pete.
> (D) He doesn't know what to do.
>
> **Sample Answer**
> ● Ⓑ Ⓒ Ⓓ

You learn from the conversation that the man is "beat," an idiomatic expression meaning "very tired." Therefore, the best answer to the question, "What does the man say?" is (A).

1. (A) put more money in his banking account
   (B) stop complaining so much
   (C) get a new job
   (D) take a loan from the bank

2. (A) after 9
   (B) before 9
   (C) before
   (D) after 12

3. (A) It is more difficult than calculus.
   (B) It is easier than calculus.
   (C) It is too difficult to speak.
   (D) It is similar to calculus.

4. (A) the man
   (B) the recently elected board
   (C) the president
   (D) the inhabitants

5. (A) in a writing class
   (B) in a math class
   (C) in a cooking class
   (D) in a chemistry lab

6. (A) at an airport
   (B) in a car
   (C) in a restaurant
   (D) in a drugstore

7. (A) The man should find it.
   (B) It costs a lot of money.
   (C) It's a good model.
   (D) It's a good deal.

8. (A) He is going to the graduation.
   (B) He will die before he graduates.
   (C) He is only kidding about graduating.
   (D) He won't go to graduation.

9. (A) see the man later
   (B) travel to Colorado with the man
   (C) travel through the mountains
   (D) travel to see the man

10. (A) His biochemistry test went well.
    (B) The woman put a smile on his face.
    (C) The woman shouldn't ask him a question.
    (D) Biochemistry makes him smile.

11. (A) two days ago
    (B) yesterday
    (C) tomorrow
    (D) two days from now

12. (A) Rhonda
    (B) John
    (C) the man
    (D) Chip

13. (A) Ron's brother
    (B) Ron and his brother
    (C) the woman
    (D) the man

14. (A) the man
    (B) the woman
    (C) Elana
    (D) Ethel

15. (A) She cannot eat any more.
    (B) She didn't mean to break the dish.
    (C) The fish doesn't look right.
    (D) She will meet him.

16. (A) dean of a college
    (B) college professor
    (C) college student
    (D) college registrar

17. (A) that a crash has blocked the road
    (B) that he use an automated teller
    (C) that she has some cash ready
    (D) that the bank is close by

18. (A) Their teacher is insane.
    (B) The woman must be joking.
    (C) The teacher's child made her mad.
    (D) The teacher was very upset.

19. (A) that they weren't leaving until dark
    (B) that they were waiting for Paul's arrival
    (C) that others were going too
    (D) that they weren't visiting the park

20. (A) a campground
    (B) a kitchen
    (C) an apartment
    (D) a zoo

21. (A) why they're going to Jim's
    (B) how they'll get to the gym
    (C) why they're going to the rear door
    (D) how Jim hurt his back

22. (A) cooking instructor
    (B) chemistry lab instructor
    (C) fire fighter
    (D) home appliance salesperson

23. (A) Her blouse was professionally ironed.
    (B) It's not a very nice blouse.
    (C) Her blouse needs cleaning.
    (D) The blouse was cleaned, not ironed.

24. (A) at a lumber mill
    (B) at a lake
    (C) in a dock area
    (D) at a swimming pool

25. (A) Charles does a lot but his grades suffer.
    (B) Charles makes the most of his time.
    (C) She does not understand Charles.
    (D) She wonders how he got his jobs.

26. (A) Dawn made them all laugh.
    (B) It lasted until very late.
    (C) Everyone was home very early.
    (D) Dawn broke something at the end.

27. (A) She went swimming on the date.
    (B) Bruce needs some exercise.
    (C) She doesn't want to talk about it.
    (D) She's seeing Bruce again soon.

28. (A) that the man's graduation was unlikely
    (B) that he's doing exceptionally well
    (C) that the graduation class is large
    (D) that the man should stop gambling

29. (A) He is becoming violent.
    (B) He should come in from the yard.
    (C) He is not speaking directly.
    (D) He is lying to her about it.

30. (A) call him if she needs help
    (B) stop writing for the day
    (C) seek help for her problem
    (D) finish her project as planned

PART B

Test_2B.mov

<u>Directions</u>: On this part of the test, you will hear slightly longer conversations. After each conversation, you will hear several questions. Neither the conversations nor the questions will be repeated.

After you hear a question, read the four possible answers in this book and choose the best one. Then, on your answer sheet, find the number of the question and fill in the space that corresponds to the letter of the answer you have chosen.

REMEMBER *that you cannot take notes or write on the test pages in any way.*

31. (A) become a trainer for a sports team
    (B) pick fruit in Europe
    (C) help a professor perform research
    (D) become an assistant professor

32. (A) if he will lend her some money
    (B) if he will give her a job
    (C) if he knows of any job opportunities
    (D) if he needs to borrow money

33. (A) She is a research assistant.
    (B) She went to Europe with the man.
    (C) She did not return to school.
    (D) She told Brenda news about the man.

34. (A) She is good with money.
    (B) She won't have a lot of money.
    (C) The man should provide for her.
    (D) She threw away most of her money.

35. (A) purchase items for his trip
    (B) lend the woman some gear
    (C) tell the woman something
    (D) raft down the Colorado river

36. (A) last week
    (B) two days ago
    (C) the day after tomorrow
    (D) yesterday

37. (A) She doesn't believe he will do it.
    (B) She wants him to shop for her.
    (C) She would like to come with him.
    (D) She doesn't like it.

38. (A) shop very quickly
    (B) cancel his trip
    (C) drive to the embarkation point
    (D) plan another trip

PART C

Test_2C.mov

Directions: On this part of the test, you will hear several talks. After each talk, you will hear some questions. Neither the talks nor the questions will be repeated.

After you hear a question, read the four possible answers in this book and choose the best one. Then, on your answer sheet, find the number of the question and fill in the space that corresponds to the letter of the answer you have selected.

Here is an example.

> **On the recording, you hear:** (*listen to sample text on CD-ROM*)
>
> **Now listen to a sample question.**
>
> **In your book, you read:**
>
>   (A)   Dinosaurs of the Sahara
>   (B)   Tyrannosaurus Rex
>   (C)   A New Species of Dinosaur
>   (D)   Bipedal Carnivorous Dinosaurs
>
> **Sample Answer**
> Ⓐ Ⓑ ● Ⓓ

The best answer to the question, "What would be a good title for this talk?" is (C), "A New Species of Dinosaur." Therefore, the correct choice is (C).

REMEMBER *that you should not take notes or write on your test pages.*

39. (A) an American company
    (B) a type of work schedule
    (C) a method of systems analysis
    (D) a term for increased productivity

40. (A) Employees must work certain hours and can select others.
    (B) Employees can only work the minimum time set by the company.
    (C) Each employee decides how long and when to work.
    (D) Employees work only forty hours a week.

41. (A) Employees are often late to work.
    (B) They don't have to allow employees to leave early.
    (C) They are in a special minority.
    (D) Employees are more productive.

42. (A) extremely productive individuals
    (B) employees who prefer rigid schedules
    (C) those with heavy outside demands
    (D) those who will be absent anyway

43. (A) bands of native Alaskans who migrated south
    (B) European tribes that lived in the Bering Straits
    (C) descendants of Siberian nomads
    (D) survivors of groups who were not killed during the Ice Age

44. (A) a passage that became flooded during the Ice Age
    (B) a long wooden bridge built by the Indians
    (C) a deposit left by a glacier
    (D) the dried-up Bering Straits emptied of water

45. (A) They were fleeing the cold.
    (B) They were looking for water.
    (C) They were following animals.
    (D) They were looking for new pasture land.

46. (A) They share common ancestry.
    (B) They eat the same food.
    (C) Only the North Americans have survived.
    (D) They keep in regular contact.

47. (A) a police officer
    (B) a hotel clerk
    (C) the resident advisor in a dormitory
    (D) the host father of an international student

48. (A) four
    (B) two
    (C) one
    (D) fifteen

49. (A) Students are forbidden to use the kitchenettes at night.
    (B) Meals are provided in the cafeteria.
    (C) The kitchenettes are dirty.
    (D) The kitchenettes contain precooked food.

50. (A) to orient new students
    (B) to learn how to avoid fires in the kitchenette
    (C) to learn how to do laundry
    (D) to become independent

STRUCTURE AND WRITTEN EXPRESSION

🕑 Time allowed for this section: 25 minutes.

Directions: Structure and Written Expression Section

This section is designed to measure your ability to recognize language that is appropriate for standard written English. There are two types of questions in this section, with special directions for each type.

PART A

Directions: Questions 1–15 are incomplete sentences. Beneath each sentence you will see four words or phrases, marked (A), (B), (C), and (D). Choose the one word or phrase that best completes the sentence. Then, on your answer grid, find the number of the question and fill in the space that corresponds to the letter of the answer you have chosen. Fill in the space so that the letter inside the oval cannot be seen.

Example I

> Geysers have often been compared to volcanoes ----- they both emit hot liquids from below the earth's surface.
>
> (A) due to
> (B) because
> (C) in spite of
> (D) regardless of
>
> **Sample Answer**
> Ⓐ ● Ⓒ Ⓓ

The sentence should read, "Geysers have often been compared to volcanoes because they both emit hot liquids from below the earth's surface." Therefore, you should choose answer (B).

Example II

During the early period of ocean navigation, ----- any need for sophisticated instruments and techniques.

(A) so that hardly
(B) when there was hardly
(C) hardly was
(D) there was hardly

Sample Answer
(A) (B) (C) ●

The sentence should read, "During the early period of ocean navigation, there was hardly any need for sophisticated instruments and techniques." Therefore, you should choose answer (D).

Now begin work on the questions.

1. ----- was a wife and mother, Anne Bradstreet found time to write poetry about her life in the American colonies.

(A) She
(B) Despite she
(C) Although she
(D) Though both she

2. The worst snowstorm in American history was -----.

(A) of 1888 a three-day blizzard
(B) in 1888 there was a three-day blizzard
(C) three-day blizzard in 1888
(D) the three-day blizzard of 1888

3. Tombstone, Arizona, ----- the OK Corral shoot-out, is a well-known tourist attraction.

    (A) the scene of
    (B) that is the scene of
    (C) where was the scene of
    (D) there the scene of

4. Glassware is formed either by blowing the molten glass into shape ----- it into a mold.

    (A) and by pouring
    (B) or by pouring
    (C) besides pouring
    (D) or to pour

5. Luxury items in medieval times, -----.

    (A) only the nobility used forks
    (B) only the nobility's using of forks
    (C) forks were used only by the nobility
    (D) forks used only by the nobility

6. There was no official quartermaster in the Revolutionary Army, so everyone carried ----- own provisions.

    (A) their
    (B) his or her
    (C) its
    (D) our

7. ----- the president's appearance and charisma that gave him his initial "honeymoon" period with the voters.

    (A) It seems to have been
    (B) It seems
    (C) There seems to have been
    (D) There seems to be

8. ------ from the cash machine, you must have a valid card and the proper code number.

    (A) For getting
    (B) To get money
    (C) Having got money
    (D) To have gotten

9. To Vice President Agnew, resignation, rather than impeachment, seemed -----.

    (A) the only thing doing
    (B) the thing only doing
    (C) the only thing to do
    (D) the thing only to do

10. ----- Nebraska nor Iowa has any coastline.

    (A) Either
    (B) Neither
    (C) Both
    (D) Together

11. The Pueblo Indians of the American Southwest were excellent artisans, designing pottery, cloth, household items, and -----.

    (A) goods leather
    (B) good in leather
    (C) leathers good
    (D) leather goods

12. Only infrequently ----- arthritis lead to total incapacitation.

    (A) is
    (B) are
    (C) does
    (D) such

13. Not all historical sites that are found -----.

    (A) are highly publicized
    (B) highly publicized
    (C) of high publicity
    (D) to be highly publicized

14. Photographs should ----- only under proper conditions.

    (A) exposure
    (B) to be exposed
    (C) exposes
    (D) be exposed

15. Theodore Hesburgh is well known as the president of the University of Notre Dame, but ----- an accomplished athlete, traveler, and author.

    (A) additionally he
    (B) he is also
    (C) is more
    (D) is too including

PART B

Directions: In questions 16–40 each sentence has four underlined words or phrases. The four underlined parts of the sentence are marked (A), (B), (C), and (D). Identify the one underlined word or phrase that must be changed in order for the sentence to be grammatically correct. Then, on your answer grid, find the number of the question and fill in the space that corresponds to the letter of the answer you have chosen.

Example I

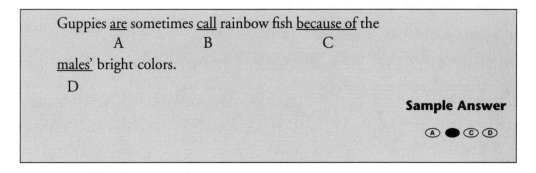

The sentence should read, "Guppies are sometimes called rainbow fish because of the males' bright colors." Therefore, you should choose (B).

Example II

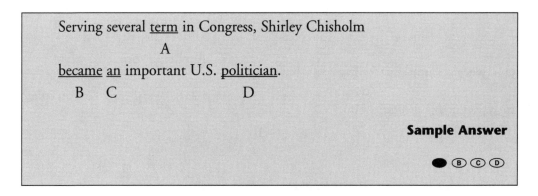

The sentence should read, "Serving several terms in Congress, Shirley Chisholm became an important U.S. politician." Therefore, you should choose answer (A).

Now begin work on the questions.

16. $\underset{\text{A}}{\underline{\text{Some}}}$ scientists believe that dinosaurs

    $\underset{\text{B}}{\underline{\text{become}}}$ extinct $\underset{\text{C}}{\underline{\text{when}}}$ a huge asteroid

    $\underset{\text{D}}{\underline{\text{fell on}}}$ the earth.

17. Earthquakes that occur under $\underset{\text{A}}{\underline{\text{or}}}$ near $\underset{\text{B}}{\underline{\text{the}}}$

    ocean $\underset{\text{C}}{\underline{\text{can to}}}$ generate tidal $\underset{\text{D}}{\underline{\text{waves known}}}$

    as tsunamis.

18. $\underset{\text{A}}{\underline{\text{It is}}}$ a well-known fact $\underset{\text{B}}{\underline{\text{that}}}$ people $\underset{\text{C}}{\underline{\text{resists}}}$

    $\underset{\text{D}}{\underline{\text{change}}}$.

19. Before the $\underset{\text{A}}{\underline{\text{invention}}}$ of $\underset{\text{B}}{\underline{\text{railroads}}}$, the

    only $\underset{\text{C}}{\underline{\text{mean}}}$ of land transportation was

    $\underset{\text{D}}{\underline{\text{the horse}}}$.

20. $\underset{\text{A}}{\underline{\text{Roses}}}$ were originally $\underset{\text{B}}{\underline{\text{cultivated}}}$ by

    $\underset{\text{C}}{\underline{\text{an early Egyptians}}}$ $\underset{\text{D}}{\underline{\text{around}}}$ 4000 B.C.

21. Bentwood, $\underset{\text{A}}{\underline{\text{who}}}$ is a wood that $\underset{\text{B}}{\underline{\text{has been}}}$

    artificially formed $\underset{\text{C}}{\underline{\text{into}}}$ a curve, is usually

    used for $\underset{\text{D}}{\underline{\text{making}}}$ furniture.

22. It is much $\underset{\text{A}}{\underline{\text{more}}}$ easier to obtain $\underset{\text{B}}{\underline{\text{a}}}$ college

    education $\underset{\text{C}}{\underline{\text{these}}}$ days $\underset{\text{D}}{\underline{\text{than}}}$ it was 20

    years ago.

23. $\underset{\text{A}}{\underline{\text{Even though}}}$ the difference $\underset{\text{B}}{\underline{\text{between}}}$

    the percentages of male and female doctors

    has narrowed $\underset{\text{C}}{\underline{\text{appreciably}}}$ in recent years,

    the number of men in that profession is

    always likely to remain $\underset{\text{D}}{\underline{\text{the highest}}}$.

24. $\underset{\text{A}}{\underline{\text{At one time}}}$, $\underset{\text{B}}{\underline{\text{alligators}}}$ up to 19 feet

    in $\underset{\text{C}}{\underline{\text{long}}}$ inhabited $\underset{\text{D}}{\underline{\text{the}}}$ southeastern United

    States.

25. $\underset{\text{A}}{\underline{\text{In}}}$ spelunking terminology, the term

    "twilight zone" $\underset{\text{B}}{\underline{\text{refers}}}$ to the

    $\underset{\text{C}}{\underline{\text{not dark completely}}}$ section of $\underset{\text{D}}{\underline{\text{a cave}}}$.

26. <u>Perhaps</u> <u>was</u> the <u>complimentary</u>
        A   B
    biography he had written <u>about Lincoln</u>
                                     C
    that secured Dean Howell's 1861
    appointment <u>as</u> U.S. consul in Italy.
                D

27. Nutritional <u>needs</u> can be <u>convenience</u>
              A   B
    represented by a pyramid, <u>with</u> the most
                           C
    important foods <u>at</u> the bottom.
                  D

28. An oligopoly is a small combination of
    <u>business</u> <u>interests that</u> work with one
       A   B
    <u>the other</u> <u>to control</u> a product or service.
       C   D

29. A <u>determined</u> hunter, a wolf may cover
        A
    dozens <u>of miles</u> <u>the day</u> in search of its
           B   C
    <u>prey</u>.
     D

30. Gloucester, Massachusetts, along with
    <u>many</u> New England <u>coastal</u> towns, depended
     A   B
    <u>with</u> the success of the cod <u>harvest</u>.
     C   D

31. Every cell <u>carry</u> the <u>genetic</u> material
               A   B
    <u>to produce</u> a complete <u>organism</u>.
       C   D

32. The metric system <u>serves</u> a <u>simple</u>,
                    A   B
    <u>universal</u> standard of <u>measurement</u>.
     C   D

33. The Dakota, being <u>one of the</u> oldest
                     A
    buildings in New York City, <u>it</u> was
                         B
    designated <u>a</u> historical <u>landmark</u>.
        C   D

34. Skiing <u>on</u> the Alps <u>calls for</u> a pair of
         A   B
    <u>well-exercised</u> legs and a <u>thickly padded</u>
       C   D
    pocketbook.

35. A budget <u>is</u> a <u>detailing</u> statement of
            A   B
    revenues and expenditures for a <u>certain</u>
                               C
    period <u>of time</u>.
        D

36. For <u>half century</u>, George Dallas <u>played</u> a
          A   B
prominent <u>role in</u> local, <u>regional</u>, and
             C   D
national political events.

37. Amber, one of the <u>first</u> <u>substances</u> used
                         A   B
<u>decorating</u>, is a <u>fossilized</u> resin.
   C   D

38. <u>Modern</u> airplanes <u>are able to</u> fly very
   A   B
<u>highly</u> because they have <u>pressurized</u> cabins.
  C   D

39. Queen Victoria, <u>who</u> reigned <u>in 1837</u> to
                 A   B
1901, ruled England <u>during</u> <u>its</u> transition
                  C D
from an agricultural to an industrial
society.

40. Spencer Tracy <u>is</u> remembered for his
               A
<u>serious</u> dramatic roles, as <u>well for</u> his
  B   C
comedy films <u>with</u> Katharine Hepburn.
           D

READING COMPREHENSION

🕐 **Time allowed for this section: 55 minutes.**

<u>Directions</u>: In this section you will read several passages. Each one is followed by several questions about it. For this section, you are to choose the one best answer, (A), (B), (C), or (D), to each question. Then, on your answer grid, find the number of the question and fill in the space that corresponds to the letter of the answer you have chosen.

Answer all the questions following a passage on the basis of what is stated or implied in that passage.

Read the following passage.

One of the most successful communal experiments in the New World was that of the Shakers, a sect that fled from England to
Line New York State in 1774 in order to escape
(5) religious bigotry. In America, they adopted the name Shaker, once used derisively by the English to describe the dance they performed when in a state of religious ecstasy. At the movement's peak, in the decade prior
(10) to the Civil War, there were 6,000 Shakers in 18 communities throughout the eastern states. Since then, however, the Shakers have almost dwindled away. Today, only two active Shaker communities remain, with a
(15) total membership of eighteen, all female. The Shakers are resigned to the death of their sect, as they have never believed that everyone could be persuaded to share their beliefs.

Example I

> Where did the Shaker movement begin?
>
> (A) The eastern states
> (B) The New World
> (C) New York
> (D) England
>
> **Sample Answer**
>
> Ⓐ Ⓑ Ⓒ ●

Jim: Great. The Sahara is so wonderful to see. During the day everything looks white, but when the sun is low, in the morning or when the sun is setting, it's positively _____ to see the colors and shapes, and the incredible size of the sky. And it was good in other ways, too.

Kyle: What do you mean?

Jim: I had such a good time talking to the people who live there. _____, they are among the kindest and friendliest people I've ever met, although I did run into a few unpleasant characters.

The passage states that the Shaker sect fled from England to New York State in 1774. Therefore, you should have chosen answer (D).

Example II

At present, the Shakers are represented by

(A)   6,000 worldwide members
(B)   18 active communities
(C)   two remaining all-female communities
(D)   two female members

Sample Answer
Ⓐ Ⓑ ● Ⓓ

According to the passage, only two active Shaker communities remain, with a total membership of 18, all female. Therefore, you should have chosen answer (C).

Now begin work on the questions.

Questions 1–10 refer to the following passage.

Elizabeth "Betsy" Ross (1752–1836) was a Philadelphia seamstress, and, according to legend, designer of the first American flag,
Line the "Stars and Stripes," a rectangle of red
(5) and white stripes with a circle of stars in one corner. The legend of her role began in 1870, when her grandson William J. Canby presented a paper about Ross at a meeting of the Historical Society of Pennsylvania.
(10) According to Canby's paper, General George Washington visited Ross's home frequently, and Ross sewed clothes for him. One day, George Washington came to her house and asked that she design a flag for
(15) the soon-to-be-independent American nation. Ross made alterations to the rough sketch that Washington gave her, and created the first American flag.

Canby's story has become part of
(20) American folklore, but there are doubts about its accuracy. To begin with, his story was recorded 94 years after the events it describes, and was told to him when he was a small boy. Canby says Ross and
(25) Washington's meeting took place in June of 1776, but historians have found no mention of meetings about a flag in government records, or in Washington's personal diaries and writings. Finally, Canby asserted that
(30) the Betsy Ross flag was in use soon after the signing of the Declaration of Independence in 1776, but Congress did not officially adopt national colors until 1777.

Ross may not have designed the Stars and
(35) Stripes, but she definitely made flags of some kind for the new American state. The minutes of the State Navy Board of Pennsylvania for May 29, 1777 refer to "an order on William Webb to Elizabeth Ross
(40) for fourteen pounds twelve shillings, and two pence, for making ship's colours."

1. What is the best title for the passage?

   (A) William Canby and the First American Flag
   (B) The Making of the First American Flag
   (C) Betsy Ross and the American Flag: Fact or Fiction?
   (D) The Life of A Colonial American Seamstress

2. According to the passage, what was the relationship between George Washington and Betsy Ross?

   (A) They were friends.
   (B) They were romantically involved.
   (C) Betsy Ross did work for him.
   (D) George Washington was her landlord.

3. The word *rough* in line 16 is closest in meaning to which of the following?

   (A) unfinished
   (B) inappropriate
   (C) bumpy
   (D) hard

4. According to the author, Canby's story

   (A) is extremely accurate
   (B) cannot be verified
   (C) has been forgotten
   (D) is definitely false

5. The author implies that Canby's story may be inaccurate because

   (A) he might not accurately have recounted events that happened long before he was born
   (B) he deliberately falsified historical documents
   (C) George Washington was uninterested in flag design
   (D) Betsy Ross never made clothes for George Washington

6. The word *mention* in lines 26–27 could best be replaced by which of the following?

   (A) honor
   (B) sound
   (C) amount
   (D) report

7. The term *colors* in line 33 is closest in meaning to which of the following?

   (A) nation
   (B) Congress
   (C) flag
   (D) record

8. Which of the following conclusions about Betsy Ross could best be drawn from this passage?

   (A) Ross wanted to be remembered for her work on America's first flag.
   (B) Ross made flags, but she may not have designed the Stars and Stripes.
   (C) Ross was well paid for her work as a flag designer.
   (D) Ross met several times with George Washington, but he never gave her a sketch of the Stars and Stripes.

9. The word *minutes* in line 37 is closest in meaning to

   (A) time
   (B) record
   (C) payment
   (D) script

10. Where in the passage does the author tell when the Congress officially adopted the new flag?

    (A) line 1
    (B) lines 6–7
    (C) lines 32–33
    (D) line 38

Questions 11–19 refer to the following passage.

The aurora is an atmospheric phenomenon occurring near the earth's poles. Known as aurora borealis or "northern lights" in the
Line northern hemisphere, and as aurora australis or
(5) "southern lights" in the southern hemisphere, it is a kind of cosmic light show.

Although their causes are not precisely known, auroras seem to result from solar activity. The sun's outer atmosphere, or corona, can
(10) be extremely hot, up to several million degrees. Such heat causes atoms to dissolve, and changes hydrogen into plasma—free electrons and protons. Holes in the sun's magnetic field allow this plasma to escape. As the sun rotates,
(15) it throws plasma outward in a spiral. The plasma moves further and further away from the sun, eventually reaching Earth's orbit. When the plasma particles get caught in the earth's magnetic field, they travel to the magnetic
(20) poles, where, at heights of several hundred kilometers, they collide with oxygen and nitrogen atoms. This energetic activity knocks away electrons to leave ions in excited states. The ions emit radiation and create color. Then the
(25) light show begins.

The longest lasting aurora form is the arc, which may remain in the sky for several hours. An aurora can also appear as a curtain, ray, or band. In the dazzling auroral substorm, an
(30) aurora's shape may change dramatically. Green lights can fill the sky towards the pole, and end in a shimmering, folded arc with a red border at the bottom. The bottom of the arc or fold often takes a sharper form than the top part.
(35) Towards the end of the display, the shapes pale and gradually drift towards the pole.

11. What is the best title for the passage?

    (A) Fun with Auroras
    (B) Auroras: Why they Appear and What they Look Like
    (C) The Aurora Borealis: Fact and Fiction
    (D) The Solar Wind and Its Effect on the Solar System

12. The word *precisely* in line 7 is closest in meaning to

    (A) exactly
    (B) truthfully
    (C) pointedly
    (D) correctly

13. Auroras are mainly caused by

    (A) solar activity
    (B) a cosmic light show
    (C) the northern and southern hemispheres
    (D) atmospheric phenomena

14. According to the passage, the sun's corona changes hydrogen gas into which of the following substances?

    (A) oxygen
    (B) nitrogen
    (C) light
    (D) plasma

15. The word *collide* in line 21 is closest in meaning to

    (A) fall
    (B) hit
    (C) scatter
    (D) stick

16. Where in the passage does the author define the term *corona*?

    (A) line 6
    (B) line 7
    (C) line 8
    (D) line 9

17. The word *dazzling* in line 29 could best be replaced by which of the following?

    (A) attractive
    (B) pleasant
    (C) stable
    (D) spectacular

18. Which of the following generalizations about auroras could best be drawn from the passage?

    (A) They do not occur often enough to be studied by scientists.
    (B) They are brilliant displays of light resulting from particles thrown from the sun's corona.
    (C) Though they are not precisely understood, scientists can predict exactly what form they will take and how long they will last.
    (D) The Earth's magnetic field shields the poles from auroral displays.

19. As the auroral display comes to a close, it appears to
    (A) contract toward the poles
    (B) arc sharply in random direction
    (C) turn greener
    (D) develop a shimmering red border

Questions 20–29 refer to the following passage.

Andy Warhol, known chiefly as a painter, was a leader of the Pop art movement of the 1960s. Working in a collective known as "The
Line Factory," he used the process of silk screening
(5) to reproduce recognized American cultural images and icons, such as soap pad boxes and celebrity photographs. This mechanical process made the point that the painted image was mundane and the artist detached.
(10) Warhol is also known for his films, such as *The Chelsea Girls* (1966) and *Blue Movie* (1969). Some of these movies are incredibly long—more than 24 hours. In 1966 in New York City, Warhol worked with the Factory
(15) and the rock band the Velvet Underground to produce a multimedia event called "Andy Warhol Uptight." He produced the Velvet Underground's first album in 1967 and took part in the Exploding Plastic Inevitable, a
(20) twelve-person team that produced multimedia events combining film, photographs, music, lights, and dance.
His main contributions to modern American art are his invention of the artist as
(25) an impersonal agent and his role as a catalyst for many other artists. After he was shot and nearly killed in 1968, Warhol was less active. He died in 1987.

20. What is the main topic of this passage?
    (A) the Pop art movement of the 1960s
    (B) the collective known as "The Factory"
    (C) the art and life of Andy Warhol
    (D) the Exploding Plastic Inevitable

21. In lines 7–8, what does "this mechanical process" refer to?

    (A) image
    (B) icon
    (C) box
    (D) silk-screening

22. "Made the point" in line 8 could best be replaced by which of the following?

    (A) inserted
    (B) ignored
    (C) implied
    (D) provided

23. The word *mundane* in line 9 is closest in meaning to

    (A) big
    (B) fascinating
    (C) simple
    (D) ordinary

24. According to the passage, Warhol worked in all of the following media EXCEPT

    (A) collage
    (B) music
    (C) painting
    (D) film

25. Which recording group does the passage say Andy Warhol supported?

    (A) Uptight
    (B) Exploding Plastic Inevitable
    (C) The Velvet Underground
    (D) The Chelsea Girls

26. In line 25, the word *catalyst* means

    (A) activating force
    (B) destructive tendency
    (C) unwilling participant
    (D) prolific composer

27. When was Warhol nearly killed?

    (A) 1987
    (B) 1968
    (C) 1966
    (D) 1963

28. Which of the following statements would the author of this passage most probably agree with?

    (A) Warhol has had great impact with his ideas about the modern artist's role in society.
    (B) Andy Warhol's silkscreens are his greatest contribution to modern American art.
    (C) An attack on his life ended Warhol's career before he attained success.
    (D) Since Andy Warhol did his artwork in collaboration with others, his achievements do not mean very much.

29. All of the following statements about Andy Warhol are true EXCEPT

    (A) He was a pop artist.
    (B) He directed movies.
    (C) He died of a gunshot wound.
    (D) He was supportive of many artists.

Question 30–38 refer to the following passage.

The best-known theory of galactic evolution is the one originated in the 1920s by Edwin P. Hubble. According to this theory,
Line a galaxy begins as a vast accumulation of
(5) gases, chiefly hydrogen and helium, rotating about a central point. Thanks to the mutual gravitational attraction of matter, this "protogalaxy" slowly condenses into millions or, more often, billions of stars, col-
(10) lected in a gigantic, roughly spherical cloud. This is what Hubble called an "ellipsoidal" galaxy.

Over many more millions of years, gravity slowly causes such a galaxy to contract,
(15) flatten, and become increasingly congested near its center. Due to the law of the conservation of angular momentum, it also begins to rotate more and more rapidly. The centrifugal force thus generated finally scat-
(20) ters much of the material from the galaxy's outer edges many thousands of light years into surrounding space. This is how the familiar "spiral" galaxy, with its characteristic compact nucleus and its widely dis-
(25) persed, spiraling outer arms, is formed.

30. The word *originated* in line 2 is closest in meaning to
   (A) cultivated
   (B) begun
   (C) declared
   (D) proposed

31. According to Hubble, one characteristic of a galaxy at its origin is
   (A) its conspicuous lack of hydrogen and helium
   (B) its spiraling arms
   (C) a compact nucleus
   (D) its initial rotation around one point in space

32. According to the passage, a "protogalaxy"
   (A) consists of billions of spherical clouds
   (B) results from an "ellipsoidal" galaxy
   (C) is a great mass of gaseous materials
   (D) ignores the law of angular momentum

33. All of the following are true about an ellipsoidal galaxy as it ages EXCEPT
   (A) It becomes flatter.
   (B) It contracts.
   (C) It creates more hydrogen.
   (D) It develops more congested centers.

34. According to the passage, the effects of the law of the conservation of angular momentum
   (A) create congestion at the galaxy's core
   (B) scatter galactic matter into space
   (C) flatten and contract the galaxy
   (D) predict the decreasing speed of rotation

35. According to the passage, a "spiral" galaxy

  (A) can be easily observed with the naked eye
  (B) is an evenly dispersed network of galactic matter
  (C) is created by the accelerating rotation of an "ellipsoidal" galaxy
  (D) is shaped more or less like a sphere

36. In line 24, *compact* most nearly means

  (A) twisted
  (B) static
  (C) oblong
  (D) dense

37. The purpose of the passage is to describe

  (A) three theories of galactic formation
  (B) the most famous theory of the evolution of galaxies
  (C) how the laws of physics influence the behavior of galaxies
  (D) the conservation of angular momentum

38. The paragraph following this would most likely be about

  (A) how other types of galaxies are formed
  (B) what an "arm" is
  (C) the role of gravity in the creation of galaxies
  (D) how materials scatter in a galaxy

Questions 39–50 refer to the following passage.

With the rise of the great metropolis in the industrial era, city planning in the United States passed out of the hands of the architect
Line and into the hands of the technical expert.
(5) Unlike the architect, who thought of the city as a work of art to be built up with an eye towards beauty, the modern technocrat has always taken a purely functional approach to city planning; the city exists for the sole pur-
(10) pose of serving the needs of its inhabitants. Its outward appearance has no important value.

Over the span of a few centuries, this new breed of urban planner has succeeded in forever changing the face of American cities. A visit
(15) to any large city confirms the grim fact. Even a casual observer could not fail to notice that the typical urban landscape is arranged along the lines of the tedious chessboard pattern, with its four-cornered intersections and long, straight,
(20) and dull streets.

Strict building codes have resulted in an overabundance of unsightly neighborhoods in which there is only slight variation among structures. Rows of squat concrete apartment
(25) houses and files of gigantic steel and glass skyscrapers have almost completely replaced older, more personal buildings. Moreover, the lovely natural surroundings of many cities are no longer a part of the urban landscape. For
(30) the most part, the hills and rivers that were once so much a part of so many metropolitan settings have been blotted out by thoughtless construction. The lone bright spot in this otherwise bleak picture is that currently there is a
(35) rebirth of interest in architecture. Enrollments in graduate architectural programs are the highest in many years. Hopefully, this trend will continue and help pave the way for a more beautiful America of the future.

39. The primary purpose of this passage is to

    (A) show the accomplishments of the modern technical expert
    (B) point out the failures of old-fashioned architects
    (C) argue for the preservation of natural surroundings
    (D) communicate the author's preference for architects over technocrats

40. The architect had always considered cities to be

    (A) a functional place of dwelling
    (B) a work of art
    (C) in need of many tall skyscrapers
    (D) a place for experimentation

41. The tone of this passage can best be described as

    (A) disapproving
    (B) conciliatory
    (C) outraged
    (D) sorrowful

42. The reference to a "purely functional approach to city planning" in lines 8–9 serves to

    (A) demonstrate that architects and technocrats should cooperate
    (B) imply that architects are unconcerned about human comfort
    (C) show that this approach is to be desired
    (D) stress the difference between architects and technocrats

43. The word *span* in line 12 most nearly means

    (A) extension
    (B) days
    (C) bridge
    (D) stretch

44. The word *face* in line 14 most nearly means

    (A) appearance
    (B) expression
    (C) conflict
    (D) value

45. In the second paragraph, the description of cities can best be described as

    (A) tolerant
    (B) unflattering
    (C) regulated
    (D) monotonous

46. According to the passage, what is a consequence of strict building codes?

    (A) an unsightly regularity of building styles
    (B) more neighborhoods than are necessary
    (C) a lack of interested building observers
    (D) a return of the old-time architect

47. We can infer from the passage that the author sees modern architecture as

    (A) necessary
    (B) impersonal
    (C) lovely
    (D) valuable

48. The expression *blotted out* in line 32 is closest in meaning to

    (A) taken away
    (B) omitted
    (C) blocked out
    (D) made useless

49. It is most likely that the author would support which of the following?

    (A) an effort to enforce disregarded building codes
    (B) programs increasing the public's appreciation for architecture
    (C) plans to build fewer parks
    (D) a return to eighteenth-century living styles

50. The passage ends in a spirit of

    (A) anger
    (B) disgust
    (C) accusation
    (D) hope

END OF TEST. *Turn to Part Five, "Answer Keys and Score Conversion Chart," to find out how you did on this practice test. Check the Listening Comprehension script on the pages that follow if there was anything in the Listening Comprehension section of this test that you could not understand.*

SCRIPT FOR THE LISTENING COMPREHENSION SECTION
PART A (TEST_2A.MOV)

The entire script for the Listening Comprehension section of the Diagnostic Test is provided on the following pages. If you could not understand what was said in a particular conversation or talk or why you got a particular answer wrong, look it up here.

1. **(man)** Even with my full-time job, I am still having trouble making ends meet.

   (woman) You probably just need to save more.

   (narrator) What does the woman say the man should do?

2. **(woman)** Does the 4 train make local stops after 9?

   (man) Only between midnight and 7. Before then you need to take the 5 or the 6 train.

   (narrator) When does the 4 train make local stops?

3. **(man)** My most difficult course this semester is Greek.

   (woman) You obviously haven't taken advanced calculus.

   (narrator) What does the woman imply about Greek?

4. **(woman)** I was talking to this guy who told me that the rental fee will be raised again.

   (man) I thought the new committee promised the residents not to add any costs.

   (narrator) Whom does the man blame for the higher price?

5. **(man)** Make sure not to overheat the solution or it will change its composition.

   (woman) Should I remove it from the burner before adding the blue solution?

   (narrator) Where is this conversation probably taking place?

6. **(woman)** Where's the nearest gas station?

   (man) I don't know, but we better find it soon. The tank's nearly empty.

   (narrator) Where is this conversation probably taking place?

7. **(man)** Is this computer a good value for the money?

   (woman) Let me put it this way: you won't find this model at this price anywhere else.

   (narrator) What does the woman say about the computer?

8. **(woman)** Are you going to your college graduation?

   (man) Are you kidding? I wouldn't be caught dead anywhere near it.

   (narrator) What does the man mean?

9. (man)   I want to travel to Colorado to see the Rocky Mountains.

    (woman)   Me too. Maybe we can go together.

    (narrator) What would the woman like to do?

10. (woman)   Did you pass the midterm exam in biochemistry?

    (man)   Do you have to ask? Can't you tell from the smile on my face?

    (narrator) What does the man imply?

11. (man)   Did you know Kenyatta's mom and dad are coming tomorrow?

    (woman)   Yes, he told me yesterday that they'd be arriving sometime at the end of this week.

    (narrator) When do Kenyatta's parents arrive?

12. (woman)   I stopped at John's store and picked up some ice cream for Rhonda.

    (man)   That's so nice of you. It's not mint chocolate chip, is it?

    (narrator) To whom is the woman giving the ice cream?

13. (man)   Ron and his brother are planning to borrow my boat for a few days.

    (woman)   You haven't used it since Labor Day weekend, have you?

    (narrator) Who is going to use the boat?

14. (woman)   Ethel's shirt is much nicer than yours.

    (man)   Yes, but Elana has the nicest shirt of all.

    (narrator) Who has the best shirt?

15. (man)   Can I give you another piece of fish?

    (woman)   No, thanks. I can't eat another bite.

    (narrator) What does the woman mean?

16. (woman)   I've got so many papers to correct, and grades are due at the registrar's tomorrow.

    (man)   Yeah, and don't forget the departmental meeting.

    (narrator) What is the woman's occupation likely to be?

17. (man)   Hurry up, I've got to get to the bank before it closes.

    (woman)   Isn't there a cash machine nearby?

    (narrator) What does the woman suggest?

18. (woman)   I've never seen the teacher as mad as she was today.

    (man)   You're not kidding.

    (narrator) What does the man mean?

19. (man)   I'll meet you at the corner in half an hour.

    (woman)   Oh, so then we're going to the park after all.

    (narrator) What had the woman thought?

20. **(woman)** I hate all these bugs and I hate sleeping on the ground.
    (man) Oh, relax, and please help make the fire for dinner.
    (narrator) Where does the conversation take place?

21. **(man)** Let's go around to the gym's back door.
    (woman) How come?
    (narrator) What does the woman want to know?

22. **(woman)** If everyone has a beaker, a burner, and the salt mixture, we'll begin.
    (man) I think we're all set.
    (narrator) What is probably the woman's occupation?

23. **(man)** That's a really nice ironing job you did on that blouse.
    (woman) Oh no, I had it done at the cleaners.
    (narrator) What does the woman mean?

24. **(woman)** Hey, there's no running near the water. And be careful on those diving boards.
    (man) Sure, no problem.
    (narrator) Where does the conversation take place?

25. **(man)** Charles is graduating early even though he has two part-time jobs.
    (woman) What I don't understand is how he does all that and still manages to get great grades.
    (narrator) What does the woman imply?

26. **(woman)** Did the party go on for long last night?
    (man) Only until the crack of dawn.
    (narrator) What does the man say about the party?

27. **(man)** Well, aren't you going to tell me about your date with Bruce?
    (woman) Oh, go jump in a lake!
    (narrator) What does the woman mean?

28. **(woman)** What did the registrar say?
    (man) He said I had one chance in a million to graduate this year.
    (narrator) What did the registrar mean?

29. **(man)** So now do you know how I feel about it?
    (woman) No I don't, and I wish you'd stop beating around the bush.
    (narrator) What does the woman imply?

30. **(woman)** If I write one more word I'm going to go crazy.
    (man) Well, you'd better call it a day then.
    (narrator) What does the man want her to do?

PART B (TEST_2B.MOV)

(narrator) *Questions 31 through 34 are based on the following conversation:*

(man) Brenda, hello. It's good to see you again.

(woman) Thanks, it's great to see you too. I heard that you might not be back this semester. Jane told me that you were going to France this fall to work on the grape harvest.

(man) Well, I thought about it but then I decided that I'd really like to graduate with my class. Also, I got a job as Professor Simpson's research assistant and I really need the money.

(woman) I know what you mean about needing the cash. Do you happen to know of any decent job openings?

(man) Well, I've heard they need an assistant trainer for the varsity basketball team. But as a computer science major I guess you're not really qualified.

(woman) I'll say. It looks like I'll be pinching pennies again this year. See you later. Hey, any chance you'll buy me lunch?

31. What job did the man decide not to do?

32. What does the woman ask the man?

33. Which of the following is true about Jane?

34. What does Brenda say about her financial situation?

(narrator) *Questions 35 through 38 are based on the following conversation.*

(woman) Are you ready for our rafting trip down the Colorado river?

(man) Well, I hate to tell you this, but I haven't gotten any supplies. I meant to stop by the camping store last week, but it slipped my mind.

(woman) I can't believe it! And we're supposed to leave in two days. How do you think you will manage to get everything you need?

(man) I was hoping maybe you could lend me some of your gear. And I thought that while we were driving to the starting point of the raft trip, we could stop by a camping store.

(woman) Mister, you've got another think coming. I've got absolutely nothing extra for you to borrow. My clothes certainly won't fit you. And we've got to drive straight to the embarkation point.

(man) I guess you're right. I'll have to
back out at the last minute.
(woman) Or else get busy shopping.

35. What did the man forget to do?

36. When are the man and woman supposed
to leave?

37. How does the woman feel about the man's
suggestion to shop on the road?

38. What does the man say that he might do?

PART C (TEST_2C.MOV)

(narrator) *Questions 39 through 42 are based on the following talk in an economics class.*

Thanks to a new work schedule called flextime, almost 13 percent of all American companies enjoy flexible working hours. At a company on flextime, each employee must work a minimum number of hours each week at times determined by the company. But each employee is free to decide how many hours more than that he or she will work. The employee is also able to decide the exact time when he will put in these "freely chosen" hours. Companies that have switched to flextime schedules have found that employee absenteeism has decreased. Also, employee lateness is no longer a problem, and productivity has increased. Employees prefer flextime because they don't have to worry as much about being late to work, nor do they need permission to leave early. Perhaps more of our companies will switch to flextime when they see how well it works. It seems to have benefits for employees and employers alike.

39. What is flextime?

40. How does flextime work?

41. Why do companies like flextime?

42. What kind of employee would benefit most from flextime?

(narrator) *Questions 43 through 46 are based on the following lecture.*

The question of who the American Indians are and how they came to live in North America has long puzzled scientists. The most popular modern theory says that the Indians came from Siberia to Alaska when the Bering Strait was not underwater. At that time there was a land bridge between Asia and America. This "land bridge" was a result of the fact that much of the water that used to cover the region became frozen in glaciers during the Ice Age. This left the land dry and bare. With the water gone, wandering bands of Siberian tribes simply walked over from what is now modern Russia to what is now the modern U.S. They were probably in pursuit of the herds of animals which were their primary source of food. From northwest Alaska, they then traveled south and east to populate North, Central, and South America.

43. Who are the American Indians thought to be?

44. What was the "land bridge" mentioned in the lecture?

45. According to the lecture, why did the early Indians probably come to the North American continent?

46. What can be inferred about the natives of North, Central, and South America?

(**narrator**) *Questions 47 through 50 are based on the following lecture.*

Hello and welcome to Northern State University. I know that for many of you this will be the first time that you have lived away from home, so I will be the person primarily responsible for making sure that your adjustment to independence is smooth. Let me start by telling you about the services you will be using here at Healey Hall. You will find laundry facilities located in the east wing of each floor. Each laundry room has two washers and two dryers. The washers and dryers do not take coins but instead require tokens. A washer takes one token per load and the dryer will give you 15 minutes of drying per token. If you have any problem with the machines, you should report it to your floor's resident advisor. Each floor also contains a small kitchenette for use by everyone on that floor. We assume that you will be eating most of your meals in the cafeteria, so the kitchenettes were really designed simply for heating up precooked foods and preparing small snacks. Because everyone will be using the kitchenette, please remember to clean up after yourself and, of course, always remember to turn off the stove right after you use it.

47. Who is probably speaking?

48. How many washers does each floor have?

49. What can we infer from the passage?

50. What is the main purpose of this talk?

PART FIVE:

ANSWER KEYS AND SCORE CONVERSION CHART

ANSWER KEYS FOR THE PRACTICE TESTS

DIAGNOSTIC TEST (PRACTICE TEST ONE)

Listening Comprehension

1. C	6. D	11. B	16. D	21. D	26. C	31. C	36. B	41. B	46. A
2. B	7. C	12. B	17. C	22. D	27. B	32. A	37. A	42. A	47. D
3. A	8. A	13. A	18. D	23. D	28. A	33. B	38. D	43. C	48. B
4. D	9. C	14. A	19. A	24. D	29. D	34. B	39. B	44. A	49. B
5. B	10. B	15. B	20. B	25. C	30. A	35. D	40. C	45. B	50. C

Structure and Written Expression

1. D	6. A	11. B	16. D	21. A	26. B	31. D	36. D
2. A	7. D	12. C	17. B	22. A	27. A	32. B	37. B
3. D	8. D	13. B	18. A	23. D	28. D	33. C	38. D
4. B	9. A	14. C	19. C	24. A	29. D	34. B	39. B
5. D	10. C	15. A	20. B	25. B	30. D	35. A	40. C

Reading Comprehension

1. B	6. C	11. C	16. D	21. C	26. D	31. C	36. A	41. C	46. A
2. D	7. A	12. C	17. A	22. B	27. C	32. C	37. B	42. D	47. C
3. A	8. C	13. B	18. D	23. A	28. B	33. A	38. A	43. B	48. B
4. A	9. B	14. D	19. A	24. C	29. D	34. A	39. B	44. C	49. D
5. D	10. A	15. C	20. C	25. C	30. C	35. B	40. D	45. D	50. D

PRACTICE TEST TWO

Listening Comprehension

1. A	6. B	11. C	16. B	21. C	26. B	31. B	36. C	41. D	46. A
2. D	7. D	12. A	17. B	22. B	27. C	32. C	37. D	42. C	47. C
3. B	8. D	13. B	18. D	23. A	28. A	33. D	38. B	43. C	48. B
4. B	9. B	14. C	19. D	24. D	29. C	34. B	39. B	44. D	49. B
5. D	10. A	15. A	20. A	25. B	30. B	35. A	40. A	45. C	50. A

Structure and Written Expression

1. C	6. B	11. D	16. B	21. A	26. A	31. A	36. A
2. D	7. A	12. C	17. C	22. A	27. B	32. A	37. C
3. A	8. B	13. A	18. C	23. D	28. C	33. B	38. C
4. B	9. C	14. D	19. C	24. C	29. C	34. A	39. B
5. C	10. B	15. B	20. C	25. C	30. C	35. B	40. C

Reading Comprehension

1. C	6. D	11. B	16. D	21. D	26. A	31. D	36. D	41. A	46. A
2. C	7. C	12. A	17. D	22. C	27. B	32. C	37. B	42. D	47. D
3. A	8. B	13. A	18. B	23. D	28. A	33. C	38. A	43. D	48. C
4. B	9. B	14. D	19. A	24. A	29. C	34. B	39. D	44. A	49. B
5. A	10. C	15. B	20. C	25. C	30. D	35. C	40. B	45. B	50. D

PRACTICE TEST SCORE CONVERSION CHART

To determine your approximate TOEFL score, follow these steps.

1. After finishing a test, check your answers by using the answer keys given after each test. Determine the total number of correct answers for each section of the test. This is called your *raw score.*

2. Once you have obtained your raw score, use the conversion table in this section to get a *scaled,* or *converted score,* for each section of the TOEFL. This is all you need to do to work out your score on the two paper-based practice exams in this book.

3. To find out how you did on the computer-based TOEFL practice test, go through steps one and two above and then turn to the TOEFL Concordance Tables provided in the chapter in the introduction entitled "Getting Started." These tables will tell you how your converted scores compare to scores on the new computer-based exam.

For example, suppose your raw scores were:

> Listening: 39
>
> Structure and Written Expression: 25
>
> Reading: 28

In this case you would use the conversion chart to get converted scores of:

> Listening: 54
>
> Structure and Written Expression: 49
>
> Reading: 44

To calculate your overall cumulative TOEFL score for this exam, do the following:

➤ Add the converted scores you achieved for each of the three sections.

➤ Multiply this number by 10.

➤ Then, divide this number by 3.

Following our example, we would get:

$$54 + 49 + 44 = 147$$
$$147 \times 10 = 1470$$
$$1470 \div 3 = 490$$

This imaginary test taker's approximate TOEFL score on the paper-based exam is 490. On the computer-based exam, according to the TOEFL Concordance Table, the test taker would have scored approximately 160.

CONVERSION CHART

Section I Listening Comprehension		Section II Structure and Written Expression		Section III Reading Comprehension	
Raw Score	Converted Score	Raw Score	Converted Score	Raw Score	Converted Score
50	68	40	68	50	67
49	64	39	68	49	65
48	62	38	68	48	63
47	60	37	62	47	62
46	59	36	60	46	60
45	58	35	58	45	59
44	57	34	56	44	58
43	57	33	55	43	57
42	56	32	54	42	56
41	55	31	53	41	55
40	55	30	52	40	54
39	54	29	52	39	53
38	53	28	51	38	52
37	53	27	50	37	52
36	52	26	49	36	51
35	52	25	49	35	50
34	51	24	48	34	49
33	51	23	47	33	48
32	50	22	47	32	47
31	50	21	46	31	46
30	50	20	45	30	45
29	49	19	45	29	45
28	49	18	44	28	44
27	48	17	43	27	43
26	48	16	42	26	43
25	47	15	42	25	42
24	47	14	41	24	41
23	46	13	39	23	40
22	46	12	38	22	39
21	45	11	36	21	38
20	45	10	34	20	37
19	44	9	31	19	36
18	44	8	27	18	35
17	43	7	26	17	34
16	42	6	25	16	33
15	41	5	24	15	32
14	40	4	23	14	30
13	39	3	21	13	29
12	38	2	20	12	29
11	35	1	20	11	28
10	33	0	20	10	28
9	32			9	27
8	31			8	26
7	30			7	25
6	29			6	24
5	28			5	24
4	28			4	23
3	27			3	22
2	26			2	21
1	25			1	21
0	24			0	20

NOTES

About

Educational Centers

Kaplan Educational Centers is one of the nation's premier education companies, providing individuals with a full range of resources to achieve their educational and career goals. Kaplan, celebrating its 60th anniversary, is a wholly-owned subsidary of The Washington Post Company.

TEST PREPARATION & ADMISSIONS

Kaplan's nationally-recognized test prep courses cover more than 20 standardized tests, including entrance exams for secondary school, college and graduate school as well as foreign language and professional licensing exams. In addition, Kaplan offers private tutoring and comprehensive, one-on-one admissions and application advice for students applying to graduate school.

SCORE! EDUCATIONAL CENTERS

SCORE! after-school learning centers help students in grades K-8 build academic skills, confidence and goal-setting skills in a motivating, sports-oriented environment. Kids use a cutting-edge, interactive curriculum that continually assesses and adapts to their academic needs and learning styles. Enthusiastic academic coaches serve as positive role models, creating a high-energy atmosphere where learning is exciting and fun for kids.With nearly 40 centers today, new centers continue to open nationwide.

KAPLAN LEARNING SERVICES

Kaplan Learning Services provides customized assessment, education and training programs to K-12 schools, universities and businesses to help students and employees reach their educational and career goals.

KAPLAN PROGRAMS FOR INTERNATIONAL STUDENTS AND PROFESSIONALS

Kaplan services international students and professionals in the U.S. through *Access America*, a series of intensive English language programs. These programs are offered at Kaplan City Centers and four new campus-based centers in California, Washington and New York via Kaplan/LCP International Institute. Kaplan and Kaplan/LCP offer specialized services to sponsors including placement at top American universities, fellowship management, academic monitoring and reporting, and financial administration.

KAPLOAN

Students can get key information and advice about educational loans for college and graduate school through **KapLoan** (Kaplan Student Loan Information Program). Through an affiliation with one of the nation's largest student loan providers, **KapLoan** helps direct students and their families through the often bewildering financial aid process.

KAPLAN PUBLISHING

Kaplan Books, a joint imprint with Simon & Schuster, publishes titles in test preparation, admissions, education, career development and life skills; Kaplan and *Newsweek* jointly publish the highly successful guides **How to Get Into College** and **How to Choose a Career & Graduate School**. *SCORE!* and *Newsweek* have teamed up to publish **How to Help Your Child Succeed in School**.

Kaplan InterActive delivers award-winning, high-quality educational products and services, including Kaplan's best-selling **Higher Score** test-prep software and sites on the Internet (**http://www.kaplan.com**) and America Online. Kaplan and Cendant Software are jointly developing, marketing and distributing educational software for the kindergarten through twelfth grade retail and school markets.

KAPLAN CAREER SERVICES

Kaplan helps students and graduates find jobs through Kaplan Career Services, the leading provider of career fairs in North America. The division includes **Crimson & Brown Associates**, the nation's leading diversity recruiting and publishing firm, **The Lendman Group and Career Expo**, both of which help clients identify highly sought-after technical personnel, and sales and marketing professionals.

COMMUNITY OUTREACH

Kaplan provides educational resources to thousands of financially disadvantaged students annually, working closely with educational institutions, not-for-profit groups, government agencies and other grass roots organizations on a variety of national and local support programs. Also, Kaplan centers enrich local communities by employing high school, college and graduate students, creating valuable work experiences for vast numbers of young people each year.

Want more information about our services, products, or the nearest Kaplan center?

HERE

Call our nationwide toll-free numbers:

1–800–KAP–TEST
(for information on our live courses, private tutoring and admissions consulting)

1–800–KAP–ITEM
(for information on our products)

1–888–KAP–LOAN*
(for information on student loans)

(Outside the U.S.A., call **1-212-262-4980**)

Connect with us in cyberspace:
On **AOL**, keyword **"Kaplan"**
On the Internet's World Wide Web, open **"http://www.kaplan.com"**
Via E-mail, **"info@kaplan.com"**

Write to:
Kaplan Educational Centers
888 Seventh Avenue
New York, NY 10106

SEE THE "USER'S GUIDE FOR THE COMPUTER-BASED TOEFL CD-ROM" IN THE FRONT OF THIS BOOK FOR SYSTEM REQUIREMENTS AND INSTRUCTIONS ON HOW TO USE THE SOFTWARE.

SOFTWARE LICENSE/DISCLAIMER OF WARRANTIES

COPYRIGHT INFORMATION FOR CD-ROM

Technical Support for this CD-ROM is available Monday through Friday 6 A.M.–6 P.M. EST at 1-970-339-7142.